The Camden House History of German Literature

Volume 6:

Literature of the Sturm und Drang

The Camden House History of German Literature

Volume 6

The Camden House History of German Literature

Vol. 1: Early Germanic Literature and Culture
Edited by Brian Murdoch and Malcolm Read,
University of Stirling, UK

Vol. 2: German Literature of the Early Middle Ages
Edited by Brian Murdoch, University of Stirling, UK

Vol. 3: German Literature of the High Middle Ages
Edited by Will Hasty, University of Florida

Vol. 4: Early Modern German Literature
Edited by Max Reinhart, University of Georgia

*Vol. 5: Literature of the German Enlightenment
and Sentimentality*
Edited by Barbara Becker-Cantarino, Ohio State University

Vol. 6: Literature of the Sturm und Drang
Edited by David Hill, University of Birmingham, UK

Vol. 7: The Literature of Weimar Classicism
Edited by Simon Richter, University of Pennsylvania

Vol. 8: The Literature of German Romanticism
Edited by Dennis Mahoney, University of Vermont

Vol. 9: German Literature of the Nineteenth Century, 1830–1899
Edited by Clayton Koelb and Eric Downing,
University of North Carolina

*Vol. 10: German Literature of the Twentieth Century:
From Aestheticism to Postmodernism*
Ingo R. Stoehr, Kilgore College, Texas

Literature of the Sturm und Drang

Edited by
David Hill

CAMDEN HOUSE

First published 2003
by Camden House

Camden House is an imprint of Boydell & Brewer Inc.
PO Box 41026, Rochester, NY 14604–4126 USA
and of Boydell & Brewer Limited
PO Box 9, Woodbridge, Suffolk IP12 3DF, UK

ISBN: 1–57113–174–4

Library of Congress Cataloging-in-Publication Data

Literature of the Sturm und Drang / edited by David Hill.
    p. cm. — (Camden House history of German literature; v. 6)
Includes bibliographical references and index.
ISBN 1–57113–174–4 (alk. paper)
    1. German literature—18th century—History and criticism. 2. Sturm
und Drang Movement. I. Hill, David, 1943–. II. Series.

PT317 .L58 2003
830.9'006—dc21
                                                                 2002010539

A catalogue record for this title is available from the British Library.

This publication is printed on acid-free paper.
Printed in the United States of America.

Contents

Illustrations

Acknowledgments

I should like to thank the Deutsches Theatermuseum, Munich, the Freies Deutsches Hochstift, Frankfurt am Main, and the Taylor Institution, Oxford, for permission to reproduce illustrations.

Quotations from the German are provided in the original, but English translations, which, unless otherwise stated, are by the respective contributors, are to be found in the endnotes that follow each essay.

I should also like to thank all those involved in the preparation of the volume for their encouragement and help, in particular Bruce Duncan, Howard Gaskill, Jim Hardin, Susanne Kord, Matthias Luserke, Jim Walker, and Daniel Wilson.

D. D. H.
August 2002

Abbreviations

GAL　*German Aesthetic and Literary Criticism: Winckelmann, Lessing, Hamann, Herder, Schiller, Goethe,* ed. H. B. Nisbet (Cambridge, etc.: Cambridge UP, 1985).

G-CW　*Goethe's Collected Works,* 12 vols., eds. Victor Lange et al. (New York: Suhrkamp, 1983–89).

G-HB　Goethe, *Briefe: Hamburger Ausgabe,* 4 vols., eds. Karl Robert Mandelkow and Bodo Morawe (Hamburg: Wegner, 1962–67).

G-MA　Goethe, *Sämtliche Werke nach Epochen seines Schaffens: Münchner Ausgabe,* 21 vols., eds. Karl Richter et al. (Munich: Hanser, 1985–99).

G-U　Heinrich Wilhelm von Gerstenberg, *Ugolino,* ed. Christoph Siegrist, Universal-Bibliothek, 141 (Stuttgart: Reclam, 1977).

H-SW　Johann Gottfried Herder, *Herders sämmtliche Werke,* 33 vols., ed. Bernhard Suphan (Berlin: Weidmann, 1877–1913).

K-SD　Friedrich Maximilian Klinger, *Sturm und Drang,* ed. Jörg-Ulrich Fechner, Universal-Bibliothek, 248 (Stuttgart: Reclam, 1970).

K-W　Friedrich Maximilian Klinger, *Werke: Historisch-kritische Gesamtausgabe,* 6 vols. to date, eds. Sander L. Gilman et al. (Tübingen: Niemeyer, 1978–).

L-WB　Jakob Michael Reinhold Lenz, *Werke und Briefe,* 3 vols., ed. Sigrid Damm (Leipzig: Insel, 1987).

S-NA[1]　Friedrich Schiller, *Werke: Nationalausgabe,* 41 vols. to date, eds. Julius Petersen et al. (Weimar: Böhlau, 1943–).

SuD　*Sturm und Drang:* The Soldiers, The Childmurderess, Storm and Stress, *and* The Robbers, ed. Alan C. Leidner, German Library, 14 (New York: Continuum, 1992).

---

[1] The reworked version of vol. 5 is referred to as "5N."

Illustration by Daniel Chodowiecki to an edition of Bürger's "Lenore."
Courtesy of Taylor Institution, Oxford.

Introduction

David Hill

The Sturm und Drang and the
Idea of a Literary Period

THE PRESENT VOLUME OFFERS a wealth of basic information about the Sturm und Drang, together with a series of in-depth examinations of some of the most important themes associated with it. Histories of literature conventionally use a single-stranded narrative in order to organize information about literary texts and locate them within a historical development.[1] The present volume provides this basic orientation, especially in this first, introductory chapter, but the following chapters offer a variety of perspectives on the Sturm und Drang by scholars adopting different approaches and placing different emphases. This format allows a range of arguments to be developed. Authors and texts, ideas and forms are not reduced to lists; they are introduced not merely because they are intrinsically or historically important but because they are part of an argument that shows why they are important. Indeed, no history is merely an accumulation of facts: it always consists of hypotheses about the way in which the relationships between the facts may be reconstructed. This volume attempts to respond to the multidimensionality and complexity of authors and texts, ideas and forms, and is able to illuminate them by presenting them in different essays within different argumentative frameworks. The reader is thus drawn into current debates about the Sturm und Drang, and, although the detail of scholarly argument is not placed in the foreground, it is hoped that the volume conveys something of the complexity, the uncertainty, and the excitement of all historiography.

The expression "Sturm und Drang," usually translated as "Storm and Stress," is used today in two ways in English: in a nonspecific, metaphorical sense it suggests an exuberant outburst of youthful energy, while, more specifically and originally, it refers to a particular period or style in German literary history that flourished in the 1770s.[2] As the first meaning suggests, the literary period was one in which, in both their writings and their lifestyle, a group of young men challenged the conventions of what seemed to them a staid and narrow-minded society. The most prominent of these was the young Johann Wolfgang Goethe (1749–1832), but they also included several other authors whose lives and achievements will be briefly reviewed in the next section of this chapter. Among them is Friedrich Maximilian Klinger (1752–1831), who gave the movement its name by changing the title of his play of 1776, *Der Wirrwarr* (Confusion), to *Sturm und Drang* on the insistence of his friend Christoph Kaufmann (1753–95), who may have been thinking of Hamlet's "very torrent, tempest, and, as I may say, whirlwind of your passion" (act 3, scene 2).[3] Both terms, "*Wirrwarr*" and "Sturm und Drang," suggest — correctly — that the writers of the Sturm und Drang were more interested in creative energy than in order. Similarly, the writers of the Sturm und Drang, or "Stürmer und Dränger," were also known to contemporaries as the "*Kraftkerle*"[4] or "*Genies*" (geniuses).

The definition of any historical epoch is a problematic enterprise. Literary periods and trends do not have distinct, self-evident boundaries. They represent an attempt, either by contemporaries or by successors, to identify a common style or a common set of ideas that marks off one phase in a complex and relatively gradual evolutionary process. The use of a literary period is, therefore, always an act of interpretation that involves the insertion of caesuras and the selection and ordering of information. But, however problematic and provisional the definition of a period is, it is nevertheless an essential tool that gives shape to a history of literature and allows us to see beyond the individual text to the wider pattern. What is important is to recall that the identification of this wider pattern is part of an act of interpretation and is, therefore, provisional. We have learned to be wary of monothematic "grand narratives" and are conscious that all judgments at all levels need continually to be renegotiated, because the basis on which judgments are made is subject to continual historical change, and because all interpretations are partial in the sense that they prioritize certain meanings at the expense of others. Each literary period is a complex network of ideas and styles that cannot be reduced to one linear "story" but is made up of many crisscrossing themes and styles that fit into various overlapping patterns, and may perhaps best be approached, as in the present volume, by several interlocking studies.

Looking back over the way historians have described the Sturm und Drang,[5] it is, nevertheless, possible to discern with varying degrees of consistency and certainty a core repertoire of themes, motifs, and stylistic features. Not all of these will be found in every text, or maybe even in every writer, but enough of them will be for the overarching term "Sturm und Drang" to be helpful. There will be debates about where to draw the boundaries of the Sturm und Drang, but these debates are less useful for their conclusions than for the insights they provide into the defining core of the movement. There will be authors and texts that are typical of the Sturm und Drang in certain respects, but less so in others. Moreover, there is a developmental dimension to this problem, inasmuch as what was typical of the Sturm und Drang changed at various stages in the movement, and scholars have therefore on occasion refined the idea of the Sturm und Drang by identifying a distinct number of phases within it — a practice that, of course, has the same benefits and problems as the use of the literary period in the first place.

Other thresholds are also to be borne in mind. It is arguable whether the Sturm und Drang should be restricted merely to literature. The characteristics of Sturm-und-Drang writing are to be found in speculative essays and private letters as much as in plays and poems. Beyond this, there is a philosophical dimension to the Sturm und Drang, although it is not normal to speak of the Sturm und Drang as a phase in the history of philosophy. Histories of music, on the other hand, do acknowledge a Sturm und Drang, but at the same time there is a debate about whether the musical Sturm und Drang should be considered as belonging to the Sturm und Drang proper, albeit at its periphery, or whether it is merely a parallel phenomenon, perhaps the product of the same social and cultural environment.[6] The visual arts are a slightly different matter. The sketches by Goethe and Jakob Michael Reinhold Lenz (1751–92) reveal real talent, and there was a time when Goethe thought that his future might lie in art rather than in literature. Friedrich Müller (1749–1825) was known as "Maler" Müller (Müller the Painter) because he was as at home in his painting, and particularly his sketches, as he was in his writing, and in both media he reflects the enthusiasm of the Sturm und Drang for nature together with an interest in the realistic portrayal of everyday life.[7] Heinrich Füssli (1741–1825), known as Henry Fuseli after he moved to England, began as a writer but is remembered today for his paintings, which, by contrast with the work of Müller, reflect the extravagant imaginative flair of the Sturm und Drang (for example, in "The Nightmare").[8] Both Müller and Füssli excelled as writers and also as artists, but although there are connections between what they achieved in each medium, it is not common to think of the Sturm und Drang as a phase in art history.

The Writers of the Sturm und Drang within the Development of German Culture in the Eighteenth Century

The intellectual landscape of eighteenth-century Germany within which the Sturm und Drang so rapidly achieved prominence in the early 1770s was a particularly complex one. A context is provided by the European Enlightenment, a broad social and cultural movement that had emerged around the beginning of the century and insisted on focusing on this world rather than the next. Alexander Pope (1688–1744) formulated the idea in his *Essay on Man* (1733): "Know then thyself, presume not God to scan; / The proper study of Mankind is Man."[9] Strongly influenced by deism, the writers of the Enlightenment in general did not doubt the existence of God, and certainly those in Germany did not. They thought of God as a creator whose existence guaranteed the ultimate order of the world, but they turned their attention away from the transcendental, which we could not know, and sought to build up a system of reliable human knowledge based on the faculties of mankind: our five senses and our reason. They rejected the tendency to interpret this world in terms of the next or to derive knowledge from the elaboration of established authorities such as the ancients or the Bible. Instead, they turned a questioning, skeptical eye on the world around them. They saw the natural world as worthy of serious investigation, and one of the things that marked off the beginning of the Enlightenment was the way that it combined empiricism with rational analysis to fuel the natural sciences. Through science people felt increasingly able to appreciate some of the perfection with which the creator had constructed the universe. At the same time, technology revealed its potential for further improvement, and the writers of the Enlightenment looked forward to a more humane society, that is, a society that granted us happiness and allowed our God-given human qualities to flourish. What was new was an understanding of God as the creator of a world that had within it the elements of perfection, rather than thinking of God as standing apart from, and occasionally intervening in, an impenetrable vale of tears. At the same time, the idea of progress was applied to man as a social and moral being in whom folly and prejudice will eventually be eroded by reason and tolerance. There was, thus, also a sociopolitical dimension to the Enlightenment. In terms of knowledge, the Enlightenment attempted to look beyond the meanings that things had been given a priori by external authorities to what one could discern, by the application of the human faculties, those things really were. The correlate of this idea was that the true identity of people was determined by their individual merit rather than the status they inherited — for example, through their social class. The Enlightenment saw the foundation of modern scientific ways of thinking about the natural world, but it also saw the evolution of modern ways of thinking about the relationship between the individual and society.

As we move on through the eighteenth century to the Sturm und Drang, the picture becomes complicated as the entanglements of terminology and interpretation come to the surface. Older literary histories tended to present the Sturm und Drang as a reaction against the Enlightenment, an outburst of irrationalism in an ordered, rationalist world. They used the term "Enlightenment" in a narrow sense to refer to the rationalist (and, in Germany, to some extent empiricist) traditions of culture between — approximately — 1720 and the 1770s, after which they saw the decline of these traditions in the Late Enlightenment (from the 1770s until the end of the century). More recent critics have drawn attention to the continuities between the Enlightenment and the Sturm und Drang and have seen the Sturm und Drang as a particularly radical set of attempts to achieve the emancipation of the self, which was, indeed, a central goal of the Enlightenment. They have, thus, used the term "Enlightenment" in a broader sense and discerned within it a number of trends and projects. These strands include not only the narrow sense of Enlightenment but also the Sturm und Drang, "*Empfindsamkeit*" (Sentimentalism, or Sensibility), and the Late Enlightenment. From this perspective, the last third of the eighteenth century appears as a fragmentation of the Enlightenment: the Sturm und Drang was one of the splinters that resulted and was characterized not so much by its specific rejection of rationalism as by its rejection of all assumptions about the parameters within which emancipation should be sought. The Sturm und Drang is, therefore, not a period in the history of culture in the way that, for example, the Renaissance or the Enlightenment are; it is not a turning point in the evolution of culture. Even to call it a "movement" may imply more cohesion and purpose than is appropriate. The Sturm und Drang is represented by a relatively small number of texts; they are important not because they represent a necessary stage in the development of German culture but because of the quality of the writing they contain and because of the radicalism, the complexity, and the incisiveness of their analysis of the human spirit on the threshold of modernity.

The advantage of this approach to the treatment of periodization is that it makes it easier to integrate into a history of literature the great variety of styles of writing and thinking that are to be found in eighteenth-century German literature. Many writers who were active within the Enlightenment in its narrower sense also wrote in what is called the rococo style, which adopted the anacreontic conventions of celebrating wine, women, and song.[10] This style has been rather underresearched, because its frivolity and mild eroticism conflict with the high seriousness and the middle-class inwardness that have often been considered typical of eighteenth-century literature in Germany. In particular, it does not quite fit the traditional image of the Enlightenment: although the rococo is oriented toward the things of this world, it turns away from the somewhat prim and worthy correctness that is often associated with the mid-century Enlightenment.

On the other hand, scholars who were intent on tracing the evolution of an independent national literature placed an emphasis that was all the greater on the historical role of Friedrich Gottlob Klopstock (1724–1803) and the sentimental style of writing he developed around the middle of the century, known as "*Empfindsamkeit.*" His emphasis on emotion has been related to the Sturm und Drang, and the boundaries between the two are often indistinct, both in terms of style and at a personal level. Writers in the sentimental style, however, had a preference for an ecstatic and elevated but rather abstract tearfulness. They liked to see themselves as bards or prophets, and there was often a religious as well as a nationalistic note to their writing. What lies behind Sentimentalism and, indeed, all eighteenth-century literature in Germany is a broad cultural movement associated with Pietism, an intensely inward religious revival dating from the beginning of the century. The Pietists sought religious meanings in everyday life, and to the extent that they took religious feeling away from the church they were part of the process of secularization; but at the same time they gave everyday experiences the intensity and the transcendental meaningfulness that had previously been the province of religion, and thus they fueled a new intensity of the inner life in literature.

If the 1770s were the decade of the Sturm und Drang, then they were also the decade of Sentimentalism: the first collected edition of Klopstock's odes was published in 1771, and the best known of his disciples formed an association, the so-called Göttinger Hainbund (Göttingen League of the Grove), in 1772 in an oak grove outside Göttingen. A letter from Johann Heinrich Voss to Ernst Brückner of August 4, 1773 describes how they celebrated Klopstock's birthday, reading his poetry, drinking wine, and burning the works of Christoph Martin Wieland (1733–1813), the main representative of the rococo style of writing and the bête noire of both the Göttinger Hainbund and the Sturm und Drang.[11] The rococo style of writing was at this time becoming less popular, though its influence was still felt. The 1770s were also the time of that concluding representative moment of the middle phase of the Enlightenment (*the* Enlightenment in the narrow sense), the dispute of Gotthold Ephraim Lessing (1729–81) with Goeze over the role of reason in religion. Lessing's belief that our human faculties were a surer basis for judgment and for humane behavior than external authorities such as the church or even the Bible inspired him to write *Nathan der Weise* (Nathan the Wise, 1779). Lessing, Wieland, and Klopstock dominated the literary scene in Germany in the 1760s and 1770s, although their concerns rapidly began to be regarded as old-fashioned by a younger group of writers, the new avant-garde: the Sturm und Drang.

Most accounts of the Sturm und Drang agree that it had a preliminary phase that was dominated by the explosion of intellectual energy in the work of Johann Gottfried Herder (1744–1803).[12] Herder came from the northeastern reaches of the German cultural world. He was born in Mohrungen (now Morag) in East Prussia, studied theology at Köngisberg (now Kaliningrad, Russia), and in 1764 was appointed to a teaching post in Riga. There he began writing essays on all aspects of cultural history. Herder had a voracious appetite for ideas, and it is not easy specify sources for his arguments, but the two greatest influences on his writing were probably Johann Georg Hamann (1730–88) and Jean-Jacques Rousseau (1712–78). If Herder was the father of the Sturm und Drang, then Hamann was its grandfather. Hamann, who lived in Königsberg, where Herder met him during his studies, turned to religion but did so in a way that was to be typical of the Sturm und Drang, in that for him the love and knowledge of God encompassed the love and knowledge of the whole of creation. Structural links clearly exist between these views and the Enlightenment belief in God as the creator whose hand could be seen in the wonder of the world; but for Hamann the godliness of the world was to be found in its present wonder, not in the fact that it pointed to a past moment of creation. Second, the godliness of the world was something to which the whole person, not merely the individual's intellectual faculties, could and should respond. Correspondingly, Hamann believed that the God-given medium of language should communicate not so much through explanation and argumentation as through allusion and association. Hamann's visionary style of writing is peppered with references to the most diverse of sources and is notoriously difficult to read, but it is scarcely possible to imagine the Sturm und Drang feeling for a secularized holiness of nature or the style of its prose writing without Hamann, both mediated mainly through Herder.

Despite their criticism of French cultural values, several French authors were admired by the writers of the Sturm und Drang. These authors include Louis-Sébastien Mercier (1740–1814)[13] but, above all, the Genevan Rousseau, whose two *Discourses* of 1750 and 1755 develop a radical critique of the contemporary world as artificial and degenerate, and paint, by contrast, a picture of a more primitive, more natural social order whose wholeness and authenticity we must recover.[14] Herder was clearly captivated by Rousseau's vision of an alternative to the falseness of the present world, and, with his special interest in language and culture, he found in folk song, and folk culture in general, the remnants of a more natural, more organic way of life. In his essay "Auszug aus einem Briefwechsel über Ossian und die Lieder alter Völker" (Extract from a Correspondence on Ossian and the Songs of Ancient Peoples), which he published in a volume he edited that was almost a manifesto of the Sturm und Drang, *Von deutscher Art und Kunst* (Of German Character and Art, 1773), Herder analyzed the artificiality of modern writing and contrasted it with folk song — or, at least, poetry in the folk style — which, he argued, was the direct expression of the life of a culture.[15] One of the starting points of this essay is, typically, Herder's description of his personal experience of reading Ossian, the Celtic bard, on the sea journey he undertook from Riga to Paris in 1769. By contrast with the faith of Enlightenment writers in the progress of history from the less to the more civilized, Herder's writing thus contains an element of cultural pessimism. Herder was, however, like Rousseau, a child of the Enlightenment, and his writings, like Rousseau's, are full of suggestions as to how reforms might be introduced that would counteract the tendencies of the age. He kept notes of his thoughts on this voyage and published them as *Journal meiner Reise im Jahre 1769* (Journal of My Journey in the Year 1769, published 1878), which contains proposals of improvements that should be made to everything from school curricula to literary cultures and national economies. Herder combines his historical pessimism with such moments of hope in *Auch eine Philosophie der Geschichte zur Bildung der Menschheit* (One More Philosophy of History for the Education of Mankind, 1774) but adds a crucial third perspective, historical relativism. He suggests here that history is an organic process in which each element of a culture can only be understood in terms of its function for the whole, and at times he speaks of cultures as organisms that have a natural life cycle. Herder does not resolve the tensions between the different historiographies embedded in this work, and maybe he felt that it would be wrong to impose an artificial harmony that would obscure the insights that each approach might offer. All of Herder's writing has something fragmentary, open, and provisional about it, because it reflects his restless energy as a generator of ideas.

Herder's essay on Shakespeare (also published in *Von deutscher Art und Kunst*) similarly combines enormous enthusiasm with an emphasis on the need to understand Aristotle and Shakespeare within their respective cultural contexts. Herder was not the only author at this time who built on Lessing's argument that German culture was closer to English than to French culture and that Shakespeare was, therefore, a more appropriate model for German writers. Heinrich Wilhelm von Gerstenberg (1737–1823) achieved renown in the late 1750s and the 1760s as a poet capable of writing both in the rococo and in the sentimental style influenced by Klopstock, but in his *Briefe über Merkwürdigkeiten der Litteratur* (Letters on Noteworthy Aspects of Literature, 1766–67) he used the example of Shakespeare to argue that rules for the composition of literature (and, therefore, by implication, the normative aesthetics of neoclassicism) can only inhibit the direct free expression of genius, the sole guarantor of true poetry. In his tragedy *Ugolino* (1768) the diction of the characters draws on Sentimentalism, but this is undercut by the almost gothic violence of the plot, in which traditional kinds of dramatic conflict have given way to the macabre portrait of a father and his three sons starving to death in prison. Ambivalent as it is, *Ugolino* must be reckoned the first drama of the Sturm und Drang.

The central figure of the Sturm und Drang — at least from 1770 until his move to Weimar late in 1775 — was Goethe. As a student in Leipzig (1765–68) Goethe had begun writing poetry predominantly in the rococo style, and his collection of poems *Neue Lieder* (New Songs, 1769) already shows notable signs of subtlety and a responsiveness to nature. Yet, his Sturm und Drang writing of two years later is so strikingly original that one looks for external stimuli, however partial the explanations they are likely to offer. First, scholars have often made connections between the new sensitivity to his inner self and the illness that prompted Goethe's hurried departure from Leipzig in the late summer of 1768, together with his withdrawal from active social life and, most important, his close contact with Pietist friends of the family, under whose influence the convalescent came to empathize with some of their intense, inward religious faith. The second essential experience was his meeting with Herder in the fall of 1770 in Strasbourg, where Goethe had gone to complete his legal studies in the spring. Herder, who was working on his *Abhandlung über den Ursprung der Sprache* (Treatise on the Origins of Language, completed 1770, published 1772), was being treated for an eye condition and had to spend time in a darkened room. Goethe visited Herder soon after the latter's arrival in September, and there developed during the winter of 1770–71 a series of almost daily meetings, during which Goethe received the most intense initiation into the world of ideas Herder was opening up.

At the same time, other new experiences so crowded in on Goethe's life that they cannot easily be placed in sequence. Under Herder's influence Goethe became engrossed in the writers who were to play an important part in the Sturm und Drang, all of whom were seen as somehow primitive and closer to nature. These included Homer; Ossian, whom he translated; and, above all, Shakespeare. He was fascinated by the cathedral in Strasbourg, which seemed to have a harmony the modern world had lost and that he tried to evoke in his essay "Von deutscher Baukunst" (On German Architecture), included in *Von deutscher Art und Kunst*. In the countryside of Alsace, Goethe began to show the intensity with which he could respond to nature, and he copied down for Herder folk songs from the oldest inhabitants of the villages. In one idyllic village, Sesenheim (now Sessenheim), he met and fell in love with a pastor's daughter, Friederike Brion. This was also a time of great creativity, as Goethe discovered a style of writing that expressed a new intensity of individual feeling. Goethe's poems of this period are driven by an energy and a directness that were quite new in German literature, and this is the time, too, when he began working on later masterpieces such as *Götz von Berlichingen* (1773) and *Faust* (part 1, 1808; part 2, 1832). Nor should one forget Goethe's skill as an artist, which is demonstrated by numerous sketches of landscapes and portraits of friends. At the same time as he was experiencing this outburst of creativity, Goethe began to establish a wide network of friends who were inspired and encouraged by him and whom he helped in many practical ways. This was the literary avant-garde formed by young men who felt that they were engaged in a common enterprise with Goethe. Reviewers were often unable to distinguish the works of Goethe, Lenz, and Klinger; and because these men engaged in intense discussions of work in progress, there is a sense in which at least some of their productions were collaborative ventures. In Strasbourg, Goethe dined regularly with a circle of friends, among whom were such promising writers as Johann Heinrich Jung (1740–1817), Heinrich Leopold Wagner (1747–79), and, a little later, Lenz.

Jung was also known as Jung-Stilling or Stilling from the family name he gave himself in what was effectively an autobiography narrated in the third person. The first volume in particular, *Heinrich Stillings Jugend* (The Youth of Heinrich Stilling, 1777), composed at Goethe's instigation, shows the sensitivity and clarity of self-observation that Pietism could induce, even and especially among the lower social classes; and although it is more commonly included in the tradition of Sentimentalism than the Sturm und Drang, the fact that it was published by Goethe illustrates the connections between the two styles. Lenz also had a Pietist background and had been destined for the Church by his father, but he broke off his theological studies at Königsberg and traveled to Alsace in 1771. There, in a furious burst of energy, he read voraciously at the same time as translating Plautus and Shakespeare, writing essays on literary theory and theology, and composing the plays for which he is chiefly remembered today, *Der Hofmeister* (The Tutor, 1774), *Der neue Menoza* (The New Menoza, 1774), and *Die Soldaten* (The Soldiers, 1776). Lenz's ability to combine humor with an unflinching insight into the way social pressures distort humanity, together with a vision of the depths and potential of that humanity, inspired Georg Büchner in the 1830s and continue to inspire authors and composers in our own time. Lenz is best known as a playwright, but, like Goethe and, later, Schiller, he also made important contributions to poetry and to narrative forms, notably *Zerbin* (1776) and *Der Waldbruder* (The Hermit, written 1776). Wagner is known primarily for one play, *Die Kindermörderin* (The Infanticide, 1776), which, like *Die Soldaten* and *Faust* (which Goethe accused Wagner of plagiarizing), is a document of the Sturm und Drang concern for the tragic consequences of the seduction and desertion of middle-class girls by men of higher social status. As in many other Sturm und Drang plays, however, the gesture of protest against all restrictions to self-fulfillment is accompanied by an insight into a network of social and psychological factors that is so complex that simple moral judgments on individuals are no longer possible.

Goethe was awarded his licentiate and left Strasbourg in August 1771 to pursue a law career based in Frankfurt. There he met Johann Heinrich Merck (1741–91), who at the beginning of the next year took over the review journal *Frankfurter Gelehrte Anzeigen* and invited Goethe to become a regular contributor. There followed nearly four years in which Goethe was active as a lawyer, including a period working at the imperial court in Wetzlar, but he gives the impression that he devoted his energies to his friendships and his writing. He traveled widely, and among the friends and collaborators in this intellectual and creative turmoil that was the core of the Sturm und Drang are a number of key figures, including Johann Caspar Lavater (1741–1801), Klinger, and Maler Müller.

Lavater was a Swiss minister who acted, like Goethe, as an important mediator between members of the Sturm und Drang circle and the broader, looser group of writers in the sentimental tradition, many of whom, including Goethe, he recruited into his investigation of physiognomics. In his *Physiognomische Fragmente* (Physiognomic Fragments, 1775–78) Lavater attempted to correlate the facial features of people and even of animals with their character, believing that he could thereby demonstrate the unity of God's creation. Contemporaries recognized a certain naiveté in Lavater, but they also admired the energy with which he pursued the question of the relationship between essential inner forms and their expression. Goethe's ambivalence about Lavater's otherworldliness is summed up in his contrast between himself as a "Weltkind" (child of the world) and Lavater as a prophet (*G-MA*, 1.1: 247). Equally revealing of the enthusiasm rather than the discrimination of the Sturm und Drang is a man whom Lavater acclaimed as a genius: the Swiss Christoph Kaufmann, who lived the life of a Sturm und Drang genius, complete with extravagantly "natural" dress, but, as far as we know, wrote almost nothing.

By contrast with most members of the circle, Klinger came from a poor background, and he received not only encouragement but also financial support from Goethe when he went to study at the University of Giessen. Klinger seems to have thrown himself with enthusiasm into both the lifestyle and the writing style of the Sturm und Drang. Some of his plays, such as *Otto* (1775) and *Das leidende Weib* (The Suffering Wife, 1775), show their dependence (on *Götz von Berlichingen* and *Der Hofmeister*, respectively), but *Die Zwillinge* (The Twins, 1776), *Sturm und Drang*, and *Simsone Grisaldo* (1776) are full of the sometimes rather unfocused intensity that has come to be seen as characteristic of the movement. Friedrich Müller worked in various literary genres and published an incomplete version of the Faust story, *Fausts Leben, dramatasiert: I. Teil* (Faust's Life, Dramatized: First Part, 1778), but increasingly devoted his main energies to his sketches and his painting.

Goethe's life was marked not only by these collegial friendships, intense though they often were, but also by a series of relations with women that were situated somewhere between friendship and love. In Wetzlar Goethe met Charlotte Buff, and he drew on the experience in his novel *Die Leiden des jungen Werthers* (The Sorrows of Young Werther,[16] 1774), which caused a furor because of its sympathetic insights into the mind of young man who commits suicide as a result of a hopeless love affair. There date from these years a host of poems that, at least in the first instance, reflect immediate emotional experiences, and several major plays. The most significant among the latter was *Götz von Berlichingen*,[17] a historical drama in the most extravagant Shakespearean manner that, together with *Werther*, established Goethe's reputation well beyond his circle of friends and admirers. There were also rather more conventional domestic dramas, including *Clavigo* (1774), *Stella* (1776), and the "Singspiel" *Claudine von Villa Bella* (1776). Of possibly greatest significance, however, was an early draft of *Faust*. *Faust* itself did not appear in print until 1808, and then only as part 1; but this draft, known rather imprecisely as the "*Urfaust*" (Original Faust), of which a copy was discovered in 1887, is a valuable indication of the progress Goethe had made on the project before he moved to Weimar.[18] He also began work on *Egmont*, though it did not appear until 1788, after he had completed it in Italy.

In 1775 Goethe formed an attachment to Lili Schönemann, the daughter of a Frankfurt banking family, and this time he seems to have been seriously tempted by the prospect of marriage; but to settle down, accommodate himself to the materialism of her family, and above all, so it seemed, put an end to the excitement of self-discovery was more than he could bear. Feeling that he had to leave Frankfurt, he set off for Italy when the invitation to join the court of Weimar that he had been led to expect failed to turn up. Duke Karl August's emissary, however, caught up with him in Heidelberg and took him to Weimar, where they arrived on November 7. This date marks the beginning of the end of the Sturm und Drang. The circle of colleagues known as the Sturm und Drang was held together by friendship and admiration and by shared values and attitudes that found expression not only in writing (imaginative literature, essays and reviews on a broad range of topics in the arts, and letters, which were often passed on to still other friends) but also in their behavior. They cultivated an exuberance that had the no doubt intended effect of causing something of a scandal. When, for example, in the early summer of 1775 the brothers Christian (1748–1821) and Friedrich Leopold (1750–1819) Stolberg, noblemen and authors in the sentimental tradition, and a friend persuaded Goethe to join them on a trip that took them to Switzerland, all four had suits made consisting of the blue coat and yellow waistcoat and trousers that Werther was famous for wearing in Goethe's novel and that had become almost a badge of the new sensibility.[19]

When Goethe first arrived in Weimar, he continued this extravagant lifestyle. He gradually distanced himself from such wild abandon, however. In a complicated and not unambiguous process his values and his writing began to change,[20] and the end of this core phase of the Sturm und Drang was marked when Lenz and Klinger, both of whom had come to Weimar in the summer of 1776 in the hope of finding employment or patronage, were expelled in disgrace. There are many hypotheses, and we shall probably never know exactly what provoked the rift in each case, but the context is clear: Goethe was developing away from the attitudes and values that lay behind the Sturm und Drang. After this falling out, both Lenz and Klinger had difficulty gathering their lives together. The rejection by Goethe, the friend he idolized, probably provoked the mental breakdown that Lenz suffered about a year later; and Klinger had an unsettled and apparently unhappy few years before he established a career in Russia in 1780, by which time his lifestyle and his interests were already changing in a direction similar to Goethe's. When Wagner died in 1779, it seemed as if the Sturm und Drang had run its course.

Goethe was the key figure in the Sturm und Drang, and the most vivid account of the movement is to be found in his *Aus meinem Leben: Dichtung und Wahrheit* (From My Life: Poetry and Truth, 1811–33), the first part of an uncompleted autobiographical project, which covers the period up to Goethe's departure for Weimar at the end of 1775. *Dichtung und Wahrheit* has had a decisive influence on the formation of the literary canon in Germany, both in terms of Goethe's evaluation of the Sturm und Drang and in the selection of individuals he chooses to discuss. Thus, there are a number of women writers of the period who share some characteristics of Sturm und Drang writing — for example, Christiane Karoline Schlegel (1739–1833), Marianne Ehrmann (1755–95), and Sophie Albrecht (1757–1840); but they are not mentioned by Goethe and have been largely excluded from the canon. Only recently have feminist critics begun to demand a reevaluation of them.[21] In other respects, too, *Dichtung und Wahrheit* reflects the perspective of the older Goethe, whose portrayal of the Sturm und Drang reflects his experience of what seemed to him the dangerous collapse of values in the French Revolution and among the Romantics, who, he felt, paid too little attention to the demands of life in the real world.

It is not easy — and maybe not entirely possible — to escape the dominance of *Dichtung und Wahrheit* when writing of the Sturm und Drang, but we should recognize that each member of the circle has his own biography, his own concerns, and his own style, and contemporary views may be better represented in letters or, for example, in Lenz's *Pandämonium Germanicum* (written 1775; published 1819), a kind of satirical comment on the literary scene that includes most of its real authors as characters. The Sturm und Drang consists of a set of intertwining fates, and, as has become clear, there are many links to authors who might more conventionally be linked with the sentimental style of writing, which in the 1770s came to be focused on the Göttinger Hainbund. Johann Anton Leisewitz (1752–1806) was a member of the Göttingen circle but wrote one play, *Julius von Tarent* (Julius of Tarentum, 1776), that explores further the Sturm und Drang motifs of the rivalry of brothers and the distortions of nature that are implied by the attempt to subordinate feelings to institutions such as family or state. Gottfried August Bürger (1747–94) bridged the Göttingen and Sturm und Drang circles and helped to develop the idea of folk poetry — particularly in his ballads, of which the most celebrated, "Lenore" (1773), was inspired by Herder and by the mood Goethe had created in *Götz von Berlichingen*. Bürger thus played an important role in creating the German tradition of the art ballad in the folk style: a narrative poem, often involving a fast-moving sequence of scenes characterized by action and direct speech and usually with a twist that is either gruesome or supernatural or both. Bürger's is also an interesting case because it demonstrates the sharpness of social criticism that was possible in the Sturm und Drang. In general, the writers of the Sturm und Drang were impelled by an urge to protest against the aesthetic and moral values of a social world that they felt had become deadeningly oppressive; but their criticisms tended not to be overtly political. Two writers did, however, show how far they were willing to go in their confrontation with the political powers: Bürger and Christian Friedrich Daniel Schubart (1739–91), who is remembered for his poetry, his editorship of the *Deutsche Chronik* (German Chronicle, 1774–77), and the ten years of imprisonment he earned through his insubordination. Both writers, typically, stand at the edges of the Sturm und Drang.

Schubart's career was marked by the two outstanding features of the part of Germany from which he came, Swabia: a middle-class culture that was strongly influenced by Pietism, and a notoriously oppressive and authoritarian ruler, Karl Eugen, Duke of Württemberg. Both also played a crucial role in the life of Friedrich Schiller (1759–1805), who visited Schubart in prison. There has been debate about whether or not the early work of Schiller should be included in the Sturm und Drang as a final phase of its evolution. As a student, Schiller was an avid reader of Shakespeare and Rousseau and of the plays referred to above as the core of the Sturm und Drang, and his first-hand experience of tyranny at Karl Eugen's academy, the Karlsschule (Karl's School), seems to have made the young Schiller's criticisms all the stronger. There is thus in his early writing a spirit of turbulence and protest, matched by emotional outbursts, that is reminiscent of the Sturm und Drang. On the other hand, while the stage directions are often extravagant, the structure of the plays is more balanced, and they seem to exist in a world where moral judgments are valid and necessary. *Die Räuber* (The Robbers, 1781), for example, takes up the motif of fraternal conflict; but whereas Klinger had ended *Die Zwillinge* in an orgy of destruction, with the murderous insanity of the main brother and his sacrificial death at the hands of his own father, Schiller's resolution is the brother's recognition of his own moral failures and his decision to hand himself over the authorities. In *Die Räuber*, but also in *Die Verschwörung des Fiesco zu Genua* (The Conspiracy of Fiesco of Genoa, 1783) and *Kabale und Liebe* (Intrigue and Love, 1784) and in his poems, Schiller, like Schubart, is emphatic in his social and moral criticism and includes stylistic elements and motifs that tend to be associated with a wide range of styles, from the Enlightenment or the sentimental style of writing as much as the Sturm und Drang: the present volume is based on the assumption that, whether or not one decides to include Schiller in the Sturm und Drang, a discussion of the Sturm und Drang would be incomplete if it did not take account of his early writing. The story of the long-drawn-out composition of *Don Carlos, Infant von Spanien* (Don Carlos, Infant of Spain, 1787), which he had begun in 1782, is the story of Schiller rethinking his aesthetic and philosophical values and moving into the phase of his life where he could, from about 1794, form the working alliance with Goethe that is the basis of what is known today as Weimar Classicism.

The Sturm und Drang and the Search for Self-Realization in Eighteenth-Century Germany

The Sturm und Drang shares several features with the tradition of sentimental writing in England and France that is sometimes called Pre-Romanticism,[22] but it was different in important ways that make it a specifically German phenomenon. The political events of the eighteenth century, however, give few clues as to the reasons for the cultural distinctiveness of Germany. Despite the Seven Years' War (1756–63), which reflected the growth of Prussia and sparked off debates about national identity, the eighteenth century was predominantly a period of outward calm in German history. The background of the literary rebellion of the Sturm und Drang is to be found, rather, in the underlying shifts in the structure of society.

Germany did not exist as a nation in the eighteenth century. To call the Sturm und Drang German is to refer not to a nation but to the cultural traditions of the German-speaking part of Europe, including some of Switzerland and the Baltic States; but even this formulation is approximate — not least because, in the early and middle parts of the century, the aristocracy generally preferred French: only the lower and middle classes regularly spoke German. Instead of a nation, there were more than three hundred separate political entities, which varied greatly in size and kind. The Holy Roman Empire provided a political frame-work that acted as a counterbalance to political fragmentation, but its powers were so limited, and its procedures so cumbersome, that it was unable to act as an effective centralizing force.

The dominant political system in the German states was feudal ab-solutism, under which all power was concentrated in the monarch. (By contrast, the free imperial cities — such as Frankfurt, where Goethe grew up — owed allegiance directly to the emperor and were governed by an elite of wealthy families.) By comparison with medieval feudalism, the central administrative system of each territory was more fully developed and was overseen by a cabinet of ministers who advised the monarch. The aristocracy increasingly played the part of senior administrators, acting on behalf of the monarch within a structure that was coming to look more and more like the apparatus of the modern state. They were assisted at the lower levels by an army of educated administrators, which began to form an important element within the middle classes beside the merchants and entrepreneurs, who were also increasing in economic importance. Although these sections of society tend to interest historians because their role changed so fundamentally during the eighteenth century, it should not be forgotten that the German lands remained predominantly agricultural: about three-quarters of the population were peasants with a low standard of living and level of education.

Many of these features could be found elsewhere in Europe, but three related factors distinguish the German situation. First, the frag-mentation of the German states, exacerbated by the tendency toward centralization within each of them, contrasted with the centralization of France and England, which allowed the development of large-scale trade focused on a substantial metropolitan capital. Second, visitors from abroad felt that Germany was backward in comparison with England and France. The economy had struggled to recover from the devastation of the Thirty Years' War (1618–48), communications were poor, trade and manufacturing were underdeveloped, and social divisions were sharp. Third, the middle classes, whose advance at this time is often taken as an indicator of social and economic progress, were weak by comparison with their counterparts in England and France. They grew in numbers and importance during the century, despite the restrictions of the guild system and the political fragmentation, which, accompanied by high import duties and a fragmentation of currencies and trading regulations, made it difficult to expand production; but they remained largely excluded from the world of politics.

Historians who have tried to account for the emergence in the twentieth century of a society capable of perpetrating the horrors of the Holocaust have often argued that the route by which Germany attained modern nationhood was exceptional, and they trace the origins of Germany's "*Sonderweg*" (special route) back to these distinguishing features of Germany in the eighteenth century.[23] In doing so, they counter a history based on heroic nationalism but in the end often reproduce its structure, albeit with reversed moral evaluation; they exaggerate the uniqueness of Germany in both the twentieth and the eighteenth centuries and suppose a normal development against which German history is an aberration. In both versions the Sturm und Drang appears as a crucial moment in the emergence of a German national identity that was to achieve its fulfillment in the twentieth century, the moment when the ideals of the court were rejected in favor of a newly discovered *Volk* (people), when outer forms, manners, "*Zivilisation*," were rejected in favor of German "*Innerlichkeit*" (inwardness) and "*Kultur*" (culture): it is symptomatic that English has no adequate translation of either word. This is, with either a positive or a negative moral judgment placed on it, the legend of Germany as the land of poets and thinkers — the dissatisfied, idealistic, Faustian Germany.

To read the Sturm und Drang in this way is not entirely wrong. The movement was marked by a gesture of dissatisfaction with the proprieties of a culture that had begun to seem superficial and alien and a wish to discover alternative, more authentic values among the common folk and in nature. It is not entirely wrong to regard the Sturm und Drang either as a key moment in the emancipation of modern German literature or as a self-indulgent evasion of the duty of humans to understand and improve the world, as a moment of liberation or as a moment of withdrawal. These two approaches are, in the end, compatible with each other: the Sturm und Drang is both a radicalization of the European Enlightenment and a failure to realize its potential. Eighteenth-century

European culture is more complex, however, and the Sturm und Drang is more deeply embedded in it than either approach tends to suggest. There are close links in terms of style, ideas, and personalities between the Sturm und Drang and other examples of eighteenth-century writing, ranging from Laurence Sterne (1713–68) and Rousseau to Klopstock and his admirers. Before Gerstenberg, Herder, or Goethe, it was Lessing who defended Shakespeare, and it was Lessing who argued that artistic production was more than merely the intelligent application of rules. To exaggerate the divide between the Sturm und Drang and the Enlightenment is to simplify each of them and to abstract them from the remarkable proliferation of styles that characterizes eighteenth-century German literature.

Norbert Elias resolves these issues by looking at the functions of culture in this society and arguing that the multiplicity of competing styles of thinking and writing that are characteristic of the eighteenth century can be interpreted as so many attempts by a middle-class intelligentsia to find an adequate means of self-expression in a world whose cultural framework was governed, as was the political framework, by the aristocracy.[24] The middle classes were beginning to coalesce as a social group, and the intelligentsia was a kind of ideological avant-garde that attempted to define their shared identity against the cultural hegemony of the aristocracy. Another way of putting it is to say that a new realm of public discourse was beginning to evolve.[25] Sociological terms such as "middle class" and "aristocracy" are, of course, abstractions and do not do justice to the diversity of each of these social groups, to the regionalism of Germany, or to the shifts that took place during the century, such as, for example, the cautious absorption by the courts of elements of middle-class culture. They do, however, allow us to identify a common theme behind the otherwise bewildering variety of styles, and they acknowledge the political undertones of eighteenth-century literature in Germany.

Despite its frequent negative portrayals of the values of the court, eighteenth-century literature tends not to engage in what we today would regard as political issues, such as foreign policy or questions of representation or taxation. The middle classes tended to concede decision-making power to the courts and seem to have preferred to feel that they were engaging in a higher moral realm that gave them a surer legitimacy. Christian Fürchtegott Gellert's novel *Leben der schwedischen Gräfin von G**** (Life of the Swedish Countess of G***, 1747–48) shows how a combination of reason and virtue and generosity and steadfastness allows the hero and heroine to overcome the problems of the world, which take the form, in the first instance, of the wickedness and vanity of the court. This is a pattern that recurs through much German literature of the eighteenth century. A set of values that is associated with the possession of power and is often, but not always, explicitly linked to the world of the court is contrasted with values that relate to the nonpolitical self and that, however problematic they may be shown to be, especially in the later part of the century, nevertheless reflect an inner, private merit. This contrast between acquired and attributed status is overlaid by the Christian connotations of spirit and body, albeit with the additional twist formulated in Max Weber's "Protestant Ethic" thesis that success in this world could be interpreted as evidence that one was destined for salvation.

The moral criticism of individuals who hold power is, therefore, not uncommon, and to the extent that individuals are presented as representatives of a social class one may claim that the literature is challenging their legitimacy and is political. On the other hand, these matters are not addressed in a systematic way as political issues: solutions are not presented in terms of political or social reform, and would-be reformers are often shown to be in their own way as problematic as the representatives of the system with which they are in conflict. Different styles of writing seem to have reflected different attitudes toward the basis on which the identity of a self-aware middle-class could be laid. What unites the Pietist tradition and the rationalist tradition, despite all their differences, is their rejection of tradition and authority and, indeed, of all truths and values that are not validated by the individual. It may even be suggested, albeit rather schematically, that what is sometimes called "Enlightened Absolutism," a form of absolutism that claimed to incorporate reason and virtue into the workings of the state, made it necessary for the writers we label as Sturm und Drang to abandon the terrain of reason and virtue and declare that genuine merit took the form of authenticity, of truth to oneself and to nature.

At the same time, these values reflect an anxiety about change, which may help to explain why, despite the urgency of its protests, there is something conservative about the Sturm und Drang. What was beginning to emerge in the eighteenth century, headed by the middle classes, was a highly differentiated economy based on competition and money, instead of community and tradition: society was fragmenting — or reforming. By comparison with England, where the industrial revolution was well under way, there was little technological innovation in eighteenth-century Germany; but there were the beginnings of the social reorganization of work, which, combined with the expansion of state administration, may have made German writers particularly sensitive to the phenomenon we now know as alienation, the feeling of estrangement that comes from losing one's place in a self-sustaining community. There was thus a feeling of loss, also experienced as a feeling of no longer belonging. At the same time there is, as in Rousseau, a feeling, expressed with different degrees of confidence by different authors on different occasions, that it may yet be possible to overcome alienation. Three realms are particularly important for the writers of the Sturm und Drang in this respect: nature, the community, and the individual.

The idea of nature was used, as it is today, in two senses. On the one hand, it refers to the essential features of a being, as when we talk about a person's true nature. On the other hand, it can be applied to the landscape. The rhetoric of the Sturm und Drang tended to idealize both meanings, but it also united them in the argument that the landscape was the true, natural physical world inasmuch as it had not been made artificial by being subordinated to the intelligence of human beings. Admittedly, the distinction is not a precise one, because working with nature does not necessarily imply alienation; and both Rousseau and the writers of the Sturm und Drang were capable of idealizing a peasant farmer who is one with the land, or a gardener who is sensitive to nature, because they in some sense participate in the oneness of nature that for these writers had acquired a moral value.

The same kind of argument could be used to legitimate the feelings of German national identity that emerged in the Sturm und Drang. In part, these feelings derived from the fact that, as Elias argues, the aristocratic culture to which the middle-class intelligentsia was opposed was a culture that was to a great extent (at least until the end of the century) oriented toward France, was articulated in the French language, and subscribed to French neoclassical norms. The emancipation from these cultural values and this aesthetic could, therefore, at the same time be expressed with less offense as an anti-French cultural movement. Moreover, to write in German in a German tradition was to be truer to one's identity as a German than to adopt foreign and socially alien models. The term "nationalism" should, however, be used with caution, because it would be wrong to attribute to the Sturm und Drang the kind of nationalism found in Germany in the nineteenth and twentieth centuries, which represented the demands of a national entity for increased power and influence: in the eighteenth century there was no such national unit, and the desire for one was as much the expression of other concerns about class identity and the essence of selfhood. For the Sturm und Drang it was important that the individual should be integrated into a community, and feelings of nationhood were an extension of this desire.

The search for self-realization, or true selfhood, was perhaps the most fundamental urge of the Sturm und Drang, and the idea of the nation is in some ways a reflection of the idea of the self, a fragmented being for whose fulfillment they longed. This is at root the phenomenon known as individualism, one of the key features of modern consciousness. On the one hand, the differentiation of society and the competition to demonstrate merit means that life becomes enriched as people become conscious of themselves as individuals different from other people. On the other hand, the same process means the fragmentation of society and the isolation of individuals who no longer feel that they are part of an integrative community.[26] Reason, order, the norms of polite society, and the other dimensions of the world against which Sturm und Drang figures tend to try to assert themselves are all characterized by their claim to universality and, thus, to the suppression of the individual. One of the achievements of the Sturm und Drang is the sensitivity with which they were able to register the restrictions placed on the individual.

The Challenge to Neoclassical Norms in the Sturm und Drang

The writers of the Sturm und Drang were often known at the time, by friends and foes alike, as the "*Genies.*" The idea of genius was not new in the Sturm und Drang. It had a long history in aesthetics, and writers of the previous generation had already moved away from the constructivist aesthetics associated with Johann Christoph Gottsched (1700–1766). Lessing, in particular, had recognized the value of imagination and inspiration in artistic creation. What distinguishes the writers of the Sturm und Drang is the priority they give this concept, attributing to the genius of the creative artist powers of judgment that transcend all traditional norms and expectations and specially the so-called "rules," which derived their authority from Aristotle, as interpreted by the writers of the French neoclassical tradition. Herder, borrowing an image from the English writer Edward Young (1683–1765), observed that crutches help the sick but hinder the healthy: similarly, aesthetic rules can help an incompetent writer produce a play that at least has the virtue of correctness, but a true genius will cast them aside and allow his writing to be determined only by what he knows to be right (*H-SW*, 5: 183).

Lavater's response to the idea of genius is as ecstatic and incoherent as is appropriate for a being who is capable of transcendental cognition:

Menschengötter! Schöpfer! Zerstörer! Offenbarer der Geheimnisse Gottes und der Menschen! Dollmetscher der Natur! Aussprecher unaussprechlicher Dinge! Propheten! Priester! Könige der Welt . . . die die Gottheit organisirt und gebildet hat — zu offenbaren durch sie sich selbst und ihre Schöpfungskraft und Weisheit und Huld. *Offenbarer der Majestät aller Dinge, und ihres Verhältnisses zum ewigen Quell und Ziel aller Dinge: Genieen* — von euch reden wir![27]

It is not surprising that, with this kind of preference for associative and emotive rhetoric, the writers of the Sturm und Drang should have been accused of arbitrary and self-indulgent subjectivism. Lenz, however, argues that liberation from the rules allows the genius to write as he must: what is arbitrary for Lenz is the neoclassical idealization of nature that denies what nature objectively is and what art objectively requires (*L-WB*, 2: 648).

Goethe's Werther makes it clear that the debate about the rules is about more than artistic creation when he introduces the analogy of society, where laws may prevent abuses but never in themselves produce greatness:

Man kann zum Vorteile der Regeln viel sagen, ohngefähr was man zum Lobe der bürgerlichen Gesellschaft sagen kann. Ein Mensch, der sich nach ihnen bildet, wird nie etwas abgeschmacktes und schlechtes hervor bringen, wie einer, der sich durch Gesetze und Wohlstand modeln läßt, nie ein unerträglicher Nachbar, nie ein merkwürdiger Bösewicht werden kann; dagegen wird aber auch all Regel, man rede was man wolle, das wahre Gefühl von Natur und den wahren Ausdruck derselben zerstören! (*G-MA*, 1.2: 205)[28]

The letter continues with a telling comparison between art and love, both of which, Werther says, must be free of external constraints if they are to be authentic; and it ends with a vision of the supremacy that genius will finally assert:

O meine Freunde! warum der Strom des Genies so selten ausbricht, so selten in hohen Fluten hereinbraust, und eure staunende Seele erschüttert. Lieben Freunde, da wohnen die gelaßnen Kerls auf beiden Seiten des Ufers, denen ihre Gartenhäuschen, Tulpenbeete, und Krautfelder zu Grunde gehen würden, und die daher in Zeiten mit dämmen und ableiten der künftig drohenden Gefahr abzuwehren wissen. (*G-MA*, 1.2: 206)[29]

In all three realms — the organization of society, the organization of the private life, and art — Werther contrasts an inner necessity with the restrictions of outer forms. The former is in each case associated with a force of nature, the flood water, which sweeps aside human constructs.

It is notable that the human constructs mentioned here are all ones which represent an attempt to appropriate nature, either by the intensive cultivation of useful and presumably marketable crops or else by building a summer-house which will allow the civilized, protected enjoyment of a civilized nature. The phrase "die gelaßnen Kerls" (respectable fellows) suggests the smug disregard for nature, an application to the individual of these attempts to civilize nature: "*gelassen*" was one of those key words used by Gellert to refer to the essence of virtue, the ability to remain composed and unaffected by whatever circumstance threw at one. What was for Gellert (and again for Goethe later in his life) civilization and order is for Werther little more than a desperate and in the end futile attempt to control nature.

What has emerged from this passage in Goethe's *Werther* is a model of repression, accompanied by hints of the possibility that the natural order of things might be restored; and it is not difficult to understand how later readers could have seen connections with the French Revolution, which broke out less than twenty years after the novel appeared. Indeed, the writers of the Sturm und Drang thought of themselves, and were thought of, as radical, Goethe himself later spoke about the Sturm und Drang as a revolution (*G-MA*, 16: 522), and it is true that arguments about the violent restoration of the natural order were later used to legitimate the French Revolution. Although this passage from *Werther* contains images of the forces of nature destroying an ordered society, however, it does not express them in terms of conflict between social classes: what is threatened seems to be society as such, or even existence. At the beginning of his novella *Der arme Spielmann* (The Poor Minstrel), which first appeared in the journal *Iris* for 1848, the year of European revolutions, Franz Grillparzer (1791–1872) compares the mass of the people streaming in through the city gates with flood waters, but the social connotations here in *Werther* over seventy years earlier are less specific. What Werther envisages, if one can reduce it to a rudimentary social content, is the collapse of a fragile, overcivilized order that stands in the way of true love, true art, true greatness, and nature. This is criticism of society as such, rather than of particular social institutions. Some writers of the Sturm und Drang, notably Lenz in his work on the relationship between the army and civil society, did develop proposals for institutional reform; but although it is possible to discern in these proposals quite fundamental social criticisms, the proposals themselves concern practical measures for improving efficiency, and even the aggressive tone adopted by Bürger and Schubart was directed against abuses of the system rather than the system as such.

What is revolutionary about the authors of the Sturm und Drang is less their politics than their acceptance of passion, both in the literary figures they created and in their style of writing. Their essays, no less than their more strictly literary works, adopt a poetic style that demands a response from the reader's emotions and imagination. There is an argument to be found in these texts, and often a subtle and complex one, but it is conducted in the form of a sequence of impressions, usually with an "I"-figure in the foreground. This style allows them to be informal in tone and to cover an emotional range from the sarcastic to the ecstatic. They demand, in the first instance, an empathetic reader who can respond with equal enthusiasm, rather than a carefully reflecting reader concerned with the balance of arguments. This characteristic is found equally in the plays, the poems, and the narrative fiction. The language of the characters in Sturm und Drang plays often has the same kind of intensity that breaks up the syntax and threatens to disrupt communication. Guelfo in Klinger's *Die Zwillinge,* for example, gazes out of the window at the sunset, and his emotions stir to the point where he forces a kiss on Kamilla, the fiancée of the brother who is also his mortal enemy:

> Die letzten Sonnenstrahlen durch die Bäume her — Ich möchte mich in die Feuerhelle dort schwingen, auf jenen Wolken reiten mit vergoldetem Saume! — Kamilla! *Faßt sie an der Hand.* Ach! und ich bin wieder so hin — ich möchte diese Feuerwolken zusammenpacken, Sturm und Wetter erregen und mich zerschmettert in den Abgrund stürzen! — Kamilla! Kamilla! Kamilla! *Küßt sie heftig.* (*K-W,* 2: 104)[30]

This style of writing is associative: the dashes indicate the leaps of imagination which link ideas whose relationship is not explicit, and the exclamation marks indicate an intensity which goes beyond the precise dictionary meaning of words. This is the disjointed stammering of a man who is overwhelmed by emotion, whose words and images are gestures rather than an abstract medium for communicating clear and distinct ideas. Klinger is here, in the violence of the language as much as in the violence of the kiss Guelfo forces on Kamilla, deliberately rejecting the coherent, balanced, and, in the end, idealizing language demanded by the French neoclassical tradition. We would scarcely guess that in this passage Guelfo is responding to Kamilla's comments on the beauty of the evening. He is so turned in on himself that he answers her with a monologue: his actual communication with her reaches its climax in his repetition of her name and in the rapelike final gesture.

Nevertheless, it would be wrong to give the impression that all writing in the Sturm und Drang is of this kind. There are many passages and many whole plays, including plays by Klinger and Goethe, where the language used is not experimental in this kind of way, or is only rarely so; but it remains a potential in the Sturm und Drang and indicates the priority given to truth of expression. Even here, though, we have to be careful, for, as has been suggested, an appreciation of Guelfo requires that we should be able to identify sufficiently with the emotional logic behind his outbursts but, at the same time, that we should retain a perspective that recognizes what is happening — how, for example, communication is distorted and Guelfo uses the language of love (the kiss) to express anger at his brother. In the case of *Werther*, the first-person utterances of Werther himself in his letters are moderated by a more reflective editor who is from the beginning aware of the suicide to which Werther's excesses are leading him; and so here, too, there is a level at which the reader is invited to empathize with an emotional, not always coherent character, but also a level at which the reader is offered a more distanced, balanced perspective. To call this irony would be going too far in most cases, but there is a sense in which the writing of the Sturm und Drang involves "putting on" a particular style. This feature is particularly evident in the private letters of Sturm und Drang writers, where it is possible to watch them changing mode according to the person to whom they are writing and the persona they are adopting. In general, there is a self-awareness to the Sturm und Drang that we are likely to miss if we simply take the expression of emotion at face value.

Guelfo's kiss shows, in a play that follows the neoclassical conventions relatively closely, the way in which the Sturm und Drang places greater emphasis on action on stage, shown by stage directions, which here indicate violence. The French neoclassical tragedy of Jean Racine (1639–99), which was still a guide to good taste — that is, to aristocratic good taste — in eighteenth-century Germany, avoided action on stage and laid the whole weight of the play in the words: beautiful words that articulated with clarity and elegance the attitudes of the characters and expressed a confidence in the ability of language to communicate complete meanings. The writers of the Sturm und Drang were more often skeptical about the power of language to communicate clear meanings,[31] and specifically language in the modern, supposedly civilized world, where the reification of language has become a further symptom of the alienation of the individual from his true self and from nature. Faust uses this point to extend the topos of the unknowability of God when Gretchen asks him to define his religious beliefs, and he replies that any name would do because none is adequate:

Nenn's Glück! Herz! Liebe! Gott!
Ich habe keinen Namen
Dafür. Gefühl ist alles
Name Schall und Rauch. (*G-MA*, 1.2: 174)[32]

Linguistic form is cast in doubt because it inhibits the expression of a true content, and similarly Goethe's early poetry contains several examples of neologisms that stretch the existing language by making the reader's imagination create the link between the elements of compound words such as "*Knabenmorgen Blütenträume*" (*G-MA*, 1.1: 231).[33]

The same principle applies to the way in which the writers of the Sturm und Drang rejected the forms of drama deriving from the neoclassical tradition, which Goethe described as fetters preventing him from expressing himself truly and freely (*G-MA*, 1.2: 412). He admired, by contrast, Shakespeare's ability to avoid abstraction and, at the same time, to release an audience's imagination. The precise historical setting of *Götz von Berlichingen* is essential to what the play is about, and Goethe would have been unable to give us this broad portrait of society over a period of years if he had not looked to Shakespeare rather than to the French neoclassical tradition in his treatment of time, place, thematic unity, and the spectrum of society he presents. Lenz too, in *Der Hofmeister* and *Die Soldaten*, was able to offer such subtle analyses of social relations only because of his disregard of the neoclassical conventions. Not all plays of the Sturm und Drang are so extreme, however. In some cases the practical considerations of performance acted as a restraint. With *Die Zwillinge*, for example, Klinger entered and won a competition for an original play that could be easily performed. He therefore used a small cast and offered a limited view of the social world, however immoderate the behavior of the characters. Gerstenberg's *Ugolino* is an interesting and characteristically transitional play. The stage represents the room in the tower where the father and his three sons are imprisoned, and the time is the time it take a man to starve to death, so that, although in technical terms Gerstenberg follows the unities to the letter, they are not allowed to play the traditional role of abstracting and idealizing but are built into the action of the play.

The emphasis on the plastic expression of content rather than on the acceptance of preordained forms is also reflected in the lyric poetry of the Sturm und Drang, particularly that of Goethe. He was able to draw on Klopstock's experiments with free verse. His great verse hymns, such as "Prometheus," "Ganymed," or "Mahomets Gesang" (Song for Mohammed),[34] have no regular meter and no regular pattern of stanzas. In these poems, which were based on contemporary interpretations (or misinterpretations) of Pindar (522–442 B.C.), Goethe creates the impression that the intensity of feeling — and the poems all in one way or another deal with attempts to overcome the distance between our existence as ordinary mortals and some transcendental realm — sweeps aside the pattern of alternations that characterizes poems written in regular meters and stanzas.

In several ways, then, the writers of the Sturm und Drang attempted to resist the imposition of external forms. Lenz's parting shot when he was dismissed from Weimar was contained in a letter to Herder: "Wie lange werdt Ihr noch an Form und Namen hängen" (*L-WB*, 3: 517).[35] This letter dates from the end of November 1776, and Lenz seems to have felt betrayed, or at least misunderstood, as a result of the compromises Goethe was by now making. Little more than a year earlier, however, before he moved to Weimar, Goethe had, in fact, developed the most subtle critique of form that the Sturm und Drang produced. It appeared in a supplement he wrote to Wagner's translation (1776) of Louis-Sébastien Mercier's *Du Théâtre*, and here he argued that outer formal constraints should be disregarded but that doing so would not of necessity lead to an absence of form: the work of art still had a shape and a structure, but it was the shape and structure that the content inherently adopted, not one that was superimposed. He called this its "inner form" (*G-MA*, 1.2: 491) and made it clear that the concept could be applied not only to poetry and drama but also to painting, on which the subsequent sections of the supplement focus.[36] These insights seem to go back to Goethe's encounter with Herder, who had criticized the first draft of *Götz von Berlichingen* as being "nur gedacht" (too intellectual) (*G-HB*, 1: 133). He seems to have meant that, despite the progress Goethe had made, the language of his characters still does not articulate them as beings: it tends too much to impose on them the dramatist's analysis of the principles behind their behavior. Herder addressed the question of the relationship between form and content in his *Über die neuere Deutsche Litteratur* (On More Recent German Literature, 1767–68) when he discussed the problem of the poet who somehow has to use a black line on white paper to communicate something of a different order, namely, feeling. He wrote of the decline of modern poetry and the dangers of separating form from content when we read the ancients,

> wenn wir Gedanken und Worte in ihnen abgetrennt betrachten: nicht das Schöpferische Ohr haben, das die Empfindung in seinem Ausdrucke, in vollem Tone höret; nicht jenes Dichterische Auge haben, das den Ausdruck als einen Körper erblickt, in welchem sein Geist denkt und spricht und handelt. (*H-SW*, 1: 396)[37]

After reading these words Goethe wrote to Herder: "doch ist nichts wie eine Göttererscheinung über mich herabgestiegen, hat mein Herz und Sinn mit warmer heiliger Gegenwart durch und durch belebt, als das wie *Gedanck* und *Empfindung* den *Ausdruck* bildet" (*G-HB*, 1: 133).[38] The idea of inner form seems to refer to the result of the process Goethe here describes with the word *bilden*.

At the same time as they were experimenting in free verse, both Goethe and Lenz also wrote many poems that are more regular in meter; but even in these the shape of the poem is more flexible and follows the flux of individual feeling, not the kind of lightly tripping foreground rhythm of, for example, the rococo poems of Friedrich von Hagedorn (1708–54). In Goethe's "Maifest" (Mayfest), for example, intensity of feeling forces the sentence over the grammatical break one would normally expect at the end of a stanza:

> So liebt die Lerche
> Gesang und Luft,
> Und Morgenblumen
> Den Himmels Duft,
>
> Wie ich dich liebe
> Mit warmen Blut,
> Die du mir Jugend
> Und Freud und Mut
>
> Zu neuen Liedern,
> Und Tänzen gibst!
> Sei ewig glücklich
> Wie du mich liebst!
> (*G-MA*, 1.1: 163)[39]

The simple enthusiasm of this poem reflects a debt to the folk style that became highly popular in the Sturm und Drang. The regular meter it shares with them, which is quite different from the free verse of the hymns, is, nevertheless, forceful and expressive. The closest imitations of the folk style are the narrative poems — of which ballads are but one, albeit typical, example — which are written in simple, sometimes colloquial language, with a tight metrical and stanzaic pattern. They often include direct speech and tend to focus on a sequence of individual moments in a narrative, thus reproducing what Herder called the "leaps and gaps and sudden transitions" (*GAL*, 160; "Sprünge und Würfe," *H-SW*, 5: 197) that he considered typical of folk poetry. Inasmuch as they exhibited formal regularity, these poems were felt to express the natural force that derived from their primitive wholeness.

The Discovery of the Self in the Sturm und Drang: Goethe's *Werther*

The Sturm und Drang did not, in general, indulge in formlessness for its own sake but insisted, and sometimes made a show of insisting, that a content should express itself directly in its own way, without the distortions produced by the imposition of preordained formal devices. This requirement is a vision more than a consistently held system of beliefs, and it applies to several important realms other than art. Older histories of literature, which often reduced the Sturm und Drang to their own celebration of irrationalism erupting into a world of rationalism, were able to point, for example, to such key words as *Genie, Herz,* and *Gefühl* and argue that they imply an assertion of the value of nonrational forms of cognition. Moreover, the characters who assert the primacy of feeling, Werther, Faust, or Guelfo, are often contrasted with other characters, Albert, Wagner, and Ferdinando, who in their rather puny way think that calm, ordered reflection can usefully resolve the problems that feeling throws up. These characters, it is claimed, are being used to show the inadequacy of the Enlightenment in the narrow sense of the term.

This may, indeed, be the meaning of the lamp that Faust's assistant, Wagner, holds when he enters: a source of light, but one that pales into insignificance after the overwhelming apparition of the *Erdgeist* (Earth Spirit). Götz, too, can be interpreted as resisting the incursions of rationalism represented in the court of the Bishop of Bamberg. The first scene set at the court, sandwiched between two scenes devoted to the portrayal of Götz's values, includes a discussion of Roman Law, whose bureaucratic rationalism is a challenge to feudal law and reveals a style of behavior characterized by aggressive cleverness, contrasting with the warmth evident in Götz's family. The spirit of Bamberg is in some ways concentrated in the figure of Adelheid, whom we first meet at the beginning of the second act engaged in the rationalist's game, chess, and agreeing to manipulate other people, notably Weislingen, in exactly the same way that she manipulates the figures on the chessboard. A more complex critique of rationalism is found in the work of Lenz, who, more than most Sturm und Drang writers, also devoted his energies to schemes for moral improvement and political reform. He includes in his dramas apparently sympathetic figures who have an intellectual understanding of what is happening. While other characters are carried away by emotion or delusion, or both, the Geheimrat (Privy Councilor) in *Der Hofmeister* or Eisenhardt or the Gräfin La Roche in *Die Soldaten* have plausible explanations of the social and psychological mechanisms at work; but they all remain incapable of taking any action that helps the situation. Understanding is an aspect of social privilege and, thus, part of the problem rather than its solution.

It is, therefore, true that in the Sturm und Drang we meet a series of characters with intellectual skills who are either clever or sensible rather than spontaneously emotional, and that these characters are shown to be weak or manipulative or both. They represent a much wider range of features, however, than the term "rationalism" would suggest. What is significant about them, rather, is that they are unable to engage the whole of what it means to be human, including not only the intellect but also feeling and imagination. This theme is evident in the cases where book learning is contrasted with spontaneous knowledge, as it is with several characters Werther meets who have studied art or nature but have no feeling for them. It is equally one-sided to reduce the emotionality of the so-called heroes of the Sturm und Drang to an ideal of irrationalism. Although they are frequently emotional, and at times violently so, it is not even certain that they are closer to their natural selves, even if this is their ideal. Faust, Werther, and Guelfo all tend to indulge themselves in emotion. The first scene of *Die Zwillinge* — rather like the first scene in which we see Karl in Schiller's *Die Räuber* — is a scene in which the hero, who has been drinking wine, is being read heroic stories from Plutarch, suggesting that there is something artificial, almost studied, about the grand gestures of despair he allows himself. Werther — again fueled by books — suffers from morbid introversion, and Faust's obsessive energy seems to contrast with the genuine naturalness of Gretchen.

Examples such as these also suggest that we should be wary of assuming that these texts present an unquestioning celebration of the heroic individuals they portray. The gestures of the characters may at times be heroic, but the authors consistently show the problematic nature of these gestures. Few plays of the Sturm und Drang have happy endings: comedy was not their forte. In Lenz the exception proves the rule: his three major plays are labeled comedies and do have apparently happy endings; but in their different ways these happy endings are false — their resolutions of their conflicts are so inappropriate that, in effect, they mock the idea that the conflicts of real life could have such neat resolutions. The plays themselves undercut the optimistic rhetoric with which they end and show that happy endings are ever only that: rhetoric. It is more common for the plays of the Sturm und Drang to end in catastrophe: the Sturm und Drang project is consistently shown to fail. The Sturm und Drang protagonist has a certain heroic grandeur that derives from a refusal to accept the normal constraints of life; but the texts criticize this refusal in many ways, not least in the fact that it so rarely actually leads to self-realization.

The Sturm und Drang tends to present people who attempt unsuccessfully to assert their individuality. They confront a world that is held together by some kind of order that they experience as repressing or restricting their individuality. This order is of various kinds, but it usually also takes the form of a particular social order — either the family or society at large; but it may also refer to the idea of society as such or even to our existence as human beings. In the case of *Götz von Berlichingen*, which is set at about the time of the Reformation, Götz is attempting to insist on a way of life and a set of values that are being eroded by the structure of a new, emerging society; the problems represented by *Faust*, too, are related to the emergence of the modern world. But it is just as common for the plays of the Sturm und Drang to focus on a contemporary domestic interior with little explicit reference to a broader historical continuum. One of the new and challenging features of these plays was that they showed the family not as a refuge to which the individual could withdraw from society but as one further dimension of the world that inhibited the individual. In Gellert's *Schwedische Gräfin von G**** the middle-class nuclear family (even if inhabited by aristocrats) seemed almost to have moral value in itself as a place where one might escape the machinations of the court. But even here, Lessing had led the way in his *Emilia Galotti* (1772). The primary social conflict is, again, between a predatory court and a rural aristocracy that is imbued with middle-class values and puts a premium on virtue; but Lessing shows how the moral purism of the father, Odoardo, contributes to the catastrophe. In the plays of the Sturm und Drang the primary conflict is often located within the family. It can appear as the foolish or selfish father, or as a conflict between son and father; or it can take the form of the man who hates his brother, leading to the motif of fratricide, which came to be seen as characteristic of the Sturm und Drang. In all of these — closely related — cases there is scarcely a hint of the moral authority that the family had for earlier generations of the Enlightenment and to which Odoardo Galotti so desperately appeals. Moral authority has been reduced to something arbitrary that the younger generation finds merely inhibiting. The Sturm und Drang can, thus, be regarded as expressing the frustrations of adolescence, encapsulated in the cry of the appropriately named Robert Hot in Lenz's *Der Engländer* (The Englishman,

1777): "Weg mit den Vätern!" (*L-WB,* 1: 330).[40] More than that, though, the family has become a place where generational conflict represents the struggle of the individual to acquire authentic individuality.[41]

It would be wrong, however, to suggest that the struggle for self-realization in the Sturm und Drang meant simply the struggle against fathers, brothers, or the family in general. In some cases these criticisms were linked to broader criticisms of society. In *Die Soldaten,* for example, Lenz shows how a whole range of social institutions — the family, the military, the class system, the gender system — produce a series of interlocking pressures within which it becomes, in practice, impossible to assert a true identity: Lenz suggests that, at least in the corrupt world in which we live, there is no such thing as a true identity separate from these particular social roles. In other cases we are, perhaps, less certain about the political connotations that are intended by the presentation of a conflict within the private realm. Do, for example, Guelfo's jealousy of his brother and his belief that his brother does not deserve the family inheritance represent a broader criticism of primogeniture and, thus, of feudal society?[42] The air of frustration that the play exudes seems too unfocused, and Guelfo's belief in the legitimacy afforded by his own physical prowess seems too closely linked to his self-indulgent posturing, for him to act as an effective channel for specifically antifeudal sentiments.

In many cases the protest against the family is linked not so much to protest against a specific social or political structure, or even against "tyranny," as against an imprecisely defined "other" that may take the form of the hierarchical order known as the family but may also take many other forms, including the ideological world of established, polite society. It is the reasonableness of an order that has been nurtured on the Enlightenment belief in reason but has lapsed into smugness and whose reasonable tolerance has become repressive tolerance because it denies the emotional depth of protest or the need for action. The writers of the Sturm und Drang manage to convey the complexity of the ways, both direct and indirect, in which the individual is prevented from finding self-fulfillment. What the Sturm und Drang helps us to understand, then, is the perspective of the subject experiencing frustration. This is an individual who is trying to discover and assert his, or less often her, individuality: it is someone trying to be — but first to discover — him- or herself. The scope of such a project is at times so immense and so unspecific that it seems as if it is existence itself that locks the individual into contradictions that prevent self-discovery and self-realization. When the eponymous hero of Klinger's *Otto,* in a moment of despair, calls himself a

"Wurm mit der Riesenseele" (*K-W*, 1: 49),[43] he identifies the fundamental discrepancy between his aspirations and the existential self they threaten to engulf.

The Sturm und Drang deals centrally with the problem of individualism and is, thus, a reflection of a distinctive feature of modern consciousness. The problem of individuation finds expression in one way or another in every representative work of the Sturm und Drang, but its paradigmatic statement is Goethe's *Werther*. The plot of this novel, which emerges from letters written by Werther, mostly to his friend Wilhelm, revolves around his hopeless love for Lotte. While the institutionalized forms of relationship sanctioned by society progress from the engagement of Lotte and Albert in the first part of the novel to their marriage in the second, Werther is cast in the role of the outsider. He is also, correspondingly, the one who is more sensitive and more preoccupied with his own feelings, and he acts as a contrast to his more conventional rival, Albert. At the beginning of the second part of the novel Werther breaks away and takes a post as secretary to an ambassador; but here, too, he comes into conflict with convention. He is irritated by the shallowness and the intrigues of court life; he is even prevented from expressing himself in his own style of language. In the end he is so humiliated by the way people respond to his failure to observe the niceties of class distinctions that he abandons this attempt to find a place for himself in the world and returns to Lotte. Werther's consciousness of himself as an outsider excluded from the realms of love and work, or private and public, drives him to shoot himself. At the same time he conspires in this exclusion through his insistence on "being himself," but his focus on the essential, "natural" inner self, intensified by the feeling of exclusion, also reveals to him a whole new dimension of individual, interior experience: "Ich kehre in mich selbst zurück, und finde eine Welt!" (*G-MA*, 1.2: 203).[44] Werther is in this way the only character in the novel who discovers himself; but, of course, this enrichment of his life is also the symptom and the cause of his inability to find an accommodation with the outside world, and shortly after asserting the idea of the authentic inner life, he recalls the "sweet" feeling of freedom: that it is always possible to choose death.

The first part of the novel provides a context for the burgeoning of Werther's love by placing him in an idyllic natural setting where he has been sent on a commission from his mother, and it opens with a gesture of joyful separation: "Wie froh bin ich, daß ich weg bin!" (*G-MA*, 1.2: 197).[45] The world that is described in the following pages is, thus, a distinctive one in which Werther is able to feel in harmony with the whole of nature, and the incipient pantheism of these descriptions, such as the one in the second letter (May 10), is an indication that he is enjoying the vision of an existence free from alienation. At a strictly economic level, the delights of eating the cabbage he has grown himself are contrasted with the empty activity of work at court (*G-MA,* 1.2: 217–18). He adds a rather generalized (Rousseauist, Herderian) historical dimension by describing his environment as paradise and associating the women who collect water from a well with an existence belonging to Old Testament times. Further realms in which Goethe develops images of a "natural" inner essence to which Werther turns, away from the institutions of modern society, include art (authentic responsiveness is obstructed by knowledge about art) and children (who have not yet been spoiled by learning).

Werther feels a particular affinity for children, and the fact that Werther sees Lotte in a nurturing role at important moments, including their celebrated first meeting, suggests that there is something of the child in him, too. Whether he is more childlike or childish is less clear. The modern reader may feel irritated by Werther's self-indulgence, but Goethe shows how inevitably his behavior follows from the fact that he insists on taking himself seriously as an individual and how this attitude enriches his life as well as isolating him and, in the end, depriving his identity of meaning. The novel shows the inherent contradictions of individualism: it is the symptom of a social group asserting the importance of areas of experience that the culture of "enlightened absolutism" had suppressed but that, if taken to their extreme, involve loss of contact with any social group. To absolutize the inner self is to deny life. It may not, therefore, be entirely wrong to say that Werther is destroyed by the society in which he finds himself, but this claim requires qualification. First, it would be wrong to deduce from its destruction that Werther's life is meaningless or valueless; even if Werther fails in a sense, his sensitivity and perceptiveness have allowed him to discover a unique richness of experience. Second, Goethe embeds the portrayal of a specifically German eighteenth-century society, with its absolutist court and its common-sense rationalism but also with its sensitivity to nature and its Klopstockian sentimentalism, in an analysis of the idea of society as such. We are never sure whether the particular is an example of the general, or whether the general is being invoked — as a poetic device (by Goethe) or as a form of legitimation (by Werther) — to give emphasis to the particular. Indeed, it is this marriage of precise observation with an awareness of philosophical or existential depths that is so characteristic of Goethe's writing.

The intensity with which Goethe captures Werther's inward responses to the world around him is reflected in the form of the novel. Although the editor who has gathered together Werther's letters provides the framework, the greater part of the text consists of these letters; and for large stretches of the novel Werther's point of view dominates our perception of the narrated events. There are, it is true, hints of alternative perspectives in the reported comments of other characters, including Wilhelm, as well as in the editorial contributions, but the novel revolves around the subjectivity of Werther himself. It is a novel about an "I" presented predominantly by and through an "I." In *Werther* Goethe adapted the form of the epistolary novel practiced by Rousseau and Samuel Richardson (1689–1761) so as to concentrate on the individualism of Werther himself. Whereas the first-person novel is more often written from the point of view of a narrator looking back over a life at distant events, *Werther* uses letters to convey the immediacy and directness of events that have just happened. They are little bursts of energy, like the stanzas of a ballad, and the fluctuating pace of the novel, both in the alternation of narrative and reflection in the individual letters and in the overall pattern of the work, is managed by Goethe with consummate skill. He enhances the sense of the inevitability of Werther's decline by contrasting the ecstatic moments of discovery and self-discovery that particularly mark the earlier parts of the novel with Werther's gradual realization that the self he has begun to discover can never be fully actualized. As it becomes clear to him that he has no place in society, nature begins to appear as destructive; and the warmth and energy of the first pages, set in May and June, give way to the coldness and death of autumn and winter some eighteen months later. The ecstatic early letter of May 10 itself ends with a warning of the mental, social, and indeed existential collapse that is to come: "Mein Freund — Aber ich gehe darüber zu Grunde, ich erliege unter der Gewalt der Herrlichkeit dieser Erscheinungen" (*G-MA*, 1.2: 199).[46] Werther's own development is supported and reflected by a number of stories or motifs in the second part that refer back to the first part but are now marked by death and decline. The walnut trees Werther had admired have been cut down, and the minister with whom he had sat under them has died; Hans has died, and his father's hopes of money have been disappointed; the landscape that had once seemed so rich and harmonious is now bleak.[47] The world seen through Werther's eyes declines in the same way that Werther's own mental state declines.

The effect is that the reader feels constrained to identify with the "I" of Werther and to empathize with his isolation and his introverted idealism. This was clearly the reaction of contemporaries who devoured the novel with such enthusiasm and made it perhaps the first cult novel of the modern world. They found in it a tragic portrait of their own emerging individualism, presented with a realism that was no doubt intensified by the knowledge that real events in Wetzlar lay behind it. On the other hand, the reader is also able to recognize that this "I" is a character in the novel, and not one that demands uncritical identification, let alone imitation. Werther is self-obsessed and self-indulgent, he speaks of nursing his heart as if it were a sick child (*G-MA*, 1.2: 200), and we suspect that there may be more than a little truth in Lotte's observation that he is so attracted to her only because she is unattainable (*G-MA*, 1.2: 279): we doubt whether Werther could ever escape from his solipsism enough to participate in a genuinely two-way relationship, let alone whether he could ever really participate in the domesticity for which part of him (as also part of Faust) longs. Goethe walks a tightrope here. In the 1787 edition of the novel Goethe shifted the balance by adding passages which encouraged readers not to identify too closely with Werther, perhaps for fear of encouraging a fashion for suicide — Christel von Lassberg had supposedly thrown herself into the Ilm with a copy of *Werther* in her pocket — but, although in *Dichtung und Wahrheit* Goethe describes the composition of the novel as an act of liberation, a confession that gave him a new life, it is clear from later comments, including a conversation with his secretary, Johann Peter Eckermann, in January, 1824, that he had embedded within *Werther* the formulation of a life-threatening individualism that he continued to find unsettling.

Rousseau integrated his analysis of individualism into his philosophy of history. In his first *Discourse* he presented a portrait of the modern world in which people are alienated from each other and from themselves. He contrasts this society, which is based on appearances, with the ideal of a former existence in which actions counted more than words and in which it was possible to be oneself. In the second *Discourse* he examines more closely the transition from the so-called state of nature to the present state of corruption and detects in the ownership of private property the seeds of moral collapse. This is a historical narrative, a story of loss that suggests the promise of recovery. Many texts of the Sturm und Drang have hidden within them, in one way or another, the hope of a different existence. A certain number of them, such as *Götz von Berlichingen*, express these ideas in terms of a historical development; but more commonly they are content to present individualism as an opportunity and a problem in its own terms. Their more discursive texts, on the other hand, are, despite all the incoherence of their enthusiastic speculations, marked by their focus on the historical nature of ideological phenomena. Lenz's plays, for example, do not in general refer to a historical transition of this type; but his essays, in particular his *Anmerkungen übers Theater* (Notes on the Theater, 1774), show that he considered that the definition of the distinction between tragedy and comedy depended crucially on our present situation within a historical continuum. Historical kinds of argumentation are central to the essays of Herder, who was in many ways the founder of the modern idea of cultural history. Herder looked to folk culture as a repository of values that had not yet been wholly eroded by the modern world. His analysis of the evils of civilization is similar to Rousseau's and is marked by a similar contrast between authenticity and artificiality, but he showed greater interest in language and literature (or folk song) as bearers of cultural values:

> Wir sehen und fühlen kaum mehr, sondern denken und grüblen nur; wir dichten nicht über und in lebendiger Welt, im Sturm und im Zusammenstrom solcher Gegenstände, solcher Empfindungen; sondern erkünsteln uns entweder Thema, oder Art, das Thema zu behandeln, oder gar beides — und haben uns das schon so lange, so oft, so von früh auf erkünstelt, daß uns freilich jetz kaum eine freie Ausbildung mehr glücken würde. (*H-SW*, 5: 183)[48]

Herder made it clear that his understanding of folk poetry was not narrowly defined, and he was content to include individually authored poems as folk songs as long as they represented a direct and authentic expression of the self. By the same kind of argument Herder was able to claim that the Bible was holy and true not because it contained factually correct historical records or even because it contained an objectively valid morality but because it was deeply imbued with poetic truth. What was important for him was the authentic poetic essence, and at the end of his essay on Shakespeare, Herder welcomed *Götz von Berlichingen* (though not by name) as a monument to Shakespeare that would keep the spirit of poetry alive in a degenerate land.

The End of the Sturm und Drang

To accept the term *Sturm und Drang* as the designation of a literary period or trend is to imply that a series of individual texts have a certain coherence, and this introductory survey has attempted in a selective fashion to focus on some of its defining elements. First, despite all the differences and variations, there is an inner consistency to the ideas, motifs, and styles of the Sturm und Drang. Second, the history of the culture of the period has a certain coherence: that is, however cautious we need to be, it is, nevertheless, possible to suggest some of the reasons why the Sturm und Drang emerged at a particular juncture. There is a complex interplay between different levels of explanation, ranging from the ideological needs of certain social strata to, for example, the circumstances that contrived to make Goethe and Herder, this Goethe and this Herder, meet in Strasbourg in the autumn of 1770. At the same time, there are bound to be many imponderables whenever we approach such questions of causality: such is the nature of historical explanation, and such is the nature of creativity. The elucidation of factors is, nevertheless, an important task, and it needs also to be applied to the ending of the Sturm und Drang. If this view of the world had a certain inner consistency, and if the general conditions were ripe for it in 1770, why was that no longer the case in 1776 or 1786? Again, one must expect a range of explanations operating at different levels and shot through with imponderables. They involve individual decisions and fates, they involve processes of individual maturation, but somehow, the excitement of discovery and protest came to seem no longer quite so relevant. The writings of the Sturm und Drang were radical in their critique of the parameters that their predecessors had accepted, they were critical of all such restraints, and they were, despite all their posturing, critical of themselves. This kind of radicalism had somehow ceased to be interesting by the late 1770s; there are certainly signs that it had ceased to be heroic. The Sturm und Drang was clearly past its zenith by the time the writers of the Sturm und Drang began writing parodies of their movement.

The Sturm und Drang was not always quite as serious as some scholars have made it out to be, and there was an element of parody, or at least of jovial, often ironic rambunctiousness in the fashion for dressing up in the Werther "uniform," or, for example, in Goethe's adoption of a pastiche of sixteenth-century German when sending a copy of *Götz von Berlichingen* to Friedrich Wilhelm Gotter (*G-MA*, 1.1: 215–16). Parody, satire, and irony were also essential to the way in which literary arguments were conducted. When Friedrich Nicolai (1733–1811) responded to *Werther* by writing an alternative ending, *Freuden des jungen Werthers* (Joys of Young Werther, 1775), and a sequel, *Freuden Werthers des Mannes* (Joys of Werther the Man, 1775), that satirized the principles on which Goethe's novel had been built, Goethe, in turn, wrote a short poem, "Freuden des iungen Werthers" (*G-MA*, 1.1: 263–64), in which he mocked the banality of Nicolai's common-sense solution by suggesting that for Nicolai, Werther's problem was nothing much more than constipation. Things were changing, however, when they applied this intentionally rather crude kind of satire to their own works. The year 1778 saw the first performance of *Der Triumph der Empfindsamkeit* (The Triumph of Sentimentalism), in which Goethe mocked the falseness of an obsession with nature and love. Admittedly, he does not distinguish here between the fashion for sentimental writing and the Sturm und Drang; but when the exquisitely beautiful doll with which Oronoro has fallen in love is unpacked, it is found to contain only straw and books: among these are not only novels by Johann Martin Miller (1750–1814) and Rousseau but also Goethe's own *Werther*. Scarcely any more systematic but in its own way equally amusing and equally self-critical is Klinger's *Plimplamplasko, der hohe Geist (heut Genie)* (Plimplamplasko, the Lofty Spirit [Called "Genius" in Our Era])[49] of 1780. Written in an archaic German, a parody of the Sturm und Drang enthusiasm for the sixteenth century, and illustrated with correspondingly crude woodcuts, it is an outlandish satire on the desperate craving for originality that characterized the literary movement of which Klinger had himself been a part less than five years earlier.

After this, it would seem, the only kind of Sturm und Drang writing that was possible was that of the young Schiller, who in his early plays expresses much of the discontent and the striving that is characteristic of the Sturm und Drang but includes a strongly moralizing element and arranges denouements with conciliatory gestures that suggest a possible resolution of the conflict. The endings of the Sturm und Drang plays written during the 1770s, even when they offer resolutions, at the same time tended to question the finality of those resolutions.

Notes

[1] The following are probably the most useful single-authored studies of the Sturm und Drang: Hermann August Korff, *Geist der Goethezeit*, 5 vols. (Leipzig: Koehler & Ameland, 1954–57), especially vol. 1; Roy Pascal, *The German Sturm und Drang* (Manchester: Manchester UP, 1953); Andreas Huyssen, *Drama des Sturm und Drang: Kommentar zu einer Epoche* (Munich: Winkler, 1980); Edward McInnes, *"Ein ungeheures Theater": The Drama of the Sturm und Drang* (Frankfurt am Main, Bern & New York: Lang, 1987); Matthias Luserke, *Sturm und Drang: Autoren — Texte — Themen*, Universal-Bibliothek, 17602 (Stuttgart: Reclam, 1997); Bruce Duncan, *Lovers, Parricides, and Highwaymen: Aspects of Sturm und Drang Drama* (Rochester NY: Camden House, 1999); Ulrich Karthaus, *Sturm und Drang: Epoche — Werke — Wirkung* (Munich: Beck, 2000). Also invaluable is Nicholas Boyle, *Goethe: The Poet and the Age*, vol. 1: *The Poetry of Desire (1749–1790)* (Oxford & New York: Oxford UP, 1992). Each of these works has something important and individual to say about the Sturm und Drang, and none of them could be called conventional; but their accounts of the Sturm und Drang are complemented by the greater open-endedness and thematic depth for which we have aimed here.

[2] See Duncan, 2. My own analysis of the Collins-Cobuild Bank of English suggests that when used in a nonspecific sense in English, the term most commonly appears in contexts relating either to the arts or to childhood.

[3] See Karthaus, 107.

[4] Translated by Jeremy Adler as "tough guys" in *The Blackwell Companion to the Enlightenment*, eds. John W. Yolton et al. (Oxford: Blackwell, 1991), 507. *Kraft* means "power" or "force"; *Kerl* is an informal word for a person.

[5] See the essay by Gerhard Sauder in this volume.

[6] See the essay by Margaret Stoljar in this volume.

[7] See Müller's sketch of Heidelberg castle following this introduction.

[8] See Füssli's "The Nightmare" following this introduction.

[9] *The Poems of Alexander Pope*, ed. John Butt (London: Methuen, 1963), 516.

[10] The term derives from the Greek poet Anacreon (sixth century B.C.), claimed as a model by this tradition.

[11] *Der Göttinger Hain*, ed. Alfred Kelletat, Universal-Bibliothek, 8789–93 (Stuttgart: Reclam, 1967), 359.

[12] See the essay by Wulf Koepke in this volume.

[13] Mercier's *Du Théâtre ou Nouvel Essai sur l'Art Dramatique* of 1773 was translated by Wagner and published anonymously as *Neuer Versuch über die Schauspielkunst*, with a supplement by Goethe (Leipzig: Schwickert, 1776); rpt. ed. Peter Pfaff (Heidelberg: Schneider, 1967).

[14] Respectively, *Discours sur les sciences et les arts* and *Discours sur l'origine et les fondements de l'inégalité*.

[15] See the essay by Howard Gaskill in this volume.

[16] Later editions drop the "s" on "Werthers." "*Leiden*" may be translated not only as "sorrows" but also as "suffering" and even as "passion" (in the sense of "the Passion of Christ").

[17] An earlier version, *Geschichte Gottfriedens von Berlichingen mit der eisernen Hand, dramatisiert* (History of Gottfried von Berlichingen with the Iron Hand, Dramatized) was written in 1771 but was not published until after Goethe's death.

[18] Subsequent references to *Faust* will, unless otherwise stated, refer to this draft version. Goethe first published extracts from his work on the project in 1790 as *Faust: Ein Fragment* (Faust: A Fragment), which contains later additional material but also omits material from the "*Urfaust*" version that eventually found its way into *Faust I*. Margarete's name is abbreviated as "Gretgen" in "*Urfaust,*" as "Gretchen" in *Faust I*.

[19] When Lenz traveled from Darmstadt to Frankfurt with Merck on his way to Weimar in 1776, Klinger rode out to meet them wearing the Werther "uniform."

[20] See the essay by W. Daniel Wilson in this volume.

[21] See Kirsten Krick, "Storm and Stress / Sturm und Drang," in *The Feminist Encyclopedia of German Literature*, eds. Friederike Eigler and Susanne Kord (Westport, CT & London: Greenwood, 1997), 495–96, and the essay by Susanne Kord in the present volume.

[22] The term has fallen out of general use because of its implication that this writing only acquires its significance through what followed it.

[23] See, for example, Helmuth Plessner, *Die verspätete Nation*, 2nd ed. (Stuttgart: Kohlhammer, 1959).

[24] Norbert Elias, *Über den Prozeß der Zivilisation: Soziogenetische und psychogenetische Untersuchungen*, 2 vols., 6th ed. (Frankfurt am Main: Suhrkamp, 1978), 1: 1–64.

[25] See Jürgen Habermas, *Strukturwandel der Öffentlichkeit: Untersuchungen zu einer Kategorie der bürgerlichen Gesellschaft* (Neuwied & Berlin: Luchterhand, 1962).

[26] Ferdinand Tönnies famously uses the terms "*Gesellschaft*" (society) and "*Gemeinschaft*" (community) to distinguish between the modern world and its more integrated predecessor.

[27] Johann Caspar Lavater, *Physiognomische Fragmente zur Beförderung der Menschenkenntniß und Menschenliebe*, 4 vols. (Leipzig & Winterthur: Weidmann & Steiner, 1775–78), 4: 83 (emphasis in the original): "*Human gods! Creators! Destroyers! Revealers of the secrets of God and of men! Interpreters of nature! Speakers of unspeakable things! Prophets! Priests! Kings of the world* . . . which the Godhead has organized and formed — in order to reveal through them itself, its creative energy and wisdom and graciousness. *Revealers of the majesty of all things and of their relation to the eternal source and goal of all things: geniuses* — it is of you that we speak!"

[28] "Much may be alleged in favor of rules; about as much as may be said in favor of middle-class society: an artist modeled after them will never produce anything absolutely bad or in poor taste, just as a man who observes the laws of society and obeys decorum can never be a wholly unwelcome neighbor or a real villain. Yet, say what you will of rules, they destroy the genuine feeling of Nature and its true expression!" (*G-CW*, 11: 11).

[29] "O my friends! why is it that the torrent of genius so seldom bursts forth, so seldom rolls in full-flowing stream, overwhelming your astounded soul? Because, dear friends, on either side of the stream sedate and respectable fellows have settled down; their arbors and tulip beds and cabbage fields would be destroyed; therefore, in good time they have the sense to dig trenches and raise embankments in order to avert the impending danger" (*G-CW*, 11: 11).

[30] "The last rays of the sun coming through the trees — If only I could sweep into the brightness of that fire or ride on those golden-edged clouds! — Kamilla! (*Grasps her hand.*) Ah! I am so carried away again — if only I could pile together these fiery clouds, summon up wind and storm, and cast myself, shattered, into the abyss! Kamilla! Kamilla! Kamilla! (*Kisses her violently.*)."

[31] See Bruce Kieffer, *The Storm and Stress of Language: Linguistic Catastrophe in the Early Works of Goethe, Lenz, Klinger, and Schiller* (University Park & London: Pennsylvania State UP, 1986).

[32] "Call it what you will — / Happiness! Heart! Love! God! / I have no name to give it! / Feeling is everything, / Name is but sound and smoke" (*G-CW*, 2, 89).

[33] The individual elements of this phrase from the poem "Prometheus" mean, respectively, "young man," "morning," "blossom," and "dreams": their syntactical relationship is ambiguous, but a literal rendering might be "the blossomlike dreams of youths in the morning of their life." It is all the bolder for the fact that it runs across the end of a line of verse.

[34] The dating of all three poems is uncertain, but they were probably written between 1773 and 1775.

[35] "How much longer are you people going to go on clinging to forms and names?"

[36] See my "The Inner Form of *Aus Goethes Brieftasche*," in *Goethe at 250: The London Symposium. Goethe mit 250: Londoner Symposium,* eds. T. J. Reed et al. (Munich: Iudicium, 2000), 109–20.

[37] "If we read thoughts and words separately in them, if we do not listen with a creative ear, that hears the fully tonal quality of the sensation in its expression, if we do not have the poetic eye that perceives the expression as a body in which its spirit thinks and speaks and acts."

[38] "But nothing came to me like a divine vision, nothing enlivened my heart and my mind with warm, holy presence like the idea that *expression* is shaped by *thought* and *sentiment*."

[39] "So does the lark love / Song and the blue, / And morning flowers / The heavenly dew, // So do I love you, / With hottest blood, / Who give me youth's gladness / And brace my mood // New songs to be making, / New dances to know: / Be happy for ever / In loving me so" (*G-CW*, 1: 13).

[40] "Away with fathers!"

[41] See the essay by Karin Wurst in this volume.

[42] Thus Olga Smoljan, *Friedrich Maximilian Klinger: Leben und Werk* (Weimar: Arion, 1962).

[43] "Worm with the soul of a giant."

[44] "I turn within myself and find there a world!" (*G-CW*, 11: 9).

[45] "How glad I am to have got away!" (*G-CW*, 11:5).

[46] "O my friend — but it will destroy me — I shall perish under the splendor of these visions" (*G-CW*, 11: 6).

[47] The 1787 version adds the story of the farm laborer, which is also much darker when it reappears toward the end of the novel.

[48] "We scarcely see and feel any longer: we only think and brood. Our poetry does not emerge from a living world, nor exist in the storm and confluence of such objects and feelings. Instead we force either our theme or our treatment or both, and we have done so for so long and so often and from our tenderest years that if we attempted any free development, it would scarcely prosper" (*GAL*, 159).

[49] Friedrich Maximilian Klinger, *Plimplamplasko der hohe Geist*, ed. Peter Pfaff (Heidelberg: Schneider, 1966). Some of the earlier chapters were written in collaboration with Lavater and Jakob Sarasin (1742–1802).

Drawing of Heidelberg Castle by Friedrich ("Maler") Müller.
Pen and ink, before 1778. Courtesy of Freies Deutsches Hochstift,
Frankfurt am Main.

"The Nightmare," by Johann Heinrich Füssli.
Courtesy of Freies Deutsches Hochstift, Frankfurt am Main.

Sturm und Drang Passions and Eighteenth-Century Psychology

Bruce Duncan

> On life's vast ocean diversely we sail,
> Reason the card, but passion is the sail.
> Alexander Pope

IN FRIEDRICH MAXIMILIAN KLINGER'S play *Sturm und Drang* the aptly-named Wild complains,

> Es ist mir wieder so taub vorm Sinn. So gar dumpf. Ich will mich über eine Trommel spannen lassen, um eine neue Ausdehnung zu kriegen. Mir ist so weh wieder. O könnte ich in dem Raum dieser Pistole existieren, bis mich eine Hand in die Luft knallte. (*K-SD*, 8–9)[1]

This mixture of melancholy and violence in a Sturm und Drang work comes as no surprise. Nor does the heat with which Karl von Moor rejects his effete times in Schiller's *Die Räuber:*

> Pfui! pfui über das schlappe Kastraten-Jahrhundert, zu nichts nütze, als die Thaten der Vorzeit wiederzukäuen und die Helden des Alterthums mit Kommentationen zu schinden und zu verhunzen mit Trauerspielen. Da verrammeln sie sich die gesunde Natur mit abgeschmackten Konvenzionen, haben das Herz nicht ein Glas zu leeren, weil sie Gesundheit dazu trinken müssen — belecken den Schuhputzer, daß er sie vertrete bei Ihro Gnaden, und hudeln den armen Schelm, den sie nicht fürchten. (*S-NA*, 3: 21)[2]

Critics may debate when the Sturm und Drang began and ended, what political attitudes it espoused, who belonged to it, or even whether it actually constituted a movement at all, but all agree that it evinces strong emotion. Extreme passion is, in fact, so closely identified with the Sturm und Drang that modern usage has extended the name, even in English, beyond eighteenth-century German literature to any period or state of emotional turmoil. For many years, literary histories routinely defined the so-called Age of Genius largely by its passions, differentiating them from the Enlightenment's cold reason. Today this opposition seems false — not because it asserts emotion's importance for the Sturm und Drang, but because it wrongly assumes that the Enlightenment denigrated feeling. Scholars now typically see the Sturm und Drang less as a counterweight to the Age of Reason than as a development within it.[3] They agree that the passions of the Sturm und Drang, no matter how extremely articulated, do not contradict the Enlightenment's project; rather, they conform to the whole eighteenth century's consuming interest in the sources, nature, and uses of human feeling. The Sturm und Drang writers are not rebels against their own time but participants in the eighteenth-century discourse of the emotions. Wild's or Karl Moor's outpourings may have shocked eighteenth-century audiences in their extremeness, but they still fall within the bounds of contemporary notions of the passions.

The idea of a passionless Age of Reason still lingers,[4] but most current scholarship agrees that emotion vivifies the whole of the late eighteenth century. The Enlightenment, it is now recognized, was as much an Age of Feeling as an Age of Reason, and for the most part it saw its purpose in the reconciliation of the two. To understand the Sturm und Drang in its context, however, we need to go further and recognize that the Enlightenment did even more than simply give feelings their due; it increasingly defined its entire project through the prism of emotion. As metaphysics and theology lost their primacy during the course of the eighteenth century, the discourse of passion moved in to take their place under such rubrics as *Anthropologie, Psychologie,* and *Seelenkunde* (the study of the soul).[5] Epistemology, ethics, and aesthetics more and more developed their basic premises in analyses of the soul and its relationship to the affects and sensations. We can observe a somewhat analogous phenomenon in our own time — for example, in the interest of cultural studies in the body and in the concern of the cognitive sciences with brain functions. As in the Enlightenment, the emotions are today being viewed not only as personal and inward, but also as social and physical, phenomena.[6]

In adopting this approach, eighteenth-century writers saw themselves as taking a significant step forward in human understanding, both by overcoming the inherent insufficiencies of older theories and by recognizing the advances being made in empirical psychology. In praising Shakespeare's understanding of character, for example, Samuel Johnson (1709–84) marveled at the depth of insight that the playwright had been able to achieve in an age that "had not yet attempted to analyze the mind, to trace the passions to their sources, to unfold the seminal principles of vice and virtue, or sound the depths of the heart for the motives of action. All those enquiries, which from that time that human nature became the fashionable study . . . were yet unattempted."[7]

Almost any randomly selected text from the eighteenth century can attest to the fashionableness of psychology. In 1739 both David Hume's (1711–76) *Treatise of Human Nature* and Alexander Gottlieb Baumgarten's (1717–62) *Metaphysica* proposed that psychology, because it contains the fundamental principles of theology, aesthetics, logic, and the practical sciences, be considered part of metaphysics.[8] Twenty years later Johann Georg Sulzer (1720–79) recommended that philosophers turn their attention to empirical psychology, "da die Kenntniß der menschlichen Seele der edelste Theil der Wissenschaft ist" (since knowledge of the human soul is the noblest part of the sciences).[9] By 1776 a similar assertion in Johann August Eberhard's (1739–1809) influential *Allgemeine Theorie des Denkens und Empfindens* (General Theory of Thought and Feeling) had become a commonplace:

> Das wichtigste Studium des Menschen ist der Mensch selbst, seine Neigungen, seine Leidenschaften. Die wichtigsten Beobachtungen, die er über sich anstellen könnte, wären gerade diejenigen, die er über seine Empfindungen und Leidenschaften anstellt, über ihre Entstehung, ihre Verwandtschaft, ihre Umwandlung, Wachsthum und Abnahme; denn davon hängt die ganze Kenntniß unserer selbst, sofern sie uns zu unserer moralischen Bildung, zur Lenkung unseres Willens nützlich seyn kann, am meisten ab.[10]

And at the end of the century the Scottish philosopher Dugald Stewart (1753–1828) could approvingly claim, "In our universities, what a change has been gradually accomplished. . . . The Studies of Ontology, of Pneumatology, and of Dialectics, have been supplanted by that of the Human Mind."[11] This development takes many forms and is marked by sometimes heated disagreements about the nature, origin, and significance of human emotions, but the participants in the discussions share a currency of images that lend their endeavors a certain overall unity. One notion that they hold in common throughout the entire century is that they are engaged in a radical redefinition of the soul's relationship to the body, an undertaking that has fundamental consequences for the whole human condition. And, despite the many years of inquiries that have preceded their efforts, they view themselves as pioneers. As the French writer Louis-Sébastien Mercier put it, "Die menschlichen Leidenschaften gleichen den neuentdeckten Südländern, in welchen man einige Schritte gethan hat, die aber noch unbekannt und fast ganz noch erst zu durchlaufen sind."[12]

Present-day depictions of this investigative process, especially as it took place in Germany, tend to be misleading, because they describe developments in terms of clear oppositions, such as those between followers of René Descartes (1596–1650) and John Locke (1632–1704) or of Locke and Gottfried Wilhelm Leibniz (1646–1716). They often posit simple antitheses between rationalists and irrationalists or lump together the "pre-Kantians." Things were, in fact, more complex. Where modern observers see rivalries between whole theoretical systems, theorists of the eighteenth century, especially its second half, grew increasingly impatient with "school philosophies" and inclined to eclectic "popular philosophies" that selected individual observations and perceived bits of wisdom from larger structures, measuring them against practical experience. These gleanings then served at most as raw material for induction. As Eberhard put it in 1776,

> Der erste und vortheilhafteste Schritt, den man durch die neuesten Bemühungen dazu gethan hat, die Weltweisheit aus dem Himmel der Schulen herabzuziehen, und in die menschliche Gesellschaft einzuführen, ist wohl allerdings dadurch geschehen, daß man angefangen hat, sich mit den Empfindungen der menschlichen Seele näher bekannt zu machen, über dieselben Beobachtungen anzustellen, und diese Beobachtungen durch die Verbindung mit einer unverwickelten und lichtvollen Theorie fruchtbar zu machen. (4–5)[13]

The discourse in which the resulting sundry theories participate serves to unite them, even if variations are evident. Much of the shared vocabulary stems from earlier understandings that were being preserved through traditional texts, while the words themselves acquired new meanings. Thus, older taxonomies such as the four humors or concepts such as the animal spirits persisted, even though physiological advances had discredited them. "Soul" continued to designate the central object of examination, even while assumptions about its nature and functions underwent radical revisions.[14] This is not to deny the existence of competing schools of thought, only to say that developments were far from linear, and that anachronistic inconsistencies can be found even within the individual theories. Nor did all contemporaries necessarily see themselves to be embracing new ways and abandoning old ones. Recalling the mood of the times before his move to Strasbourg, Goethe begins book 9 of *Dichtung und Wahrheit* by quoting what he labels a typical call addressed to the youth of his generation, urging them to gain their insights into the hidden corners of the human heart and its passions by abandoning abstruse formal studies and returning to nature and the active life. The passions, Goethe recalls, were to become the Sturm und

Drang generation's primary object of study (*G-MA*, 16: 382–83). Though the process he describes differed from Eberhard's methodological investigations, both, in fact, participated in the same project. Similarly, Herder's *Abhandlung über den Ursprung der Sprache* claims itself reluctant to embrace modern scientific developments, arguing that advances in physiology threaten holistic understandings of the psyche: "Sollte die Physiologie je so weit kommen, daß sie die Seelenlehre demonstrirte, woran ich aber sehr zweifle, so würde sie dieser Erscheinung manchen Lichtstral aus der Zergliederung des Nervenbaues zuführen; sie vielleicht aber auch in Einzelne, zu kleine und stumpfe Bande vertheilen" (*H-SW*, 5: 6).[15] But in the preceding paragraph Herder has already placed himself among progressive thinkers by describing "die Mechanik fühlender Körper" (the mechanics of sentient bodies), the concept that makes modern physiology possible in the first place. In fact, he took a lively interest in the scientific research of the time, especially the work of Albrecht von Haller (1708–77) and Charles Bonnet (1720–93).

Obviously, concern with the origins, nature, and effects of human emotions did not begin in the eighteenth century. The Enlightenment thinkers themselves were conscious of engaging in an inquiry stretching back to the ancient Greeks. But the process underwent a decided shift in the later part of the seventeenth century. As Charles Taylor describes it, "For the ancients, the passions were understood primarily through their relevance to the moral life. This was seen to lie principally in their being implicit appreciations of the goodness or badness of some end or state of affairs."[16] That is to say, right thinking consisted of insight into the world's meaningful order. Emotions could, at one extreme, benefit moral action by urging conformity to this order, or, at the other, they could enslave reason and, thus, bar access to the good life. In the best case they remained docile, allowing reason to work unobstructed; philosophers could then achieve insight into the moral order that lay outside themselves and, in turn, encourage or control the passions appropriately. Even if seekers such as St. Augustine turned within themselves to find manifestations of the higher order, they were, in the end, looking for an external, objective reality. Renaissance thinkers, too, considered the cosmic order to be the measure of all things, "because it exhibits Reason, Goodness; in the theological variant the Wisdom of God" (160). With Descartes, however, a fundamental transformation takes place. Reason is still preeminent, and the passions are still, by and large, barriers to right thinking; but the defining order ceases to be based wholly outside the self. The cosmos no longer embodies the ideal order — at least, not in the sense that reason's first goal is to conform to it. The Cartesian revolution "throws the individual thinker back on his responsibility, requires him to build an order of thought for himself, in the first person singular" (182). The result is not solipsism, however: individuals must still exercise their reason according to universal criteria. But the reference point has shifted dramatically.

Descartes famously bought the preeminence of an individual's reason at the cost of disassociating it from the material world; and the unbridgeable gap between body and soul haunted German psychology throughout the following century, with no one ever finding a satisfactory solution to the incompatibility. Christian Wolff's (1679–1754) theory, dominant until about 1750, postulated two complementary forms of psychology, one empirical, the other rational.[17] The former served two primary functions: to provide a base from which to argue the existence of the soul, which is the entity that thinks, wills, and desires, and to demonstrate "that bodily and mental actions occur simultaneously" (Corr, 259). What Wolff could never do, even to his own satisfaction, was account for the relationship between these two kinds of action. He made do by suggesting three possible hypotheses to explain the *commercium mentis et corporis*. In the first, body and soul do not actually interact but run parallel to each other in a preestablished harmony. This theory seems particularly hard to credit today; but when Leibniz first offered it, it bore a comforting resemblance to the accepted Renaissance doctrine of correspondences between this world and the cosmos. In fact, the notion persisted in one form or another until late in the eighteenth century (see Taylor, 160–92, and Mattenklott, 28–29). The second hypothesis accepted Descartes's proposal of a "continually acting cause," the notion that each and every correspondence between body and soul results from a divine miracle. This explanation was, of course, also supported by a strong religious tradition. The third hypothesis, while more appealing to materialistic philosophers, held little explanatory power. It simply posited an as yet undiscovered force ("*vis*") that moves between the two essentially distinct entities.

Wolff himself pointed out how unsatisfactory all three explanations were, since none was capable of demonstration. And by the middle of the century, as more and more thinkers concluded that abstract conjectures about the soul's essence led to a dead end, they increasingly turned away from speculation and toward observations of bodily responses to sensation. This change was not necessarily in direct opposition to Wolff, although some philosophers defined it that way. Johann Nicolaus Tetens (1736–1807), for example, specifically objected to Wolff's "geometrical genius,"[18] and opposing camps developed during some dramatic disputes within the Berlin Academy around mid-century. It should, however, be remembered that Wolff's system left considerable room for empirical psychology, so that Baumgarten, Georg Friedrich Meier (1718–77), and Moses Mendelssohn could still be counted among his followers even as they legitimated knowledge derived from sensation. Still later in the century, Wolff's psychology did not seem wholly irrelevant; tradition continued to require syllogistic deductions, and empirical studies based their legitimacy, at least in part, on the assumed parallelism between body and soul. Observing the former, it was still felt, led to an understanding of the latter.

Not only the insufficiencies of speculative reasoning precipitated a turn toward empiricism. Scientific advances in physiology affected notions about how the soul and body interact. Luigi Galvani's (1737–98) electrical experiments were not made known until 1791, but scientists such as Hermann Boerhaave (1668–1738), Julien Offrie de La Mettrie (1709–51), and Lazzaro Spallanzani (1729–99) had already demonstrated material effects in the body. Another impulse came from a new appreciation of subjective knowledge, for which Eberhard's essay of 1776 credits discoveries about bodies' secondary characteristics, specifically colors. Physiologists, he points out, had determined that colors are not independent realities but exist only as they are perceived through the senses. This recognition led, in turn, to an acknowledgment of the senses' importance and an increased effort to understand them (8). Eberhard's reference to "discoveries" seems to imply certain recent color experiments of the time,[19] but he also cites Leibniz's extension of the categories of "*Klarheit*" (clarity) and "*Deutlichkeit*" (distinctiveness) to describe primary qualities, which, he claims, thus advanced physiology beyond Locke.[20] Locke had, of course, introduced to Germany the notion that sensations, not innate structures, form the mind; but we can also point to a strong empirical strain that already existed in German thought, beginning perhaps with Christian Thomasius (1655–1728) and continuing throughout most of the century. Today that tradition is largely forgotten, overwhelmed by the later presence of Immanuel Kant; but at the time it exerted some influence, and thinkers who gave weight to sensual phenomena were tapping into an approach that already seemed legitimate.[21]

Finally, the turn toward empiricism had a political aspect. Just as post-Gottschedian literary critics deliberately moved away from French models and embraced British ones, so, too, did philosophers such as Tetens reject French "reasoning philosophy" and identify "observational" philosophy with British sources (Barnouw, "The Philosophical Achievement," 308).

Again, it is important to emphasize that discussions about the emotions did not advance along a continuum. While they often reflected contemporary developments, they simultaneously preserved outmoded concepts and designations, mixing scholastic reasoning and orthodox beliefs with scientific experiment. Goethe's description of his youthful self caught between two literary epochs applies equally well to the world of psychology: "so viel Neues [drängte] auf mich ein . . ., ehe ich mich mit dem Alten hätte abfinden können, so viel Altes [machte] sein Recht noch über mich gelten . . ., da ich schon Ursache zu haben glaubte, ihm völlig entsagen zu dürfen" (G-MA, 16: 305).[22] But in all the apparent chaos, a shared set of references served to unify eighteenth-century psychologists by defining the discourse of the passions. One can meaningfully speak with Thomas Saine of a "Gedankenkomplex" (constellation of thought) in which most thinkers of the time found themselves at home.[23]

One particular text, already cited here several times, serves well as an exemplar. In 1775 the Berlin Academy awarded its prize to Johann August Eberhard for his Allgemeine Theorie des Denkens und Empfindens, which was published the following year. The academy had called for a theory of thought and sensation that would describe and explain the relationship between these "two powers of the soul," as well as their influence on genius and character (Eberhard, 14–15). Although Eberhard is counted among Mendelssohn's followers, his "general theory" taps into a variety of traditions; and his book, despite the academy's charge, lacks systematic rigor. A kind of compendium of then-dominant concepts, it belongs to the genre of popular philosophy; no other book, says Sommer (232), offers a better example of the general state of psychology at the time.

Eberhard begins his argument with the assertion that the soul is a simple substance. This conventional formulation (found, among many other places, in Mendelssohn's influential Phädon, 1767) gives the soul both immortality and materiality. His next task is to establish thought and feeling as aspects of the same "Grundkraft" (fundamental power) of this soul, "das Bestreben Vorstellungen zu haben" (33: the striving to have representations). Here Eberhard advances two kinds of argument. The first is speculative: to make possible any sort of moral order, we have to assume that thought and feeling affect one another. But if the soul is a simple, and hence unalterable, substance, this relationship is imaginable only if the two functions are part of the same unity. Therefore, that must be the case.

In his second form of argument, however, Eberhard appeals to physiological observations, as well as to the Leibnizian notion of harmony, to characterize the relationship between body and soul:

> Wenn auch die einfachste, abgesondertste Vorstellung nach der Harmonie, die zwischen Leib und Seele ist, und wodurch diese beyden Theile zu Einem Menschen vereinigt werden, doch ihre, wie wohl unbemerkte begleitende Bewegung in dem gegliederten Körper haben muß: so gilt der Schluß nun umgekehrt von der Menge solcher harmonischen Bewegungen in dem Körper auf die Menge der vereinigten Elementar-Vorstellungen, die sich zu Einer starken Empfindung oder Gemüthsbewegung in der Seele vereinigen. Wenn in dem Zustand des Denkens nur einige Nerven des Kopfes geschäftig sind: so ist hingegen in dem Zustande starker Empfindungen die Erschütterung der Nerven so stark, daß sie sich dem ganzen System mittheilt, die Adern erweitert oder zusammenzieht, dem Blute entweder die Ergießung nach den andern Theilen des Körpers verschließt, oder den Rückweg nach dem Herzen versperrt, den so bewegten Menschen entweder in Furcht erbleichen, oder in Scham und Zorn erröthen läßt, ja endlich sich den Muskeln mittheilt, und den ganzen Körper in unfreiwilligen Verzukkungen zusammenzieht. (52–53)[24]

Eberhard fails to describe the source of this harmony between body and soul, relying mainly on the momentum of tradition to justify it. Others of his contemporaries, however, including Ernst Platner (1780–1818) and Jakob Friedrich Abel (1751–1829), Schiller's teacher, embrace a theory of material ideas. According to this theory, each idea in the soul has its physiological equivalent, an *idea materialis* that literally leaves its impression on the brain. These ideas make up an individual's memory. Stored in this fashion, they are available to thought; but they also randomly stimulate each other, producing inspired leaps, involuntary associations, and sudden insights within the soul. As Riedel points out (433–34), this theory presents nothing less than a "physiological subconscious" in which the body, not the soul or intellect, gives rise to associated thoughts. Such an acceptance of purely physical experience is, however, not new. Mendelssohn had already praised the soul's immediate delight in the body's harmonious response to sensual pleasure in 1755: "Alle diese Wirkungen erfolgen aus einem wundervollen mechanischen Triebe, bevor sich noch der denkende Theil des Menschen in das Spiel mischt."[25] Mendelssohn attaches particular value to this phenomenon and even complains that thought, by its very nature, can negate the enjoyment precipitated by such agreeable feelings. Nevertheless, the unreflective kind of pleasure that he approvingly depicts occupies an order lower than that of distinct ideas. To later advocates of material ideas, however, sensual experience is richer than what the thinking soul affords. Eberhard in effect agrees, albeit without recourse to this theory. Although his stated purpose is to establish equivalencies between thought and feeling and to demonstrate their common origin, and although he also worries about possible imbalances in the soul that could injure reason,[26] he shifts the primary emphasis toward the emotions, especially in the realm of aesthetics.

One consequence of his analysis is a blurred distinction between objective and subjective knowledge. In bold type he asserts, "daß die Seele bey dem Denken den Gegenstand, womit sie sich beschäftigt, als außer sich befindlich ansieht; hingegen bey dem Gebrauch der Empfindungskraft mit ihrem eigenen Zustand zu thun zu haben glaubt" (45).[27] In other words, the thinking subject, capable of clear and distinct representations, distinguishes itself from the objects of its thought, imagining them to exist externally. This distinction convinces the thinking subject that it is active and free, since it not only sees itself as separate from the object of its thought but can also imagine alternative actions (31–44). With feeling, especially strong feeling, the effect is reversed: sensation is such a mixed and immediate phenomenon that the resulting representations remain *"verworren"* (confused; in Leibniz's terminology, *"confusus"*), and the subject cannot distinguish itself from them. On the one hand, Eberhard seems to consider this differentiation to be one of degree, saying that the more confused a perception is, the less a sentient being can differentiate itself from its cause (47–48). On the other hand, he attributes the differentiation to the very nature of thought and feeling. But either way, the difference is one of perception, not essence.

Not only is thought's "objectivity" a subjective phenomenon, but its clarity can lead to an impoverishment of perception, at least in the realms of aesthetics and ethics. Thoughts or concepts (*"Begriffe"*), here thought of as distinct representations, exist individually; if two appear at the same time or even in close succession, they weaken one another. Sense impressions, on the other hand, even contradictory ones, can strengthen each other's effects within the soul:

> *Ihre Totalempfindungen werden durch alle solche Partialempfindungen verstärket, die genug gemeinschaftliche Bestimmungen haben, um unter einer Hauptvorstellung begriffen zu werden, aber auch genug besondere Bestimmungen, um die Anzahl der Partialempfindungen in der Totalempfindung zu vermehren.* (150–51; emphasis in the original)[28]

To explain what he means by "*Hauptvorstellung*" (main representation), Eberhard gives two examples: if I enter St. Peter's Cathedral with a heavy heart, my mood and my appreciation of the church's magnificence, being dissimilar, weaken each other. When, however, my visit is characterized by a variety of related sense impressions, such as the sound of music, the smell of incense, and so forth, then these fragmentary sensations augment one another (151–58). This relatedness is not, Eberhard emphasizes, an intellectually unifying concept but an overarching compatibility of contrasting impressions. In art, for example, some combinations strengthen one another: black and white or red and green in proximity, dissonance and consonance or pain and pleasure in sequence. If any of these contrasting pairs are reduced to a single idea, however, the effect is weakened (152).

In emphasizing the partial nature of these individual apprehensions, Eberhard harks back to Leibniz's notion of "*petites perceptions*," "obscure" representations that were also central to Sulzer and Abel. These "*Teilvorstellungen*," as Sulzer labeled them, have several important features. As we have already seen, they augment one another, accounting for feeling's superior power. We saw above Eberhard's description of unified partial representations that are unified into a single powerful feeling or emotion within the soul. He offers "persistence of vision," the phenomenon that makes cinema possible, as a simile for this effect: discrete visual images tend to last longer in the eye than in reality, so that when presented in rapid succession they appear as one continuous movement — Eberhard's illustration is a glowing coal swung on the end of a cord (56–57). Not only individuals, but whole groups can be moved by this accumulation of emotional power: a minor grievance can suddenly cause a people to revolt against a tyranny under which it has silently suffered for years (126).

"*Petites perceptions*" do not gain force just by simple accumulation, however. Association also plays a role. Eberhard points to impressions that might by themselves seem insignificant but that evoke strong emotions when they join together synecdochically with other experiences. A small stimulus, such as the sight of a particular dress, can evoke overwhelming feelings of sadness by bringing back the image of a lost love (113). This associative power helps to explain a further phenomenon, one that earlier ages attributed to outside causes such as evil spirits: our occasional propensity to act against our own principles or self-interest. When we unthinkingly undertake such an action, which on reflection surprises us, we can be sure that unarticulated feelings that are stored in our memories have been at work (129–30). In 1759 Sulzer had advanced the idea that the "darker" representations constitute a hidden force that can prove superior to our will, and Riedel credits him with conceiving of the Freudian slip and even of a rudimentary form of the unconscious (435).

"*Teilvorstellungen*" can accumulate associative power and are perceived subjectively because they are "*verworren*" — that is, the distinctions among them are undefined. But some sense impressions are less distinct than others. The sentient subject differentiates itself less from those feelings that it acquires through smell, taste, and touch than through the less confused feelings gained from sight and hearing (Eberhard, 48). These last two senses convey a relative distinctness that invites intellectual activity, an abstraction of the self from the perceived object. One is reminded here of Herder's praise of the haptic sense in his *Plastik:* "Ein blos Fühlender ist in sich selbst eingeschlossen: seine Empfindungen gehören ihm unmittelbar zu und sind mit seinem Ich verbunden. Das Auge wirft uns weit aus uns weg" (*H-SW*, 8: 97).[29] And, as Wilkinson and Willoughby show, when Herder took the young Goethe in hand in the winter of 1770–71 and proposed to him "a doctrine of the psyche which assumed the closest possible interdependence between sense perception and the mental activities of knowing, feeling, and willing," he especially urged his charge to abandon his bird's-eye view of life and involve himself through touch.[30]

The idea of partial perceptions has crucial implications for the aesthetics of the Sturm und Drang. The goal of art, virtually all theorists in the second half of the eighteenth century agree, is to arouse emotion, although they might argue about what kinds of feeling are appropriate. Earlier theories postulated that this effect is best achieved through the imitation of nature, a notion that never entirely disappears. But through the kinds of differentiation that Eberhard makes between the categories of thought and feeling, of distinct and confused representations, and of objective and subjective impressions, mimesis relinquishes much of its importance to the expressiveness of the feeling soul (see Sommer, 218–19). At the same time, emotion is not an end in itself but the means by which art influences its recipient. Christian Ludwig Willebrand (1750–1837), for example, states that the arousal of the passions is the poet's highest art; but he goes on to add, "Durch die wirkt er auf die Seele des Lesers, übt unumgeschränkte Gewalt über sein Herz, bemächtigt sich jeder Empfindung, und lenkt sie nach seinem Gefallen."[31] In the process, feeling does not replace thought, since both are in the end only different aspects of the soul's basic function (which is "to have representations"); rather, feeling achieves art's purpose more profoundly.

Mendelssohn makes an analogous argument in his "Gedanken vom Ausdrucke der Leidenschaften" (Thoughts on the Expression of the Passions).[32] He distinguishes between arbitrary and natural signs as conveyers of emotion: arbitrary signs merely describe a passion, while natural signs convey it immediately and, hence, more powerfully, especially on the stage. More than some of his contemporaries, Mendelssohn sees danger in this phenomenon and urges the playwright to limit natural signs to a complementary role; above all, the theater should eschew actions that affect the audience so strongly that natural signs overwhelm the arbitrary ones (264). Mendelssohn is, of course, aware that the actor's "natural" signs are, in fact, imitations of the body's emotional responses, not the real thing. But the perceived effect is the same. As Tetens says, the artistic genius can create the inner impression of a phenomenon even where the outward phenomenon does not exist. He cites the analogy of color perception, an area in which he himself conducted experiments. Green light rays, he points out, are a simple, indissoluble phenomenon of nature that cannot be reconstructed from other elements. But if we mix yellow and blue light, we achieve the subjective impression of green. We perceive both kinds of green as the same phenomenon, even though the new "green" is materially different and capable of being broken down again into its component parts of yellow and blue.[33]

Although the perceived effect — green — is the same, there is a crucial distinction in the process of perception (or, we might say, the nature of the representation). In the first case our "*Vorstellung*" (representation) of spectral green is of a material substance that lies outside ourselves, and our soul is exercising what Tetens identifies as one of its two basic functions: receptivity. In the second case the "object" of perception, being a subjective construct, seems to lie wholly within our soul. The process of representation does not refer to an object outside ourselves. Tetens labels this second function "spontaneity." Hume ascribes this spontaneous quality to passion in general, which he calls "an original existence" that "contains not any representative quality" (Sommer, 415); Tetens, in contrast, focuses on the nature of the soul's function, on the fact that the soul perceives itself as processing a subjective sense impression.

According to Sommer (277–78), these two qualities, spontaneity and receptivity, represent the two main directions that psychology took in eighteenth-century Germany. For Leibniz, the soul was wholly spontaneous because it generated representations without outside influence; the empiricists, on the other hand, stressed the sensual origins of thought, ascribing only the power of receptivity to the soul. Tetens tried to combine both qualities.

One area in which spontaneity is possible is the aesthetic realm, where the self-sufficient soul is free to make its representations independent of the world outside itself. This aesthetic distance is what Mendelssohn means when he insists that arbitrary signs should have the ascendancy over natural ones in literature: he is not trying to suppress emotion; rather, he is urging poets to recollect their emotions in tranquility, to separate their passions from the objective source of those passions. Schiller makes a similar point when he criticizes Gottfried August Bürger's lack of "idealization": "Die Empfindlichkeit, der Unwille, die Schwermut des Dichters sind nicht bloß der *Gegenstand,* den er besingt, sie sind leider oft der *Apoll,* der ihn begeistert" (*S-NA,* 23: 255).[34] Schiller will, of course, later extend this notion of disinterested emotion in *Über die ästhetische Erziehung des Menschen in einer Reihe von Briefen* (On the Aesthetic Education of Man in a Series of Letters, 1795).

Virtually all eighteenth-century theorists agree that the quality of genius, with which all Sturm und Drang writers identify themselves, is marked by passion. But, as Schiller's teacher, Abel, puts it, "Nicht jede schnelle Reizbarkeit der Seele, nicht schnell verfliegende Hize, nicht aufbrausende Wuth, nicht jene convulsivische Bewegung des Körpers, sind Zeichen des ächten Geniefeuers."[35] Genius, as Eberhard says (214), does not content itself with the already established relationships among things but creates an original world in the aesthetic realm through bold combinations of partial perceptions. In Tetens's description of the poetic process,

> Alsdann drängen sich Empfindungen und Ideen so ineinander und vereinigen sich zu neuen Verbindungen, dass man sich viel zu wenig vorstellt, wenn man die Bilder, die von diesen Poeten in ihrer lebendigen Dichtersprache ausgehaucht sind, für nichts anders als für eine aufgehäufte Menge von nebeneinander liegenden und schnell aufeinander folgenden einfachen Empfindungsideen ansieht. In ihren neuen selbstgemachten zusammengesetzten Ausdrücken geben sie die einzelnen Züge an, aus denen das Gemälde bestehet, aber selbst die Art, wie sie die Worte hervorbringen, beweist, dass die bezeichneten Züge in der Phantasie, wie die vermischten Farben, ineinander getrieben und miteinander vermischt sind.[36]

In other words, genius — and, hence, art in its highest form — does not simply arouse emotions. Instead, it invites the soul to take pleasure in the lively exercise of its most profound functions. Tetens's "*Spontaneïtaet*" is the soul's engagement in the free play of its faculties, similar to Schiller's later notion of "*Spiel*" (play). From this standpoint, the subject matter of a literary work, its reference to external reality, is of secondary importance. Its goal is the complete and self-contained engagement of the soul through an inspired combination of confused perceptions. The Sturm und Drang writers refer to this self-sufficiency when they praise the wholeness of a work of art. What Goethe calls Shakespeare's "*Raritäten Kasten*" (peep show; *G-MA*, 1.2: 413) is a world unto itself, one in which we stretch our emotional capacity.

This intent is clearly compatible with the Enlightenment's aim to encourage the practice of "*Mitleid*" (pity) in a theatrical setting, to exercise certain emotions within an aesthetic space abstracted from the real world. Where Gottsched earlier insisted that drama present only behavior that is either worthy of emulation or else held up to ridicule, Mendelssohn goes further and recognizes the necessary distinction between morality within and outside of the theater. He admits that drama presents "untrue" passions, but he says that it does so to achieve its higher purpose of arousing compassion (see Luserke, *Die Bändigung der wilden Seele*, 176). He even acknowledges the delight we can take in staged evil, attributing our pleasure to our recognition of the difference between imperfection and the ideal. The Sturm und Drang not only accepts this notion but proposes a more radical version in which relatively daring passions presented for their own sake. When Lessing objected to illogical parts of the plot of *Ugolino*, Gerstenberg replied that his play was concerned only with "a starvation."[37] The assumption here is that the arousal of any passion creates a general benefit. Lenz relies on a similar notion in his *Briefe über die Moralität der Leiden des jungen Werthers* (Letters on the Morality of The Sufferings of Young Werther, written 1774–75; published 1918). Rejecting the accusation that Goethe's portrayal of suicide could corrupt impressionable youth, he claims that the experience and exercise of many kinds of passion lend the soul empathy and, ultimately, balance. Werther's contribution — the contribution of every poet — is to acquaint us with unnamed passions and feelings of which we are only darkly aware; Lenz announces that he has presented his copy of *Werther* to a young woman in the complete confidence that it will educate her heart to feelings that will ensure her future husband's happiness (*L-WB*, 2: 676–77, 682).

Although Lenz's defense of the arousal of passion in *Werther* seems radical, he ultimately returns to the standard insistence on feeling's didactic function, to the assumption that emotions constitute a social good. Several strains of thought support this assumption. The idea of moral sensibilities, first articulated by Anthony Ashley Cooper, first Earl of Shaftesbury (1621–83) and Francis Hutcheson (1694–1746) and then incorporated into the general concept of "*Empfindsamkeit*" (sentiment), suggests that properly cultivated emotions are our most reliable moral guides. In earlier times, when reason reputedly received its direction from its insight into the natural order, altruistic feelings had little importance — except, perhaps, in their absence. With the rise of sentiment, however, nature as it is experienced within the individual becomes the norm, replacing, or at least rivaling, rational insight into the nature of the cosmos. This development gives the emotions a whole new value. "What changes is not that people begin loving their children or feeling affection for their spouses, but that these dispositions come to be seen as a crucial part of what makes life worthy and significant" (Taylor, 292). Indeed, this sort of sentiment attains such importance that playwrights increasingly portray tragic conflict in the context of family relationships, where "natural feelings" are at their strongest. Some modern critics suppose that Sturm und Drang dramatists set their plays within the domestic sphere as a conscious or unconscious compensation for their political frustrations: unable or unwilling to articulate the class conflicts of their age, they reduce the contradictions to less significant rivalries between brothers or between fathers and sons (see Duncan, 30–39). But it is also possible to see just the opposite effect at work, to suppose that the eighteenth century's staged familial discord can represent an intensification of tragic conflict, reflecting the dramatist's effort to evoke the strongest possible emotion. In the 1680s, for example, English playwrights, presumably less inhibited politically than their German counterparts, regularly locate highly charged material in family settings, even when the subject is the Roman Republic: "Both Whig and Tory plays construct pathos-rich cross-generational relationships that favor the sacrifice of the volatile son" (Ellison, 29).

Today we are more likely to find such familial relationships trivial, because we tend to separate private feeling from larger public issues; but the eighteenth century saw the two spheres as interconnected: the affective qualities of the soul are formed within the tension between societal strictures and individual desires. The goals of human striving are not preordained; rather, they develop within the conflict between the subjective and the objective. The soul is the location for both the integrative power that constructs an individual entity and the integration of that entity into the societal whole.[38] Where modern observers might squirm at the open displays of emotion that characterize Enlightenment sentiment, eighteenth-century audiences were more inclined to see feelings as "transsubjective entities"[39] and to take this emotional responsiveness not only as a sign of individual authenticity but also as a declaration of interconnectedness.

This bivalence helped to inspire the enthusiastic interest in empirical psychology that marked the last decades of the century. In his *Vorschlag zu einem Magazin einer Erfahrungs-Seelenkunde* (Proposal for a Magazine for Experiential Psychology), written in 1782, Karl Philipp Moritz (1756–93) envisioned a compendium of individual psychological analyses; general moral principles, he claimed, are abstracted from individuals.[40] Contributors were to begin with minute observations of their own inner workings, stressing that which might seem insignificant. They would then extend their observations to even the most idiosyncratic individuals of all ages. Finally, a compendium of multiple reports from careful observers would produce an experiential psychology that would represent a huge practical advance over previous efforts (794–95).

The proposed magazine appeared annually from 1783 to 1793. Its success testifies to the breadth of the century's shift from predominantly speculative analyses of the soul's functions to empirical observations of individual case studies. Despite these differences in approach, however, Moritz's *Magazin zur Erfahrungsseelenkunde* continues important assumptions that characterize almost all eighteenth-century considerations of the emotions: that feelings not only enrich life but are the basis of a legitimate and profound form of knowledge; that this kind of knowledge is necessary to any understanding of aesthetics or ethics; that emotions have their origins in individual experiences that are personal and sensual; but at the same time, that shared or communicated feelings are the glue of all social structures. For all its youthful fervor, and for all the revolutionary zeal that observers have ascribed to it, the Sturm und Drang does not depart from these assumptions. Its articulations of feeling, even when extreme, still fall within the bounds of the established eighteenth-century discourse.

Notes

[1] "My mind is so numb again. Completely apathetic. I want be stretched over a drum, to give me a new dimension. My heart aches again. Oh, if I could just vegetate in the barrel of this pistol until some hand blew me away."

[2] "Pah! To hell with this century of eunuchs, good for nothing but chewing over past deeds, flaying ancient heroes with learned commentaries and perverting them in tragedies. They block up their healthy nature with tasteless conventions, and don't have the heart to empty a glass because they'd have to drink to good health — they kiss the bootblack's ass in the hope he'll put in a good word for them with His Grace, and they torment any knave they're not afraid of."

³ For example, Andreas Huyssen, *Drama des Sturm und Drang: Kommentar zu einer Epoche* (Munich: Winkler, 1980), 47–54. For some definitions of the Sturm und Drang, see my *Lovers, Parricides and Highwaymen: Aspects of Sturm und Drang Drama* (Rochester NY: Camden House, 1999), 1–9; Matthias Luserke, *Die Bändigung der wilden Seele: Literatur und Leidenschaft in der Aufklärung* (Stuttgart: Metzler, 1995), 223–28, and *Sturm und Drang: Autoren — Texte — Themen*, Universal-Bibliothek, 17602 (Stuttgart: Reclam, 1997); Gerhard Sauder, "Die deutsche Literatur des Sturm und Drang," in *Europäische Aufklärung*, 2, ed. Heinz-Joachim Müllenbrock (Wiesbaden: AULA, 1984), 327–78; Manfred Wacker, *Schillers "Räuber" und der Sturm und Drang: Stilkritische und typologische Überprüfung eines Epochenbegriffs* (Göppingen: Kümmerle, 1973); Hans-Gerd Winter, "Antiklassizismus: Sturm und Drang," in *Geschichte der deutschen Literatur vom 18. Jahrhundert bis zur Gegenwart*, vol. 1.1, ed. Viktor Žmegač (Königstein: Athenäum, 1978), 245–56. See also the introduction and the essay by Gerhard Sauder in the present volume.

⁴ In 2000 Amartya Sen still felt the need to disprove it: "East and West: The Reach of Reason," *New York Review of Books* 47 (2000): 34–35. One vestige is Richard van Dülmen's study of the early modern period, which still describes the Enlightenment as a movement that subjects public and private life to the rules of reason, declaring war on all physicality, passion, and sensuality: *Kultur und Alltag in der frühen Neuzeit* (Munich: Beck, 1994), 3: 216. Compare Robert W. Jones, "Ruled Passions: Re-Reading the Culture of Sensibility," *Eighteenth-Century Studies* 32 (1999): 395.

⁵ See Wolfgang Riedel's introduction to *Jacob Friedrich Abel: Eine Quellenedition zum Philosophieunterricht an der Stuttgarter Karlsschule (1773–1782)* (Würzburg: Königshausen & Neumann, 1995), 421. For some larger studies of this phenomenon in Germany, see Gabriele Dürbeck, *Einbildungskraft und Aufklärung: Perspektiven der Philosophie, Anthropologie und Ästhetik um 1750* (Tübingen: Niemeyer, 1999); Mareta Linden, *Untersuchungen zum Anthropologiebegriff des 18. Jahrhunderts* (Bern & Frankfurt am Main: Lang, 1976); Gert Mattenklott, *Melancholie in der Dramatik des Sturm und Drang*, 2nd ed. (Königstein: Athenäum, 1985); Gerhard Sauder, *Empfindsamkeit*, vol. 1: *Voraussetzungen und Elemente* (Stuttgart: Metzler, 1974); Hans-Jürgen Schings, *Melancholie und Aufklärung: Melancholiker und ihre Kritiker in der Erfahrungsseelenkunde und Literatur des 18. Jahrhunderts* (Stuttgart: Metzler, 1977); Hans-Jürgen Schings, ed., *Der ganze Mensch. Anthropologie und Literatur im 18. Jahrhundert* (Stuttgart: Metzler, 1992); and Robert Sommer, *Grundzüge einer Geschichte der deutschen Psychologie und Aesthetik von Wolff-Baumgarten bis Kant-Schiller* (Würzburg, 1892; rpt., Amsterdam: Bonset, 1966).

⁶ See Julie K. Ellison, *Cato's Tears and the Making of Anglo-American Emotion* (Chicago: U of Chicago P, 1999), 5. Neurobiologists are beginning to use positron emission tomography to locate sites of the various emotions — a desideratum for several thousand years and, according to Joseph LeDoux, still "the holy grail" of neuroscience: *The Emotional Brain: The Mysterious Underpinnings of Emotional Life* (New York: Simon & Schuster, 1996), 73–103. See Richard D. Lane and Lynn Nadel, eds., *Cognitive Neuroscience of Emotion* (New York: Oxford UP, 2000).

⁷ Samuel Johnson, *The Yale Edition of the Works of Samuel Johnson*, 16 vols. to date (New Haven: Yale UP, 1958–90), 7: 88; see Christopher Fox, ed., *Psychology and Literature in the Eighteenth Century* (New York: AMS, 1987), 1.

[8] Alexander Gottlieb Baumgarten, *Metaphysik* (Halle: Hemmerd, 1783), § 368; this edition is of Baumgarten's own translation of the original Latin *Metaphysica*, which was published in 1739, the same year as Hume's *Treatise*.

[9] Quoted by Hans Adler, "Aisthesis, steinernes Herz und geschmeidige Sinne: Zur Bedeutung der Ästhetik-Diskussion in der zweiten Hälfte des 18. Jahrhunderts," in *Der ganze Mensch: Anthropologie und Literatur im 18. Jahrhundert,* ed. Hans-Jürgen Schings (Stuttgart: Metzler, 1992), 98.

[10] Johann August Eberhard, *Allgemeine Theorie des Denkens und Empfindens* (Berlin: Voß, 1776; rpt., Frankfurt am Main: Athenäum, 1972), 141: "The most important study of man is man himself, his inclinations, his passions. The most important observations he can make of himself would be precisely those that he makes of his emotions and passions, of their origins, their relatedness, their transformation, growth and decrease; for mostly on this does our self-knowledge depend, to the extent that it can serve our moral development, the directing of our will."

[11] Quoted by Roy Porter, *The Creation of the Modern World: The Untold Story of the British Enlightenment* (New York & London: Norton, 2000), 183. Pneumatology is the study of spiritual beings or phenomena.

[12] "The human passions are like the newly discovered lands of the South, in which we have taken a few steps, but which still remain unknown and almost wholly unexplored." [Louis-Sébastien Mercier,] *Neuer Versuch über die Schauspielkunst* [translated by Heinrich Leopold Wagner] (Leipzig: Schwickert, 1776; rpt., ed. Peter Pfaff, Heidelberg: Schneider, 1967), 277.

[13] "The first and most advantageous step undertaken most recently to haul philosophy down from the scholarly heavens and introduce it into human society has most likely come about because we have begun to gain a closer acquaintance with the feelings of the human soul, to observe them, and to make these observations fruitful by combining them with a straightforward and illuminating theory." See Riedel, 408–15.

[14] In normal usage during this period, "soul" refers to that which animates the body and simultaneously serves as the seat of the feelings, emotions, and perceptions, as well as of the desires and passions they engender: Johann Heinrich Campe, *Wörterbuch der Deutschen Sprache, Erster Theil, A- bis -E* (Braunschweig: Schulbuchhandlung, 1807), 4: 368; see Sommer, 60–70. Christian Wolff subscribed to the conventional wisdom when he considered the soul to be "an immaterial simple substance" (Richard Blackwell, "Christian Wolff's Doctrine of the Soul," *Journal of the History of Ideas* 22 (1961): 339–54, here 346). Compare Lucretius's assumption that the soul was an assemblage of very fine atoms. With the increased tendency toward empirical analyses in the eighteenth century, the soul came to be defined largely as a set of functions, rather than as an entity: Günther Mensching, "Vernunft und Selbstbehauptung: Zum Begriff der Seele in der europäischen Aufklärung," in *Die Seele: Ihre Geschichte im Abendland,* eds. Gerd Jüttemann et al. (Weinheim: Psychologie Verlags Union, 1991), 217–35, here 218–20. And, of course, more radical thinkers such as La Mettrie were willing to dispense with the soul altogether. In the nineteenth century scientists largely replaced "soul" with "brain." For the Pietistic characterization of the soul, see Michael Reiter, "Pietismus," in *Die Seele,* 198–213. On the question of vestigial taxonomies, see Alan T. McKenzie, *Certain*

Lively Episodes: The Articulation of Passion in 18th-Century Prose (Athens: U of Georgia P, 1990), 77–88; compare Ralph Häfner, "'L'âme est une neurologie en miniature': Herder und die Neurophysiologie Charles Bonnets," in *Der ganze Mensch,* 392–93.

[15] "Should physiology ever progress to a point where it can demonstrate psychology — which I greatly doubt — it would derive many a ray of light for this phenomenon, though it might also divide it in individual, excessively small, and obtuse filaments." The English translation is by Alexander Gode, *On the Origin of Language* (New York: Ungar, 1966), 87–88; see also Sommer, 89, and Häfner.

[16] Charles Taylor, *Sources of the Self: The Making of Modern Identity* (Cambridge, MA: Harvard UP, 1989), 283. See also McKenzie, 24–54.

[17] On Wolff, see Blackwell's study, and Charles A. Corr, "Christian Wolff and Leibniz," *Journal of the History of Ideas* 36 (1975): 241–62.

[18] On Tetens, see Jeffrey Barnouw, "The Philosophical Achievement and Historical Significance of Johann Niclas Tetens," *Studies in Eighteenth-Century Culture* 9 (1979): 301–35.

[19] Possibly the experiments in pigment mixing conducted by Jakob LeBon in 1730, Tobias Mayer in 1758, and Johannes Lambert in 1772; see Richard Kremer, "Innovation through Synthesis: Helmholtz and Color Research," in *Hermann von Helmholtz and the Foundations of Nineteenth-Century Science,* ed. David Cahan (Berkeley: U of California P, 1993), 205–228, here 221.

[20] Eberhard, 9. Leibniz's hierarchy of "representations" (ideas presented to or by the mind) remained authoritative throughout the eighteenth century. A rough synopsis: an obscure representation (*"dunkel," "obscurus"*) cannot be distinguished from others, nor can its object be articulated; a clear (*"klar," "clarus"*) representation is distinguishable, but it remains confused (*"verworren," "confusus"*) until its distinguishing characteristics can be described through reason, at which point it starts to become distinct (*"deutlich," "distinctus"*). See Jeffrey Barnouw, "The Cognitive Value of Confusion and Obscurity in the German Enlightenment: Leibniz, Baumgarten, and Herder," *Studies in Eighteenth-Century Culture* 24 (1995): 29–50, here 29–33; and Raimund Bezold, *Popularphilosophie und Erfahrungsseelenkunde im Werk von Karl Philipp Moritz* (Würzburg: Königshausen & Neumann, 1984), 19.

[21] Barnouw, "The Philosophical Achievement," 301–7. Lewis White Beck regrets that Tetens, the most accomplished of the German empirical thinkers, wrote "his philosophy as if it were psychology"; he failed to go in the same direction as Kant, "and thereby missed the boat": *Early German Philosophy: Kant and His Predecessors* (Cambridge MA: Harvard UP, 1969), 414–15.

[22] "A great many new things intruded before I had learned to deal with the old ones, and a great many old things continued to exercise their hold over me even though I thought I was justified in renouncing them completely" (*G-CW,* 4: 214).

[23] Thomas P. Saine, *Die ästhetische Theodizee: Karl Philipp Moritz und die Philosophie des 18. Jahrhunderts* (Munich: Fink, 1971), 52.

[24] "If even the simplest, most isolated representation must, according to the harmony that exists between body and soul, and through which these two parts are united to form a single individual, have its accompanying, even if unperceived, movement in

the articulated body; so it must in turn be concluded from the set of such harmonious movements in the body, that the set of unified partial representations are unified into a single powerful feeling or emotion within the soul. In the condition of thought, only a few cerebral nerves are active; in the condition of strong emotion, in contrast, the nervous shock is so strong, that it conveys itself to the whole system, dilating or contracting the blood vessels so that the flow of blood to other parts of the body is obstructed, or its return to the heart is blocked, so that the affected person grows either pale with fright or red with shame or anger; indeed, it conveys itself to the muscles, and the entire body involuntarily contracts in spasms."

This kind of observation had become common by the 1770s. Riedel's survey concludes that the "*psychologia empirica*" increasingly dominated the second half of the eighteenth century under various labels. While Abel practiced "*empirische Psychologie*," Johann Georg Sulzer referred to "*Experimentalphysik der Seele*" (experimental physics of the soul), Johann Gottlieb Krüger to "*Experimental-Seelenlehre*" (experimental study of the soul), and Karl Philipp Moritz to "*Erfahrungsseelenkunde*" (experiential psychology). Psychological studies flooded the German book market in a variety of forms, and it is, Riedel insists, no exaggeration to call the Late Enlightenment the epoch of empirical psychology (431–32).

[25] Moses Mendelssohn, *Gesammelte Schriften*, 24 vols., eds. F. Bamberger et al. (Stuttgart-Bad Canstatt: Fromann, 1971–97), 1: 84: "All of these affects emerge from a miraculous, mechanical drive before the thinking part of a human being comes into play."

[26] He discusses therapeutic measures by which reason can be restored to someone who is overwhelmed by passion (117–19), offering prescriptions almost the same as Aspermonte's advice in Leisewitz's *Julius von Tarent*. See also Julius's claim that "unsre Seele ist ein einfaches Wesen": Johann Anton Leisewitz, *Julius von Tarent: Ein Trauerspiel*, ed. Werner Keller, Universal-Bibliothek, 111 (Stuttgart: Reclam, 1965), 5.

[27] "That the soul engaged in thought conceives the object with which it is occupied to be outside itself; in contrast, when the soul makes use of its emotional powers, it believes itself to be occupied with its own condition."

[28] "Its totality of sensations is strengthened by all the partial sensations that have enough shared determinants to cause them to be classified within a main representation, but which also have enough particular determinants to increase the number of partial sensations in the totality of sensation."

[29] "Someone perceiving only through touch is closed in on himself: his feelings are an immediate part of himself, are bound together with his ego. Our eye throws us far outside of ourselves." The quotation is from "Studien und Entwürfe zur Plastik" (Studies and Sketches on Sculpture), written in 1769. Compare Johann Jakob Engel's "Die Bildsäule" (The Statue), first published in 1775, which builds on Bonnet's and Etienne Bonnot de Condillac's (1715–80) fable of a statue acquiring consciousness through the senses. Mendelssohn and Johann Karl Wezel (1747–1819) take up the same topic later. Engel begins with smell and hearing but eventually concludes that each of the senses has its own, albeit limited value, and that each is a worthy subject of study in its own right: Johann Jakob Engel, "Die Bildsäule" (1775), *Schriften*, 1: *1801–1806* (Frankfurt am Main: Athenäum, 1971), 335–55.

[30] Elizabeth M. Wilkinson and Leonard A. Willoughby, "The Blind Man and the Poet: An Early Stage in Goethe's Quest for Form," in *German Studies Presented to Walter Horace Bruford* (London: Harrap, 1962), 29–57, here 36–46.

[31] Quoted by Luserke, 212: "In this way he affects the reader's soul, exercises unbounded power over his heart, gains control over every feeling, and directs them as he will."

[32] Mendelssohn, *Gesammelte Schriften*, 2: 259–65.

[33] Sommer, 274–77. When Leibniz discussed green as a mixed color, he was apparently unaware that it could also be spectral; see Barnouw, "Cognitive Value," 31.

[34] "The poet's sensitiveness, vexation, and melancholy are not merely the *object* of his song; unfortunately, they are often the *Apollo* that inspires him."

[35] Riedel, 198: "Not every sudden irritability of the soul, nor fleeting ardor, nor fermenting fury, nor every convulsive bodily movement signifies the true fire of genius."

[36] Johann Nicolas Tetens, *Philosophische Versuche über die menschliche Natur und ihre Entwicklung* (Leipzig: Weidmanns Erben und Reich, 1777), 125, quoted by Sommer, 276: "Then the sensations and ideas interpenetrate one another and unite in new combinations in such a way that one does not do justice to these images, which have been expressed by these poets in living, poetic language, by viewing them merely as an accumulation of simple emotional ideas either set next to each other or following each other in quick succession. In these newly crafted, combined expressions, these poets present the individual strokes of which the painting consists, but even the way in which they bring forth these words proves that the characteristic strokes have, like mixed colors, been pressed into each other and mixed together."

[37] Gotthold Ephraim Lessing, *Sämtliche Schriften*, 23 vols., eds. Karl Lachmann and Franz Muncker (Stuttgart: Göschen, 1886–1924), 19: 254.

[38] See Christoph Wulf, "Präsenz und Absenz: Prozeß und Struktur in der Geschichte der Seele," in *Die Seele*, 5–12, here 7.

[39] Adela Pinch, *Strange Fits of Passion: Epistemologies of Emotion, Hume to Austen* (Stanford CA: Stanford UP, 1996), 19.

[40] Karl Philipp Moritz, *Werke*, 2 vols., eds. Heide Hollmer and Albert Meier (Frankfurt am Main: Deutscher Klassiker Verlag, 1999), 1: 794.

Herder and the Sturm und Drang

Wulf Koepke

Herder in Histories of Literature

HISTORIES OF GERMAN LITERATURE present Johann Gottfried Herder as one of the intellectual fathers of the Sturm und Drang. The *Brockhaus* encyclopedia of 1957 summarized the matter for a general readership by saying that the Sturm und Drang received its theoretical foundation, above all, from Johann Georg Hamann and Herder.[1] "Hamann und Herder" was a typical formula in this context. Four texts by Herder are mentioned: *Journal meiner Reise im Jahre 1769; Auch eine Philosophie der Geschichte zur Bildung der Menschheit;* and his two contributions to *Von deutscher Art und Kunst,* the Ossian essay and "Shakespear." These should, we are told, be regarded as marking the birth of the Sturm und Drang.

Journal meiner Reise im Jahre 1769, also known as the *Reisejournal,* was not published until much later; *Von deutscher Art und Kunst* appeared in 1773; *Auch eine Philosophie der Geschichte zur Bildung der Menschheit* in 1774; and, while Goethe and Lenz read these texts, their impact on others is in many cases less certain. It is, therefore, only partly true that Herder formulated ideas and beliefs that other writers then received from him. Herder may have articulated what was "in the air" and what corresponded to the aspirations of the younger generation. Nevertheless, two questionable statements seem to perpetuate themselves: that Hamann and Herder share all their fundamental beliefs and that the writers of Goethe's generation were inspired by them. Hamann's writings, cryptic and "private" as they were in an age of clarity in public discourse, were known and read only by a few, although Herder did his best to make Hamann a household word in his circles. Moreover, he differed from Hamann on fundamental points of theology, a difference that became evident when Herder's essay *Über den Ursprung der Sprache,* written in 1770 and published in 1772, opted for a human and not a divine origin of language.

Even though he praised some of Goethe's early writings and Lenz's major plays, Herder never considered himself part of an exclusive movement — let alone the spiritual head of it. During the heyday of the Sturm und Drang, Herder lived in Bückeburg in almost total isolation, far from cultural and economic centers such as Frankfurt am Main, Leipzig, Göttingen, and Hamburg. Herder's tastes were catholic: he admired Klopstock and Klopstock's poetry, he considered Lessing Germany's greatest writer after Klopstock, and he liked some of Wieland's writings. But at that time he did not consider himself primarily a poet and literary critic. He was concerned with the text of the Bible, with theological and homiletic questions, with the training of ministers and the educational system, with the philosophy of history, with the propagation of the writings of the Dutch philosopher François Hemsterhuis (1721–90), and also with the collection, translation, and publication of folk songs. The two works of this period that were closest to his heart were *Älteste Urkunde des Menschengeschlechts* (The Oldest Document of the Human Race, 1774) and *Auch eine Philosophie der Geschichte zur Bildung der Menschheit*. Although *Von deutscher Art und Kunst* has been considered by many a "manifesto" of the new movement for a "German" art and literature, it was, in Herder's eyes, an "occasional" publication without lasting significance — "einige Fliegende Blätter" (a few loose leaves), as the subtitle indicates. Scholars and literary histories have generally considered the *Älteste Urkunde des Menschengeschlechts* an embarrassment and have made much of the two Herder essays in *Von deutscher Art und Kunst;* but even if we allow for Herder's habit of downgrading his new works and lowering the expectations of his readers, his own view of his writings of the Bückeburg period of 1771–76 differs fundamentally from that of later critics, especially German critics. Herder's later writings on the Old Testament, however, notably *Vom Geist der Ebräischen Poesie* (On the Spirit of Hebrew Poetry, 1782–83), were in a different style and spirit. He never came back to the *Älteste Urkunde,* while *Auch eine Philosophie der Geschichte zur Bildung der Menschheit* was superseded by his magnum opus, *Ideen zur Philosophie der Geschichte der Menschheit* (Ideas on the Philosophy of the History of Mankind, 1784–91).

Critics attribute many fundamental aspects of Sturm und Drang thinking to the impact of Herder: the affirmation of emotionality — and, more generally speaking, irrationality — over abstract thinking and a rationalistic view of life and the universe; the affirmation of the "genius" and of "original" creativity not bound by the rules of a prescriptive aesthetic theory, specifically, the three unities in drama; the advocacy of free-verse poetry and of expressiveness over a beautiful and elegant style;

and truth, including naturalistic prose, over beauty. A true work of art is, for Herder, the creation of a genius, not the fulfillment of rules and conventions by a person of talent and erudition.

Herder's models of great literature — Homer and Sophocles in Greek antiquity; Shakespeare; the realistic English novel from Henry Fielding to Oliver Goldsmith, in particular Laurence Sterne; Rousseau; Denis Diderot; Lessing; Klopstock; even folk songs — were neither formless, spontaneous, nor "original." Goethe's Werther, too, is forever raving about nature, but he experiences nature with Homer and Ossian in his pocket and with Klopstock's "Die Frühlingsfeier" (Celebration of Spring), and he praises the authenticity of Goldsmith's *The Vicar of Wakefield* (1766). He quotes the Bible abundantly, and his last reading before his suicide is the latest event in German letters in 1772, Lessing's *Emilia Galotti*. Herder and the Sturm und Drang writers lived in the context of the entire European literature, philosophy, and theology of the time.

The prevalent views of the connections between Herder and the Sturm und Drang go back to the lasting impact of Goethe's account in *Dichtung und Wahrheit*. Popular history demands to be personalized. In the cultural tradition of the Germans the Sturm und Drang, the first German youth movement (the first of many), and maybe the *"Deutsche Bewegung"* (German Movement)[2] itself, had its real inception in the encounter of the ailing Herder and the youthful student Goethe in Herder's inn "Zum Geist" in Strasbourg in the fall of 1770, vividly narrated by Goethe in his autobiography. Herder the mentor is associated with the gestation of the *Faust* drama, with Goethe's new tone in poetry, with an iconoclastic circle of friends in Strasbourg around Goethe that may be more *"Dichtung"* than *"Wahrheit,"* more poetry than truth. He is associated with the inspiration of Goethe the genius through a new view of language, with a new understanding of Shakespeare, the Bible, Homer, and all of this led to the evolution of the greatest genius of German letters, Goethe. In this picture of the creation of the genius Herder plays an ambiguous role: he is the inspiring mind, but also the negative critic, sometimes the destructive and sarcastic Mephisto. He is generous with his gifts and insights but equally envious that he does not possess Goethe's creative ability. Thus, the drama unfolds that will be played out over more than three decades until Herder's death in 1803: a drama of attraction and repulsion between these two great men, in which Goethe the classicist will always have the upper hand and the "better press." According to this narrative, Herder, unlike Goethe and Schiller, was unable and unwilling to mature to classicism. Instead, he remained in a posture of futile opposition and envy toward the achievements of the Weimar alliance of Schiller and Goethe and regressed into a sterile Enlightenment attitude.

This was the consensus of the majority of the critics until quite recently, and it followed the views of Schiller himself. This personal drama reaches far beyond the Sturm und Drang, but Goethe's later account of its beginning diagnosed its course from the perspective of Herder's last years. Shoehorned into the myth of Weimar, the place of Herder in literary history is still overshadowed by the tradition of partisan opinions generated by the various cultural and political movements of the nineteenth and twentieth centuries. In order to place Herder in the framework of the Sturm und Drang and to discuss his views on poetry, history, language, and society as a theoretical expression or "foundation" of the philosophy of life espoused by the Sturm und Drang, it is first necessary to analyze both Herder's writings of the earlier 1770s as his own Sturm und Drang and to consider his personal relations with writers of the Sturm und Drang, notably Goethe and Lenz.

Herder's Sturm und Drang

In May 1769 Herder abruptly quit his post as a teacher and preacher in Riga and sailed to France. He spent the first four months in Nantes, ostensibly to gain fluency in French. His subsequent stay in Paris was short and uneventful. Even Diderot, whose writings he respected so much, cannot have made a lasting impression on him as a person. The only real gain from this stay was a firsthand acquaintance with much visual art, primarily sculptures and statues, which helped to clarify the ideas he later developed in his *Plastik* (Sculpture, 1778). Herder accepted the position of tutor to the Prince of Holstein-Gottorp on the latter's Grand Tour; he hoped that it would give him the opportunity for an educational journey through Europe, particularly to Italy and England. But after six weeks of traveling Herder resigned his position and went to Strasbourg, where he hoped that the well-known surgeon Lobstein would cure him of an eye ailment. The cure, which included several painful operations, lasted for many months. During this time he met Goethe and finished his essay *Über den Ursprung der Sprache,* which received a prize from the Berlin Academy of Sciences. In May 1771 Herder went to work as a consistorial councilor and court preacher to Graf Wilhelm von Schaumburg-Lippe in Bückeburg. He was lonely and depressed for the first two years, but his mood changed markedly when he married Caroline Flachsland in the spring of 1773. It was in Bücke-

burg in 1773 and 1774 that Herder published the writings associated
with the Sturm und Drang. His publications during his first years in
Weimar — for instance, the collections of folk songs of 1778–79 — were
based on the work done in Bückeburg.

In Nantes, where he had led a rather isolated life, Herder had written down an assessment of his previous years and outlined plans for the
future. These plans included the future school curriculum in Riga, to
which he still planned to return, but in larger part they concerned future
publications and the dream of his own role as a reformer of Russia. This
unfinished "diary," the *Reisejournal,* was never meant for publication.
Parts of it were published in 1846 by one of Herder's sons, and the
entire text did not appear until 1878. It was, therefore, only with Rudolf
Haym's seminal biography, which began to appear in 1877,[3] that Herder
scholars began to have full access to this crucial text. In Friedrich Wilhelm Kantzenbach's biography we read that the *Reisejournal* is "das
lebendigste Selbstbekenntnis, das Herder uns hinterlassen hat. Es geht
dabei nicht um eine Reisebeschreibung, sondern um eine Konfession aus
vollem Herzen, ohne Rückhalt, ganz im Sinne des Sturm und Drang,
dessen prophetischer Botschafter Herder in diesen Aufzeichnungen ist."[4]
Considering this description, which is typical of many, we will not be
surprised to find very little on the voyage itself, except some often-
quoted "philosophical" reflections; but we are surprised to find that the
confession takes up so little space. Herder seems to start out in the manner of pietistic autobiographies; but soon and, as it seems, with relief he
returns to his book plans and his pedagogical and political visions. Herder faults himself for too much reading and writing and missing out on
"real" life, but it seems that for him only reading and writing provide
access to life. The *Reisejournal* is an abundant source for the genesis of
Herder's ideas and later writings; it shows also a man torn between the
needs for action and for writing. At the time of the *Reisejournal* he
thought that his field of activities had been too confining; but later, after
the experiences of Bückeburg and Weimar, he knew that a self-governing
city such as Riga provided much more opportunity for action than the
petty principalities of Germany. Herder was an ambitious man. He
wanted to be remembered as the reformer of a state or, at least, of its
educational system. He compared himself with Martin Luther, and he
never abandoned the feeling that he was wasting his time with trivial
tasks, especially during the later Weimar years.

The bulk of the text of the *Reisejournal* discusses books he had read,
French books in particular, and his own plans for books. In later years
Herder wrote about the value of self-observation and autobiography, but

the "confession" that Kantzenbach attributed to him was something that he never, in fact, contemplated. And he had no urge to publish the *Reisejournal*. He was always mindful of his position in society: that of a church administrator and pastor who has to be careful about his appearance, who represents an important institution that is under attack and that needs to be defended.

Herder's Sturm und Drang writings proper were typically published anonymously, continuing the game of denial that he had played, much to his regret, with his *Kritische Wälder* (Critical Groves, 1769). One of the primary contradictions of this complex person and writer was his penchant for biting criticism and satire, which earned him the nickname "Swift" in the Strasbourg circle, and his extreme sensitivity to counterattacks. This sensitivity began with his feuds with Christian Adolf Klotz in *Kritische Wälder* and culminated in the Bückeburg years in his controversies with August Ludwig Schlözer and Johann Joachim Spalding. Herder later relented and kept his biting wit to himself or his circle of friends, but it still caused frictions, especially with Goethe. In his writings between 1773 and 1776 Herder appeared as one who insists on taking the opposite view to that of the best-known authors of the age: he attacked the Voltairean vein of philosophy of history, especially the notion of "progress"; he challenged the entirety of contemporary theology with a totally new approach to the text of the Bible; and he opposed the ruling notion of literature and literary theory with his view of Shakespeare and his praise of folk songs.

One of the strikingly provocative features of Herder's writings from this period is his style. It is highly rhetorical: there are many question marks and exclamation marks; there are even more dashes, sometimes indicating incomplete phrases; and there are gestures that indicate that here is a writer offering new revelations to an audience that he expects to have a closed mind. His phrases are often teasing; rhetorical questions abound, promising statements that will not come; they always challenge the authorities of the day; they demand a totally new approach and perspective. This could only come across as arrogant, as the voice of one who claimed to know the absolute truth, and common-sense Enlighteners such as Friedrich Nicolai resented it. Nicolai had invited Herder, as the author of the *Kritische Wälder,* to review books for his *Allgemeine Deutsche Bibliothek,* which Herder did for several years; but Nicolai found it hard to tolerate the style Herder adopted in, for example, his reviews of Gerstenberg's *Ugolino,* Klopstock's poetry, and "bardic" lyric poetry. (Herder's reviews have subsequently been praised as the beginning of a new style, examples of an empathetic identification with the text as opposed to coldly critical distance and prescriptive dogmatism.) The Nicolai connection came to a quarrelsome end in 1774 with a sarcastic letter by Nicolai on the style of the *Älteste Urkunde*. In later years Nicolai repeatedly provoked Herder, beginning with his polemical collections of folk songs *Ein feyner kleyner Almanach vol schönerr echterr liblicherr Volkslieder, lustiger Reyen unndt kleglicher Mordgeschichten, gesungenn von B. Gabryell Wunderlich* (1777–78).[5] Nicolai knew Herder's Ossian essay and Gottfried August Bürger's *Herzensausguß über Volkspoesie* (Outpourings of the Heart on Folk Song, 1776), which was inspired by the essay, and he knew that Herder was preparing his own collection of folk songs. After breaking with Nicolai, Herder rushed his two volumes of *Volkslieder* (Folk Songs, 1778–79) into print; the seminal collection later became known as *Stimmen der Völker in Liedern* (Voices of the Peoples in Songs) after it was republished under that title in 1807 by Johannes von Müller. Among those who were not fooled by Herder's rather overblown rhetoric was Lessing, who read Herder's texts carefully and, even in disagreement, considered them stimulating.

In 1773 Herder published a collection of five essays and gave it the title *Von deutscher Art und Kunst*. Hans Dietrich Irmscher describes it as the programmatic statement of the Sturm und Drang but stresses that it owes its origins to chance.[6] Herder and Johann Joachim Bode, the translator of major English novels and also a publisher in Hamburg, wanted to give Herder's Ossian essay, originally destined for a discontinued journal, more weight and context. Herder added his essay "Shakespear"; Goethe's "Von Deutscher Baukunst" (On German Architecture), on Erwin von Steinbach and the Strasbourg cathedral; excerpts from "Versuch über die Gothische Baukunst" (Essay on Gothic Architecture, 1766), by Paolo Frisi; and parts of the introduction to the *Osnabrückische Geschichte* (History of Osnabrück), by Justus Möser, which Herder called "Deutsche Geschichte" (German History). Herder mentioned Frisi's and Möser's names but neither his own nor Goethe's. He placed his own essays first, giving them more weight and intimating that the rest were fillers to give him enough pages for a book.

Herder's and Goethe's contributions have always overshadowed the rest. Herder's inclusion of Möser's text makes good sense, as Möser insisted on the Germanic traditions in German history and, in addition, called for a "universal" history, meaning a history encompassing the interplay of all societal areas — law, religion, political and military events, and culture. Only this interplay would give a true picture of the past and of its significance for the present. Herder's excerpt highlights Möser's emphasis on honor and property and the liberty of the independent landholders as the only sound basis for a well-balanced and truly free society. Möser preferred traditional laws and customs to abstract rules and bureaucracies and local and regional control to a centralized imperial administration. He has been called conservative, but in the context of the absolutism of the eighteenth century the demand for a more participatory government is better described as reformist.

The inclusion of the Frisi essay is surprising, as it is a rather dry dissertation on the advantages and disadvantages of various types of domes and on the architectural problems of the pointed arch. Frisi's understanding is that gothic architecture was the product of the decline of ancient Roman architecture, but that it produced remarkable buildings, sometimes with "mixed" designs — that is, both antique and gothic. His prime example is the cathedral in Milan. One cannot really say that Frisi is hostile to the gothic style, but he clearly prefers Palladio. Remarkably, he claims a German origin for the gothic style, and sees both the gothic and the Moorish architecture of Spain as noteworthy antitheses to the neoclassical "norm." Herder wanted to contrast Goethe's enthusiastic praise of Erwin von Steinbach with an unemotional analysis of such structures, and he was not sure whether such youthful enthusiasm as Goethe's was justified. He himself refused to reject the norm of antiquity in such a flagrant manner. This refusal is indicated by his footnote between the two essays: "Der folgende Aufsatz, der beinahe das Gegentheil und auf die entgegen gesetzteste Weise behauptet, ist beigerückt worden, um vielleicht zu einem dritten mittlern Anlaß zu geben" (*H-SW*, 5: xx).[7] Maybe that third essay would offer an investigation into the real principles of beautiful architecture. Herder did not agree with the legend that the gothic style had a German origin; he liked to trace it back to Moslem Spain.

The word *deutsch* in the title of the collection has been at the center of many controversies and interpretations. It is clear from these texts, as well as from Herder's other writings, that the word did not designate the political entity of the Holy Roman Empire but the entire non-Roman, non-Mediterranean tradition in Northern Europe, Great Britain in particular, including the Scots and Irish. He was concerned about the evolution of a new national literature and its orientation. He emphasized, both with his title and in the texts, an alternative to Roman models and to French norms, and, with the reference to Möser, an affirmation of the indigenous traditions of the Germans in their laws, constitutions, customs, and family structures.

Herder's Ossian essay is the first and by far the longest of the contributions. Although Herder was an enthusiastic believer in the authenticity of the Ossianic epics, this essay does not deal with them as such but only with their recent translation in hexameters by Michael Denis, which appeared in 1768. The Ossian text cannot be translated in the manner of Klopstock's *Messias* (The Messiah), Herder argues, because "Oßians Gedichte *Lieder, Lieder des Volkes, Lieder* eines ungebildeten sinnlichen Volks sind, die sich so lange im Munde der väterlichen Tradition haben fortsingen können" (*H-SW*, 5: 160).[8] Denis's Ossian is, therefore, beautiful; it is well done; but it is not Ossian. As proof, Herder offers comparisons with old songs that appear in Shakespeare or in English collections. He insists that the closer these songs, especially the "Lieder der Wilden" (*H-SW*, 5: 168; songs of savages), are to the oral tradition, the less polished they must be. Herder's examples include the famous "Edward" ballad and songs from Latvia and the Lapps, as well as "Odins Höllenfahrt" (Odin's Descent into Hell). The specimens underscore the Nordic bent of his essay and show the impact of the fashion for things bardic. Subsequently, Herder turns to original German songs from olden times. His examples include Goethe's "Heidenröslein" (Little Heath-Rose), and he insists on counting religious songs among folk songs. To emphasize the poetic dignity of folk poetry he offers a long lament from Greenland as an example of a model elegy. The essay has no real conclusion, and this fact is not changed by the later postscript. But Herder has made his point. Although his views about the authenticity of Ossian are problematic, he had offered a most stimulating description of what ancient folk songs all over the world must have been, had shown that such songs existed in Germany, and had urged that their examples should invigorate the poetry of his own day.

The impact of Herder's ideas on the development of the German *Lied* and the ballad was enormous; but in spite of its suggestive tone, the impact of his essay on Shakespeare is not so easily defined. Herder's purpose was to justify the form and content of Shakespeare's plays through the historical context of the Elizabethan age. Sophocles had written the perfect drama for his time and his stage in Athens, and Shakespeare reached perfection in his own age and on his own stage precisely because he did not imitate the drama of antiquity, as the French did, but did what his society demanded. Inevitably, Herder's concluding reflection must be: is it right, or is it possible, to "imitate" Shakespeare in our time? Are Shakespeare's texts not also documents of a past age that we have difficulty understanding? Historical empathy has its narrow limits, especially in the case of productive reception, and the Germans should not do with Shakespeare what the French had done with Euripides and Seneca. Shakespeare could, however, he believed, still be revived in an original way, and the proof was Goethe's *Götz von Berlichingen,* which Herder praises in his essay, though without mentioning names. The Germans, Herder argues, had begun to appropriate Shakespeare, but, as the reception of *Hamlet* showed, the translations reflected the age and the beliefs of the translators rather than those of Shakespeare.

Herder was concerned with the text of the Bible throughout his life, and the whole complex of divine revelation through the word, the poetic word in particular, was central to his thinking. Hamann's dictum, "Poesie ist die Muttersprache des Menschengeschlechts,"[9] has to be understood in a religious sense: the language of revelation was poetic. Eighteenth-century theology had tried in various ways to harmonize the words of the Bible with the discoveries of the sciences. A major stumbling block proved to be the story of creation in Genesis, which was contradicted by the multiplying evidence of a long and slow evolution of plants, animals, and the earth itself. Physico-theology, the theology based on the evidence of design in nature, offered various ways of harmonizing the natural sciences with the Bible, but Herder rejected such compromises between revelation and reason or experience. He was convinced that scientific methods could never reach back to the very beginning of humankind and of the world. The text of the Bible was the expression of an early sensuous people and their need for images to understand the invisible God.

Herder made several assumptions that would remain fundamental to his philosophy of history. One was the origin of humankind in one place and from one group — in other words, from Adam and Eve. A second assumption was that geographically the origin of the human race was to be found in the Orient and that it was in Oriental texts, if anywhere, that it would be documented. Herder used the term *"Morgenland"* for the Orient and was attracted by the analogy of the origin of the world with the morning, the rising sun, dawn, the *"Morgenröte."* For Herder, basing himself on deficient and sometimes misleading information about ancient Oriental texts, the Book of Genesis in the Bible was the oldest, the most original documentation of the origin of the human race. He struggled with an adequate understanding of the biblical text. In spite of Martin Luther's great work, he felt it incumbent on himself to produce his own translation — a work he never accomplished, although he translated poetic texts in *Vom Geist der Ebräischen Poesie* and also translated the Song of Songs. The *Älteste Urkunde* must be considered, on one level, as a new translation of Genesis.

During his Riga years Herder had made extensive studies of what he called the archaeology of the Orient, and in Strasbourg he told Goethe about them. In Bückeburg, Herder returned to the subject, and when he was on leave in Göttingen and buried in books from that library, he wrote to Christian Gottlob Heyne in mid-February, 1772, "daß ich in einem Stücke, das wir alle auswendig wissen, eine Rune gefunden zu haben glaube, die ich für das älteste Symbolgebäude des menschlichen Geschlechtes mit dem Zeugniß des ganzen Alterthums angeben kann;"[10] this "rune" leads to "den Ursprung des Buchstaben, den ersten Schlüssel der Aegyptischen Hieroglyphe, Mythologyie u.s.w." (*H-B*, 2: 134).[11] This was a kind of epiphany or revelation; and, as far as the hieroglyph was concerned, Herder was to remain impervious to all doubts and criticisms.

The story of creation is equally the story of the first instruction of the human race, and what Herder means by the term *hieroglyph* is a symbol predating the separation of writing and picture, through which God instructed the first humans. The origin of the human race, of human language, and of human knowledge is bound together in this one moment of divine presence and impact, in this revelation. Reason is not an antagonist of revelation: it is the outcome of revelation.

Herder's claim was bound to raise questions, especially since he emphasized that after thousands of years of examinations and investigations, he was the first who had the insight that would change the whole of theology. Herder did not pursue this claim after its initial rejection, but it continued to provide the unstated basis for his views on religion and on history. To do justice to this much maligned text, it is fair to consider in greater detail the concept of the rune, which Herder later renamed the "hieroglyph." Herder develops it in steps, after commenting on his version of the Genesis text. The hieroglyph binds together time and space as it represents the pictograph of the seven days of creation: light, earth and water, creatures of the earth and the sky, high and low, and, finally, the Sabbath. Herder's creation story is dominated by the motif from Genesis, "And God said, let there be light: and there was light." In the beginning there was dawn, "*Morgenröte*." Herder's first concern is, as always, to find the unifying principle in the disparate sequence of events. The unifying point is found in the origins — the origin of language, the origin of the history of the human race. The scientific and scholarly view of the world was, for Herder, characterized by fragmentation, by the lack of a point of view that would bring order, proportions, and harmony into the chaos that scholars had created for themselves.

The theologians of Herder's day and of later times have rejected his speculations and claims. Nevertheless, he inspired others — poets, in particular — who felt that his account of the creation of nature and the human race had a deeper meaning for them as an analogy to the power of poetic creation.[12] Herder was averse to the dominant trends of his age, and, as a fundamental critic of the methods and goals of scholarship, he did not want to add to the growing body of learned information. He wanted to cut through the secondary and tertiary literature and reopen the path to the sources — to reality. In his contribution to historiography, which in his Sturm und Drang years was represented above all by *Auch eine Philosophie,* he opposed, on the one hand, the emerging professional or academic historical research as lacking a unifying point of view, and he also disagreed sharply, on the other hand, with the optimistic narratives of philosophies of history that adhered to the principle of "progress" and that saw the present age as the highest point in the evolution of humankind. Recently Isaak Iselin from Switzerland had found wide acceptance with his *Philosophische Muthmassungen über die Geschichte der Menschheit* (Philosophical Speculations on the History of Humankind, 1764; new edition, 1770). Herder, in his conception of a unified philosophy of human history, thought to replace the principle of progress with that of self-contained epochs. Herder's book, which he later called a pamphlet, bears the subtitle *Beytrag zu vielen Beyträgen des Jahrhunderts* (Contribution to Many Contributions of the Century), indicating its critical and polemical nature. The work is celebrated for its exposition of the theory that historical periods correspond to the life stages of the individual human being: childhood, youth, maturity, and old age. Herder pursued this analogy through ancient history, from the childlike stage of the Patriarchs and the Egyptians through the youthful culture of the Greeks to the manhood of Roman civilization. He modified it later by arguing that each civilization reached a certain stage of its development and remained there. For instance, Chinese culture had remained in a childlike stage — a widespread prejudice of Herder's age.

To go beyond the history of the ancient world demands different categories, as the history of Europe was based on the combination of the Roman tradition, the dominance of the Germanic peoples, and Christianity. Encouraged by Möser, Herder's evaluation of the Middle Ages was fairer than that of his Enlightened predecessors; and in spite of his praise of Luther's achievements, Herder was much more balanced in his views of the modern age as he leveled two major criticisms against it: the dominance of absolutist rulers and the pervasiveness of mechanical principles. For Herder, the philosophy, the laws and constitutions, the bureaucracy, and the military all obeyed the mechanical principle. Mechanical thinking favors utilitarian rationalism over all other human faculties and creates states of rulers and puppetlike subjects that are hostile to any individuality and original creativity.

These objections give impetus to Herder's main point that it would be foolish to call the present age the best of all times. In fact, for Herder there is a balance in history: what an age gains on the one hand, it loses on the other. It is impossible to ask which age of human history was or could be the happiest or most perfect: progress means loss, and imperfection is the human condition. The outstanding trait of the present age of "enlightenment" is its arrogance, and this is especially true for Europe. The Europeans are foolish to consider their civilization the yardstick of human accomplishments.

In his laments and his polemics Herder is in danger of seeing human history as a process of degradation and decadence from an original golden age. There is an antidote, however: he retains his faith in divine providence. In spite of all suffering, all senseless violence and human error, there is order behind the seeming chaos that we are unable to see because our perspective cannot encompass the whole of human history. We can only see some fragments and, at best, make some general assumptions, mainly through analogies. There is also a strongly critical attitude toward the state that has been criticized by prominent scholars such as Friedrich Meinecke[13] and that leads to the ideal of a stateless community, which could be called anarchism. For Herder, absolutist rulers and their arbitrary methods of government represented the negative consequences of the mechanical powers of bureaucracies and standing armies.

Auch eine Philosophie contains many elements of historicism, that is, the idea that each historical period and each civilization is an end in itself and has to be judged by its own criteria; and historicism implies a critique of Eurocentrism: the European values of today cannot be the yardstick for an evaluation of other civilizations. Herder maintains the analogy between the course of a civilization or epoch and the development of a living being from birth through maturity, old age, decay, and death. States with an artificial structure resulting from wars and conquests can maintain themselves beyond their "natural" age, but they will eventually die. Herder was looking for more "natural" or organic units of human communities than states. These he called "nations"; each is united by a common history, customs, traditions, and language. At no point, however, does Herder equate linguistic borders with political boundaries. What he has in mind are culturally cohesive, nonaggressive republics with participatory governments. This is scarcely the ideal to which the nationalisms of the nineteenth and twentieth centuries conformed.

Herder and Other Writers of the Sturm und Drang

The connection between Herder and Goethe is a ubiquitous topic in literary histories and in biographies of Goethe and Herder; it has generated studies of various specific problems, but by no means as many as one might expect. Since the relationship lasted from 1770 until Herder's death in 1803, it underwent many changes and phases. The best-known part is the encounter in Strasbourg, when the young student Goethe considered Herder his mentor, and his letters to Herder of 1771–72 testify to the warmth of his attachment, even after a harsh critique by Herder of the first version of *Götz von Berlichingen*. Herder, however, wrote to Caroline Flachsland on March 21, 1772, in a much more detached manner, "Göthe ist wirklich ein guter Mensch, nur äußerst leicht u. viel zu leicht, u. Spazzenmäßig, worüber er meine ewige Vorwürfe gehabt hat . . . auch glaube ich ihm, ohne Lobrednerei, einige gute Eindrücke gegeben haben, die einmal wirksam werden können."[14]

After Goethe settled in Weimar, the opportunity arose to appoint Herder to the position of general superintendent, consistorial councilor, and court preacher — to the relief of Herder, who longed to leave Bückeburg and whose appointment as a professor of theology in Göttingen had just run into insurmountable obstacles. Some correspondence resulted, and it reveals the continuation of Herder's close attachment to Goethe. Herder arrived in Weimar on October 1, 1776, and stayed for the rest of his life. A closer friendship between Herder and Goethe developed in 1783 and lasted for a decade before being overshadowed by political disagreements after the French Revolution. With Goethe's and Schiller's alliance in 1794 and their programmatic journal *Die Horen,* Herder's estrangement from Goethe grew: in addition to various personal conflicts, the later Herder's concept of literature and literary culture was diametrically opposed to that of Weimar Classicism.

Outsiders had good reasons for considering Herder part of the Frankfurt circle of Sturm und Drang writers. He contributed fourteen reviews to the iconoclastic year of 1772 of the *Frankfurter Gelehrten Anzeigen,* edited by Johann Heinrich Merck, Goethe, and Goethe's future brother-in-law Johann Georg Schlosser. Contrary to the typical reviews of the time, especially in the *Allgemeine Deutsche Bibliothek,* which attempted to be objectively informative, Herder made a point of being partisan, of either praising or condemning. He praised François Hemsterhuis, still virtually unknown in Germany, and he condemned J. D. Michaelis (1717–91), a prominent Bible scholar in Göttingen. But his most conspicuous controversy involved the Göttingen historian August Ludwig Schlözer, who published in 1772 an outline and guide for his course on universal history. Herder was not only irked by the arrogance of someone claiming to have his own history but also found no unity or spirit in the compilation. Herder's piece was most provocative and aroused Schlözer's anger, moving him to write an entire book, a sequel that was designed to refute Herder's few pages and punish the impertinent reviewer (by name) as an incompetent amateur. Herder did not respond, but a number of passages in *Auch eine Philosophie* show that he had read the book, and he refuted it in his own way without mentioning Schlözer.

The most conspicuous collaboration of Herder and Goethe during these years was Herder's inclusion of Goethe's "Von Deutscher Baukunst" in *Von deutscher Art und Kunst*. Goethe's enthusiastic piece was a eulogy of Erwin von Steinbach and his greatness, embodied in the greatness of his building, Strasbourg cathedral. Goethe celebrates Erwin as the genius who, like Herder's Shakespeare, was able to unify, to make a whole, out of disparate parts. Goethe recalls how he approached the cathedral with neoclassical prejudices and was overwhelmed by its warmth and unity. He compares the building to a tree reaching to the heavens, contrasting it with the "regular" arcades and pillars of classical monuments. We must, he argues, reject the prejudice against the word "gothic" and accept the work of genius, free from the dictates of one single prescriptive taste. Goethe's polemic turns against French theoreticians and regulatory aesthetics that generate mechanical principles and rules. Goethe did not republish this enthusiastic piece until 1824.

At the end of his "Shakespear" essay Herder praised an unnamed friend for his dramatization of the times of the German knights, mentioning Goethe's *Götz von Berlichingen;* but he was even more direct in his praise of other works by Goethe from this period. Somewhat surprisingly, he applauded *Stella* in its first version and recommended the play to others.[15] In 1775–76 he spoke highly of Goethe and his talents; for instance, in a letter to Hamann he referred to Lenz as Goethe's younger brother (*H-B*, 2: 188). Goethe's response to Herder's publications in the early Weimar years seems to have been cool; but during the period of their renewed friendship Goethe was one of the first readers of the *Ideen,* and Herder responded to Goethe's interest in the natural sciences and to the progress of *Wilhelm Meisters Theatralische Sendung* (Wilhelm Meister's Theatrical Mission, written circa 1777–85, published 1911). He was also helpful in the editing of Goethe's collected works, which were published during his time in Italy. While the alliance between

Goethe and Schiller has received close scrutiny, based on their correspondence and on Eckermann's reports, the friendship of Herder and Goethe deserves new investigation — especially the lasting impact of Herder's ideas on Goethe beyond their estrangement and beyond Herder's death in 1803.

The connection between Herder and Lenz was short but intense. It fell in the years of Lenz's greatest productivity and prominence, 1775 and 1776. They saw each other once, briefly and under unfavorable circumstances, when Herder arrived in Weimar in October, 1776, and Lenz was about to be banished from the court. In his letter of March 9, 1776, Herder is already trying to give the self-doubting Lenz more confidence: "Und Du, was zitterst Du, wie ein Irrlicht zu erlöschen. In Dir is wahrlich Funke Gottes, der nie verlöscht u. verlöschen muß. Glaube!" (*H-B*, 3: 256).[16] Herder was instrumental in securing the publication of *Die Soldaten,* and he praised *Der Hofmeister* and *Der neue Menoza.* But he was also familiar with Lenz's problems as the son of a stern Lutheran minister trying to find his own way both professionally and in his religion. Herder's writings from the Bückeburg period, particularly those on the Bible, were a new point of orientation for Lenz. For Lenz, Herder could have been a father figure, and he defended Herder's controversial writings both publicly and privately — for instance, against his father, who disapproved of his son's relationship with an unorthodox clergyman who had the reputation among theologians of being a "Socinian." Herder was opposed by the clergy in Bückeburg, in Weimar, and among the professors of theology in Göttingen, who prevented his appointment as university preacher. Herder acknowledged with gratitude Lenz's sympathetic reading of his *Älteste Urkunde* and *Auch eine Philosophie.* Lenz referred to Herder in the prologue to his *Meynungen eines Layen den Geistlichen zugeeignet* (Opinions of a Layman Dedicated to the Clergy, 1775), and Herder repaid the compliment with a footnote on *Der neue Menoza* in the second volume of *Älteste Urkunde.* In Lenz's *Pandämonium Germanicum* Herder appears as someone who thinks positively of Lenz's talents and encourages him. Lenz's essays, such as "Versuch über das erste Principium der Moral" (Essay on the First Principle of Morality, written 1771–72), show his proximity to Herderian views, and their ideas on Shakespeare and tragedy are close. Although Herder appears mostly as the giver, the dialogue with a searching mind such as Lenz's might under other circumstances have developed into the kind of give-and-take relationship on which he thrived.

Johann Caspar Lavater, a minister in Zurich, was known for his *Aussichten in die Ewigkeit* (Prospects of Eternity, 1768–78); for his effusive style in his correspondence with many personalities of his day, including Goethe; and, later, for his monumental *Physiognomische Fragmente,* an extremely controversial demonstration of the way in which faces and skulls express the personality, that sold widely in spite of its high price and grew to four huge volumes. During the period under consideration Lavater enticed Herder into engaging in a regular correspondence. Herder was not a born letter writer,[17] and he hesitated for a long time before he entered into the correspondence with Lavater, who became notorious when he publicly challenged Moses Mendelssohn in 1769 either to refute Bonnet's *Apologie des Christentums* (Apology for Christianity, just translated by Lavater) or to convert. But in his depressing isolation in Bückeburg, Herder wrote a long letter to Lavater, dated October 30, 1772, followed by others in which he wrestled with his major problem: his attempt to find access to revelation through a poetic, divinely inspired language — Klopstock is mentioned again and again. After his marriage in the spring of 1773, Herder's exchange with Lavater becomes more collegial in character and concerns publications and theological ideas. Lavater was repeatedly hurt by Herder's criticisms of his writings; but they were well meaning and constructive, and Herder did his best to restore harmony. In the end, after Herder's move to Weimar and his turn to practical concerns, Lavater came to dislike Herder's *Briefe, das Studium der Theologie betreffend* (Letters Concerning the Study of Theology, 1780–81), and their ways parted. In Bückeburg, Herder found in Lavater's *Aussichten in die Ewigkeit* passages that appealed to his needs, and he found a correspondent who gave him the opportunity to express some of his religious strivings. Herder connected the idea of physiognomics with the ideas on sculpture that he formulated in his *Plastik,* but Lavater's *Physiognomische Fragmente* assumed only a modest role in the dialogue between the two men.

Scholarship and the Image of Herder

German scholarship has, for the most part, emphasized Herder's earlier works and has seen his publications after the *Ideen* as products of a mind in decline and one that was unwilling and unable to advance with the changing times. Until at least 1945 the Sturm und Drang was regarded as the first period of a new national German literature that resulted from transcending the Enlightenment; Herder's achievement was seen in this light, and his late works seemed to fall back into Enlightenment patterns that had long been overcome by Goethe and Schiller and the Romantics.

Herder's views were defined as antirationalistic, as a philosophy rooted in feeling; but this strength was also considered his weakness: he never arrived at the clarity and purity of Goethe's classicism. In other words, Herder's achievements were never considered without a comparison with Goethe — a comparison in which he was bound to lose. As scholars noted, he left a work rich in seminal ideas but a work of fragments, of unfinished projects. He never wrote the great work that would crown and unify all his endeavors. The focus on Goethe led to a relative neglect of Herder's religious and theological writings and to a neglect of Herder's own poetic production, except for his translations.

Herder was active in many domains, and research on him has, therefore, been conducted in many areas: linguistics, aesthetics and literary theory, literary history, anthropology, historiography, geography, theology, psychology, and philosophy. For the most part these branches of scholarship have remained separate, without much profiting from each other — which is certainly contrary to Herder's own spirit and procedures. Nevertheless, the overall image of Herder, largely influenced by Goethe's account in *Dichtung und Wahrheit*, is evident everywhere. It has made of Herder a genius of intuition and historical/cultural empathy who felt and thought many things that later research by sober scientists would have to sift through, examine, and reassess. What remains true is that Herder stands at the crossroads between the man of universal knowledge and the professional specialists in the sciences who were developing at the universities. In this respect he resembles Goethe. For the Sturm und Drang period, scholars stress three contributions by Herder: his call for the creation of a new national literature; his initiation of a new historical consciousness and hermeneutics; and his controversial Bible studies and theology, the last passed over by many historians and literary scholars.

Work on editions of Herder's works began soon after his death, initiated by his widow, Caroline. They were supplemented by testimonials and, later, a wealth of information and documents on his life and works. Heinrich Düntzer and other nineteenth-century Germanists worked on the letters, and Herder's *Sämtliche Werke*, edited by Bernhard Suphan and his team of collaborators, appeared in thirty-three volumes between 1877 and 1913 (*H-SW*). During the same period Düntzer and Anton Eduard Wollheim da Fonseca produced a twenty-four-volume edition of Herder's works;[18] they reprinted the first editions, whereas Suphan took Herder's final versions as definitive. Suphan's edition was praised as a model for critical editions, and it provided the basis for Herder scholarship in the late nineteenth and all of the twentieth century; but from today's perspective many problematic editorial decisions are apparent. The recent edition by the Deutscher Klassiker Verlag (1985–2000) contains indispensable new material and important commentaries.[19]

Critical Herder scholarship began with an unsurpassed achievement: the biography by Rudolf Haym published in two volumes, 1877 and 1885, which was able to make use of the first volumes of the Suphan edition and much unpublished material. This monumental work contains a wealth of information and many incisive observations and evaluations. At the same time, it reflects, as it must, the political, cultural, and stylistic prejudices of its author, including his condemnation of *Die Älteste Urkunde* as frighteningly formless, hurried, immature, and unreadable (1: 587).

The scholar who followed Haym in his intention of presenting the "whole" Herder was Eugen Kühnemann.[20] He was less interested in facts and individual analyses of texts than in a unified picture of Herder's personality and creativity. By contrast with Haym's nineteenth-century liberalism, Kühnemann reflects the impact of Friedrich Nietzsche, together with the intense German nationalism of his day. Comparing Herder, once again, with Goethe, he considers Herder's tragedy to be a decisive lack of vitality that prevented him from creating the great work he had in mind. Kühnemann stands at the beginning of the tradition of the history of ideas, which preferred generalities and initiated a tendency to disregard Herder's texts, declaring them vague and contradictory, in favor of a general view of his personality and his philosophy of life.

The hundredth anniversary of Herder's death in 1903 generated a wide-ranging discussion of Herder's idea of "*Humanität*" in which writers of all persuasions, including socialists, participated. In 1907 a rather short section on Herder in Meinecke's *Weltbürgertum und Natio-nalstaat* defined Herder's political attitude as suitable for a "*Kulturnati-on*" (cultural nation), a new concept at the time, but argued that this was now an anachronism, since vital and aggressive "*Staatsnationen*" (state nations) were needed. Herder was too soft, too feminine, too weak for such a "manly" view of history. This view of Herder perpetuated itself through the first half of the century. On the other hand, Meinecke credited Herder's *Auch eine Philosophie* with the breakthrough to truly historicist thinking, a mode of thought that views past epochs in their own right and without prejudice.[21] Such a view of history, he argues, does more justice to the history of Germany, especially when it sees, as Herder did, the nation as the core unit of human communities and the moving force in history. Meinecke's and Kühnemann's image of Herder, modified by Josef Nadler in 1924[22] and Max Kommerell in 1928,[23] legitimized

Herder as the herald of the nation and of a true conception of history but declared him too soft, too humanistic, to be a direct model to be followed in the present. This characterization was echoed in publications during the period after 1933 by such writers as Gerhard Fricke,[24] Benno von Wiese,[25] and Wolfdietrich Rasch.[26]

Herder's association with the idea of the nation meant that it took a long time after 1945 to liberate him from the liabilities of the past. Scholarship in the German Democratic Republic (GDR) approved his concepts of folk art and history and declared Herder part of the great movement of European Enlightenment, rather than someone who had either opposed or transcended it, and it revalued his later political views in the light of his positive attitude toward the French Revolution. This revaluation called for a reinterpretation of the Bückeburg period as a phase of the Late Enlightenment rather than the onset of a German national revival.

The most comprehensive attempt to see Sturm und Drang as a movement in its own right came from British scholars who were unburdened by the need of German studies in Germany to justify and define German classicism or to see its origins in nationalistic terms. They had a keener eye for the foreign influences on the Sturm und Drang and had the necessary distance to see in it a unity that the Germans were not always able to perceive. Roy Pascal[27] treated the Sturm und Drang as a group movement, including Herder, Merck, Goethe, Lenz, and Klinger, with authors such as Maler Müller, Wagner, and Leisewitz at the periphery and close to groups such as the Göttinger Hainbund and personalities such as Lavater and Friedrich Heinrich Jacobi. "Herder's unhappy temperament gives us perhaps the deepest insight into the psyche of the Sturm und Drang" (12), says Pascal; it "mirrors a cultural crisis, the conflict within his century" (19).

Pascal is highly critical of the political philosophy implied in *Auch eine Philosophie*, although he acknowledges that Herder showed a concern for individual welfare. He agrees that the *Älteste Urkunde* was "the most important statement of Herder's religious views" (95) in this period but sees it also as "a crisis in Herder's thought" (95). It represented an attempt to return to simple faith, accentuated by the intensity of an "all-sided experience" (100). Herder's turn from "thinking" to "feeling" and "doing," which included the immersion in nature — first in the *Reisejournal,* then in many poems and in *Vom Erkennen und Empfinden der menschlichen Seele* — Pascal sees as informing Goethe's early work on *Faust* and his poems. He describes *Auch eine Philosophie* as the "profound expression of the glory and the tragedy of the Sturm und Drang" (232); but the achievement of the Sturm und Drang, for Pascal, lies ultimately in its poetry and dramas.

In his 1952 study of the Sturm und Drang, H. B. Garland[28] downplays Herder's impact on Goethe: "Herder accelerated processes which Goethe would have completed eventually of his own accord" (26). Herder is characterized as "a powerful mind and striking, if unsatisfactory, personality" exemplifying "romantic impatience with reality" (14–15). Herder's response to Shakespeare was purely "emotional"; *Von deutscher Art und Kunst* was "repetitive and elliptical, slipshod and obscure" and may not have had the impact that is often claimed for it, but "its symptomatic and evidential value" is considerable (18–19). Garland argues that the lack of clarity and substance in Herder's ideas diminished their impact, and he relegates Herder to one of the "forerunners" of the movement together with Klopstock and Hamann: all in all, Herder comes across as inferior to Gerstenberg and, of course, Klopstock.

Robert T. Clark published his lifetime study of Herder in 1955[29] and largely determined the image of Herder in the United States for the second half of the twentieth century, especially since the scarcity of English translations makes the secondary literature even more important for all except those few who can read Herder's difficult texts in the original.

A new impetus for Herder scholarship in the Federal Republic of Germany and in the United States developed in the 1970s and manifested itself in conferences and in the foundation in 1985 of the International Johann-Gottfried-Herder Society, which publishes a yearbook that includes a Herder bibliography. One of the features of more recent Herder scholarship is its closer attention to the words of Herder's texts and their meanings. Whereas more attention has been given to the later Herder and to Herder's struggle against Kant's critical philosophy, there have been several publications on philosophical and psychological issues in the work of the earlier Herder, as well, with a clear emphasis on the antecedents, implications, and impact of his theory of language.

Surprisingly, most of the studies of the relationship of Goethe and Herder have dealt primarily with positivistic questions of details of their life and work; Hans Dietrich Irmscher's article on their lifelong attraction and repulsion is a foray into new territory.[30] There has been even less interest in the results of the short but intense correspondence between Herder and Lenz; but at a time when the Sturm und Drang is considered less as a "movement" of a whole generation than as the totality of the affinities of loosely connected small groups of writers, personal exchanges seem to take on greater significance. This emphasis can serve to define more precisely Herder's uniqueness in the group. He was, at the same time, part of other groups: he was on friendly terms with Lessing, Mendelssohn, and Matthias Claudius; he tried to cooperate with Friedrich Nicolai; and he was embroiled in several theological controversies.

An earlier German tradition had seen the Sturm und Drang as a youth movement: the German version of "Pre-Romanticism," a first phase leading to the greater achievements of Weimar Classicism and Romanticism.[31] The opposite view involves the integration of the Sturm und Drang into the European Enlightenment as part of the Late Enlightenment, as Ehrhard Bahr has formulated it.[32] This perspective emphasizes the continuity of historical developments and considers the Sturm und Drang as a final, innovative phase of the Enlightenment, leading into the new epoch of Romanticism. Moreover, the impact of French and English philosophers is emphasized. While it is generally acknowledged that Herder's view of history, together with that of Möser, had great significance for Goethe's generation of writers, it is primarily in Herder's concept of language and its evolution that the most productive energies seem to lie. Furthermore, the Sturm und Drang can be seen as the awakening of a new awareness of the self, a self-reflection and self-consciousness that are not sufficiently defined by the term "subjectivity." It is evident in the writings of Goethe and Lenz but equally in Herder's poems and in some passages from his *Reisejournal,* and his *Vom Erkennen und Empfinden der menschlichen Seele* (On the Cognition and Sensation of the Human Soul, 1778) can serve as a theoretical underpinning of this new awareness of the self.

Literary scholars tend to consider Herder's views and ideas as unchanging, although they generally acknowledge considerable modifications from the Riga to the Bückeburg and then to the Weimar period. The question arises in this context whether it was really the Bückeburg period that made Herder the seminal figure for German letters, as scholars have maintained. During the nineteenth century Herder's most popular work in Germany, by far, was *Der Cid* (1803). Internationally, his reputation rested mainly on his *Ideen,* while Goethe's memories of Herder centered on his personality and on their conversations. To get a clearer picture of Herder's writings and achievements, they have to be disentangled from many prejudices and established clichés.

The Herder scholarship of the last thirty years has shown that many discoveries can be made through a closer reading of Herder's texts. This is true of his Sturm und Drang period as much as for any other period of his life. It has also become evident that a reading of Herder without preordained comparisons, such as "Hamann and Herder," "Goethe and Herder," or "Kant and Herder," is productive and clears the way for a fresh look at these essential relationships. Furthermore, the writings of the Bückeburg period should not be limited by the label "Sturm und Drang." They represent a distinct period in Herder's work, but are also the continuation of previous ideas and trends and not without a continuation in Weimar. The first requirement is, therefore, openness. It needs to be remembered that Herder's poetic writings from the period, his poems and a cantata such as *Brutus* (1774), do not conform to the image of Sturm und Drang poetry, which is primarily determined by Goethe. In investigating the Sturm und Drang connections, critics have been primarily concerned with the style of the prose writings. While the consensus that Herder provided the philosophical underpinnings of the Sturm und Drang seems to be unchanged, it is still not clear exactly how much of an impact his works had on the young writers, especially those beyond his personal acquaintance. The phrase "Herder and the Sturm und Drang" often conceals more than it reveals: each of these three areas of debate — Herder, the Sturm und Drang, and the relationship between Herder and the Sturm und Drang — is considerably more complex than has often been acknowledged.

Notes

[1] *Der große Brockhaus* (Wiesbaden: Brockhaus, 1957), 11: 309.

[2] The term, which refers to the revival of a German national culture at the end of the eighteenth century, was popularized by Heinz Kindermann in his *Durchbruch der Seele: Literarhistorische Studie über die Anfänge der "Deutschen Bewegung" vom Pietismus zur Romantik,* Danziger Beiträge, 1 (Danzig: Kafemann, 1928).

[3] Rudolf Haym, *Herder nach seinem Leben und seinen Werken dargestellt,* 2 vols. (Berlin: Gaertner, 1877–85).

[4] "The liveliest confession that Herder has left us. It is not a travelogue but a confession, flowing without restraint from the fullness of his heart, wholly in the spirit of the Sturm und Drang, whose prophet Herder shows himself in these sketches to be." Friedrich Wilhelm Kantzenbach, *Johann Gottfried Herder in Selbstzeugnissen und Bilddokumenten,* Rowohlts Monographien, 164 (Reinbek: Rowohlt, 1979), 39–40.

[5] The title, which is in a deliberately old-fashioned German, may be translated "A Splendid Little Almanac Full of Beautiful, Charming and Genuine Folksongs, Jolly Tunes and Pitiful Street Ballads sung by B. Gabryell Wunderlich."

[6] Hans Dietrich Irmscher, ed., *Von deutscher Art und Kunst,* Universal-Bibliothek, 7497 (Stuttgart: Reclam, 1968), 163.

[7] "The following essay, which makes almost the opposite claims, and does so in the most antithetical way, has been included in order, perhaps, to give rise to a third, lying between these two."

[8] "Ossian's poems are *songs, songs of the people, songs* of an uneducated, sensual people, which paternal tradition could sustain as songs."

[9] "Poetry is the mother tongue of the human race." From *Aesthetica in nuce,* in Johann Georg Hamann, *Sämtliche Werke: Historisch-kritische Ausgabe,* 6 vols., ed. Josef Nadler (Vienna: Herder, 1949–53), 2: 197.

[10] "That I believe I have found in a piece that we all know by heart a rune that, basing myself on the evidence of the whole of antiquity, I can claim to be the oldest symbol structure of the human race."

[11] "The origins of the alphabet, the first key to Egyptian hieroglyphs, mythology, etc."

[12] The best example is Goethe's letter to Schönborn of June 8, 1774, in which he comments on the *Älteste Urkunde.*

[13] Friedrich Meinecke, *Weltbürgertum und Nationalstaat* (1908), rpt. in his *Werke,* vol. 5 (Munich: Oldenbourg, 1969).

[14] "Goethe is truly a good man, he is just extremely easy-going, much too easy-going and sparrowlike, which I repeatedly reproached him over . . . and without boasting, I think I can say that I have given him a few good ideas that will play their part in due course." Herder, *Briefe: Gesamtausgabe, 1763–1803,* 10 vols., eds. Karl-Heinz Hahn et al. (Weimar: Böhlau, 1977–96), 2: 154. This edition of Herder's letters will henceforth be abbreviated *H-B.*

[15] He wrote, for example, to Johann Georg Zimmermann in a letter of March 23, 1776: "Welch ein Paradiesisch Stück seine Stella!" ("What a heavenly play his *Stella* is!" *H-B,* 2: 260).

[16] "And you, why are you anxious about losing your light, like a will-o'-the-wisp? You truly have the spark of God, which never goes out and must never go out. Have faith!"

[17] Apart from the letters he wrote on official business and the intense exchange of letters with Caroline, Herder corresponded with Hamann, with Christian Gottlob Heyne in Göttingen, with Gleim, and with his publisher Hartknoch. There were also temporary affinities expressed in letters to Zimmermann and Merck.

[18] *Herder's Werke,* 24 vols., eds. Heinrich Düntzer and Anton Eduard Wollheim da Fonseca (Berlin: Hempel, n.d.).

[19] Herder, *Werke,* 10 vols., eds. Günter Arnold et al. (Frankfurt am Main: Deutscher Klassiker Verlag, 1985–2000).

[20] Eugen Kühnemann, *Herders Leben* (Munich: Beck, 1895), much expanded and modified in the second edition, *Herder* (Munich: Beck, 1912).

[21] Friedrich Meinecke, *Die Entstehung des Historismus,* 2 vols. (Munich & Berlin: Oldenbourg, 1936).

[22] Josef Nadler, "Herder oder Goethe?" (1924); rpt. in his *deutscher geist/deutscher osten: zehn reden,* Schriften der Corona, 16 (Munich, Berlin, & Zurich: Oldenbourg, 1937), 127–40.

[23] Max Kommerell, *Der Dichter als Führer in der deutschen Klassik* (Berlin: Bondi, 1928).

[24] Gerhard Fricke, "Das Humanitätsideal der klassischen deutschen Dichtung und die Gegenwart: Herder," *Zeitschrift für Deutschkunde* 48 (1934): 673–90.

[25] Benno von Wiese, *Herder: Grundzüge seines Weltbildes* (Leipzig: Bibliographisches Institut, 1939); Wiese, "Der Philosoph auf dem Schiffe, Johann Gottfried Herder," in *Zwischen Utopie und Wirklichkeit: Studien zur deutschen Literatur* (Düsseldorf: Bagel, 1963), 32–60.

[26] Wolfdietrich Rasch, *Herder: Sein Leben und Werk im Umriß* (Halle: Niemeyer, 1938).

[27] Roy Pascal, *The German Sturm und Drang* (Manchester: Manchester UP, 1953).

[28] H. B. Garland, *Storm and Stress* (London: Harrap, 1952).

[29] Robert T. Clark, *Herder: His Life and Thought* (Berkeley & Los Angeles: U of California P, 1955).

[30] Hans Dietrich Irmscher, "Goethe und Herder im Wechselspiel von Attraktion und Repulsion," *Goethe-Jahrbuch* 106 (1989): 22–52.

[31] The classical formulation of this view is to be found in Hermann August Korff, *Geist der Goethezeit*, 5 vols. (Leipzig: Koehler & Ameland, 1954–57). Korff tried to overcome the irksome overlapping of shorter periods in literary history with the broader concept of the "age of Goethe."

[32] Ehrhard Bahr, ed., *Geschichte der deutschen Literatur: Kontinuität und Veränderung. Vom Mittelalter bis zur Gegenwart*, vol. 2, *Von der Aufklärung bis zum Vormärz* (Tübingen: Francke, 1988).

Ossian, Herder, and the Idea of Folk Song

Howard Gaskill

IN DECEMBER 1761 (but dated 1762) there appeared in London a volume titled *Fingal,* consisting of an eponymous epic prose poem in six books accompanied by sixteen shorter pieces, all attributed to the third-century Scottish Gaelic bard Ossian, son of Fingal, and translated into English by one James Macpherson. This work literally fulfilled the promise of an earlier publication, *Fragments of Ancient Poetry, Collected in the Highlands of Scotland, and translated from the Galic or Erse Language,* which had appeared in Edinburgh in June 1760 to much acclaim and the demand that the translator search for the lost whole of which some of the "fragments" were allegedly part. A hero featured in *Fingal,* but not in the earlier collection, is Dargo, "king of spears," who plays a role in the poem "Calthon and Colmal." In a note to that poem Macpherson writes:

> Dargo, the son of Collath, is celebrated in other poems by Ossian. He is said to have been killed by a boar at a hunting party. The lamentation of his mistress, or wife, Mingala, over his body, is extant; but whether it is of Ossian's composition, I cannot determine. It is generally ascribed to him, and has much of his manner; but some traditions mention it as an imitation by some later bard. — As it has some poetical merit, I have subjoined it.
>
> The spouse of Dargo came in tears: for Dargo was no more! The heroes sigh over Lartho's chief: and what shall sad Mingala do? The dark soul vanished like morning mist, before the king of spears: but the generous glowed in his presence like the morning star.
>
> Who was the fairest and most lovely? Who but Collath's stately son? Who sat in the midst of the wise, but Dargo of the mighty deeds?
>
> Thy hand touched the trembling harp: Thy voice was soft as summer-winds. — Ah me! what shall the heroes say? for Dargo fell before a boar. Pale is the lovely cheek; the look of which was firm in danger! — Why hast thou failed on our hills, thou fairer than the beams of the sun?

The daughter of Adonfion was lovely in the eyes of the valiant; she was lovely in their eyes, but she chose to be the spouse of Dargo.

But thou art alone, Mingala! the night is coming with its clouds; where is the bed of thy repose? Where but in the tomb of Dargo?

Why dost thou lift the stone, O bard! why dost thou shut the narrow house? Mingala's eyes are heavy, bard! She must sleep with Dargo.

Last night I heard the song of joy in Lartho's lofty hall. But silence now dwells around my bed. Mingala rests with Dargo.[1]

I have quoted this "lamentation" of the widow of Dargo because it seems to me a useful starting point for illustrating some of the problems and pitfalls still to be successfully negotiated by mainstream accounts of the Sturm und Drang. The poem is one of the first of a handful from Ossian chosen for translation by Johann Gottfried Herder and included in letters to his fiancée, Caroline Flachsland, in 1770/71.[2]

Herder's enduring enthusiasm for Ossian was first prominently expressed in the seminal essay "Auszug aus einem Briefwechsel über Oßian und die Lieder alter Völker," written in 1771 and published in 1773 as by far the most substantial contribution to that manifesto of Sturm und Drang values, *Von deutscher Art und Kunst*. It is an enthusiasm that has embarrassed generations of sympathetic critics who have faced the tricky task of arguing the originality and validity of Herder's insights while explaining how these came to be underpinned by a self-evident forgery. How could someone with such a fine awareness of the qualities of "primitive" poetry have been taken in by Macpherson's impudent fraud? For that, apparently, is what we now know it to be, and its inauthenticity — according to the common assumption — was already obvious to the more discerning of Herder's own contemporaries. Accordingly, he is usually represented as choosing to cling to a cherished illusion rather than accept plain and painful evidence. This is, in fact, a grotesque distortion. Far from being a naïve and gullible dupe, Herder was quite capable of entertaining doubts as to the absolute authenticity of Macpherson's Ossian, particularly as epic, though he (rightly) never seriously regarded it as totally fraudulent. Whatever his parti pris, he always made strenuous efforts to keep himself abreast of the Ossianic debate, so that by the time he came to write his second major essay on the subject, "Ossian und Homer," which appeared in Schiller's *Horen* in 1795, he was, according to Alexander Gillies (149), undoubtedly better informed on the authenticity question than any other German intellectual of the day. And that means rather better informed than those modern critics who still choose to condescend to him. For, insofar as Macpherson's work is based on genuine indigenous Gaelic sources, these are, in the main, popular ballad adaptations of traditional material and would, indeed, correspond to what Herder understood by "*Volkslied*" (folk song).[3] The lamentation of the widow of Dargo is a case in point. In Macpherson's day it was still sung by thousands in the Highlands and Islands, and his rendering of it is probably as close as he ever gets to literal translation.[4] Given that the song is tucked away in a footnote to a minor poem in *Fingal,* Herder ought, perhaps, to be congratulated for his powers of divination — all the more so, given that he was dependent on a translation of a translation. For despite the misinformation still to be found in secondary literature and even in editions of Herder, at the time he sent the Ossianic poems to Caroline he as yet had no access to the English. As Gillies (80–82) showed in 1933, they are, in fact, reworkings of extracts taken from the published German translations of Michael Denis (1768–69), of which Herder possessed a review copy. Unfortunately, Gillies's work is too often bypassed by modern critics and editors.[5]

It is true that Herder's interest in folk song predates any direct acquaintance with Ossian. Although this interest goes back to the mid-1760s, it was not until late in 1771 — some months after the completion of the first essay — that Goethe lent Herder a copy of an original, the *Works* edition, which he had found in his father's library in Frankfurt. Until then, Herder was dependent on German and French versions. It also predates his direct acquaintance with another text that was of enormous importance for him, Thomas Percy's collection *Reliques of Ancient English Poetry: Consisting of old heroic Ballads, Songs and other Pieces of our earlier Poets (chiefly of the Lyric Kind), together with some few of later date* (1765). It was not until early August 1771 that that Herder received a copy on loan through the good offices of Rudolf Erich Raspe (1737–94). Though now best known as the progenitor of the Münchhausen tall stories, Raspe was an extremely influential reviewer in the 1760s and was one of the first in Germany to draw attention to the significance both of Ossian and of the *Reliques.*[6]

These two works, which extensively underpin Herder's essay and owe much of their huge impact in Germany to it, might at first seem to be strange bedfellows. After all, Percy's "owlish" antiquarianism, with the emphasis firmly on manuscripts, serves the design of constructing a text-based Gothic (English) historical tradition to confront and refute Macpherson's impudent recovery of a glorious Celtic (Scottish) past from suspect and unverifiable oral sources.[7] And despite condescending acknowledgment of the "pleasing simplicity, and many artless graces" of the ballads, Percy is at pains to use chronological order within each of the three volumes of his collection "to show the gradual improvements of the English language and Poetry from the earliest ages down to the present"[8] — hence the inclusion of songs from Shakespeare, Raleigh, Thomas Deloney (1543–1600), and, in the final volume, modern imitations of traditional ballads by poets such as William Shenstone (1714–63). By contrast, with Macpherson earliest is definitely best: the third-century geriatric bard Ossian, the last of a race of heroes, laments the decline and extinction of an ancient culture and bewails the dawn of an age of pygmies: "Often have I fought, and often won in battles of the spear. But blind, and tearful, and forlorn I now walk with little men. O Fingal, with thy race of battle I now behold thee not. The wild roes feed upon the green tomb of the mighty king of Morven" (*PO*, 79). The great superiority of Ossian's poetry to that produced by subsequent Gaelic literary culture (the client bards of the clan chiefs) is repeatedly emphasized in Macpherson's notes. Percy is overtly concerned to shield his readership from the more barbarous features of his sources, notably by concealing their fragmentary nature and smoothing over apparent incoherence — so, for instance, the 201 lines of "Sir Cauline" become 392 in Percy's version, the avowed intention being "to connect and compleat the story in the manner which appeared to him most interesting and affecting."[9] Again by contrast, Macpherson deliberately attempts to convey something of the patina of ancient poetry, not only by underlining the fragile and fragmentary nature of transmission — he can resort to Shandyesque devices such as rows of asterisks introduced at a particularly gripping point in the narrative[10] — but also, and above all, by fulfilling contemporary expectations of the "primitive" *genus abruptum*. These are articulated in exemplary fashion by Hugh Blair in his enormously influential "Critical Dissertation on the Poems of Ossian":[11]

> The manner of composition bears all the marks of the greatest antiquity. No artful transitions; nor full and extended connection of parts; such as we find among the poets of later times, when order and regularity of composition were more studied and known; but a style always rapid and vehement; in narration concise even to abruptness, and leaving several circumstances to be supplied by the reader's imagination. (*PO*, 354)

These stylistic features — in particular, the use of parataxis and asyndeton, the paucity of syntactic co- and subordination — are even accentuated by Macpherson in the *Poems of Ossian* of 1773, the last edition to emerge from his hands. Quite clearly, though, Macpherson, too, is concerned to "please a polished age" (*PO*, 50), and insofar as he makes use of authentic Gaelic sources (which is much further than is generally

supposed), he is extremely selective, ruthlessly pruning anything suggestive of vulgarity, ribaldry, or primitive superstition that might detract
from the dignity of Ossian. For his attitude toward his native culture is
characterized by a mixture of pride and self-conscious defensiveness, and
all the while he writes too much with the metropolitan bigot in mind,
the sort of person who would scoff at the very notion of bare-arsed
Highland savages being able to produce poetry of any kind, let alone
full-blown epics. To a degree Macpherson may well himself initially have
believed that such had at one time existed and that he was justified in
correcting and amending corrupt tradition, filling in gaps and specula-
tively "restoring a work of merit to its original purity."[12] Nor did he make
any great secret of his own part in this process of imaginative reconstruction.[13] Herder was well aware of these facts and could, in any case,
see that most of the original *Fragments* had later been worked into larger
wholes. He never doubted that Macpherson had been responsible as
translator for — at the very least — considerable embellishment of his
Gaelic sources. Nor could he seriously doubt that the kernel of *Ossian*
was just as valid a product of indigenous Scottish Highland literary
culture as were his beloved "Edward," and other Border ballads included
in Percy's collection, products of the Scottish Lowlands. The edition of
Reliques Herder possessed was that of 1767, the second, in which Percy
publicly admitted (for the only time) to having been converted to a
belief in the authenticity of *Ossian,* though privately he made no bones
about how much it went against the grain to do so.[14]

From the above it ought to be clear that there can be no real justification for playing down the role of Ossian in the development of Herder's thinking about folk song. Instructive, and all too typical, is Roy
Pascal's comment (offered without irony) on the Ossian essay: "Fortunately Herder then escapes from Ossian, and all the pitfalls of this forgery, and quotes Shakespeare's *Come away Death.*"[15] Even if, as Orsino
in *Twelfth Night* suggests, this is a traditional song, it is embedded in a
sophisticated play, and it is difficult to see why it should self-evidently
represent a better choice for Herder's purposes. If Macpherson's part in
the composition of the Ossianic poetry is greater than he pretends, then
he is at least utilizing indigenous sources — just like Shakespeare, in fact,
and just as modern Germans should be doing, according to Herder.[16]
For he is less interested in folk song for its own sake — he (wisely) never
attempts a precise definition — than in promoting the literary qualities
he sees embodied in it.

Herder was not, of course, by any means the first to argue that
popular poetry and song had its own charms and merits of which the

literate and educated would do well to take note. The fear of ridicule that led him to delay the publication of his own collection of *Volkslieder* until the late 1770s also meant that when he did so, he was careful to preface it with positive comments on folk song from earlier authorities such as Montaigne, Sidney, and Addison.[17] The two Lapp songs, given in Latin by Johannes Scheffer in his *Lapponia* of 1673, had been the occasion for Addison's enthusiasm in the *Spectator* in 1712, and they continue to resurface in the form of translations and adaptations, particularly from the middle of the eighteenth century onwards (for instance, in the Parisian *Journal Etranger*, 1755–56). Ewald von Kleist's free translation of one of them, first published in 1758 and using Elizabeth Rowe's version ("A Laplander's Song to his Mistress") as its source, quickly established itself as a modern German classic. Herder quotes the whole of the Lapp poem in his Ossian essay, but not in his own or Kleist's German. In fact, he uses the German rendering given by Michael Denis in the third volume of his *Ossian*, which opens with the translation of Blair's "Critical Dissertation." In the original Blair quotes the poem in a footnote and prefaces it with the comment:

> Surely among the wild Laplanders, if any where, barbarity is in its most perfect state. Yet their love songs which Scheffer has given us in his Lapponia, are a proof that natural tenderness of sentiment may be found in a country, into which the least glimmering of science has never penetrated. To most English readers these songs are well known by the elegant translations of them in the Spectator, N°. 366 and 406. I shall subjoin Scheffer's Latin version of one of them, which has the appearance of being strictly literal. (*PO*, 547)

Leaving aside the question of how Blair could possibly judge the literalness of Scheffer's translation (into Latin from a Swedish version supplied by the Lapp Olaus Sirma) any better than that of Macpherson from the Gaelic, two points should be emphatically made here. One is that it is quite astonishing that — despite his assurance that he is giving the poem "aus der dritten Hand" (at third hand) — critics have persisted in crediting the German translation in the Ossian essay to Herder. As he later showed in the *Volkslieder*, when he had direct access to Scheffer, he could do much better than Denis. And had he had an English edition of Ossian at his disposal when writing his essay, he could have translated from Scheffer's text via Blair, for Denis gives only his own translation, not the Latin.[18] And if critics have failed to look at Denis's Ossian translation, despite the fact that Herder's essay consists to a large extent of a broadside against its failings, one should not be surprised — and this is the second point — that the true significance of Blair's "Dissertation" for Herder has been largely ignored.[19]

It was in the form of Denis's translation that Herder first encountered Blair's essay in its entirety, but he had been familiar with it in extracts and paraphrase for several years.[20] It is clear that he repeatedly reread it and that it confirmed his intuitions and influenced his thinking not just about Ossian but about "primitive" poetry in general. Blair was a critic after Herder's own heart, a model of the nonprescriptive, empathetic approach. He is praised as such in Herder's review of volumes two and three of Denis's translation.[21] Not that Blair is alone in that respect: he is one of an impressive list of "English" authorities, including Thomas Blackwell. It was Blackwell who, in his *Enquiry into the Life and Writings of Homer* (1735), first publicly adumbrated and articulated many ideas that became commonplaces of primitivist discourse and so conditioned the reception of Ossian.[22] Among the many aspects of the work that proved to be influential were the depiction of Homer as a wandering bard, an oral poet-performer,[23] singing of a turbulent world of which he is himself a product and has personal experience, and drawing on a home-grown mythology transmitted orally, particularly in song; the constant insistence on the virtues of *originality* and its superiority to imitation; the feeling that with the establishment of civilization the time had passed when it was possible to write poetry of the highest order ("what marvellous Things happen in a well ordered State?"[24]); the assertion that language has a primarily emotional origin; that poetry, being humanity's earliest form of expression, is fundamentally the expression of emotion; and the conception of poetic creation as an inspired process in which human beings temporarily transcend their rational faculties. The language used by people in early societies lends itself to poetry, for they naturally use "metaphors of the boldest, daring and most natural kind," and "their Passions are sound and genuine, not adulterated and disguised, and break out in their own artless phrase and unaffected Stile. They are not accustomed to the *prattle*, and little pretty *forms* that enervate a polished Speech."[25] The notion of the authenticity and integrity of early human beings in their direct expression of emotions, unsullied by dissimulation and calculation; the observation that language is diminished by polishing and sophistication; and the conviction of the superiority of poetry that is recited and sung over the dead letter of what is written and read — all of this was grist to Herder's mill. The message was reinforced and mediated — both to Herder and to Macpherson himself — by Blair:[26]

Irregular and unpolished we may expect the productions of unculti-
vated ages to be; but abounding, at the same time, with that enthusiasm, that vehemence and fire, which are the soul of poetry. For many
circumstances of those times which we call barbarous, are favourable to
the poetical spirit. That state, in which human nature shoots wild and
free, though unfit for other improvements, certainly encourages the
high exertions of fancy and passion. . . . [Men's] passions have nothing
to restrain them: their imagination has nothing to check it. They display themselves to one another without disguise: and converse and act
in the uncovered simplicity of nature. As their feelings are strong, so
their language, of itself, assumes a poetical turn. Prone to exaggerate,
they describe every thing in the strongest colours; which of course renders their speech picturesque and figurative. Figurative language owes
its rise chiefly to two causes; to the want of proper names for objects,
and to the influence of imagination and passion over the form of expression. Both these causes concur in the infancy of society. Figures are
commonly considered as artificial modes of speech, devised by orators
and poets, after the world had advanced to a refined state. The contrary
of this is the truth. Men never have used so many figures of style, as in
those rude ages, when, besides the power of a warm imagination to
suggest lively images, the want of proper and precise terms for the ideas
they would express, obliged them to have recourse to circumlocution,
metaphor, comparison, and all those substituted forms of expression,
which give a poetical air to language. An American chief, at this day,
harangues at the head of his tribe, in a more bold metaphorical style,
than a modern European would adventure to use in an Epic poem.[27]

In the progress of society, the genius and manners of men undergo
a change more favourable to accuracy than to sprightliness and sublim-
ity. As the world advances, the understanding gains ground upon the
imagination; the understanding is more exercised; the imagination,
less. . . . Men apply themselves to trace the causes of things; they correct and refine one another; they subdue or disguise their passions; they
form their exterior manners upon one uniform standard of politeness
and civility. Human nature is pruned according to method and rule.
Language advances from sterility to copiousness, and at the same time,
from fervour and enthusiasm, to correctness and precision. Style becomes more chaste; but less animated. (*PO*, 345)

As the reference to the American Indian chief makes clear, societies
develop at different rates, so that some still in their infancy may be encountered "at this day." Hence, the references not only to early poetry,
including the by now ubiquitous "Death-song of Regner Lodbrog" —
of which Blair translates substantial parts and quotes all twenty-nine
stanzas in the Latin of Olaus (Ole) Wormius (Worm)[28] and which is duly
mentioned by Herder — but also to contemporary societies, such as that

of the Lapps, where "barbarity is in its most perfect state." In a much-quoted passage in his Ossian essay Herder praises the language of the "savage":

> Sie wißen aus Reisebeschreibungen, wie stark und fest sich immer die Wilden ausdrücken. Immer die Sache, die sie sagen wollen, sinnlich, klar, lebendig anschauend: den Zweck, zu dem sie reden, unmittelbar und genau fühlend: nicht durch Schattenbegriffe, Halbideen und symbolischen Letternverstand (von dem sie in keinem Worte ihrer Sprache, da sie fast keine abstracta haben, wissen) durch alle dies nicht zerstreuet: noch minder durch Künsteleien, sklavische Erwartungen, furchtsam-schleichende Politik, und verwirrende Prämeditation verdorben — über alle diese Schwächungen des Geistes seligunwissend, erfassen sie den ganzen Gedanken mit dem ganzen Worte, und dies mit jenem. Sie schweigen entweder, oder reden im Moment des Intereße mit einer unvorbedachten Vestigkeit, Sicherheit und Schönheit, die alle wohlstudierte Europäer allezeit haben bewundern müßen, und — müßen bleiben laßen.

If you are looking for traces of such genuine eloquence ("*Beredsamkeit*") in our own society, he says, you certainly will not find it among those who play the scholar: "unverdorbne Kinder, Frauenzimmer, Leute von gutem Naturverstande, mehr durch Thätigkeit, als Spekulation gebildet, die sind, wenn das, was ich anführte, Beredsamkeit ist, alsdenn die Einzigen und besten Redner unsrer Zeit" (*H-SW*, 5: 181–82).[29]

Such eloquence has, of course, nothing to do with the smooth and orderly progression of ideas. On the contrary, this expressive energy, issuing directly, as it does, from the whole man — body, heart, and mind in unison — is incompatible with the logically structured, cold abstractions of philosophical prose. One of the most famous phrases in Herder's essay is "Sprünge und Würfe" (literally: leaps and tosses), which he sees as characteristic of folk poetry:

> Alle Gesänge solcher wilden Völker weben um daseiende Gegenstände, Handlungen, Begebenheiten, um eine lebendige Welt! Wie reich und vielfach sind da nun Umstände, gegenwärtige Züge, Theilvorfälle! Und alle hat das Auge gesehen! Die Seele stellet sie sich vor! Das setzt Sprünge und Würfe! Es ist kein anderer Zusammenhang unter den Theilen des Gesanges, als unter den Bäumen und Gebüschen im Walde, unter den Felsen und Grotten in der Einöde, als unter den Scenen der Begebenheit selbst. (*H-SW*, 5: 196–97)[30]

It is easy enough to see this as an unwarranted generalization arising from gaps and omissions in the narrative line — hiatuses in the train of thought, which are characteristic of older ballads — and to present Herder as making a virtue of the vagaries and contingencies of oral transmission. There may be some truth to the charge — but not much, unless one is determined to exaggerate his originality; for a taste for what Adam Smith called the "loose and broken manner," as exemplified in Pindar, "the most unconnected," was clearly developing by the middle of the eighteenth century. And this taste undoubtedly had to do with the growth of Sentimentalism (in Germany, "*Empfindsamkeit*") and the reaction against arid rationalism. All too lucid order and connection come to be associated with shallowness of feeling and absence of inspiration. As Smith observes: "The higher the Rapture, the more broken is the expression."[31] What has been called rhetorical diasparaction (literally "torn to pieces") is seen as *the* appropriate form to indicate elevated emotion.[32] And it could be shown to have a biblical pedigree. In 1753 Robert Lowth had published his lectures *De sacra poesi Hebraeorum* (On the Sacred Poetry of the Hebrews), finding in that poetry a fiery spirit too ardent to be confined by rule, expressing itself in bold metaphors, and advancing through syntactic parallelism and repetition, rather than the logical progression of ideas.[33] Divine inspiration is such that "the nature of the prophetic impulse . . . bears away the mind with irresistible violence, and frequently in rapid transitions from near to remote object, from human to divine."[34] And rapid transitions, or "schnelle Übergänge" (to quote an early German review of Macpherson's *Temora*),[35] are precisely what are to be expected from "primitive" poetry, ancient or modern. When the first authentic Gaelic ballad appeared in English, four years before Macpherson's *Fragments,* the translator presented it as the product of "simple and unassisted genius, in which energy is always more sought after than neatness, and the strictness of connexion less adverted to than the design of moving the passions and affecting the heart." (He also compared it to Homer.)[36] As early as September 1760 Anne Robert Jacques Turgot (1727–81) had drawn attention to the "style oriental" of Macpherson's *Fragments* (though like Blair after him he regards it as characteristic of a certain stage in human development, rather than as the product of a particular region[37]). He draws attention to "cette marche irrégulière, ces passages rapides et sans transition d'une idée à l'autre" (this irregular progression, these rapid leaps, without transition, from one idea to another).[38] And of course, as already mentioned, Blair himself was not slow to find in Ossian "a style always rapid and vehement; in narration concise even to abruptness, and leaving several circumstances to be supplied by the reader's imagination" (*PO,* 354). In his analysis of the language of Sturm und Drang Eric Blackall argues that "it is not until the Ossian essay that we find any close description of poetic language.

Here however we are given a full description, the most specific description of the *Sturm und Drang* ideal of language." But he also suggests that when Herder talks of Ossian's being "abgebrochen in Bildern und Empfindungen" (*H-SW*, 5: 159: abrupt [broken-off] in imagery and sentiment), this is "a new point and represents a contrast to the rationalistic (and ultimately Ciceronian) ideal of *connexio*."[39] It does, indeed, represent such a contrast; but as we have seen, it is hardly new. Nor does Herder claim that it is, since he is well aware of the established association between what he calls "Sprünge und Würfe" and the so-called oriental style, its fire and prophetic enthusiasm, also the perceived wild irregularities of the Pindaric ode.[40] But he also knew that virtually anyone commenting on Ossian would also remark on it — including, indeed, the bête noire of Herder's own essay, Michael Denis. For despite the (for Herder) totally inappropriate choice of smooth-flowing Klopstockian hexameters to render the rough bard, Denis was quite capable of recognizing that Ossian is "kurz, und abgerissen" (laconic and abrupt).[41]

Though this is not the impression one receives from much secondary literature, Harold T. Betteridge is probably correct in saying that Herder actually breaks no new ground in his Ossian essay but that "it remains, by virtue of its subject-matter and the spirited manner of its exposition, the most important and most influential of his polemical writings."[42] And this evaluation applies not least to his highlighting of "*Sprünge und Würfe*." That it could be positively inspirational is proved by its most impressive exemplification in Goethe's early version of *Faust* (c. 1775). As Pascal observes: "Its construction is like that of a ballad, springing from scene to scene, without the detail and complex transition of real events. It is, indeed, nature focused in a burning-glass; nature intensified, nature transformed: art."[43] Its fragmentariness is clearly for the most part by design, and — comparing *Urfaust* with *Faust I* — many may feel that the play is all the better for it. (I think particularly of the way in which, in the first version, Mephisto just suddenly appears without explanation, and we are left to work out for ourselves the precise nature of the devil's relationship with Faust.)

Related to this advocacy of the *genus abruptum* in Herder's essay is the rejection of regulated word order.[44] The emphasis on inversion in the Ossian essay and elsewhere is, again, not startlingly original, though it has its own particular resonances within the context of German. In his preface to Macpherson's *Fragments* Blair had declared: "The translation is extremely literal. Even the arrangement of the words in the original has been imitated; to which must be imputed some inversions in the style, that otherwise would not have been chosen" (*PO*, 6). This claim is echoed by Macpherson himself at the end of the "Dissertation" preceding *Fingal:* "And all that can be said of the translation, is, that it is literal, and that simplicity is studied. The arrangement of the words in the original is imitated, and the inversions of the style observed" (*PO,* 52). And it is, of course, true that the liberties taken in Ossian with the conventions of word order in English prose are designed to suggest Gaelic (which is a verb-subject-object language), causing Percy to mock what he called a studied affectation of Erse idiom. An illustration of what he might have been thinking of is provided by a passage from *Temora:* "Now is the coming forth of Cathmor, in the armour of kings! Dark-rolled[45] the eagle's wing above his helmet of fire. Unconcerned are his steps, as if they were to the chace of Atha. . . . Sudden, from the rock of Moi-lena, are Sul-malla's trembling steps" (*PO,* 271). Interestingly, if it were, indeed, strictly literal (and nowadays nobody would claim that it is), it would be an early example of foreignizing, as opposed to domesticating, translation: in other words, rather than aiming for naturalness in the target language, the exoticism and alterity of the original is preserved by the adoption of deliberate "translatorese." The lesson was not lost on Goethe and Herder when they came to translate into German portions of the Gaelic specimen that Macpherson offers of the seventh book of *Temora* (*PO,* 329–41), armed with little more than an Irish-English dictionary.[46] But then, inversion was also frequently invoked to underline the distinction between emotional and logical order. It is something Herder discovers everywhere in the poetry that is dearest to him, whether foreign or German, the Song of Songs or the hymns of Luther.[47] Or, of course, Ossian and folk song. As Blair tells us of "Lodbrog": the poetry "is wild, harsh and irregular; but at the same time animated and strong; the style, in the original, full of inversions, and, as we learn from some of Olaus's notes, highly metaphorical and figured" (*PO,* 349).[48] Inversion, which had been condemned in Luther by that literary pope, arch-rationalist, and upholder of neoclassicistic values, Johann Christoph Gottsched, becomes a principle of stylistic liberation, suggesting spontaneous and passionate expression directly from the heart, as opposed to the flat, colorless, calculated language of the age of reason. This principle is nicely illustrated in Goethe's *Die Leiden des jungen Werthers* of 1774. In the letter of December 24 Werther comments on the pedantry of the legate ("der Gesandte"), for whom he works. The spontaneous, inspirational manner in which Werther writes is not at all to his taste. He insists on proper syntactic links — so no adventurous ellipsis or asyndeton — and, of course, has rigid ideas as to how complex sentences should be structured: "von allen Inversionen die mir manchmal entfahren, ist er ein

Todfeind" (*G-MA*, 1.2: 248: of all inversions which sometimes escape me he is a sworn enemy). Goethe's *Werther* enjoyed enormous contemporary popularity both in Germany and beyond. In the protagonist's idealization of "unspoiled children, women, folk of a sound natural sense, minds formed less by speculation than by activity,"[49] we can clearly see the influence of Herder (a conduit for Blackwell, Rousseau, his own mentor Hamann, and, no doubt, countless others). But we can also see that influence in the crucial role the novel accords to Ossian.

The significance of the months in Strasbourg in 1770–71, during which the young Goethe closely associated with Herder and adopted him as a mentor, cannot be overstressed. Though his relationship with the older man later became strained, his autobiography *Dichtung und Wahrheit* contains a just and generous tribute:

> Ich ward mit der Poesie von einer ganz andern Seite, in einem andern Sinne bekannt als bisher, und zwar in einem solchen, der mir sehr zusagte. Die hebräische Dichtkunst, welche er nach seinem Vorgänger *Lowth* geistreich behandelte, die Volkspoesie, deren Überlieferungen im Elsaß aufzusuchen er uns antrieb, die ältesten Urkunden als Poesie gaben das Zeugnis, daß die Dichtkunst überhaupt eine Welt- und Völkergabe sei, nicht ein Privaterbteil einiger feinen gebildeten Männer. (*G-MA*, 16: 440)[50]

As Pascal observes, Herder "remained a man of the study and pulpit. . . . If he restored folksong to the rank of poetry, he left it to others to go among the common people and collect their songs."[51] And this Goethe himself did, returning with twelve ballads collected from the lips (or rather, throats — *"Kehlen"*) of old Alsatian women, as he writes to Herder in September 1771 (the younger people apparently preferred more trashy modern stuff). How much his own poetry was subsequently influenced by the so-called genuine article (and "authenticity" is a term that tends to be derided by modern ethnologists), or rather by Herder-inspired Platonic ideas of what it could and should be, cannot be decided here. But it does seem likely that in his most "popular" ballads, such as "Der König in Thule" (The King of Thule) and, in particular, "Heidenröslein" (The Heath Rose), Goethe was not so much directly modeling his poetry on traditional popular song as he was himself decisively helping to enshrine the norms by which "folksiness" came to be judged.[52] And he had inherited these norms from Herder. Herder it was who also encouraged Goethe's intense (if not prolonged) preoccupation with Ossian.

It is clear that, contrary to the claims often made in secondary literature, Goethe's acquaintance with Ossian predates his meeting with Herder by at least two years and possibly by an appreciably longer time.[53]

But it is not until the Strasbourg period that the blind bard becomes more than a convenient repository of images and begins to assume a major role in Goethe's literary life. It is, admittedly, virtually certain that he did not have an English edition of Ossian with him at the time, since he would scarcely have concealed it from Herder.[54] Nor would the various translations he made — the *Songs of Selma* for Friederike Brion and extracts from the Gaelic specimen for Herder — have had to wait until after he left Strasbourg for Frankfurt in August 1771. So Herder would have been mediating Ossian to Goethe via the medium of Denis, and possibly other German and French translations. The impact went deep, and, despite Goethe's later expressions of alienation from Ossian's nebulous world, it left its mark not just on his Sturm und Drang work.[55] But naturally, what he produced in the first few years of the 1770s provides the most plentiful harvest for anyone searching for Ossianic motifs. This is true not only of the poetry — for instance, the famous ode "Prometheus" owes a clear debt to Macpherson's "Carric-thura" (*PO*, 158–65) both in its opening image of the thistle-topping boy and also in the theme of heroic defiance of the deity — but also of the plays: it is not difficult to imagine the eponymous hero of *Götz von Berlichingen* as a battle-scarred Fingalian warrior, like Ossian himself the last of his race, surrounded by "little men";[56] and, of course, it is true of the novel *Werther*, fully seven percent of which (in the 1774 version) is taken up with translation from Ossian. It is Werther's reading aloud of his own rendering of most of the *Songs of Selma*, and a poignant passage from "Berrathon," that unbearably heightens the emotional tension between Werther and Lotte and precipitates the catastrophe. Whatever Herder's essay had done to promote the ancient bard, Goethe's inclusion in the novel of stunningly good translations of Macpherson at his best contributed mightily to raising Ossian to the status of a cult text both in Germany and beyond. And to ensure its wider dissemination, Goethe collaborated with his friend Merck on a pirated reprint of the English.[57] (It was this edition that Lenz used for his complete translation of *Fingal* in 1775–76, about which, until relatively recently, critics have tended to be strangely silent.)[58]

In the preface to the first volume of his *Evergreen*, a collection of traditional songs and ballads published in Edinburgh in 1724 (and one of Herder's sources for his *Volkslieder*), Allan Ramsay informs us that

When these good old "Bards" wrote, we had not yet made use of imported trimming upon our Cloaths, nor of foreign embroidery in our writings. Their "Poetry" is the product of their own country, not pilfered and spoiled in the transportation from abroad: Their "Images" are native, and their "Landskips" domestick; copied from those Fields and Meadows we every day behold.[59]

Herder's hopes for the discovery of indigenous good old German bards, displaying similar authenticity and originality, were not to be fulfilled. The German content of his *Volkslieder* proved to be somewhat meager and was offered apologetically, at that. But regrettable as this was, in a sense it did not matter. Though he would no doubt have preferred a rejuvenation of German literature from within its own resources, the qualities he was concerned to promote could easily be found elsewhere. And as Pascal points out, he personally responded more ardently to the poetry of the Old Testament, Homer, Shakespeare, the Scottish ballads and Spanish romances, Ossian and the Edda than he did to ancient or medieval German poetry.[60] What German writers had to learn from such texts was to be similarly productive and inventive in relation to their own environments, to express their own experience and "living world." They were to emulate, not imitate. His essays in *Von deutscher Art und Kunst* (on Shakespeare, as well as Ossian and the poetry of ancient peoples) represent an enormously powerful synthesis of the best contemporary thought on such matters. And there is little point in caviling about Herder's choice of models. You cannot keep Percy and the Edda, while rejecting or ignoring Ossian. In this respect, Herder's — and the Sturm und Drang's — bequest to the Romantic generation is an integrated package, with Ossian playing a major role. German literary history has been peculiarly unwilling to acknowledge that fact, but it is high time that it did.[61]

Notes

[1] *The Poems of Ossian and Related Works,* ed. Howard Gaskill (Edinburgh: Edinburgh UP, 1996), 174–75, henceforth cited in the text as *PO*. This edition is based on the two-volume *Works of Ossian* (London: Beckett & de Hondt, 1765), the version used by Herder and Goethe for their translations (and by Goethe for the pirated edition of the English he produced with Merck in 1773/74).

[2] See Alexander Gillies, *Herder und Ossian* (Berlin: Junker & Dünnhaupt, 1933), 25–26, 80–81.

[3] For Macpherson's sources and the uses he makes of them, see Derick Thomson, *The Gaelic Sources of Macpherson's "Ossian"* (Edinburgh: Oliver & Boyd, 1952); cf.

Donald E. Meek, "The Gaelic Ballads of Scotland: Creativity and Adaptation," in *Ossian Revisited,* ed. Gaskill (Edinburgh: Edinburgh UP, 1991), 19–48.

[4] For comments on the poem, see Thomson, *Gaelic Sources,* 55. The "lamentation" is one of the "Ancient Galic Poems" picked up in the Highlands by the Irish bishop Matthew Young and published — in a version even closer to Macpherson's than that used by Thomson — in the *Transactions of the Irish Academy* 1787.

[5] See my essay, "'Aus der dritten Hand': Herder and His Annotators," *German Life and Letters* 54 (2001): 210–18. Particularly culpable in this respect are Grimm and Gaier, respectively editors of volumes two and three of the modern Frankfurt edition: Johann Gottfried Herder, *Werke,* 10 vols. (Frankfurt am Main: Deutscher Klassiker Verlag, 1985–2000).

[6] Raspe produced the earliest German extended review of *Fingal* in the *Hannoverisches Magazin* 92 (1763) and translations from it that same year in issues 94–97. His review of the *Reliques,* containing the call for a German Percy, appeared in the *Neue Bibliothek der schönen Wissenschaften und freyen Künste* in 1766.

[7] See Nick Groom's excellent *The Making of Percy's Reliques* (Oxford: Oxford UP, 2000), especially chapter 3 (61–105). It is one of the abiding myths of the Ossianic controversy that Macpherson claimed to have translated the bulk of the poetry from manuscripts. Though he did make some important written finds — including *The Book of the Dean of Lismore,* one of the two most important collections of authentic "Ossianic" lays — he affected to despise them and emphasized the superiority of oral tradition.

[8] *Reliques of Ancient English Poetry* (London: Dodsley, 1765), 1: ix-x.

[9] *Reliques* 1: 36.

[10] See, in particular, *Cath-loda* (*PO,* 308–10, 328).

[11] First published separately in 1763, this work was appended in extended form to the *Works* edition of Ossian in 1765. It is too easy to forget, and difficult to overestimate, the enormous prestige Blair came to enjoy in Europe and even beyond: his *Lectures on Rhetoric and Belles Lettres* (1782) went into its second French edition in 1821, its third Dutch in 1832, and its third Spanish in 1816–17, and was even influential in South America; Hamann thought it a "magnificent work," and among Blair's many German admirers was Jean Paul. Clearly, the public support and commitment of a man of Blair's stature and reputation contributed a great deal to the success of Ossian.

[12] Andrew Gallie (in whose house Macpherson stayed and worked on his materials on his return from the first prospecting trip to the Highlands and Islands), as quoted in Henry Mackenzie, ed., *Report of the Committee of the Highland Society of Scotland, appointed to inquire into the Nature and Authenticity of the Poems of Ossian* (Edinburgh: Constable, 1805), 44.

[13] Cf. his comment in the preface to the first edition of *Fingal:* "I was not unsuccessful, considering how much the compositions of ancient times have been neglected, for some time past, in the north of Scotland. Several gentlemen in the Highlands and isles generously gave me all the assistance in their power; and it was by their *means I was enabled to compleat the epic poem*" (*PO,* 36; my italics). Also Macpherson's note to the second epic: "By means of my friends, I collected since all the broken frag-

ments of Temora, that I formerly wanted; and the story of the poem, which was accurately preserved by many, enabled me to reduce it into that order in which it now appears. The title of Epic was imposed on the poem by myself" (*PO, 479*).

[14] *Reliques* (1767), 1: xlv. In his letter to Evan Evans of December 24, 1765, Percy writes: "When I was in Scotland I made great inquiry into the Authenticity of Ossian's Poetry, and could not resist the evidence that poured in upon me; so that I am forced to believe them, as to the main genuine, in spite of my teeth." He later came to the conclusion — rightly or (more probably) wrongly — that he had been tricked, so in later editions of the *Reliques* any reference to this "evidence" is suppressed. For an excellent account of this episode, showing how the ugliness of Anglo-Scottish hostility transformed a seemingly minor incident into a major cultural confrontation, see Richard B. Sher, "Percy, Shaw, and the Ferguson 'Cheat': National Prejudice in the Ossian Wars," in *Ossian Revisited*, ed. Gaskill (Edinburgh: Edinburgh UP, 1991), 204–45.

[15] Roy Pascal, *The German Sturm und Drang* (Manchester: Manchester UP, 1953), 252. This is a wonderful and magisterial account, but occasionally even Homer nods.

[16] Herder was not, in fact, particularly happy with what Percy does to Shakespeare's songs. See his note on the translation from *Hamlet* of "Opheliens verwirrter Gesang um ihren erschlagenen Vater" (Ophelia's deranged song about her murdered father) in his *Volkslieder* (Folk Songs) of 1777–78, which registers tart disapproval of a procedure justified by Percy as follows: "Dispersed through Shakespeare's plays are innumerable little fragments of ancient ballads . . . the editor was tempted to select some of them, and with a few supplementary stanzas to connect them together, and form them into a little tale." Quoted in Herder, *"Stimmen der Völker in Liedern": Volkslieder*, ed. Heinz Rölleke, Universal-Bibliothek, 1371 (Stuttgart: Reclam, 1975), 154, 426, n.115.

[17] Rölleke, 5–8.

[18] See Gaskill, "'Aus der dritten Hand.'"

[19] Two of the few to show an adequate awareness of Herder's massive debt to Blair are Gillies and Michael Maurer, *Aufklärung und Anglophilie in Deutschland* (Göttingen: Vandenhoeck & Ruprecht, 1987), 349.

[20] Particularly in Weisse's extended review in the *Neue Bibliothek der schönen Wissenschaften* (1766) and in Suard's abridged translation published in the *Variétés Littéraires* (1768).

[21] See *H-SW*, 5: 329. The word used by Herder for the type of criticism embodied by Blair is "*nachempfindend.*"

[22] In many respects precedence ought to be given to Giovanni Battista Vico, but his ideas were notoriously little known until the nineteenth century.

[23] Far from a new idea, even then. For instance, in 1715 Thomas D'Urfey had justified his collection of vulgar broadside ballads, *Wit and Mirth: Or Pills to Purge Melancholy*, with the observation that Homer himself was "but an old blind ballad-singer."

[24] Thomas Blackwell, *Enquiry into the Life and Writings of Homer* (London: Oswald, 1735), 26.

[25] Blackwell, 41, 55.

[26] Blair acted as Macpherson's mentor in 1760 and 1761, seeing the *Fragments* through the press and writing the preface, helping to raise money for the prospecting trip to the Highlands and Islands to recover the lost epic, and supervising the production of *Fingal* (literally so, in that Macpherson took lodgings immediately below Blair's house at the head of Blackfriar's Wynd in January 1761). Blackwell was principal of Marischal College Aberdeen during Macpherson's time there (1754–55); even if no evidence can be found of a direct relationship, he was definitely taught by Blackwell's pupil Thomas Reid, so that it is reasonable to assume that Macpherson would have become familiar with Blackwell's ideas and begun applying them to his native Gaelic culture.

[27] Similar arguments were later used by Adam Ferguson in his *Essay on the History of Civil Society* (1767): "when we attend to the language which savages employ on any solemn occasion, it appears that man is a poet by nature. Whether at first obliged by the mere defects of his tongue, and the scantiness of proper expression, or seduced by a pleasure of the fancy in stating the analogy of its objects, he clothes every conception in image and metaphor." Quoted in Margaret Mary Rubel, *Savage and Barbarian: Historical Attitudes in the Criticism of Homer and Ossian in Britain, 1760–1800* (Amsterdam: North Holland, 1978), 84. It will not be without relevance that Ferguson, who was involved in the Ossian project from the beginning and remained faithful to it, was a speaker of Gaelic and had some knowledge of its literary culture.

[28] See *PO*, 347–49, 543–46. Worm's *Literatura Runica* appeared in 1636 (he dates the poem 857). But it is really through Sir William Temple's "Upon Heroic Virtue" (1690) that "Lodbrog" makes its entry into general literature. Extracts were published in Paul Henri Mallet's *Introduction à l'histoire de Dannemarc* (1755); Mallet's later translator into English (*Northern Antiquities,* 1770) is Percy, who already includes the song as one of his *Five Runic Pieces* (1763); "Lodbrog" is also referred to at the beginning of Lessing's *Laokoon* (1766). It is in the context of his review of Schütze's German translation of Mallet for the *Königsbergsche Gelehrte und Politische Zeitungen auf das Jahr 1765* that Herder first mentions Ossian in print. It seems likely that it was through Blair that Macpherson was alerted to Scaldic poetry. He quotes Mallet's *Introduction* in a note to the fifth book of *Temora* (*PO,* 504), and according to Malcolm Laing in his edition of *The Poems of Ossian, &c. containing the poetical works of James Macpherson, esq., in prose and rhyme,* vol. 2 (Edinburgh: Constable, 1805), 253, 307, 332, Macpherson actually echoes "Lodbrog." In most countries, and particularly in Germany, Scandinavianism and Ossianism tend to go hand in hand and mutually reinforce each other right up to the end of the century. It was in the companion volume to the *Introduction,* his *Monumens de la mythologie et de la poésie des Celtes et particulièrement des anciens Scandinaves pour servir de supplément et de preuves à l'Introduction à l'histoire de Dannemarc* (1756) that Mallet in the very title compounded the existing confusion about the different cultures, enabling Celts, Scandinavians, and, indeed, Germans to be thrown into one big "Nordic" pot and encouraging the latter to believe that they had a proprietary interest in Ossian. Significantly, when Mallet comes to produce a revised edition of the twin volumes (1787 and 1790), he refers approvingly to the "Erse poems" and

finds in Ossian interesting confirmation of Scandinavian mythology. (Macpherson's authentic sources frequently feature martial engagements with Vikings, both home and away, and his *Fingal* is about the repulsion of an invasion of Ireland by the Scandinavian chief Swaran.)

[29] "You know from traveller's accounts how vigorously and clearly savages [in the sense of un- or pre-civilized man — HG] always express themselves. Always with a sharp, vivid eye on the thing they want to say, using their senses, feeling the purpose of their utterance immediately and exactly, not distracted by shadowy concepts, half-ideas, and symbolic letter-understanding (the words of their language are innocent of this, for they have virtually no abstract terms); still less corrupted by artifices, slavish expectations, timid creeping politics, and confusing pre-meditation — bliss-fully ignorant of all these debilitations of the mind, they comprehend the thought as a whole with the whole word, and the word with the thought. Either they are silent, or they speak at the moment of involvement with an unpremeditated soundness, sureness and beauty, which learned Europeans of all times could not but admire — and were bound to leave untouched. . . . unspoiled children, women, folk of a sound natural sense, minds formed less by speculation than activity — these, if what I have been describing is true eloquence, are the finest, nay the only orators of our time" (*GAL*, 158).

[30] "All the songs of these savage peoples move around objects, actions, events, around a living world! How rich and various are the details, incidents, immediate features! And the eye has seen it all, the mind has imagined it all! This implies leaps and gaps and sudden transitions. There is the same connection between the sections of these songs as there is between the trees and bushes of the forest; the same between the cliffs and grottoes of the wilderness as there is between the scenes of the event itself."

[31] Adam Smith, *Lectures on Rhetoric and Belles Lettres,* ed. J. C. Bryce, *The Glasgow Edition of the Works and Correspondence of Adam Smith,* 6 vols. (Oxford: Oxford UP, 1983), 4: 139–40. (The lectures were delivered in Glasgow in the 1750s.)

[32] See Susan Manning, "Henry Mackenzie and Ossian: Or, The Emotional Value of Asterisks," in *From Gaelic to Romantic: Ossianic Translations,* eds. Fiona Stafford and Howard Gaskill (Amsterdam: Rodopi, 1998), 136–52, here 145. The term *diaspar-action* is adopted from Thomas McFarland, *Romanticism and the Forms of Ruin: Wordsworth, Coleridge, and Modalities of Fragmentation* (Princeton NJ: Princeton UP, 1981), 5.

[33] Blair had thoroughly assimilated Lowth, as had Macpherson (either directly or through Blair) and, of course, Herder, too. Herder initially intended to incorporate his own translations of the Song of Songs in his *Volkslieder.* For his attempt to present the biblical book as a kind of folk song anthology, see John D. Baildam, *Paradisal Love: Johann Gottfried Herder and the Song of Songs,* Journal for the Study of the Old Testament, Supplement Series, 298 (Sheffield: Sheffield Academic P, 1999), 95–96 and passim. The *Lieder der Liebe* finally appeared in 1778. Percy had attempted his own Song of Solomon, setting it out in a form of free rhythmic verse, in 1764.

[34] Quoted from G. Gregory's translation, 2 vols. (London, 1787), 2: 85–86, by Stephen Cornford in his edition of Edward Young, *Night Thoughts* (Cambridge: Cambridge UP, 1989), 2.

[35] *Bibliothek der schönen Wissenschaften* 9 (1763): 315. The author of the review is presumably C. F. Weisse, who had been editing the journal since 1759 and who in 1766 produced the extremely influential extended review of the *Works* edition of Ossian.

[36] *Scots Magazine* 18 (1756): 15–16. The author was the Dunkeld schoolmaster Jerome Stone. It seems likely that his free translation/adaptation of the *Lay of Fraoch* may have inspired Macpherson in his Ossianic undertaking.

[37] Cf. *PO*, 347: "What we have been long accustomed to call the oriental vein of poetry, because some of the earliest poetical productions have come to us from the East, is probably no more oriental than occidental; it is characteristical of an age rather than a country; and belongs, in some measure, to all nations at a certain period. Of this the works of Ossian seem to furnish a remarkable proof."

[38] Quoted in Paul van Tieghem, *Ossian en France*, 2 vols. (Paris: Rieder, 1917), 1: 114. Early French reaction to Macpherson's work comes from some impressive authorities: apart from Turgot, one might mention Diderot — whose translation of the fragment *Shilric and Vinvela* was on sale in Paris before the end of 1760 — and Suard. Their contributions, including Suard's abridged translation of Blair's "Dissertation" (in which David Hume probably had a hand), were collected together with others in the *Variétés Littéraires* for 1768 and avidly read by Herder the following year in Nantes.

[39] Eric A. Blackall, "The Language of Sturm und Drang," in *Stil- und Formprobleme in der Literatur: Vorträge des VIII. Kongresses der Internationalen Vereinigung für moderne Sprachen und Literaturen in Heidelberg*, ed. Paul Böckmann (Heidelberg: Winter, 1959), 272–82, here 281. The main focus of this excellent essay is on the contrast and tension with the Sturm und Drang, between the articulate, flowing, expansive, highly rhetorical style, as epitomized by Klopstock, and the "inarticulate, broken, stuttering style" (275) of the Sturm und Drang, between strong and close (direct) expression of emotion.

[40] Cf. *H-SW*, 5: 197: "denn da es gewöhnlich ist, Sprünge und Würfe solcher Stücke für Tollheiten der Morgenländischen Hitze, für Enthusiasmus des Prophetengeistes, oder für schöne Kunstsprünge der Ode auszugeben. . . ." ("for since the leaps and tosses of such pieces are conventionally attributed to oriental fervor, the enthusiasm of the prophetic spirit, or the virtuoso salto of the ode. . . ."). Hence his decision to quote a "cold" Greenlander "ohne Hitze und Prophetengeist und Odentheorie" ("without fire, prophetic spirit, or theoretical knowledge of the ode").

[41] See the "Vorbericht über die vaterländische Dichtkunst" in Denis's collection *Die Lieder Sineds des Barden* (Songs of Sined [= Denis backwards] the Bard) (Vienna: Trattner, 1772), xlviii.

[42] H. T. Betteridge, "Macpherson's Ossian in Germany, 1760–1775" (dissertation, London, 1938), 294. Since only a fraction of this doctoral thesis made it into print, its impact on subsequent research has been negligible. This is a pity, since it is an example of good, thorough — if old-fashioned — positivism, containing much extremely useful information.

[43] Pascal, 289.

[44] See Blackall, 276–77.

[45] In 1773 this is changed to "dark-waves." In both cases the apparently idiosyncratic hyphen alters the stress and has the effect of making "dark" part of the verb, which therefore opens the sentence. Such constructions seem to be modeled on the natural inversions of Gaelic. As Blackall points out (274), the strongly emphasized prefixed verb is a feature of Sturm und Drang language, as, for example: "Herausgeben sollst du mir die Erstgeburt" or "Hinstürzte eine helle heiße Thräne" (Klinger). Though he calls the device Klopstockian, it is legitimate to wonder how much it might owe to Ossian. Certainly its occurrence in German translations, including Herder's own, is striking (cf. Rölleke, *Volkslieder*, 266–67: "Aufstand Krieg in den Träumen des Heers," "Auf stand sie in Mitte der Nacht"). It is most consistently adopted by Schiller's friend Johann Wilhelm Petersen in his prose translation of 1782. See my essay "Herder, Ossian and the Celtic," in *Celticism*, ed. Terence Brown (Amsterdam: Rodopi, 1996), 257–71, especially 269–70, for examples from Petersen such as: "Aufmachte sich Konnal," "Auffuhren die Krieger," "Aufschwollen die Fluthen," "Auffuhren vom Teiche die Rehe," and "Hinschwirrte der niedrichschwebende Nebel."

[46] The full story of this has yet to be told — cf. Gaskill, "'Aus der dritten Hand,'" 215. Whether the likes of Petersen knew anything about Gaelic word order is questionable. But Goethe and Herder certainly did. The translation from the Gaelic specimen, which, as it appears in the *Volkslieder*, is their combined work, contains verses such as: "Kam Schall von der Wüsten am Baum — / Konar, der König heran — / Zieht schnell schon Nebel grau, / Um Fillan am Lubar blau" (Rölleke, 265). Macpherson's English of 1765 reads: "A sound came from the desart; the rushing course of Conar in winds. He poured his deep mist on Fillan, at blue-winding Lubar" (PO, 279). A literal translation of the published German would be: "Came sound from the desert at the tree — / Conar, the king [came] up — / [he?] surrounds already with mist gray / Fillan at Lubar blue." (Needless to say, in Gaelic the adjective normally follows the noun.)

[47] For Herder's use of inversion in his *Lieder der Liebe*, see Baildam, 227–28.

[48] Cf. Blair's note: "Frequent inversions and transpositions were permitted in this poetry; which would naturally follow from such laborious attention to the collocation of words" (*PO*, 543). How this "laborious attention" may be squared with naturalness and spontaneity of expression we are not told. But then, Herder himself seems untroubled by the problem the obvious complexities of Scaldic prosody (the "136 Rhythmusarten der Skalden"; *H-SW*, 5: 165) might pose for his general argument.

[49] See *H-SW*, 5: 181–82, quoted above.

[50] "I became acquainted with poetry in a quite different way, in a different sense from before, and it was one which appealed to me very much. Hebrew poetry, about which, following the example of Lowth, he had illuminating things to say; folk poetry, the tradition and remains of which he encouraged us to search out in Alsace; the most ancient documents in the form of poetry: [all] served to prove that the art of poetry is in reality a universal gift, not the private inheritance of an intellectual elite."

[51] Pascal, 14.

[52] See Thomas Althaus, "Ursprung in später Zeit: Goethes 'Heidenröslein' und der Volksliedentwurf," *Zeitschrift für deutsche Philologie* 118 (1999): 161–88. Althaus effectively shows how through various versions the poem — which, astonishingly, owes much to Lovelace in Samuel Richardson's *Clarissa* — evolves via Herder in the direction of "naturalness."

[53] See the discussion in my essay "'Ossian hat in meinem Herzen den Humor verdrängt': Goethe and Ossian reconsidered," in *Goethe and the English-Speaking World*, eds. Nicholas Boyle and John Guthrie (Rochester, NY: Camden House, 2001), 47–59.

[54] There can be no reasonable doubt that the first time Herder had protracted sight of an English Ossian was when he received Goethe's (father's?) copy on loan toward the end of 1771. He kept it for about a year.

[55] See Gaskill, "Ossian hat in meinem Herzen . . ." for evidence of conscious and unconscious reminiscence in the work of the later Goethe.

[56] Ossianic echoes are particularly strong in the early version of the play.

[57] The first volume appeared in May 1773, the second at the end of 1774. After being taken over and continued by a commercial publisher, Fleischer of Leipzig, it sold quite well.

[58] See my essay "'Blast, rief Cuchullin . . .!': J. M. R. Lenz and Ossian," in *From Gaelic to Romantic*, 107–18.

[59] Quoted in Malcolm Chapman, *The Gaelic Vision in Scottish Culture* (London: Croom Helm, 1978), 30.

[60] Pascal, 267.

[61] The signs are propitious. Wolf Gerhard Schmidt of the University of Saarbrücken is in the final stages of a doctoral dissertation on the reception of Ossian in Germany in which — for the first time ever — its enormous significance for German Romanticism is convincingly demonstrated.

"Shakespeare has quite spoilt you": The Drama of the Sturm und Drang

Francis Lamport

THE MEETING OF GOETHE AND HERDER in Strasbourg in 1770 was probably the most momentous encounter in the history of German literature, outranking even that of Goethe and Schiller in Weimar twenty-odd years later. By that time Goethe's and Schiller's literary paths were already converging in a new form of neoclassicism. But in 1770 Herder transformed the imagination of the twenty-one-year-old Goethe, released it from the frivolities of the rococo or the artificial constraints of an earlier, outmoded neoclassicism of French origin, and revealed to Goethe new and powerful sources of inspiration: the national heritage of German culture, embodied in history, folklore, folk song, and ballad, and the free, unfettered, original, but also profoundly "national" dramatic genius of Shakespeare. Herder's own panegyric on Shakespeare appeared in its final version in his collection *Von deutscher Art und Kunst* in 1773; Goethe's address *Zum Schäkespears Tag* (For Shakespeare's Nameday) had already been delivered to a circle of like-minded enthusiasts on Goethe's return to his native Frankfurt in the autumn of 1771. Inspired by Shakespeare, Goethe declares, he hesitated not a moment in renouncing the "regular" theater and casting off the "fetters" of the supposedly Aristotelian unities of action, time, and place. Shakespeare's theater is

> ein schöner Raritäten Kasten, in dem die Geschichte der Welt vor unsern Augen an dem unsichtbaren Faden der Zeit vorbeiwallt. Seine Plane, sind nach dem gemeinen Styl zu reden, keine Plane, aber seine Stücke, drehen sich alle um den geheimen Punkt, (den noch kein Philosoph gesehen und bestimmt hat) in dem das Eigentümliche unsres Ichs, die prätendierte Freiheit unsres Wollens, mit dem notwendigen Gang des Ganzen zusammenstößt. (*G-MA*, 1.2: 413)[1]

His characters are nothing but "nature! nature!" but inspired by their creator's "Promethean" spirit, figures of "Kolossalischer Größe" (*G-MA*, 1.2: 414; colossal scale, *G-CW*, 3: 165) — we may think of Shakespeare's

Julius Caesar, who, as Cassius says, "doth bestride the narrow world / Like a Colossus" (act 1, scene 2). And Goethe had also thrown himself into the composition of a Shakespearean-style historical drama or dramatized chronicle, based loosely on the autobiography of the sixteenth-century imperial knight Gottfried (Götz) von Berlichingen, which had been published in 1731: a publication which was itself evidence of the growing interest in German history and authentic documents of the German past even earlier in the eighteenth century. The *Geschichte Gottfriedens von Berlichingen mit der eisernen Hand, dramatisiert* was dispatched to Herder in December 1771. Herder returned it with what appear to have been (as was his wont) somewhat sarcastic comments. Unfortunately, these have been lost: we have only Goethe's reply of July 1772, in which he concedes the justice of Herder's criticism "Dass euch Schäckessp. ganz verdorben" (*G-HB*, 1: 133: that Shakespeare has quite spoilt you). The criticism was unfair (though it may well have been meant in a teasing spirit), in that the Shakespeare who inspired the *Geschichte* was very much Shakespeare as Herder had taught Goethe to see him: the "national" poet, creator of a vision of history and of a rich panorama of character and action, utterly neglectful of the "rules" of neoclassical drama. But Goethe took Herder's words to heart and rapidly produced a revised and tightened-up version of the *Geschichte,* which was published in 1773 under the title *Götz von Berlichingen mit der eisernen Hand: Ein Schauspiel* (Gottfried von Berlichingen with the Iron Hand: A Play), the first and one of the greatest dramas of the Sturm und Drang proper. This time Herder was enthusiastic, and the Shakespeare essay of 1773 ends with a warm commendation of his unnamed friend and of his "monument of our own chivalric age" (*H-SW*, 5: 231).

Despite the scorn and derision of neoclassicists such as Gottsched, the would-be dictator of German literary taste in the first half of the eighteenth century, for whom the drama of seventeenth-century France — of Corneille, Racine, and Molière — represented the only possible model for the theater of the Age of Reason, interest in English drama and in its greatest practitioner had been growing in Germany for a generation or more.[2] In 1740 the Prussian ambassador to London, Johann Caspar von Borcke, had translated *Julius Caesar* into French-style alexandrine verse, and the young playwright and critic Johann Elias Schlegel (1719–49) had published his *Vergleichung Shakespeares und Andreas Gryphs,* a comparison of Shakespeare's play with the *Leo Armenius* (written 1646; printed 1650) of the German dramatist usually known by his Latinized name Gryphius (1616–64). Schlegel is critical of what he sees as Shakespeare's stylistic extravagances but recognizes

Shakespeare's powers of characterization, which will be repeatedly stressed by subsequent commentators. Lessing, in the seventeenth of his *Briefe, die neueste Literatur betreffend* (Letters Concerning the Most Recent Literature) of 1759, had thrown down the gauntlet to the neoclassicists, declaring that although Corneille had mechanically followed the model of the ancient Greek dramatists, Shakespeare had come closer to them in essentials; at the same time, Lessing had offered the suggestion, which Herder and the writers of the Sturm und Drang were to seize upon, that German drama, left to its "natural" bent, would be much more like the English than the French model. In his *Hamburgische Dramaturgie* (Hamburg Dramaturgy) of 1767–69 Lessing also praises Shakespeare's dramatic psychology, while distancing himself from his earlier praise of the "English manner," which he now declares to be overly complex and tiring (*Dramaturgie*, No. 12); but at the same time, Gerstenberg, in his *Briefe über Merkwürdigkeiten der Litteratur* (1766–67), clearly intending to follow where Lessing had led, was enthusiastically praising Shakespeare's freedom from the neoclassical rules and even from the traditional division of the dramatic genres of tragedy, comedy, and so on: "Away with the classification of drama!" he cries: call the plays what you like, "ich nenne sie lebendige Bilder der sittlichen Natur" (*G-U*, 93).[3] Gerstenberg also wrote a tragedy, *Ugolino* (1768), which is sometimes claimed as the first Sturm und Drang drama. It depicts the death by starvation of Count Ugolino and his sons, as related in Canto 33 of Dante's *Inferno:* there is virtually no action, only a gradual descent into delirium and death. Gerstenberg's play is strictly neoclassical in form, with its unchanging location in Ugolino's prison and its temporal restriction to a single stormy night — though this matching of setting and mood is itself no doubt intended as Shakespearean in spirit and was to be emulated in many plays of the Sturm und Drang proper. In the 1760s Wieland had translated twenty-two of Shakespeare's plays into German: this was the version in which Goethe, though he had a fair knowledge of English, would principally have encountered them; a complete translation by J. J. Eschenburg (1743–1820) appeared between 1775 and 1782. By this time Shakespeare had also begun to appear on the German stage,[4] albeit in versions drastically tailored to suit the "enlightened" taste of the age — which was, of course, also the case in England itself at the time. The ground was thus well prepared, in theory and even in practice, for the enthusiasm of the Sturm und Drang, of Goethe and the young dramatists who were his close contemporaries: Lenz, the third member of the Strasbourg triumvirate, whose *Anmerkungen übers Thea-ter*, the movement's other major theoretical essay, appeared in 1774;

Klinger; H. L. Wagner; Leisewitz; and Friedrich "Maler" Müller. Ten years later the first tragedies of the young Schiller — born in 1759, ten years after Goethe — bring the movement to its end.[5]

Formally speaking, *Götz* is modeled on, or at any rate inspired by, Shakespeare's history plays, as we would expect from the Shakespeare address. It traces the career of Götz, knight of the Holy Roman Empire and passionate defender of its medieval feudal privileges and liberties, against the encroachments of the dawning modern age: the increasing power of ambitious territorial princes, the bureaucratization of justice, the rise of a commercial class. Götz, described as "das Muster eines Ritters tapfer und edel in seiner Freiheit, und gelassen und treu im Unglück" (*G-MA*, 1.1: 475/632),[6] fights to defend the old Germany he knows but is betrayed by his political enemies and dies (unhistorically) in prison. An important subplot — it could even be called the plot proper, since it has more of a conventionally "dramatic" character than the story of Götz himself — encapsulates these historical conflicts at a more personal level: the vacillating Weislingen is torn between, on the one hand, his old friendship for Götz and his love for Götz's sister Marie and, on the other, the rival attractions of the court of Bamberg, principally and literally embodied in the figure of the sex- and power-hungry Adelheid. The fact that Bamberg is an ecclesiastical principality, ruled by a bishop, emphasizes the corruption of the courtly world. A large cast presents us with a complete social panorama of the age, from the emperor himself through the bishop and his courtiers, Götz and his friends and allies, peasants, merchants, down to the gypsies living in the "wild woods" (*G-MA*, 1.1: 478/642) on the fringe of the social order. The play appears at first sight (as Goethe says of Shakespeare's plays) to be shapeless and sprawling; but in fact, as in Shakespeare, the various strands of the action are skillfully interwoven and contrasted. The unities of place and time are completely abandoned. Over fifty scene changes (there are around sixty in the *Geschichte Gottfriedens*) sweep us rapidly around southern Germany, from the opening in a wayside inn, via Götz's castle at Jaxthausen in Swabia (where outdoor productions of the play are still staged), via Bamberg and Augsburg, by hill and vale and forest to the closing scenes in Götz's prison in Heilbronn. The action spans months or years — in fact, there seems to be a dual time scheme: the action on stage appears to unfold over a matter of months, while datable background events span over half a century, from the imperial pacification of 1495 through the Peasants' Revolt of 1524–25 to Götz's death, which actually occurred in 1562. Episodic scenes add further touches of historical color. The monk Brother Martin (plainly intended to suggest, but not to be identified with, Luther) adds to the chorus of Götz's admirers: "Ich danke dir Gott dass du mich ihn hast sehn lassen, diesen Mann, den die Fürsten hassen, und zu dem die Bedrängten sich wenden" (*G-MA,* 1.1: 395/556);[7] a meeting of the secret court of the *"Femgericht"* condemns Adelheid to death for adultery and murder; in the *Geschichte Gottfriedens,* where the story of Adelheid is developed at perhaps excessive length, we actually witness her death, heralded by the ghost of one of her victims. The neoclassical rules banished all physical action offstage, but here not only the siege of Götz's castle but even the Peasants' Revolt are brought before our eyes, with stage directions such as "Tumult in a village, plundering: women and old people with children and baggage, flight" and in the next scene "Two villages and a monastery are seen burning in the distance" (*G-MA,* 1.1: 636, revised version only). The subtitle *Schauspiel* ("play," but also, more generally, "spectacle") draws attention to the abandonment of traditional genre classification, even though *Götz* is arguably the most unambiguously tragic of all Goethe's major dramas. Perhaps its most original feature of all is its language. Neoclassical "decorum" or "propriety" insists on correct, dignified, and uniform speech from all characters; but in *Götz* Goethe convincingly differentiates between, for example, the affected banter of the courtier Liebetraut, the colloquial familiarity of Götz and his friends, the ungrammatical jargon of the gypsies, and the coarseness of the play's most famous, or notorious, line, replaced by dashes in later editions: Götz's invitation to the imperial envoy sent to demand his surrender to "mich im Arsch lecken" (*G-MA,* 1.1: 458/615).[8] No other drama produced by the movement can match *Götz* in range, sweep, and vitality until we come to Schiller's explosive debut in *Die Räuber.* But the mid-1770s witnessed a remarkable outpouring of works that seek in various ways to fulfill the "Shakespearean" program enunciated by Goethe and Herder: the celebration of the "colossal" hero, the liberation from the "prison" of the neoclassical rules (though it is noteworthy how often a prison, as in *Ugolino,* recurs as an actual setting in the plays), and the creation of a new realism (to use a term that did not become current until almost a century later) of character portrayal and language.

Goethe planned but did not complete a number of tragedies on the theme of the great, heroic individual: the mythical demigod-creator Prometheus, the historical "colossus" Julius Caesar, the charismatic prophet or leader in conflict with his age — Socrates or Mohammed. It is perhaps significant that the only two such plans that did eventually reach completion, *Faust* and *Egmont,* treat figures from the same historical period as *Götz:* the sixteenth century, the age of Renaissance and

Reformation, the crucible of modern Europe. Goethe had encountered the semilegendary figure of Faust, the disaffected scholar who compacted with the devil for knowledge, wisdom, pleasure, and power, in his student days in Leipzig — or even before, as the hero of popular puppet-plays that he had seen as a child. But as Lessing had observed in 1759, the popular Faust plays of the traveling players and puppet-theaters, despised by the arbiters of neoclassical taste such as Gottsched, had much that was "English" about them: they were, in fact — though Lessing appears not to have known this — ultimately descended from Marlowe's *Doctor Faustus*, which was not properly translated into German until 1818. A number of fragmentary scenes of a Faust drama date from Goethe's Sturm und Drang years, and these include an opening monologue and some episodes satirizing university life. In Frankfurt in 1772 Goethe learned at first hand of the tragedy of a young woman executed for infanticide after her abandonment by her faithless lover, who, she claimed, had seduced her with the aid of witchcraft; Goethe may even have witnessed the execution. He transmuted this incident into the balladesque "Gretchen tragedy," whose incorporation into the Faust story was a stroke of genius — though it also caused considerable formal problems, evident in his failure to complete the so-called *Urfaust* (original Faust) and still only provisionally solved in the published *Faust: Part I* of 1808. In Egmont, champion of the traditional liberties of the Netherlands, betrayed and executed by the Spanish government in 1568, Goethe found a hero of similar cast to his contemporary Götz, though of greater rank and refinement — and the tragedy, which he had almost certainly begun by 1775 but did not complete until twelve years later, is correspondingly more refined and restrained. Though *Egmont*, too, sets its hero against a broad social background, from the ordinary citizens, who open the play in one of many lively crowd scenes, to the Princess Regent of the Netherlands and her successor, the Duke of Alba; and though, again, there is an important subsidiary love interest in the relationship of Egmont and the commoner Klärchen, there is a great deal less action on stage than in *Götz*, and the play actually observes something like the spirit, if not the letter, of the neoclassical unities, taking place in a small number of locations in Brussels in the course of, it would seem, a few days or, at most, weeks. (The time scale is not precisely indicated, whereas neoclassical playwrights are always anxious to remind their audiences of their strict observance of the rules.) If Goethe had completed *Egmont* in 1775, it might have looked rather more superficially Shakespearean or *Götz*-like; but in October of that year he entered the service of the Duke of Weimar, where he was to remain for the rest of his life, and courtly discipline began to make its mark — some would say, take its toll — on the hitherto rebellious young writer of the Sturm und Drang. *Götz* and *Egmont*, however, together with the plays of Schiller's maturity, established the history play, whose ultimate inspiration undoubtedly lay in Shakespeare, as the most prestigious form of serious drama in German, dominating the nineteenth and surviving well into the twentieth century.

Several minor dramatic works completed by Goethe before his move to Weimar in 1775 show him experimenting with a wide range of forms and styles. Some farces and burlesques, which satirize contemporary fads and figures, take up the traditional, popular German form of the *Fastnachtspiel*, the carnival or Shrovetide play, associated particularly with the sixteenth-century shoemaker-poet Hans Sachs (to be hymned by Richard Wagner a century later in *Die Meistersinger von Nürnberg* as the exemplary German artist). *Das Jahrmarktsfest zu Plundersweilen* (The Lumbertown Fair, written 1773) incorporates a parody of a biblical tragedy in neoclassical style. *Pater Brey* (Father Porridge, 1774) and *Satyros, oder der vergötterte Waldteufel* (Satyros, or the Deified Wood-Devil, written 1773) satirize fashionable forms of religious enthusiasm: Goethe was at this time emancipating himself not only from literary neoclassicism but also from the Lutheran Christianity in which he had been brought up. The "farce" *Götter, Helden und Wieland* (Gods, Heroes, and Wieland, 1774) burlesques the emasculation, as Goethe saw it, of the spirit of classical Greece in Wieland's treatment of the Alcestis legend in his musical play *Alceste* (1773).[9] Goethe and his associates never wavered in their admiration for the Greek authors — Homer, Pindar, the tragedians; what they objected to was the neoclassical perversion and enfeeblement (as they believed) of the true classical spirit. "What are you doing in that Greek armor, little Frenchman (*Französgen*)," asks Goethe in the Shakespeare address; "it's too big and heavy for you" (*G-MA*, 1.2: 412). Notwithstanding the part he had played in bringing Shakespeare to Germany, Wieland remained a neoclassicist at heart. Roused from his dreams in Goethe's farce to be confronted by the "real" Hercules, a larger-than-life figure boasting loudly of his martial and sexual prowess, the fastidious Wieland can only say, "Ich habe nichts mit euch zu schaffen Koloß" (*G-MA*, 1.1: 690).[10] In considerably less exuberant style, and in no spirit of parody, two plays of 1774–75, *Clavigo* and *Stella*, adopt the fashionable form of the middle-class domestic drama ("bürgerliches Drama") introduced by Lessing, whose *Miß Sara Sampson* of 1755 is the first successful German, if not European, serious drama to present "ordinary" contemporary characters in something approaching a realistic manner. In his autobiography, *Dichtung und Wahrheit*, Goethe recalls another sharp-tongued friend, Johann Heinrich Merck (sometimes cited as a model for Mephistopheles in *Faust*), telling him not to write such rubbish ("Quark") but to leave that to others who could do it just as well (*G-MA*, 16: 706) — and, indeed, by the end of the century the domestic drama, in the hands of playwrights such as August Wilhelm Iffland (1759–1814) and August von Kotzebue (1761–1819), dominated the German stage rather than anything more ambitious or Shakespearean. *Clavigo* and *Stella*, however, have remained in the repertory of the German theater to the present day. Both have a weak, vacillating male protagonist — Weislingen advanced to center stage, as Goethe observed in a letter to Schönborn of June 1, 1774 (*G-HB*, 1: 162): a kind of antitype of the ideal Sturm und Drang hero. *Clavigo* is loosely based on the memoirs of Beaumarchais, later to achieve fame as a playwright himself with *The Barber of Seville* (1775) and *The Marriage of Figaro* (1784). Clavigo abandons the faithful Marie Beaumarchais to serve his personal ambition, encouraged by his unscrupulous friend Carlos (a Mephistopheles to his rather feeble Faust). Fernando in *Stella* abandons his first wife, Cäcilie, goes through a form of marriage with Stella, then abandons her in turn — but all three are eventually reunited in a ménage à trois. If *Clavigo* and *Stella* can claim to be more radical than the "Quark" of most contemporary domestic drama and, thus, to rank as products of Sturm und Drang, it must be by virtue of their stretching, rather than actually breaking, the conventions of the domestic form. *Clavigo* ends in a melodramatic or balladesque scene, with a torchlit nocturnal setting and offstage music, in which Clavigo breaks in on the funeral procession of the abandoned Marie, is challenged and killed by Beaumarchais, and dies on Marie's coffin. (In reality, none of the principal personages died; and Beaumarchais, for one, was not amused by Goethe's play.) The ending of *Stella* was, unsurprisingly, found shocking at the time. For a production in Weimar in 1808 the "classical" Goethe revised the ending in accordance with both moral and dramatic propriety, killing off both Stella and Fernando; but the result is not an improvement: the original problematic ending is more in keeping with the spirit of the work, which is neither tragic nor comic in the traditional sense. Commenting on Merck's criticism, Goethe observes that works such as these were intended to contribute to the development of a home-produced repertory for the German stage, to the requirements of which *Götz*, with its huge cast and extravagant scenic demands, made no concessions — if, indeed, it was composed with actual performance in mind. Such practical concerns are also evident in Goethe's interest in another popular form of the day, the play with musical numbers. Two such works were written before 1775 (later to be revised and designated "*Singspiele*" — the form that at the end of the century was to give rise to the German operas of Mozart). *Erwin und Elmire* (written 1773–75) is based on an episode from Oliver Goldsmith's popular novel *The Vicar of Wakefield*. Several performances took place in Weimar in 1776 and the Dowager Duchess Anna Amalia composed the music herself. It is a lightweight piece, its tongue-in-cheek character evident from the title page with the direction "The scene is not in Spain" (*G-MA*, 1.2: 12). Spain is, however, the setting; and a Spanish ballad source has been suggested for the second musical play, *Claudine von Villa Bella* (written 1774–75), in which something more of the spirit of the Sturm und Drang can be detected. The plot is furnished by the amorous rivalry of two temperamentally contrasted brothers: Pedro, sentimental and melancholy; and Crugantino, a wild rebel against the restrictions of conventional society — a motif we shall encounter again in some of the movement's most characteristic dramatic works. There, as we shall see, rebellion and fraternal rivalry boil over and explode in tragedy; but in *Claudine* the brothers' encounter results only in a flesh wound, and all is peaceably and harmoniously resolved in song.

By the time of his move to Weimar, Goethe seems to have moved away from the championship of characters "on a colossal scale" and the total freedom from formal and stylistic restraint he had proclaimed in the Shakespeare address and put into practice in *Götz*. It is, however, important to note the enormous range of his stylistic experimentation in these early years — history, tragedy, farce and burlesque, domestic drama, and musical play — which none of the other writers of the Sturm und Drang can match, though they all adopt and develop various of Goethe's initiatives. Goethe's linguistic experimentation should also be emphasized. Most of this work is in prose — often, as in *Götz*, of an unprecedented colorfulness and vigor. But the *Prometheus* fragment employs free verse, without regular meter or rhyme — itself a remarkable technical innovation, paralleled in some of Goethe's lyric verse of this time — while the Sachsian carnival plays employ the *Knittelvers*, the rhymed doggerel of their sixteenth-century prototypes, a "national" form that had survived in popular theater and ballad poetry and that Goethe brought back into the formal repertory of serious literature. It is used in several of the early *Faust* scenes, notably the opening monologue, together with a unique variety of other forms, both verse and prose: the completed *Faust* drama of many years later was to grow into an unparalleled compendium of poetic forms both ancient and modern, and this can be seen as the ultimate fulfillment of Goethe's early experimentation. One verse form is, however, conspicuous by its absence in this period: Shakespearean blank verse, the unrhymed iambic pentameter of the English drama. This is all the more surprising in that there had been several experiments in dramatic blank verse in German in the 1750s, including a complete translation of *Romeo and Juliet* (1758) by S. Gynaeus[11] and an "original" tragedy by Wieland, *Lady Johanna Gray* (Lady Jane Gray, 1758), which was, in fact, based closely on a play by Nicholas Rowe. Wieland had also begun his Shakespeare translations with a blank-verse rendering of *A Midsummer Night's Dream* (1762) but had found it easier thereafter to stick to prose, and it was in these prose translations that Goethe and his associates best knew their Shakespeare. (Lenz translated both *Love's Labour's Lost* and *Coriolanus* in 1774, but, again, in prose in both cases.) Prose offered the Sturm und Drang the maximum freedom from the stylistic restraints of neoclassicism; indeed, paradoxically, when Goethe does begin to employ blank verse in the mid-1780s, during his stay in Italy, it is in the interest of a classical restraint and discipline rather than the freedom and realism of the Sturm und Drang years. He thus employs it in the published version (1787) of *Iphigenie auf Tauris* (the first version of 1779 is in prose, but a prose that often seems to fall into an iambic cadence), in *Torquato Tasso* (1789), and in the "Wald und Höhle" (Forest and Cavern) monologue in *Faust,* and the spoken dialogue of the revised "*Singspiel*" versions of *Erwin und Elmire* and *Claudine von Villa Bella* is also recast in blank verse. At the same time, Schiller was independently turning from the prose of his first three plays to blank verse in *Don Carlos,* completed in 1787, again in the pursuit of what he himself described as "klassische Vollkommenheit" (classical perfection [*S-NA,* 6: 344]). And of all the dramas of the German "classical" repertory of the eighteenth and nineteenth centuries, only *Käthchen von Heilbronn* (1808), by Heinrich von Kleist (1777–1811), employs the mixture of blank verse and prose so characteristic of the plays of Shakespeare.

The theories of Goethe and Lenz (and much of the critical literature on the movement) lay great emphasis on the "great man," the "colossus," the "*großer Kerl*" or "*Kraftkerl*" — an untranslatable term often applied to the Stürmer und Dränger themselves, as well as to their dramatic heroes: *Kraft* implying strength, energy, elemental force, and vigor, *Kerl* a colloquialism for "fellow" or even "guy," which can be used, like its English equivalent, as a term either of celebration ("*großer Kerl*") or denigration ("*miserabler Kerl*"). Goethe writes of Shakespearean tragedy as depicting the clash between the freedom of the great individual and the "notwendiger Gang des Ganzen" (inevitable course of the whole). Lenz in his *Anmerkungen übers Theater* calls for the abandonment of the Aristotelian unity of action in favor of a

> Reihe von Handlungen, die wie Donnerschläge auf einander folgen, eine die andere stützen und heben, in ein großes Ganze zusammenfließen müssen, das hernach nichts mehr und nichts minder ausmacht als die Hauptperson, wie sie in der ganzen Gruppe ihrer Mithändler hervorsticht (*L-WB*, 2: 655–56)[12]

and that moves us to cry out "das ist ein Kerl!" (*L-WB*, 2: 668). This "monodic" principle, as we may call it, may certainly be seen to inspire *Götz* and *Egmont,* with their single dominating protagonists; a curious feature of the structure of *Egmont* is, indeed, that there is only one other character with whom Egmont himself appears on stage more than once — his adversary Alba's son Ferdinand, who, after a brief entry in act 4 returns to play a more important part in act 5. Klinger's first tragedy, *Otto* (1775), seems also to have been written to this formula — at any rate in intention, though the titular protagonist appears as a rather passive figure, somewhat lost amid the profusion of barely comprehensible plots and subplots that make up the action of the play; similarly, in the fragmentary "First Part" of *Fausts Leben dramatisiert* (Faust's Life Dramatized), which "Maler" Müller published in 1778, Faust himself plays only a minor role. (Klinger in later years evidently thought little of *Otto* and did not include it in his collected works; Müller in the 1820s labored to rewrite his early prose drafts into a monster eight-act blank-verse tragedy, which did not, however, see the light of day until 1996.)[13] In *Simsone Grisaldo* (1776), on the other hand, Klinger portrays a true "*Kraftkerl*," a "Herculean" figure who "vermag die Welt auf seinen Schultern zu tragen"[14] and finally triumphs over the (at times almost farcical) intrigues of his adversaries, both male and female: the play contains at least three Delilah figures, but none succeeds in trimming this Samson's mane. Here, for once, the "*Kraftkerl*" is victorious, but the mixture of potential tragedy and (not always intentional) comedy is not uncharacteristic.

Aside from this monodic form, however, some of the most memorable tragedies of the movement are based on the motif of the conflict of rival brothers of contrasting character types, which we have seen treated in light-hearted vein in *Claudine von Villa Bella.* In Leisewitz's *Julius von Tarent* and Klinger's *Die Zwillinge,* both of which appeared in 1776, a dynamic but frustrated man of action (Guido in Leisewitz, Guelfo in Klinger) is opposed to a more pacific, melancholy figure (Julius, Ferdinando); in Schiller's *Die Räuber* of 1781 the high-minded idealist Karl Moor is provoked into violent rebellion by the treachery of his evil, scheming brother Franz. The brothers are in all cases rivals for the love and affection of the same woman, like Goethe's Pedro and Crugantino, but also, and more importantly, for the love and affection of their father: the less favored brother is provoked into envy and hatred, which in Guelfo and Franz Moor attain pathological dimensions. Guido and Guelfo kill their respective brothers, and each is finally killed by his father in punishment; Franz Moor first persuades his father to disown Karl, then tries unsuccessfully to bring about his father's death, first through psychological torture and then by starvation (as in *Ugolino*), but old Count Moor finally "gives up the ghost," as the stage direction expressively has it (*S-NA*, 3: 131), on discovering that Karl has become a robber and a murderer. The three plays obviously have much in common: Klinger's was designed in deliberate rivalry with Leisewitz's and is based on the same source material, though using different names; Schiller draws on both his predecessors, while adding new accents of his own. Guelfo and both Moor brothers vent their frustrations in extravagant rhetoric — Guelfo himself asks, appropriately enough, "Was hilft das nun all, wenn ich mir mit geballter Faust vor die Stirne schlag' und mit den Winden heule — droh' und lärme, und bei alledem nur Luftschlösser, Kartenhäuser baue!" (*K-W*, 2: 22)[15] — and wild, melodramatic gesture: Guelfo smashes his reflection in a mirror; Franz Moor writhes in his chair; Karl, in the forest, charges into a tree. Leisewitz's play is generally soberer in tone. Guido, Guelfo, and Franz Moor end their lives in despair, Karl confronts and overcomes despair (the word "Verzweiflung" echoes through *Die Räuber* like a knell) by giving himself up to justice in atonement for his crimes. Schiller's play is in some ways even more sensational and melodramatic than Klinger's. *Die Zwillinge,* despite its title, is virtually monodic in form, concentrating almost entirely on Guelfo, while Ferdinando appears on stage only once; but *Die Räuber* is much more complex — a genuine double tragedy — and much more profound. It is also the only one of the three that is still regularly performed today. Interpretations of these three plays have tended to stress one of two aspects. Some critics have emphasized the psychological contrast between the brothers, holding that it represents a permanent conflict between two sides of the human personality, between action and contemplation, or head and heart, or selfishness and altruism — or even complementary aspects of a single personality: in the original version of *Die Räuber* the two brothers never meet on stage, and the two parts have often been played by the same actor, though this calls for enormous physical, vocal, and emotional resources if it is to be carried off success-fully. The two types have also been seen in a historical light as repre-senting feudal autocracy and the stirrings of "bourgeois" emancipation, or even Enlightenment and Sturm und Drang itself. But others have argued that the true center of the conflict lies between the two brothers and their father, and that this represents the breakdown of a patriarchal order, a crisis that threatens not merely the "nuclear family" but the whole social order. In the words of one recent critic, Franz Moor's words that open the play, "Aber ist Euch auch wohl, Vater? Ihr seht so blaß" (*S-NA*, 3: 11),[16] characterize not just one unhappy old man but a whole sick society.[17] While such interpretations suggest, perhaps, an excess of post-French Revolutionary hindsight, the recurrence of the motif undoubtedly indicates a feeling, probably only imperfectly articu-lated at the time, that is of more than merely personal significance.[18]

Both Leisewitz and Klinger, following their Italian sources, set their plays in late medieval or Renaissance Italy; Schiller's play in its original form takes place in eighteenth-century Germany during the Seven Years' War, though the war itself impinges little on the action. For the first performance, however, Schiller was obliged, much against his will, to consent to the director's altering the setting to the end of the fifteenth century, partly to cash in on the fashion for historical costume drama that *Götz* had initiated but also, no doubt, because the modern setting was thought too provocative — again indicating that the action does have a public, as well as a purely personal or psychological, dimension. (Both versions of the play remained current: details can be found in most mod-ern editions, though these are almost all of the original version.) Neither Leisewitz nor Klinger, however, makes much attempt at serious local color, and the same is true of Klinger's other "historical" plays with their invented plots and their vaguely fifteenth-century settings — German in *Otto*, Spanish in *Simsone Grisaldo*. There is certainly nothing of the com-plex evocation of a past age or the sense of historical movement that Goethe sought to capture in *Götz* and *Egmont*. For his part, Schiller turned to Renaissance Italy for his second tragedy, *Die Verschwörung des Fiesco zu Genua*, completed in 1782. There are hints at the broader historical context of the action, for the story is based on a real historical event; but, like Goethe in *Götz* and *Egmont*, Schiller treats the facts with considerable license, and once again the setting really serves only to furnish a colorful, exotic background to the portrayal of a "*großer Kerl*." As Schiller wrote in his program note for the first performance, Fiesco, the supposed champion of republican liberties who betrays the cause in pursuit of personal ambition, is the center ("der große Punkt") of the play, to which all other characters and strands of action gravitate "like rivers to the ocean" (*S-NA*, 4: 271; the image recalls Goethe's "Mahomets Gesang," originally intended for the unfinished tragedy but subsequently published as an independent poem). As with the other monodic tragedies of the Stürmer und Dränger, the action that "gravitates" around the central figure is complex, perhaps excessively so, and, despite Schiller's claim, is sometimes rather loosely related to him (as in the Berta-Bourgognino subplot); but Fiesco is eventually defeated not by the "notwendiger Gang des Ganzen" (the historical Fiesco was accidentally drowned at the moment of his triumph, which might have been thought to represent a kind of nemesis) but by the counterplotting of his republican adversary, Verrina. Despite its complexities, *Fiesco* is a stageworthy play, full of genuinely colorful character and incident, and Schiller is obviously trying, if not always successfully, to curb the excesses he himself had identified in *Die Räuber*.[19] We are never quite sure how seriously we should take the histrionic gestures of Guelfo or the Moor brothers; with Fiesco, Schiller is clearly presenting a deliberate play-actor on the political stage whose self-dramatization is a measure of his progressive corruption. It is a powerful and incisive character study. But it is really only with his fourth play, *Don Carlos,* that history itself begins to come into its own. Here Schiller begins his exploration (continued in his great "classical" dramas, *Wallenstein* and *Maria Stuart*) of the political and religious conflicts of the sixteenth and seventeenth centuries, of Reformation and Counter-Reformation, from which the European polity as he knew it had emerged: "die europäische Staatengesellschaft" (the European community), as he himself called it in his lecture on Universal History (*S-NA*, 17: 367), delivered in May 1789, a few weeks before the outbreak of the French Revolution that was to shake that community to its foundations. *Don Carlos* took Schiller some years to complete, and what had originally been intended as a typical Sturm und Drang celebration of a "*großer Kerl*" (totally unlike the historical figure of the unhappy Prince Carlos, son of Philip II of Spain) developed only gradually into a complex historical study. And with this achievement, and the adoption of verse and a measure of classical discipline, Schiller put the Sturm und Drang behind him.

Other plays of the 1770s employ contemporary settings, in some cases combined with a sharply critical portrayal of social relations. Their radicalism should again not be exaggerated, however: while writers such as Lenz, Wagner, and Schiller are undoubtedly concerned to expose the evils and abuses of the existing social system, their political program, if they have one, is reform rather than revolution. The way had been pointed in 1772 by Lessing, with his social tragedy *Emilia Galotti*. Lessing's plot, the seduction by an aristocrat of a woman of lower social rank, furnishes the basic formula on which the three later dramatists execute their variations; and whereas Lessing's play is set in Italy (though its petty Italian principality looks much like a typical contemporary German one), they go beyond him in adopting German characters and settings, often with recognizable real-life prototypes. If of all these plays Schiller's *Kabale und Liebe*, completed in 1783, strikes closest to the heart of princely absolutism (though only in *Emilia Galotti* is the ruling prince himself the would-be seducer), Lenz's *Der Hofmeister* and *Die Soldaten* are perhaps the most radical, both in the bitterness of their social satire, drawing closely on Lenz's personal experience, and in their dramatic form. *Der Hofmeister* was probably completed in Strasbourg in 1772 — that is, before *Götz von Berlichingen:* it appeared anonymously in 1774 and was thought by many to be the work of Goethe himself. In it the "Shakespearean" technique of a kaleidoscope of short, disconnected scenes depicting various groups of characters in various locations, which Goethe was to employ in *Götz* to create a social panorama of Germany in the early sixteenth century, is used to portray class attitudes and class relations in the eighteenth. Here, too, we already find the pair of dissenting brothers — not, however, rival sons, but fathers with differing ideas on the issue of education. The old-fashioned aristocrat Major von Berg, who wants his son to follow in his own footsteps as a soldier and a "*braver Kerl*" in the Prussian tradition (*L-WB*, 1: 43), employs the hapless "hero" Läuffer (a profoundly unheroic character) as private tutor to his children Leopold and Augusta (Gustchen). His apparently more enlightened brother, the Geheimer Rat (privy councilor), seeing that times are changing and that a broader public education is desirable, sends his son Fritz away to a university. The play's full, ironic title is *Der Hofmeister, oder Vorteile der Privaterziehung* (The Tutor; or, Advantages of Private Education); but in fact both choices lead to disaster: at home in rural Prussia, Läuffer makes Gustchen pregnant, both run away from the furious major, and Läuffer castrates himself in remorse for his seduction of (or, rather, by) Gustchen, while Fritz, away in Leipzig, is drawn into riotous student living, foolishly stands surety for a friend's debts, and finds himself in prison. A series of wildly improbable twists and coincidences (including a lottery win, the most obvious symbol of the operations of blind chance) brings about a "happy ending" in which all are reconciled and even the castrated Läuffer is betrothed to a cheerful peasant girl who is willing to forgo motherhood because, as she explains, she already has enough chickens and ducks to look after: the overall effect is bizarre and hardly optimistic. The play is subtitled a comedy ("*Komödie*," rather than the more unambiguously happy "*Lustspiel*"), but Lenz himself was uncertain what to call it; similarly, with *Die Soldaten* he wrote to the publisher asking that the designation "*Komödie*" be changed to "*Schauspiel*," but the request arrived too late. Here and in Lenz's other major "comedy" *Der neue Menoza*[20] we find a similar mixture of at least potential tragedy, contemporary social satire, black farce, and ironic incongruity, including in both cases murder and suicide onstage. Both plays employ a kaleidoscopic scenic technique to depict a chaotic society, but the satirical portrayal of upper-class irresponsibility is sharpest in *Die Soldaten*, with its aristocratic officers (a class Lenz knew at close quarters, having served as private tutor to three officer brothers from his native Baltic provinces) engaging in futile discussions of bogus profundity, playing foolish practical jokes, and seducing the daughters of respectable members of the middle class. Marie Wesener, a jeweler's daughter, throws over her middle-class suitor Stolzius in favor of the aristocrat Desportes, but he abandons her; Stolzius joins the army as a batman and poisons Desportes and himself, crying out "Marie! Marie!"; Marie's father goes in search of his errant daughter, finds her begging for her bread, and the two are "carried off half dead" by the crowd that has gathered to witness their reunion (*L-WB*, 1: 245). The play concludes with a curious epilogue in which two (supposedly) enlightened aristocrats comment on the events and discuss a scheme for organized prostitution, by which the sexual urges of the military could be appropriately channeled and respectable middle-class girls saved from ruin — a bizarre proposal that Lenz, however, seems to have meant quite seriously; after writing the play he devoted himself to working out further elaborate schemes for military reform, which he aimed to present to the Duke of Weimar or possibly even the chief minister of France: "the last scene of *The Soldiers* need not be printed," he wrote in a letter to Herder, "if I can get this thing through at Court" (*L-WB*, 1: 730). Shortly after writing this letter Lenz suffered a mental collapse, which is movingly recounted in Georg Büchner's novella *Lenz* (1839); Büchner profoundly admired Lenz and was greatly influenced by him. Lenz never completely recovered, and none of his other works met with the favorable reception *Die Soldaten* had enjoyed. They undoubtedly betray a certain eccentric or even pathological streak, particularly in their treatment of sexuality, but their social observation is acute and the problems they addressed were real enough. Both *Der neue Menoza* and *Die Soldaten* employ the same kaleidoscopic scenic technique as *Der Hofmeister;* act 4 of *Die Soldaten*, in particular, in which the action reaches its climax, is a whirl of tiny scenes including one of only six words, spoken by Marie's father: "Marie fortgelaufen — ! Ich bin des Todes" (L-WB, 1: 236).[21] The seduction of a tradesman's daughter is also the subject of Wagner's formally more conventional but still in contemporary terms shocking *Die Kindermörderin*. As the title indicates, the story here proceeds to a tragic conclusion: Evchen kills her baby — on stage, stabbing it to death with a needle as it lies in its cradle — and is condemned to death (though Wagner himself made an adaptation with a conciliatory, nontragic ending). Goethe, in *Dichtung und Wahrheit*, somewhat ungraciously accuses Wagner of plagiarizing the subject from his own Gretchen tragedy, but the two works are quite different in style, to say nothing of quality: Goethe's balladesque and intensely poetic, Wagner's prosaically realistic, though not without satirical bite. Finally, Schiller's *Kabale und Liebe* is yet another variation on the same social theme, and again combines a tragedy of relatively conventional middle-class form with a fiercely satirical portrayal of contemporary society and its abuses. The scene is a petty principality with a distinct resemblance to Schiller's native Württemberg, with a corrupt President (chief minister) who has gained his position by intrigue and murder and proposes to keep it by forcing his son to marry the Prince's mistress, and with its subjects press-ganged and sold off to fight in America to pay for the Prince's extravagances.[22] In a famous essay the critic Erich Auerbach accused Schiller of melodramatic exaggeration and "hair-raising rhetorical pathos" in his social satire,[23] but the picture is not really so far from reality and often has a sharp, ironical comic edge — as in the scenes between the cynical President and his henchman Wurm or his foppish crony von Kalb. If there is melodrama and rhetoric, it is rather to be found in the tragic love affair between the President's son Ferdinand von Walter and the musician's daughter Luise Miller.[24] The idealistic Ferdinand speaks of tearing down class barriers to marry the woman he loves; Luise knows that this is impossible. Ferdinand defies his father; Luise, after a struggle, remains loyal to hers. The play contains, in parallel and contrast, two of the father-child relationships that so appealed as a dramatic motif to Schiller and also to Giuseppe Verdi, who chose no less than four of Schiller's plays as opera libretti. Ferdinand, convinced (somewhat implausibly) of Luise's infidelity by a letter to a supposed lover that Wurm has forced her to write at his dictation, poisons her and himself with lemonade (rather than a more aristocratic choice of means — a sober, even bathetic middle-class touch). The ending draws the various threads of action together with slightly indecent haste, reminiscent of Lenz's endings but presumably not here intentionally ironic or incongruous: Ferdinand denounces Wurm, Wurm denounces the President, and the two criminals are handed over to justice, but the curtain falls on a gesture of reconciliation between the dying Ferdinand and his father. Once again, it is corruption and abuse within the system, rather than the institution of princely absolutism itself, that is attacked. Ferdinand's reforming idealism is shown (like Karl Moor's) to be impractical and even dangerous — his destructive jealousy is psychologically closely related to it — and the Prince himself remains in the background, untouched and unseen. (A controversial Berlin production of the 1960s had the stage dominated by a huge figure of the Prince, so that the human actors did, indeed, like the "petty men" of whom Shakespeare's Cassius speaks, "walk under his huge legs, and peep about" to find their perhaps not entirely "dishonorable graves.")

Lenz, Wagner, and Schiller thus made serious attempts to use the drama to address some of the specific problems of contemporary society. This is hardly the case with Klinger's *Sturm und Drang* itself, the play after which the movement came retrospectively to be known, despite the striking topicality of its setting in the American War of Independence, which began in the very year in which the play was composed. Here, as in Klinger's "historical" plays, the nominal setting serves only as an exotic backdrop for the explosive antics and extravagant rhetoric of several would-be "*Kraftkerls*," including the appropriately named hero, Wild. Curiously enough for these apostles of liberty, it appears — though it is not made very clear and, correspondingly, does not seem very important — that the characters are fighting for the English against the rebellious colonists, as, indeed, Klinger himself planned to do; he eventually achieved his military ambitions in Russia, where he had a distinguished career in the service of Catherine the Great and her successors Paul and Alexander and rose to the rank of lieutenant general. In *Sturm und Drang* we have not hostile brothers but two generations of hostile families, the Berkley and Bushy fathers and sons — the names are taken from *Richard II*, and the plot is a kind of tragicomic amalgam of *Romeo and Juliet* (though with the families eventually reconciled) and *Love's Labour's Lost* (in which three lords pursue three ladies). After much melodramatic confusion the two fathers are reconciled, and Wild — in reality, Carl Bushy — is betrothed to Jenny Berkley; but Harry Berkley, alias Captain Boyet (the name is taken from *Love's Labour's Lost*), seems for the moment determined to pursue the feud: the play thus ends on an ambiguous note.

The mixture of comedy, tragedy, and melodrama is no doubt intended to be seen as Shakespearean and is directly inspired by Lenz, but new forms of prose drama of contemporary life had already been attempted earlier in the century in France. In the 1750s Denis Diderot, now remembered for his philosophical prose works and his editorship of the great *Encyclopédie,* had published two plays and a series of theoretical essays (translated by Lessing as *Das Theater des Herrn Diderot* [The Theater of M. Diderot, 1760]) in which he suggests that various intermediary forms might be introduced between the traditional genres of tragedy and comedy — though he is opposed to the *mixture* of tragedy and comedy, which he regards as a bad habit of the English drama.[25] In 1773 Louis-Sébastien Mercier went beyond this position in his treatise *Du théâtre, ou nouvel essai sur l'art dramatique,* arguing that tragedy in the traditional sense was impossible for the modern dramatist and advocating a generically neutral form that he calls simply "drame." Wagner translated Mercier's essay in 1776 at Goethe's suggestion, but Lenz had, in effect, already established the form both in practice and in theory. In a review of his own *Der neue Menoza,* written in response to hostile criticism by Wieland, he writes, "Komödie ist Gemälde der menschlichen Gesellschaft, und wenn die ernsthaft wird, kann das Gemälde nicht lachend werden. . . . Daher müssen unsere deutschen Komödienschreiber komisch und tragisch zugleich schreiben" (*L-WB,* 2: 703).[26] The inseparable fusion of elements in Lenz's own plays is the true fulfillment of Gerstenberg's demand, "Away with the classification of the drama!" (*G-U,* 93). Lenz has been seen as the pioneer of tragicomedy,[27] of "open drama,"[28] or of "epic theatre" as defined by Bertolt Brecht, in which the "unity of action" is replaced by a multiplicity of actions moving not in a continuous straight line but in "leaps and curves"[29] or (as in *Der Hofmeister* and *Die Räuber*) with almost independent actions mirroring or paralleling each other but with a poetic unity conferred by repeated motifs and images. If the theory of the modern drama originated in France, it was in the German Sturm und Drang that it took root and bore fruit.

Lenz is regarded by many as the most modern of the Sturm und Drang writers, and it is true that his work "has received increasing attention lately for its stunning prefiguration of the theater of our own century."[30] It has not, however, apart from Brecht's tendentious adaptation of *Der Hofmeister* (1950), been much seen in actual performance. And even in their own day, though the movement caused a stir in literary and critical circles, the plays were, with the exception of Goethe's and Schiller's, less successful on the stage. Even in 1776, the year in which the movement peaked in terms of quantity of work published, only Goethe (together with Lessing) managed, according to the admittedly incomplete evidence of Reichard's *Deutsches Theater-Kalender,* to achieve productions in double figures (and *Götz* achieved only three).[31] The more radical and innovatory works were not performed. Of Lenz's plays only *Der Hofmeister* was performed in his lifetime, and that in a fairly drastic adaptation by the director F. L. Schröder; *Die Soldaten* had to wait almost a century. *Die Kindermörderin* was performed in Bratislava (Pressburg, then within the Habsburg dominions) in 1777, but was soon displaced in the public favor by an adaptation with a happy ending by Lessing's brother Karl; it was in response to this that Wagner himself rewrote his play. In the case of *Götz* and the plays of Lenz, the principal reason, apart from the squeamishness of public morality, was no doubt their impracticality from the point of view of the traditional theater, which, though not technically unsophisticated, was ill equipped to cope with so many rapid changes of decor. It may be that the plays were not written with any realistic thought of performance but only as closet dramas, *Lesedramen*, for private rather than public consumption. Wagner claimed as much for the original version of *Die Kindermörderin* ("a closet drama for thinking readers"),[32] Schiller for *Die Räuber* ("a dramatized history," *S-NA*, 3: 5) and again for *Don Carlos* (*S-NA*, 6: 495). These disclaimers are in part, no doubt, just a polite convention; but Lenz, and Goethe in *Götz*, were, indeed, probably "spoilt" by the example of Shakespeare as they understood him. Eighteenth-century German theaters had picture stages with a proscenium arch and a front curtain, with wings and backdrops for scenery: the Elizabethan type of open stage was unknown, and Sturm und Drang writers probably believed that Shakespeare cared as little for the practicalities of theatrical production as they themselves did. Herder writes of Shakespeare's plays, in contrast to those of the French school, as liberating our imagination from the physical confines of the theater; and in the concluding section of his late essay "Shakespeare und kein Ende" (Shakespeare ad Infinitum, 1826) Goethe argues that Shakespeare must be considered above all as a poet and that his plays must be drastically modified for actual stage performance. Many Sturm und Drang dramas make, indeed, a very "literary" impression, which is reinforced by their frequent use of literary quotation and allusion. Even such a stageworthy play as *Die Räuber*, for example, is full of deliberate echoes not only of Shakespeare but also of Plutarch, Homer, the Bible, Milton, and Klopstock, as well as of other dramas of the movement, as we have already noted. Satire of a specifically literary kind is also found not only in Goethe's *Götter, Helden und Wieland* and *Das Jarhmarktsfest zu Plundersweilen* (and in the slightly later *Der Triumph der Empfindsamkeit*) but also in Lenz's *Pandämonium Germanicum*, in which Goethe and Lenz himself are seen ascending a "steil'

Berg" (steep mountain; *L-WB*, 1: 248), evidently a German Parnassus or, perhaps, a literary Brocken, to reach the Temple of Fame at the summit, and encountering a motley crew of writers and critics alive and dead, including Wieland, Lessing, Klopstock, Herder, and the ghosts of Molière and (of course) Shakespeare: another work written in dramatic form, with dialogue and scenic directions, but plainly intended to be read rather than staged. On the other hand, *Julius von Tarent* and *Die Zwillinge,* which were written for a theatrical competition, make modest scenic demands and conform to the spirit, if not the letter, of the classical unities. In *Die Zwillinge* the murder of Ferdinando actually takes place offstage, in accordance with neoclassical propriety: his parents only realize what has happened when his horse is seen returning without him, with blood on its saddle — which, of course, also has to happen offstage and be observed through the open window. Goethe effectively employs a similar device in *Egmont,* where Alba in act 4 observes Egmont arriving on horseback and dismounting in the courtyard of what, unbeknown to him, is to be his prison; but *Götz,* as we have seen, calls for violent action and spectacle onstage, and Klinger's other plays are similarly unrestrained.

If the movement begins on a high note in *Götz,* it comes to an end on a threefold peak in Schiller's three prose tragedies. They sum up the essence of the Sturm und Drang: the desire for freedom both as theme and as formal principle, the motifs of fraternal hatred in *Die Räuber,* of the "*großer Kerl*" in *Fiesco,* of the conflicts of contemporary society in *Kabale und Liebe.* All three are not without some of the characteristic excesses, improbabilities, and extravagances of their predecessors, but they are written with a fire and vigor that betray the hand of a true master of the theater, and they continue to hold the stage to the present time. As a contemporary reviewer wrote of *Die Räuber,*[33] if there ever was to be a German Shakespeare, who would dominate the subsequent history of the German theater as Shakespeare has that of the English-speaking world, then this was he.

Notes

1 "A colorful gallery where the history of the world passes before our eyes on the invisible thread of time. The structure of his plays, in the accepted sense of the word, is no structure at all. Yet each revolves around an invisible point which no philosopher has discovered or defined and where the characteristic quality of our being, our presumed free will, collides with the inevitable course of the whole" (*G-CW*, 3: 164–65).

[2] See Roy Pascal, *Shakespeare in Germany 1740–1815* (Cambridge: Cambridge UP, 1937); also Hansjürgen Blinn, *Shakespeare-Rezeption: Die Diskussion um Shakespeare in Deutschland,* vol. 1: *Ausgewählte Texte von 1741 bis 1788* (Berlin: Erich Schmidt, 1982).

[3] "I call them living tableaux of moral nature."

[4] See Simon Williams, *Shakespeare on the German Stage,* vol. 1: *1586–1914* (Cambridge: Cambridge UP, 1990).

[5] The most recent critical discussion of the drama of the movement in English is Bruce Duncan, *Lovers, Parricides, and Highwaymen: Aspects of Sturm und Drang Drama* (Rochester NY: Camden House, 1999); in German, Ulrich Karthaus, *Sturm und Drang: Epoche — Werke — Wirkung* (Munich: Beck, 2000), both with further bibliographies and discussions of earlier literature.

[6] References to the two versions of the play are given in this form throughout. "The model of a knight, bold and noble in his freedom and calm and loyal in his misfortunes" (*G-CW,* 7: 66; *G-CW* includes a translation only of the second version of the play).

[7] "Thanks be to God that He has allowed me to see him, this man hated by princes, and the hope of the oppressed" (*G-CW,* 7: 7).

[8] "Lick my arse."

[9] Alcestis dies in place of her sick husband, Admetus, but is rescued from Hades by Hercules. There are operatic treatments by Handel (1734) and Gluck (1767).

[10] "I will have nothing to do with you, colossus."

[11] For samples of this and other translations, see Pascal, *Shakespeare in Germany.*

[12] "A series of actions, succeeding one another like thunderclaps, the one supporting and enhancing the other, and all flowing together in one great whole, that finally adds up to nothing more and nothing less than the main character, standing out from the whole group of his fellow actors."

[13] Friedrich Müller genannt Maler Müller, *Der dramatisierte Faust,* ed. Ulrike Leuschner (Heidelberg: Winter, 1996). The fullest edition of the early prose fragments is Friedrich Müller, *Fausts Leben,* ed. Johannes Mahr, Universal-Bibliothek, 9949 (Stuttgart: Reclam, 1979).

[14] "Is capable of carrying the world on his shoulders" (*Sturm und Drang: Dramatische Schriften,* 2 vols., eds. Erich Loewenthal and Lambert Schneider, 2nd ed. [Heidelberg: Lambert Schneider, 1963], 2: 227).

[15] "What is the use of all this, my beating my clenched fist upon my forehead and howling with the winds — threatening and storming, and for all this building nothing but castles in the air, houses of cards!"

[16] "But are you quite well, Father? You look so pale."

[17] Götz-Lothar Darsow, *Friedrich Schiller* (Stuttgart: Metzler, 2000), 3.

[18] See Stefanie Wenzel, *Das Motiv der feindlichen Brüder im Drama des Sturm und Drang* (Frankfurt am Main: Lang, 1992).

[19] See Schiller's own — anonymous — review of the earlier play, *S-NA,* 22: 115–31.

[20] The title alludes to a novel by the Danish writer Erik Pontoppidan entitled *Menoza, an Asiatic Prince who Traveled the World in search of Christians, but found Few of what he Sought* (1742, German translation 1747).

[21] "Marie run away — ! It'll kill me." Note that *L-WB* uses an earlier version of the play, in which Marie's name appears as Mariane.

[22] This practice was, in fact, a major source of income for several of the German princes in the 1770s.

[23] Erich Auerbach, "Miller the Musician," in his *Mimesis: The Representation of Reality in Western Literature* (Princeton: Princeton UP, 1974), 434–53. The German original dates from 1946.

[24] Verdi's opera based on the play retains Schiller's original title, *Luisa Millerin;* Iffland advised Schiller that *Kabale und Liebe* would be more catchy.

[25] Denis Diderot, *3° Entretien sur le Fils naturel*, in his *Œuvres esthétiques*, ed. P. Vernière (Paris: Garnier, 1959), 138n. See R. Mortier, *Diderot en allemagne* (Paris: Presses universitaires de France, 1954), 48–138.

[26] "Comedy is a depiction of human society, and if the state of society is serious, comedy cannot be a laughing matter. . . . For that reason our German dramatists must write comically and tragically at the same time."

[27] K. S. Guthke, *Geschichte und Poetik der deutschen Tragikomödie* (Göttingen: Vandenhoeck, 1961), challenged by Helmut Arntzen, *Die ernste Komödie: Das deutsche Lustspiel von Lessing bis Kleist* (Munich: Nymphenburg, 1968), 85.

[28] Volker Klotz, *Geschlossene und offene Form im Drama* (Munich: Hanser, 1960). Klotz's highly influential categorization has also been challenged: see John Guthrie, *Lenz and Büchner: Studies in Dramatic Form* (Frankfurt am Main: Lang, 1984).

[29] Bertolt Brecht, "Anmerkungen zur Oper 'Mahagonny,'" in his *Gesammelte Werke*, 20 vols. (Frankfurt am Main: Suhrkamp, 1967), 17: 1004–16. Brecht's terms *"Sprünge"* and *"Kurven"* plainly recall the *"Sprünge und Würfe"* commended by Herder.

[30] *Space to Act: The Theater of J. M. R. Lenz*, eds. Alan C. Leidner and Helga S. Madland (Columbia SC: Camden House, 1993), xiii.

[31] See K. S. Guthke, "Repertoire: Deutsches Theaterleben im Jahre 1776," in his *Literarisches Leben im achtzehnten Jahrhundert in Deutschland und der Schweiz* (Bern & Munich: Francke, 1975), 290–96.

[32] *Sturm und Drang: Dichtungen und theoretische Texte*, ed. Heinz Nicolai (Munich: Winkler, 1971), 2: 1899.

[33] C. F. Timme, review in *Erfurtische gelehrte Zeitung*, July 24, 1781; see Schiller, *Werke und Briefe*, ed. Otto Dann, vol. 2 (Frankfurt am Main: Deutscher Klassiker Verlag, 1988), 950.

The Theater Practice of the Sturm und Drang

Michael Patterson

THE PLAYS OF THE Sturm und Drang hardly impress us with their plots, which are often melodramatic; nor with their characterization, which frequently lacks depth; nor, again, with the quality of their language, which is seldom memorable. What distinguishes the drama of this period is its theatrical energy. A nation whose theater had lain semidormant under the constraints of French neoclassicism now awakened with a start, creating works that can be fully appreciated only in performance.

Ironically, however, the exciting theatricality and controversial content of the Sturm und Drang dramas made it difficult if not impossible for many of them to be staged at the time. Although premiered in 1782, Schiller's *Die Räuber* had to be adapted to a seven-act structure and was not performed as Schiller had written it until 1861. Wagner's *Die Kindermörderin* was banned from performance in Berlin and reached the stage only in the far-flung Pressburg (now Bratislava) in 1777, although, thanks to the addition of a happy ending, it was performed in Frankfurt two years later. Lenz's *Die Soldaten* fared even worse: it was not performed until 1863. What we encounter here, to my knowledge for the first time in the history of theater, is the curious spectacle of young playwrights creating works for a stage that did not yet exist.

Of course, there had been earlier writers who wrote plays without any hope or intention of having them performed; for example, the nun Hrotsvit. In the main, however, dramatists, from the ancient Greek tragedians to the playwrights of the eighteenth century, wrote for the stage they knew. While some of these writers may, like Shakespeare, have chafed at the constraints of the "hollow O," they wrote plays that were suited to the stage conditions of their time. Now, in the Sturm und Drang, playwrights were writing for the stage but making impossible demands on it. For example, Schiller's *Die Räuber* required that Karl Moor should enter on horseback and that Count Moor's castle should burn fiercely on stage. Such excesses of theatrical imagination, which challenged the theatrical conventions of the period, recur throughout the history of German theater: Goethe's *Faust,* the fairy-tale pieces of Ludwig Tieck (1773–1853), the plays of Büchner and Christian Dietrich Grabbe (1801–36), on up to many of the dramas of German expressionism and Karl Kraus's *Die letzten Tage der Menschheit* (The Last Days of Mankind, 1918–19).

In a letter to Friedrich Ludwig Schröder of October 12, 1786, Schiller recorded his dismay at the limitations of the theater of his day, declaring that he had a horror of the terrible mistreatment of plays on the contemporary stage and yearned impatiently for a theater that would give free rein to his imagination and did not inhibit the free flight of his feelings (*S-NA,* 24: 62–63). He had a long wait; for serious theater in Germany of the eighteenth century was only gradually moving toward greater realism and freedom, and it had a considerable journey to travel. Leaving aside the popular theater with its crude *Haupt- und Staatsaktionen* (plays about the sudden fall of kings and princes) performed by wandering players mainly in market squares, the theater for much of the eighteenth century in Germany — the literary theater — had been stifled by its imitation of French neoclassicism. The alliance between the actressmanager Karoline Neuber and the academic and critic Johann Christoph Gottsched between 1727 and 1740 led to a well-meaning but misguided attempt to raise the quality of German theater by following the precepts of French models. In imitation of the French alexandrine, the heavy stresses of the German language were rendered in hexameter rhyming couplets. In place of the mercurial fluidity of the French, the plodding stresses of Gottsched's *Der sterbende Cato* (The Dying Cato) of 1731 gave birth to a piece so tedious that one could only wish that Cato might die more quickly. The rules of the three neoclassical unities of place, time, and action were strictly observed and the conventional five-act structure treated as a law. Thus, when the diligent Frau Gottsched translated the three-act *Fausse Agnès* by Philippe Destouches, she wrote in some lines requiring the cast to leave the stage for coffee and later for a meal in order to create the "requisite" five acts.

In 1759 Lessing commented wittily on Gottsched's achievements:

Als die Neuberin blühte, und so mancher den Beruf fühlte, sich um sie und die Bühne verdient zu machen, sahe es freilich mit unserer dramatischen Poesie sehr elend aus. Man kannte keine Regeln; man bekümmerte sich um keine Muster. Unsere *Staats- und Helden-Aktionen* waren voller Unsinn, Bombast, Schmutz und Pöbelwitz. Unsere *Lustspiele* bestanden in Verkleidungen und Zaubereien; und Prügel waren die witzigsten Einfälle derselben . . . Und wie ging er [Herr Gottsched] damit zu Werke? Er verstand ein wenig Französisch und fing an zu übersetzen; er ermunterte alles, was reimen und Oui Monsieur verstehen konnte, gleichfalls zu übersetzen; . . . kurz, er wollte nicht sowol unser altes Theater verbessern, als der Schöpfer eines ganz neuen sein.[1]

Instead of the mistaken attempt to imitate the wholly unsuitable models of Corneille and Racine, Lessing argued that the German Genius would be set alight only by another Genius (5: 72). That other Genius was Shakespeare.

While Lessing himself showed few signs of the influence of the English "Genius" in his own play writing, his encouragement to seek inspiration in Shakespeare was to have a momentous effect on the development of German drama. One outcome, first evident in Lessing's own *Nathan der Weise* (1779), was to establish blank verse, unrhymed iambic pentameter, as the preferred form for serious drama in German. The first translations of Shakespeare into German by Christoph Martin Wieland in the 1760s had, with one exception, been into prose, however, so to the young writers of the 1770s and 1780s Shakespeare seemed even more wild and undisciplined than was, in fact, the case. The young Goethe, celebrating Shakespeare's name day in 1771, said that on discovering Shakespeare he leaped into the air and felt for the first time that he had hands and feet (*G-MA*, 1.2: 412). Shakespeare's vast panoramic vision, his apparently naïve disregard of all the classical rules of dramaturgy, his portrayal of violent incidents on stage, and his blending of the most lyrical poetry with robust comedy, all inspired the young playwrights of the Sturm und Drang to be excitingly iconoclastic in a way that was unique to European drama of the day.

The history of the German stage in the eighteenth century is one of the gradual establishment of theatergoing as a legitimate cultural activity, culminating in the bold, if failed, attempt to found a national theater in Hamburg in the late 1760s and in the glories of the Mannheim National Theater and the Weimar Court Theater in the following decades. Actors moved from being regarded as vagabonds to being treated as respected members of society, and German writers for the theater, most notably Goethe and Schiller, could now take their place among world dramatists.

In the mid-eighteenth century many courts boasted magnificent and well-equipped opera houses; but spoken drama had to be performed in makeshift theaters, often no more than a shed or the back room of a tavern. If a luxury such as heating was provided, it was usually proudly announced on the playbill as a special attraction. In time, however, the courts and certain progressive towns began to create theaters in which German drama could be performed. The standard arrangement was an oblong building with the auditorium at one end and the stage at the other. The auditorium usually had two tiers of seating, although larger theaters such as the Mannheim National Theater, with its capacity of 1,200 for a population of 20,000, boasted four tiers. The best seats, where the duke or other ruler sat with his entourage, were on the upper level (what we would call the Dress Circle), facing the stage. The rest of the court and well-to-do bourgeoisie sat at right angles to the stage down either side of the upper level, the seating often partitioned into boxes. Their view of the stage was poor, and they could not avoid looking directly into the wings diagonally opposite them, but they were compensated by having a good view of the ruler and his courtiers. The ground level (the stalls) offered seating and standing room for the less elegant members of the community, the petite bourgeoisie, students, and so on. Large chandeliers with candles provided lighting in the auditorium and remained illuminated throughout the performance.

There was almost always a small orchestra pit, from which the musicians produced incidental music or played interludes, often to cover scene changes. It was also not uncommon, even in the most serious of dramas, to introduce between the acts quite unrelated material — an opera singer singing an aria, even acrobats — and, again, the orchestra would be called upon to provide accompaniment. The stage was viewed through a proscenium arch, across which a decorative curtain was hung. The curtain was opened for the start of the performance and remained raised until the end, so that scene changes were seen by the audience. The standard arrangement of the stage decoration was a backcloth at the rear of the stage, with some seven so-called sliders on either side of the stage into which wing-pieces were slotted. The wing-pieces were painted to offer a perspective of a room or a landscape.[2] To change scenes without breaking the flow of the performance, a painted curtain was commonly introduced halfway down the stage. This arrangement allowed a scene to be played in front of the curtain, while the background scenery on the upper stage was changed. An example is seen in the stage direction at the start of act 2, scene 6 of Schiller's *Die Jungfrau von Orleans* (The Maid of Orleans, 1801), which requires the backdrop to be opened to reveal the English camp in flames.

Although this arrangement was tenaciously maintained far into the following century, it was unsatisfactory in many respects. First, the perspective could be appreciated fully only by someone sitting directly in front of the stage. Second, to maintain the perspective the objects on the backdrop had to be reduced in size: trees were a couple of meters high, and doorways were too low for any normal person to pass through, so that actors could not move far upstage for fear of dwarfing the scenery. Third, actors entered the stage by stepping between the wing-pieces, ideally beside one with a door painted on it. Johann vom Hagen complained about this often laughable practice, which had the actors sometimes exiting by the windows and reentering through a mirror, or charging through walls with aplomb, even though the room had several doors.[3] Fourth, it was common practice to paint stage properties and even furniture onto the backcloth and wings, so that actors were obliged to pluck a real rose from a painted bush or to sit in a chair beside a painted table. Finally, it was not uncommon to use stock flats and backcloths for quite dissimilar settings and even to muddle them. So a wood or a garden would frequently use the same set of scenery, or the backdrop would display the interior of a castle, while the wings displayed heavy foliage. The much more realistic box set was not introduced until the next century, mainly because its use would have made it impossible to light the stage strongly enough. For, in addition to a chandelier above the stage and footlights in front of it, each wing-piece had a row of candles and, later, oil lamps that shone light onto the stage from the side, providing essential additional illumination.

Therefore, despite the considerable improvement in staging conditions in the course of the eighteenth century, the Stürmer und Dränger, eager to write with a new passion and a new realism, were confronted with a theater practice that was normally incapable of realizing their vision. This is not to say that these playwrights were writing only to be read, that they had no wish to see their works performed. Indeed, despite the limitations of the theater of their day, one or two of their dramas provided the most exciting evenings in the theater for decades. And, while the eighteenth-century stage proved unable to cope with what seemed to be the impossible excesses of their theatrical imagination, their writing was to have a profound influence on later theater practice. Disappearing like an underground stream, the episodic structure and powerful theatricality of their plays were to resurface in the charged excitement of expressionist drama and in the work of Bertolt Brecht.

As late as 1962 Olga Smoljan could still write of Maximilian Klinger's *Otto* that the parallel conversations in one scene represent a method technically impossible for the stage, and that the multiplicity of set changes in the play exceeds the possibilities of the stage.[4] Fortunately, our present-day theater, by often returning to the simplicity of the Elizabethan stage, gives free rein to the imagination, creating a battlefield with a banner and a palace with a throne. The method by which a complex episodic play can now be staged with ease (*pace* Smoljan!) is sometimes dignified by the suspect adjective "Brechtian," and undoubtedly his influence on modern set design has been considerable. But one should not forget that he, in turn, owed much to the Elizabethans, the expressionists, and, indeed, the Sturm und Drang.

One of the earliest documents of the Sturm und Drang was Lenz's *Anmerkungen übers Theater,* which he read to a circle of friends in 1771 and published in 1774. While dealing principally with issues of composing dramatic work, some of the observations have important implications for theater practice. These relate principally to the need for multiple sets and to the style of acting. On the first, he denounced Aristotle and even more the neoclassicists for the imposition of the three unities of action, place, and time. Even Lessing had not gone as far as to challenge the authority of Aristotle. Now this twenty-year-old writer had the temerity not only to dismiss Aristotle but also to hold up, in place of the constrictions of the unities, the dramatic style of the seemingly primitive writer of doggerel *Knittelvers,* Hans Sachs. Praising the fact that Sachs's Patient Griselda is wooed, marries, becomes pregnant, and bears a child all within one act of the play, Lenz asks: "Woher das Zutrauen zu der Einbildungskraft seines Publikums? Weil er sicher war, daß sie sich aus der nämlichen Absicht dort versammelt hatten, aus der er aufgetreten war, ihnen einen Menschen zu zeigen, nicht eine Viertelstunde" (*L-WB,* 2: 669).[5] Like Sachs, Lenz places his trust in the imagination of the audience to become engaged with one individual, even when the depiction of the life of that individual ranges over many years and locations. Like Sachs, he placed "einen Menschen" (a human being) at the center of his dramas. By discovering unity in the central figure, Lenz also created a new vision of acting and costume. He was scornful of the feeble performances generated by neoclassical theater:

> da erscheinen die fürchterlichsten Helden des Altertums, der rasende Oedip, in jeder Hand ein Auge, und ein großes Gefolge griechischer Imperatoren, römischer Bürgermeister, Könige und Kaiser, sauber frisiert im Haarbeutel und seidenen Strümpfen, unterhalten ihre Madonnen, deren Reifröcke und weiße Schnupftücher jedem Christenmenschen das Herz brechen müssen, in den galantesten Ausdrücken von der Heftigkeit ihrer Flammen, daß sie sterben, ganz gewiß und unausbleiblich den Geist aufzugeben sich genötigt sehen, falls diese nicht. . . . In diesem Departement ist Amor Selbstherrscher, alles atmet, seufzt, weint, blutet, ihn und den Lichtputzer ausgenommen, ist noch kein Akteur jemals hinter die Kulisse getreten, ohne sich auf dem Theater verliebt zu haben. (*L-WB,* 2: 643)[6]

Lenz contrasts this hollow attitudinizing with the boldness and truthfulness of the Elizabethan stage: "Diese Herren hatten sich nicht entblödet, die Natur mutterfadennackt auszuziehen, und dem keusch- und züchtigen Publikum darzustellen wie sie Gott erschaffen hat" (*L-WB*, 2: 644–45).[7]

The belief that the best theater should strip nature bare led to a rejection of the ornate prettification of tragedy by French neoclassicism and its imitators and was to have a profound effect on styles both of presentation and of acting. Gradually the court costumes, in which virtually all plays were performed, came to be recognized as quite unsuitable for plays set in ancient Greece or Rome or for historical tragedies. Soon it became impossible for a Roman matron to appear in a crinoline or for a soldier to appear on the battlefield in immaculate satin breeches and coat. Much more authentic clothing was adopted, and everyday dress was worn for contemporary pieces. There was also a serious attempt to use historically correct weapons and props, which was to culminate the following century in the pursuit of total authenticity in the work of the Saxe-Meiningen troupe.

More significantly, the emphasis on naturalness led to more truthful acting, especially in Berlin, Hamburg, and Mannheim. Formal poses and hollow declamation were replaced with intensely impassioned performances, notably by a new breed of theater stars such as Ludwig Iffland and Franz Brockmann. In 1782, the year of the première of *Die Räuber,* the director of the Mannheim National Theater, Wolfgang Heribert Freiherr von Dalberg, invited his ensemble to respond to the question: "What is meant by 'natural,' and what limitations should be imposed on this in theatrical performance?"[8] Despite variations in the responses a consensus emerged: "Nature" was understood as God's perfect creation, to be represented as perfectly as possible, not as some crude reality merely to be imitated. Thus, one sees that even these progressive theater practitioners were still enmeshed in eighteenth-century idealistic thought. Nevertheless, the exhortation to portray nature truthfully resulted in a substantial shift toward actors' finding emotions within themselves, in contrast to the external approach to characterization of their predecessors (with the notable exceptions of the early "realist" performances by actors such as Konrad Ekhof and Friedrich Ludwig Schröder). This shift ultimately led to the actor's total identification with the role, as in the early writings of Konstantin Stanislavsky. Iffland argued that the creative inspiration implied in this process could only translate into effective performance if the actor made him- or herself a worthy channel for this inspiration. In a radical drawing together of life and art, he elsewhere asserted that the best means of portraying a noble figure is to be oneself.[9]

The "naturalness" of these young performers attracted a great deal of criticism — not least from Ludwig Tieck, who expressed his unhappiness at the appointment of Iffland as director of the Berlin Royal Theater in 1796. Iffland's actors, declared Tieck, were not natural but trivial, throwing away important lines and great thoughts, regarding every elevated feeling as emotional bombast and all majesty and dignity as unnatural. These worshippers of impoverished naturalism deserved as much scorn as they had heaped on their predecessors.[10] It was partly in response to these mumbled and undisciplined performances that Goethe devoted so much of his effort toward encouraging elegant movement and fine verse speaking at the Weimar Court Theater.

The impact of the Sturm und Drang on the theater practice of contemporary Germany may be detected more clearly in their general influence on these questions of presentational style than through the specific effect of their actual dramatic writing, for, as we have seen, not much of the latter actually saw the inside of a theater until many years later. A chronological survey of the dramas of the Sturm und Drang reveals little about their actual stage practice. If we begin with Goethe's *Götz von Berlichingen*, written in 1771 and published in a revised version in 1773, we note the epic breadth of the piece; its over fifty changes of scenery; its focus on a superhuman central figure; and its willingness to embrace the crudest of dialogue, which has delighted generations of German schoolboys with access to an unexpurgated edition of the text. The influence of Shakespeare is evident, but Shakespeare's stage was long gone. So when it was first produced by Heinrich Koch in Berlin in 1774, it had to be adapted by Karl Lessing, the younger brother of Gotthold Ephraim. Indeed, Goethe's name did not even appear on the playbill for the first performance. The only major theatrical innovations were that Johann Gottfried Brückner dispensed with the conventional court wig to play the title role bare-headed and that the costumes went some way toward achieving authenticity. When Schröder performed it in a heavily abridged version in Hamburg later the same year, it ran only four performances. A full-length text was not performed until 1819 — and then only in a sanitized version, adapted by Goethe for performance over two consecutive evenings at the Weimar Court Theater.

Not all the Stürmer und Dränger were so insistent on multiple set changes. Heinrich Leopold Wagner succeeded in being less demanding of stage resources, even though he tended idiosyncratically to write in six acts rather than five. His *Kindermörderin* requires a set change only at the end of each act, and apart from the first and last acts — the former of which he later cut anyway — all the action takes place in the Humbrecht household in Strasbourg. In the last act of *Die Reue nach der Tat* (Remorse after the Deed, 1775) Wagner avoids the expected change to the setting of the abbey by using the neoclassical device of a *récit* by Walz. This economy may explain why, despite the violence of his themes, Wagner had greater success in being staged than many of his contemporaries: *Die Reue nach der Tat* in Hamburg and Berlin in 1775, *Die Kindermörderin* in Pressburg in 1777, and the revised version, *Evchen Humbrecht*, in Frankfurt in 1778. Gerstenberg's *Ugolino*, if one may admit it as a Sturm und Drang piece, went even further in totally observing the unity of place and time by adopting an analytic structure of revealing the past in the present. It had enjoyed a production as early as 1769 in Berlin.

The major dramatists of the Sturm und Drang, Lenz and Klinger, however, did not fare so well, and one may speak of a genuinely theatrical impact (as opposed to the response by a reading public to a published drama) only with Schiller's *Die Räuber*. Writing to Gotter in 1775, Lenz even claimed that he did not care whether his dramas were playable (*L-WB*, 3: 356). He asserted, however, that this refusal to concern himself with the theater practice of the day proceeded not from ignorance of the requirements of the theater but from an attempt to reach for a superior form (*L-WB*, 2: 730), and, only two months after his dismissive statement to Gotter, he seems to be in favor of performance — other things being equal (*L-WB*, 3: 368). There is no actual evidence that Lenz visited the theater in his youth. Probably it was an activity that one took so much for granted that it was hardly worthy of comment, any more than a student of today would record having watched television the previous evening. It is unthinkable that a young intellectual such as Lenz would not have been a theatergoer, especially during his years in Königsberg, where the debate raged between the differing styles of the two leading theater figures of the city, Ludwig Döbbelin and Franz Schuch. Döbbelin represented the formal, declamatory style derived from Gottsched, whereas Schuch continued to use improvisation and included in his repertory challenging pieces such as Lessing's *Miß Sara Sampson* and translations of Plautus, at which Lenz himself was soon to try his hand.

When he moved to Strasbourg in 1771, Lenz almost certainly encountered the popular marionette theater, which features in *Der neue Menoza*: Zierau, an upholder of the three unities, cannot understand how his father can enjoy the crude pleasures of the "*Püppelspiel*" with its Hanswurst. The term *Püppelspiel*, in place of the more common *Pup-*

penspiel, is Alsatian dialect and points directly to Lenz's time in Strasbourg. Strasbourg was also the last home of the *Meistersinger,* and one recalls Lenz's reference to Hans Sachs in his *Anmerkungen übers Theater.* Probably the major influence of his Strasbourg theatergoing was that of the French theater, supported mainly by the French officers garrisoned in the city, who were all obliged to buy season tickets. The effects of Lenz's visits would have been both negative and positive. On the one hand, he would have observed the improbability of so-called *vraisemblance* (verisimilitude), packing incidents into one room and into twenty-four hours and, as Lessing said, depriving the audience of so many creative possibilities.[11] On the other hand, as Goethe records in *Dichtung und Wahrheit,* Aufresne, the main actor at the French theater in Strasbourg, had a major impact on the Sturm und Drang. His natural style was calm and reflective without being cold, yet he could be sufficiently violent when it was needed (*G-MA,* 16: 522).

In 1776 Lenz published the play that grew out of his association with the soldiers in Strasbourg, *Die Soldaten,* but the play had to wait almost a century before it was staged at the Burgtheater in Vienna in 1863. In 1775 he submitted an adaptation of Plautus's *Captivi, Die Algerier* (The Algerians), to Abel Seyler in the hope of performance, which Lenz felt was necessary to bring it to life.[12] Lenz then tried to interest Schröder in it, but the only copy was lost. Lenz had more success with *Der Hofmeister,* for this work was at least staged in his lifetime, albeit in a bowdlerized version.

Der Hofmeister was based on an actual incident with which Lenz had been familiar from his youth in Livonia; indeed, he retained the name of the actual family in his play. In this sense it may be accounted one of the first examples of a documentary play. The characters are, therefore, bourgeois and contemporary, and the topic of the play is of immediate social relevance, as is the case even more obviously with *Die Soldaten.* Clearly, the performers, who were thus called upon to imitate people whose behavior was familiar to the audience, were obliged to act in a naturalistic style, in a way that was not required for ancient tragedy or for a historical piece such as *Götz von Berlichingen.* To solve the staging problems posed by Lenz, Schröder put the blue pencil through many scene changes and several characters for his 1778 production in Hamburg. The five acts of the play were reduced to four; the thirty-five scenes, which range all over Germany and require thirty-one scene changes, were reduced to twenty-eight, with only nine settings, three of which were the same:

ACT ONE   Antichamber in the Berg household
           Läuffer's room

ACT TWO   A garden
           A room

ACT THREE Village school
           Room in Major Berg's house
           Village school

ACT FOUR   A pond
           Village school

Thirteen of the twenty-three characters were cut. For example, Gustchen's beloved cousin Fritz was omitted, thereby removing any rival for the tutor Läuffer and so destroying one of the sources of conflict in the play. Other major elements that were omitted for the sake of good taste were Läuffer's castration and Gustchen's pregnancy. The role of Lise, the simple girl who marries Läuffer, was cut, and the Schröder version ended happily with Gustchen marrying Läuffer, who is fortuitously ennobled. The Mannheim production of 1780, which ran with great success and was repeated for ten years, dispensed with two further locations, keeping the same setting throughout each of the first and second acts.

Despite the success of this corrupt version of *Der Hofmeister* — which, when first published anonymously, was thought of so highly that many believed Goethe to have been the author — Lenz's other plays failed to reach the stage. *Der Engländer* was not performed until 1916, *Amor vincit omnia* (Love's Labour's Lost, 1774) until 1936, *Die Buhlschwester* (The Rival in Love, completed 1772) until 1920, and *Der neue Menoza* until 1965. Thus, of his nine major original plays (as opposed to his translations of Shakespeare and Plautus), only one was performed during his lifetime, one (*Die Soldaten*) in the nineteenth century, and the rest not until the twentieth century, when, it might be said, the theater had at last caught up with Lenz's theatrical genius.

Despite involving himself more directly with the theater and giving a name to the movement, Friedrich Maximilian Klinger did not enjoy much more success. He began writing plays in 1774 in Giessen. His *Otto* of 1774, a historical piece that clearly owes a great deal to Goethe's *Götz*, has thirty-seven speaking parts and takes place in fifty-four locations. Many of the scenes are only two or three sentences long. Small wonder, then, that no director of the day attempted to stage it. On its publication in 1775 it attracted as many as seven reviews, but the majority were unfavorable. Probably it was as much the charged emotionalism of his drama about adultery as the technical difficulties (thirty changes of scenery) that prevented *Das leidende Weib* from reaching the stage. Strong emotional conflicts did not, however, stand in the way of *Die Zwillinge,* the play he submitted in response to an invitation, advertised in February 1775 by Schröder and his mother Sophie Charlotte Ackermannn, which offered twenty Louisdor for any suitable new works for the stage. Thirteen plays were submitted, of which Klinger's, closely followed by Johann Anton Leisewitz's *Julius von Tarent,* was rated the best.

Die Zwillinge made modest demands on the stage: there were no subplots within its five-act structure, and it required only eight speaking parts and six settings, only the second act having two different locations. The demand for a powerful and committed acting style was considerable, however. The character of the wronged twin Guelfo, a typically amoral, brave, and violent Sturm und Drang hero, especially, can only be realized by an impassioned performance. Grimaldi, Guelfo's loyal friend, describes him thus: "Dieser Blick! dieses Wesen! diese sich ausbreitende Menschenbeugende Gluth im schwarzen, grossen, rollenden Auge!" (*K-W,* 2: 30).[13] It was impossible to perform such a character in a formal declamatory style. It called on the flamboyantly theatrical quality seen in the famous illustration of Franz Brockmann in the "mirror scene" of act 4:[14] Guelfo, having just murdered his twin brother, stands, his legs in their spurred boots wide apart, his sword raised above his head, his hair and his sash flying, his plumed hat thrown to the ground. His body is half turned as he glimpses his own murderous features in the mirror, which he is about to destroy because he cannot bear to see his reflection.

Despite allegedly having been written in only twenty-four hours, *Die Zwillinge* was a great success, and Klinger was hailed as the "German Shakespeare."[15] Riding high on this newfound fame, Klinger headed for the Mecca of Weimar, where his revolutionary Sturm und Drang enthusiasm, especially for the American War of Independence, was now almost as great an embarrassment to the court official Goethe as the presence of the hot-headed Lenz. While at Weimar, Klinger wrote *Sturm und Drang.* Despite dealing with ten years of travels across two continents, the action, which is revealed largely in narration, is condensed into twenty-four hours and takes place in eight different locations. It was performed the following year by Abel Seyler's troupe, which Klinger had joined as dramaturge. He remained with Seyler for about a year and a half, during which he wrote a play specifically for the troupe — the closest a Sturm und Drang dramatist came to the actual theater practice of the day. The resulting play, *Stilpo und seine Kinder* (Stilpo and His Children, 1777), while being able to lay claim to treating a revolutionary theme four years before Schiller's *Die Räuber,* is, unfortunately, not one of Klinger's best, and it was not highly regarded when it premiered in Mainz in May 1779. Significantly, after *Stilpo* he turned to writing comedies and eventually gave up writing for the stage altogether, devoting himself to novels.

The most important and influential stage production of the Sturm und Drang movement took place after the end of the 1770s, the decade of their major activity. This was the premiere at the Mannheim National Theater on 13 January 1782 of Schiller's wild, iconoclastic piece written while still at school, *Die Räuber.*[16] The notoriety of the play, which had been published anonymously the previous summer, was already so great that people traveled considerable distances so as not to miss this theatrical event; some were in their seats four hours before the start. During the performance, which began at five o'clock, the theater erupted in pandemonium. The audience stamped their feet and shouted; complete strangers fell into each other's arms; fainting women had to be helped toward the exits. One eyewitness described it as a general dissolution as in the time of Chaos.[17]

In fact, the director, Dalberg, had gone some way in reducing the impact of the piece. Predictably, he had removed the most offensive and melodramatic material, such as the suicides of Franz and Schweizer and the report of nuns being raped by the robber band. He had gone further by insisting that the piece should be set not, as Schiller intended, in contemporary Germany but removed to the safer historical distance of the Middle Ages. (Indeed, when the play was performed in modern dress in Leipzig in September 1782, it was banned after the second performance.) Once again, to render the work playable on a contemporary stage, the number of scenes and locations had to be drastically reduced. The published text contains fifteen scenes and requires thirteen different settings; Dalberg reduced the action to eleven scenes with seven different settings. Even so, the premiere lasted four and a quarter hours, and twenty stagehands, in place of the usual dozen, had to be employed to effect the many scene changes and produce effects of fire and battle. Schiller recognized that in order that the tension of a performance should not be dissipated by frequent changes of scenery, it would be essential to create simpler staging requirements in the future. Thus his next pieces, *Die Verschwörung des Fiesco zu Genua* of 1782 and *Kabale und Liebe,* staged in Mannheim in 1784, require only nine and four different settings, respectively. Even his eventful historical tragedies were written with an eye for the practicalities of the stage of the day. Thus, his

Maria Stuart of 1800 provides for a single setting for each of the first three acts, while the two final acts change location only once each.

In itself, solving the technical problems thrown up by *Die Räuber* was not particularly ground-breaking. The special impact the play and its production had on the German theater was created by their youthful vitality: a play written by a schoolboy, still only twenty-two at the time of the premiere, its theme of youthful revolt against an age devoid of heroes, and a cast of actors, most of whom were still in their twenties. Dalberg, the director, was himself only thirty-one; Madame Toscani, who played Amalia, was twenty; Heinrich Beck (Kosinsky), twenty-one; and Johann David Beil (Schweizer), twenty-seven. Among the major roles only Johann Michael Boeck, thirty-eight, as Karl Moor, and, of course, figures such as Old Moor and Daniel did not fit this parade of the young. August Wilhelm Iffland, whose specialty was performing old men, played the villainous Franz Moor; Iffland was twenty-two.

Schiller admitted that he had considered the role of Franz Moor an impossibility, not really suited to the stage;[18] but Iffland's achievement in the part not only proved Schiller wrong but transformed it into one of the most sought-after in the German theater, ousting Karl, the idealistic hero of the piece, as the dominant figure. What impressed Schiller and the rest of the audience, even the critics, was Iffland's ability to internalize the emotions of Franz and so to generate acting that was both intense and truthful. Carl August Böttiger wrote at length about Iffland's achievement and cited the scene in which Old Moor and Amalia receive the false news of Karl's death.[19] Iffland leaned on the back of Old Moor's chair, his head thrust forward, his eyes bulging, as he stared at Amalia, catching every trace of pain that was tearing her apart. As Böttiger reported, no one in the audience could have escaped an involuntary shock of horror.

What Schiller learned from such moments of silent intensity in Iffland's performance was not only that Franz Moor can be a credible figure but also that the violent emotions of the Sturm und Drang did not need to be shouted loudly or reinforced by excessive action. If the emotion was genuine, and the actor able to convey it truthfully, then exclamation marks could be removed from the dialogue. The outstanding plays of Schiller's maturity, which were to become the greatest verse tragedies in the German language, revealed this lesson, learned from a young actor at a provincial theater.

Thus, while it might seem initially that the playwriting of the Sturm und Drang had little to do with the theater practice of the day, it did throw out challenges to the stage that we have begun to solve satisfactorily only in the last half century. And the few occasions when writers such as Schiller were forced to confront the practicalities of theatrical performance led them to produce works of considerable power.

Notes

[1] "When Karoline Neuber flourished, and many followed the calling to serve her and the German stage, our dramatic literature was indeed in a miserable state. Rules were unknown; there were no models to follow. Our *Staats- und Helden-Aktionen* were full of nonsense, bombast, filth and vulgar humor. Our *comedies* consisted of disguises and magic, and slapstick fights were their wittiest moments . . . And how did Herr Gottsched go to work on this? He knew a little French and began to translate; he encouraged anyone who could rhyme and understand 'Oui Monsieur' to translate as well; . . . in short, he did not wish merely to improve our old theater but to be the creator of an entirely new one" (Gotthold Ephraim Lessing, *Werke,* 8 vols., eds. Herbert G. Göpfert et al. [Munich: Hanser, 1970–79], 5: 70–71).

[2] For a more detailed account of a typical stage of the day, see Sibylle Maurer-Schmoock, *Deutsches Theater im 18. Jahrhundert* (Tübingen: Niemeyer, 1982); Michael Patterson, *The First German Theater: Schiller, Goethe, Kleist and Büchner in Performance* (London: Routledge, 1990), 26–31 and Plates 2 and 3.

[3] Johann Jost Anton vom Hagen, ed., "Über die Kochische Schauspieler-Gesellschaft," *Magazin zur Geschichte des Deutschen Theaters* 1 (1773): 72.

[4] Olga Smoljan: *Friedrich Maximilian Klinger: Leben und Werk* (Weimar: Arion, 1962), 46.

[5] "Where does this trust in the audience's power of imagination come from? Because he [Hans Sachs] was certain that they had gathered there for the very reason that induced him to perform, namely to show a whole human being not merely a quarter of an hour."

[6] "Here there appear the most terrible heroes of the ancient world, the crazed Oedipus, an eye in each hand, and a large retinue of Greek rulers, Roman burgomasters, kings and emperors, tidily coiffured with a hairnet and silk stockings, employ the most gallant expressions to inform their ladies, whose crinolines and white handkerchiefs cannot fail to break the heart of every honest Christian, that they will die, quite certainly and unavoidably will find themselves obliged to give up the ghost, unless they. . . . In this department Cupid is despot: everyone gasps, sighs, weeps, bleeds, except for Cupid himself and the candle-snuffer. No actor has ever stepped backstage without first falling in love out front."

[7] "These gentlemen did not shy away from stripping Nature utterly naked and presenting her to a chaste and respectable public just as God had created her."

[8] Max Martersteig, *Die Protokolle des Mannheimer Nationaltheaters unter Dalberg aus den Jahren 1781 bis 1789* (Mannheim: Dramaturgische Gesellschaft, 1890), 74–87. For a fuller analysis of the responses by the Mannheim ensemble, see Patterson, 33–7.

[9] See S. Troickij, *Konrad Ekhof, Ludwig Schröder, August Wilhelm Iffland, Johann Friedrich Fleck, Ludwig Devrient, Karl Seydelmann: Die Anfänge der realistischen Schauspielkunst* (Berlin: Henschel, 1949), 54.

[10] Hans Oberländer, *Die geistige Entwicklung der deutschen Schauspielkunst im 18. Jahrhundert* (Hamburg: Voss, 1898), 200.

[11] Letter of February 3, 1781: Gertrud Rudloff-Hille, *Schiller auf der deutschen Bühne seiner Zeit* (Berlin & Weimar: Aufbau, 1969), 13.

[12] Elisabeth Genton, *J. M. R. Lenz et la scène allemande* (Paris: Didier, 1966), 38–40.

[13] "This look! This being! This all-consuming, devastating fire in large black rolling eyes!"

[14] Original in the Deutsches Theatermuseum, Munich. See dust jacket for illustration of Klinger's Guelfo.

[15] Smoljan, 71.

[16] For a more detailed account of this production, see Patterson, 31–50.

[17] See Anton Pichler, *Chronik des großherzoglichen Hof- und National-Theaters* (Mannheim: Bensheimer, 1879), 67–68.

[18] Pichler, 68.

[19] C. A. Böttiger, *Entwickelung des Ifflandischen Spiels in vierzehn Darstellungen auf dem Weimarischen Hoftheater im Aprillmonath 1796* (Leipzig: Göschen, 1796), 293. See also Patterson, 47–50.

Die
R ä u b e r.

Ein Schauspiel

von fünf Akten,

herausgegeben

von

Friderich Schiller.

Frankfurt und Leipzig.

1 7 8 7.

Title page of the unauthorized second edition of Schiller's Die Räuber.
Courtesy of Taylor Institution, Oxford.

"Die schönsten Träume von Freiheit werden ja im Kerker geträumt": The Rhetoric of Freedom in the Sturm und Drang

David Hill

IN HIS ADDRESS *Zum Schäkespears Tag* (1771) Goethe uses the language of liberation to describe the moment when he recognized the genius of Shakespeare:

> Ich zweifelte keinen Augenblick dem regelmäßigen Theater zu entsagen. Es schien mir die Einheit des Orts so kerkermäßig ängstlich, die Einheiten der Handlung und der Zeit lästige Fesseln unsrer Einbildungskraft. Ich sprang in die freie Luft, und fühlte erst daß ich Hände und Füße hatte. Und jetzo da ich sahe wieviel Unrecht mir die Herrn der Regeln in ihrem Loch angetan haben, wie viel freie Seelen noch drinne sich krümmen, so wäre mir mein Herz geborsten wenn ich ihnen nicht Fehde angekündigt hätte, und nicht täglich suchte ihre Türne zusammen zu schlagen. (*G-MA*, 1.2: 412)[1]

Schiller uses a similar image of artificial constriction in his preface to *Die Räuber* when he defends his refusal to squeeze his play into "die allzuenge Pallisaden des Aristoteles und Batteux" (*S-NA*, 3: 5).[2] The drama of the Sturm und Drang may be accused of being sprawling and shapeless, but it is clear that Goethe and Schiller and their colleagues delighted in a "freer" form that they felt liberated them from the dominant neoclassical tradition, with its implications of order and propriety and, therefore, artificiality. Goethe was at the heart of a group of young writers who shared the feeling of being frustrated by the irrelevance of an older generation of writers and constrained by the conventions of polite society, which was dominated by the alien culture of the court. Freedom meant turning away from French neoclassical models to Shakespeare. As Goethe later put it in an autobiographical note characterizing the period 1769–75: "Man fühlt die Nothwendigkeit einer freiern Form und schlägt sich auf die Englische Seite" (*G-MA*, 14: 9).[3]

Goethe's address describes not only the form but also the content of Shakespeare's plays in terms of freedom: "seine Stücke, drehen sich alle um den geheimen Punkt . . . in dem das Eigentümliche unsres Ichs, die prätendirte Freiheit unsres Wollens, mit dem notwendigen Gang des Ganzen zusammenstößt" (*G-MA,* 1.2: 413).[4] This formulation could be applied to many texts of the Sturm und Drang that are structured around the struggle of an individual to achieve self-realization, and the idea of freedom was consistently used to express this urge to overcome restrictions of the self. It is a negative idea,[5] referring to that from which the individual seeks freedom, and is unspecific about what freedom actually is. It is, therefore, ideally suited as an emotionally laden gesture expressing frustration, a desperate insistence on some undefined alternative to constriction: the Sturm und Drang is a kind of protest movement, impatient with everything that limits the possibilities of the individual, and "freedom" is the name used to refer to an imagined state in which there are no such limits.

Imprisonment and freedom are core motifs in the part of *Faust* written before Goethe settled in Weimar. In his opening monologue Faust expresses frustration with the world of learning within which he has hitherto lived his life. Beyond his study he glimpses an alternative, represented, in turn, by the light streaming through the window, Nostradamus's scheme of the macrocosm, and the Earth Spirit; but none quite represents the alternative he seeks, and after each he returns in despair to his narrow gothic study, which he refers to as a prison (*G-MA,* 1.2: 135). One of the paradoxes of the Faust character is that in his attempt to achieve liberation from this narrow academic world he is attracted to Gretchen, who comes from a domestic environment that is in its own way equally restrictive. He reflects on this paradox when he creeps into her room and compares it also to a prison, but now in a tone of enthusiastic devotion: "In diesen Kerker welche Seligkeit!" (*G-MA,* 1.2: 155).[6] The play ends with Gretchen in a real prison, from which she is led to her execution. She accepts her just punishment as the will of God, rather than the freedom that Faust offers, which would in reality mean her enslavement to Mephistopheles.[7]

In the Sturm und Drang the idea of freedom is frequently linked, as here, with other realms associated with self-realization, such as love and nature. Goethe's "Bundeslied" (Fellowship Song) shows how true friendship makes us freer because it undercuts affectation, while in his early drama *Die Laune des Verliebten* (The Wayward Lover, written 1767–68, performed 1779, published 1806) the character Egle makes the point that true love depends on freedom: "Wo keine Freiheit ist, wird jede Lust getödet" (*G-MA*, 1.1: 305).[8] Goethe's poetry makes use of the literary convention that refers to commitment to one's beloved as imprisonment and nonattachment as freedom, but the poem "Der wahre Genuß" (True Enjoyment, 1769) asserts that freedom can be reconciled with commitment. This complex of metaphors is handled with particular subtlety and wit in the poem "Lilis Parck" (Lili's Park, written 1775, published 1789), in which the poet compares himself with a captive bear, which, with all its gruffness and clumsiness, is a devoted member of Lili's menagerie, enchanted by her but still capable, he claims, of asserting its natural freedom.

The Idea of Freedom in the Literature of the Eighteenth Century

Prisons and imprisonment were part of the everyday experience of life in the eighteenth century. Schubart suffered long years of imprisonment, and Goethe's portrait of Gretchen is based in part on the infanticide Susanna Margareta Brandt, who was imprisoned near Goethe's house in Frankfurt. But if the writers of the Sturm und Drang were interested in justice, at least in particular cases such as infanticide, they were less interested in the practicalities of incarceration or in penal reform.[9] Imprisonment was used, like slavery, above all as a metaphor.

The idea of freedom was established well before the French Revolution, with which it tends to be associated. In theology it was familiar from discussions of free will, and in history it was used for describing the republics of the ancient world. Theories of absolutism, too, allowed for a primal state of freedom but argued that in the social contract many freedoms had been relinquished for the common good. A residue, however, remained, and in the second half of the century voices were increasingly heard claiming that the common good positively demanded freedoms, particularly economic ones. Thus, the gradual shift away from absolutist notions of freedom as part of natural right provides the context for the increasing focus on the idea of freedom in the literary discourse of the second half of the century.[10]

There was continuity in some of the standard images of freedom, including, for example, Switzerland, which is found in authors as various as Haller, Salomon Gessner (1730–88), Lessing (*Samuel Henzi*, 1753), Schubart, Johann Peter Hebel (1760–1826), Goethe, and, of course, Schiller (*Wilhelm Tell*, 1804); but it is possible to discern relatively distinct phases in the use of the idea of freedom during the century. In the literary culture of the generation before the Sturm und Drang the idea of freedom frequently appears in the Christian sense as a quality of the divine: "where the Spirit of the Lord is, there is liberty" (2 Cor. 3: 17). In the semisecularized eighteenth century this notion takes the form of a contrast between an inner spiritual realm in which one can be free and an outer material realm in which one is unfree, and this contrast was used to buttress the attack on the values of the court by contrasting its superficiality and artificiality with the richness, authenticity, and moral probity of a middle-class sensibility. Gellert, for example, in his description of John the Baptist in prison ("Herodes und Herodias," 1748), suggests that virtue ensures an inner freedom preferable to the dependency of the court: "ein Tugendfreund liegt lieber frey an Ketten, / Als sklavisch um der Fürsten Thron."[11] The contrast between a free inner self and outer restrictive reality is characteristic of the sentimental currents within the Enlightenment and fed into the Sturm und Drang — for example, in the portrait of Gretchen. F. H. Jacobi refers in a letter to Goethe to a repressive childhood by describing it in terms of fetters, contrasted with the freedom he has now found, but he avoids both the abstract moralism of Gellert and the rhetorical gesture of finding an elegant formulation for a self-evident truth.[12] At the same time, the idea of freedom also appears in those authors who saw enlightenment itself as a process by which humankind gained freedom by using reason and discussion to dispel superstition and ignorance. The classic definition of enlightenment in this sense, Kant's essay "Beantwortung der Frage: Was ist Aufklärung?" (Reply to the Question: What is Enlightenment?) of 1784, uses the image of shackles to refer to the ingrained habits that prevent enlightenment, talks about the "Fußschellen einer immerwährenden Unmündigkeit" (shackles of enduring immaturity) and the "Joch der Unmündigkeit" (yoke of immaturity), and seeks a way of releasing what Kant calls the "Geist der Freiheit" (spirit of freedom).[13] Here, too, despite the distance from Gellert, a distinction is being made between an inner world of freedom and an outer world of unfreedom. The freedom with which Kant is concerned is what we would today call the freedom of the private citizen to express and discuss ideas, which he contrasts with the individual's duty to obey when carrying out a representative function.[14]

Nevertheless, although it is an important category, the literature of the generation before Goethe could not be said to be defined by its use of the idea of freedom. The final scenes of Lessing's *Emilia Galotti*, although they clearly contain an indictment of the Prince and his world, show more concern for justice and morality than for freedom. The house arrest of Emilia is important because of the future with which she is threatened rather than because it represents a loss of freedom in any abso-lute sense. It was only for the next generation of writers, born around 1750, that the idea of freedom and the word *Freiheit* acquired the inten-sity of a category that they felt defined their identity in some sense.

The specific features of this usage will become clearer if we first look beyond the Sturm und Drang and observe the way it developed in the 1790s in the wake of the French Revolution, when it became an ideo-logical weapon in the struggle around the values of the revolution. In the political poetry of Goethe and Schiller, or in the notes of Lichtenberg, the use of the word *Freiheit* is enough to refer the reader to debates surrounding the social and political upheaval in France. The central argument against the French revolutionary ideal of liberty, that revolu-tion merely released barbarism, was conducted in Germany by the use of two other meanings of the term. First, freedom also means license, or the abandonment of the self-control that, conservative opponents of the French Revolution felt, gives our lives order and meaning. It was thus possible to suggest that the idea of freedom leads to, or is a mask for, disorder and its correlate, despotism. On the other hand, beside this strongly negative usage, Goethe and Schiller both make use of the idea of freedom in a positive sense to refer to the free will that makes us — or in the future will make us — truly human by giving us access to a moral dimension denied to the natural world. In this sense, too, *Freiheit* is a slogan because it is being used to refer to an established discourse: the terminology of Kant's ethics. Thus, the two negatively labeled usages, the *"liberté"* of the French Revolution and license or lack of self-control, are countered by the idea that there is a true, Kantian kind of freedom that negates the French Revolution and everything for which it stands. Kant's idea of freedom is, indeed, based on the notion of resisting en-slavement by the passions, which belong to the realm of necessity, and it seems likely that one of the reasons Kantianism suddenly seemed so relevant in the 1790s was that it offered a way of reinterpreting this slogan of the French Revolution as the key to a more quietist philosophy. It did so, moreover, by means of an argument that at the same time could, in a further twist, be used to criticize the licentiousness of the ancien régime, whose corruption could be seen as a cause of the French Revolution. This politicization of the idea of freedom at the end of the century meant in some cases the amendment of Sturm und Drang texts:[15] one task for scholars of the Sturm und Drang is to reconstruct the origi-nal texts, but the more difficult task lies in reconstructing the connota-tions the idea of freedom had when the texts were first written.

Our brief historical overview suggests that there were three stages in the evolution of the idea of freedom in the eighteenth century. The transition from the first to the second is marked by the passage of one generation to the next, whereas the third stage was initiated by events in France in the early 1790s and applies to writers of all ages. The second stage, the Sturm und Drang, is the stage when the idea of freedom acquired a new rhetorical force but still lacked political specificity. One notable qualification needs to be made, however, concerning the work of Klopstock, who was born in 1724. He and his disciples in the Göttinger Hainbund (contemporaries of the Sturm und Drang) cultivated an aggressively antityrannical stance that revolved around the idea of German national liberation.[16] The opening of "Die Freiheit" (Freedom) by Friedrich Stolberg is typical:

> Freiheit! Der Höfling kennt den Gedanken nicht,
> Sklave! Die Kette rasselt ihm Silberton!
> Gebeugt das Knie, gebeugt die Seele,
> Reicht er dem Joch den feigen Nacken.[17]

The idea of freedom does here have the strong rhetorical force that is also found in the Sturm und Drang, and it is associated with gestures of protest against a frenchified courtly absolutism, but it remains abstract.[18] Personal and stylistic overlaps existed between this group and the Sturm und Drang, but the Sturm und Drang is characterized by its much more complex uses of images of restraint and liberation. No doubt some of the political pathos that the Göttinger Hainbund found in the word freedom is there, too, for the writers of the Sturm und Drang, but the latter are more interested in pursuing the social and philosophical connotations of the idea and unraveling the contradictions inherent in it. The word *Freiheit* appears most frequently in the Sturm und Drang as a linguistic gesture used by characters who want to paper over their failure to come to terms with the real world around them: imprisonment, whether literal or metaphorical, is something from which the heroes of the Sturm und Drang notably fail to escape.

One of the characteristics of the Sturm und Drang is the mixture of explosive enthusiasm and doubt. Herder rejected simplistic ideas of moral freedom and argued that the first step toward freedom was the recognition of the extent to which we are unfree:

Da ists wahrlich der erste Keim zur Freiheit, fühlen, daß man *nicht* frei sein, und an *welchen* Banden man hafte? Die stärksten freisten Menschen fühlen dies am tiefsten, und streben weiter; wahnsinnge, zum Kerker gebohrne Sklaven, höhnen sie, und bleiben voll hohen Traums im Schlamme liegen. (*H-SW*, 8: 202)[19]

This formulation also contrasts the possibility (and the necessity) of being clear about the limitations to freedom with ideas of freedom themselves, which are deceptively generalized and unrealistic. Goethe also gave — retrospective — expression to the precariousness of the idea of freedom in his account of how he and his friends responded to reading Helvétius: "Die Hoffnung . . . uns von den äußeren Dingen, ja von uns selbst immer unabhängiger zu machen, konnten wir nicht aufgeben. Das Wort Freiheit klingt so schön, daß man es nicht entbehren könnte, und wenn es einen Irrtum bezeichnete" (*G-SW*, 16: 523).[20] The problematic nature of the idea of freedom does not, however, detract from the intensity with which its absence was deplored: it is the energy and frustration of incoherent protest that fueled the Sturm und Drang. In part, this intensity may be ascribed to the political weakness of the middle classes, in particular the intelligentsia, in eighteenth-century Germany. In part, though, it reflects a deeper appreciation of the meaning of freedom: the discovery of the potential of a social class or of a nation is meaningless if separated from the emancipation of the individual in all the dimensions of existence. For this reason the Sturm und Drang has been described as a phase of the Enlightenment that focused on the anthropology of liberation.[21]

The idea of freedom is, therefore, an important motif in the writing of the Sturm und Drang, but it is only one element in a constellation of concepts revolving around the idea of self-fulfillment or self-realization. The idea of freedom is for the Sturm und Drang inseparable from the idea of overcoming alienation, alienation from society and alienation from oneself: true independence and wholeness of being are prerequisites of freedom, but sympathy for one's fellow human being, the basis of human sociability, and love, its highest realization, are also often realms in which the individual can catch a glimpse of that freedom that cannot yet become universal reality. Werther at first sees freedom as the antithesis of the world of work:

Es ist ein einförmig Ding ums Menschengeschlecht. Die meisten verarbeiten den größten Teil der Zeit, um zu leben, und das Bißgen, das ihnen von Freiheit übrig bleibt, ängstigt sie so, daß sie alle Mittel aufsuchen, ums los zu werden. (*G-MA*, 1.2: 201)[22]

This attitude soon develops, however, to the point where Werther identifies freedom with death (*G-MA*, 1.2: 204 and 256):[23] work, engagement in economic life, has come to stand for life itself, which is the antithesis of freedom.

The Idea of Freedom in the Sturm und Drang

When Werther sees freedom as release from work, he seems to be thinking with some specificity of modern forms of work, such as his own work at court at the beginning of part 2 of the novel. By contrast with this, he delights in eating vegetables he has grown himself, thinking happily of the work that has gone into them (*G-MA*, 1.2: 217–18). This is clearly unalienated labor, and it is significant that it makes Werther imagine himself into Homeric times. It is modern, alienated forms of work that have produced the division between work time and free time.

If freedom is the antithesis of modern forms of work, it is paradoxical but also symptomatic that at this time, particularly in England and Scotland, forms of work were evolving that in many ways depended on freedom: the freedom of the individual to buy or sell labor power on the market. In 1776, two years after the appearance of *Werther, An Inquiry into the Nature and Causes of the Wealth of Nations* by Adam Smith (1723–90) provided an account of the evolving economic structures. In feudal society the peasant was bound to the land and to a network of obligations that linked him with his lord, but increasingly the nexus of society was formed by exchange. This change was a transition to a social formation marked by the expansion of economic freedom through a free market in which capital and labor power meet. Although their interest in specifically economic matters was limited, the writers of the Sturm und Drang detected the signs of the social formation that Smith was learning to describe but responded differently to it. They took up and questioned the idea of the individual as an economic agent, an isolated individual in competition with other economic agents, free of a network of obligations and reduced to naked labor power. In some ways they accepted the freedoms associated with the rejection of the older courtly culture — for example, in Werther's frustration with aristocratic etiquette; but in others they saw true freedom as belonging to a more primitive world of wholeness that was being eroded by modernity.

These complexities can best be examined in individual texts, but before going on to analyze in greater detail the rhetoric of freedom in some representative works it will be helpful to consider briefly three authors who in their different ways stand at the threshold to the Sturm und Drang. The first, Jean-Jacques Rousseau, placed at the head of his *Du contrat social* (The Social Contract, 1762) the challenging assertion: "L'homme est né libre, et par-tout il est dans les fers."[24] For Rousseau the idea of freedom has a new pathos. It is linked to nature and declared to be inalienable (4: 586–87). There is, therefore, a moral imperative attached to freedom, which Rousseau conceives both humanity in general and the individual in particular to have had in an original state of nature but now to have lost. The relevance of Rousseau to the Sturm und Drang lies less in his proposal of ways in which it might be possible, through education and political reform, to restore the benefits of the state of nature than in his analysis of the interrelationship of the various dimensions of inauthenticity that characterize modern life, as particularly evident in his two Discourses and in book 2 of *Emile* (1762). For Rousseau the essential characteristic of the lack of freedom is dependence on other people. Two important points follow. First, the master is as dependent on the slave as the slave is on the master: both are unfree, and liberation is not the release of one individual from oppression but the elimination of social relationships that are distorted by inequalities of power. Second, Rousseau insists that present-day society is unfree not only because it exists as a network of mutual dependencies but also because the individual is dependent on the mass of people as society, that is, on the prejudices, the ideology that govern society.

What Herder derived from Rousseau was this notion that the idea of freedom together with the idea of nature could play a central role in an overall critique of the modern world. In his essay on Ossian and folk poetry he looks both backward and forward by presenting as an ideal the culture of more primitive peoples for whom the whole of social and economic life and the expression they gave to it remained an organic whole. He describes this state in many ways, but the idea of freedom is always part of it. For example, he enthusiastically writes about the way that the songs of a people — that is, its earliest forms of literature — will be more natural, the more natural their way of life is: "je wilder, d.i. je lebendiger, je freiwürkender ein Volk ist, (denn mehr heißt dies Wort doch nicht!) desto wilder, d.i. desto lebendiger, freier, sinnlicher, lyrisch handelnder müssen auch . . . seine Lieder seyn!" (*H-SW*, 5: 164).[25] He means that the life and, consequently, the forms of expression of such "natural" cultures are governed by inner necessity and not constricted by externally imposed norms, even internalized ones. Their forms of self-expression — most notably, their language — are free and direct, the antithesis of feeble, artificial language in which we talk about freedom and virtue at the same time as living in chains in a state of dependence and moral corruption (*H-SW*, 5: 538).

Whereas many of Herder's writings revolve, at least implicitly, around the idea of freedom by conceiving it as an essential condition of the organic, natural way of life the modern world had forsaken, Heinrich Wilhelm von Gerstenberg's *Ugolino*, which in all its contradictoriness remains one of the defining texts on the threshold to the Sturm und Drang, does so by focusing almost obsessively on the absence of freedom, so that the play is little more than an extended portrait of the imprisonment and gradual starvation of Ugolino and his three sons. All thought of escape is illusory. Although the oldest son makes a daring attempt, he soon reappears in a coffin, having been caught and poisoned, with now only a few minutes to live. Ugolino's letter to his wife, another gesture of reaching beyond the confines of the tower, is intercepted by his enemies and drenched in poison, so that his wife, too, is killed and brought on stage in a coffin. And even the human spirit is seen to be incapable of transcending imprisonment: Gerstenberg shows how hunger drives Ugolino to close his eyes to what is really happening, and at the end he kills his second son under the illusion that he is killing Ruggieri, the rival who has condemned them all to die.

There is no dramatic conflict in the traditional sense of the term, because Ruggieri is a shadowy figure who remains offstage, outside the tower; nor is there tragic guilt. It would be possible to read the play literally as simply a portrait of the psychological consequences of imprisonment and starvation, but Gerstenberg uses the situation as a metaphor to suggest a whole range of ways in which our lives are constricted. The patriarchal nuclear family, far from being the source of order, nurture, and love, is shown in a state of collapse as the antithesis of these values. The authority of the father is damaged, the relationship between the brothers is threatened by jealousy, and Gerstenberg sets up the most grotesque perversion of family relations when Anselmo tries to take a bite from the breast of his dead mother as she lies poisoned in her coffin, after which he is killed by his father. The family is a place of violence and noncommunication. The isolation of the characters is marked by monologues in which they talk to themselves and by moments of hallucination in which they fail to recognize each other. There is none of the integral private realm Gellert had blithely posited. The claustrophobic prison in which they are trapped can be taken to represent the family, individuality, or human existence, and should probably be taken to represent all three. Imprisonment represents for Gerstenberg lack of freedom in all its manifestations, including our inability to conceptualize the means by which we might become free.

Gerstenberg's reflections on freedom are distinguished from those of Klopstock or Friedrich Stolberg by being more concrete and more complex, and his idea of freedom is more problematic. Nature and freedom as they exist outside the tower and, supposedly, at the heart of the family, seem impossibly remote. So, too, does the language of authentic experience. The characters speak in a way that is often more reminiscent of earlier literary styles in which Gerstenberg had also worked, the rococo and the sentimental: here it is as artificial and unrealistic as the ideals it encodes. Thus, for example, Ugolino uses the language of sentiment to address his sons, "Euch in dieser reizenden Vertraulichkeit beisammen sehn ist Erquickung zum Leben!" (*G-U*, 51),[26] unaware that just before he arrived two of them were at each other's throats and the third was denying his father's existence.

Goethe

Goethe's *Götz von Berlichingen*[27] also ends with the hero dying in prison; and the emphasis of this play, too, is on the idea of freedom, given particular intensity and emphasis by Götz's dying words, "Himmlische Luft. — — Freiheit! Freiheit!" (*G-MA*, 1.1: 653).[28] Here, too, a certain lack of clarity about the causality leading to the hero's death creates the impression of a necessary decline. This lack of clarity is produced by the fragmentation of the plot, so that Marie's success in persuading Weislingen to revoke the death sentence does not prevent Götz's death, and by several formulations, especially toward the end of the play. When speaking to his wife, Elisabeth, in prison he lists the elements of his identity that have been denied him:

> Suchtest du den Götz? Der ist lang hin. Sie haben mich nach und nach verstümmelt, meine Hand, meine Freiheit, Güter und guten Namen. Mein Kopf was ist an dem? . . . Und jetzt ist's nicht Weislingen allein, nicht die Bauern allein, nicht der Tod des Kaisers und meine Wunden. — Es ist alles zusammen. Meine Stunde ist kommen. (*G-MA*, 1.1: 651)[29]

This is partly psychological, for it has been clear at least since the middle of the play that Götz is losing his confidence, and even his first speech is a complaint about the exhaustion that the maintenance of his freedom costs him. He feels increasingly that he does not belong in the world, that he is no longer himself. But the impression created by these despairing lists is more than psychological: it is that there is no longer a place in the world for Götz or for the values he represents,[30] and it is reinforced by the image of the Emperor — and the Empire — losing power, sickening, and dying.

Götz represents a way of life that is being eroded by a new world. This correspondence allows Goethe to explore a wide range of values by associating them to the old and the natural (Götz) or to the new and the artificial (the court of the Bishop of Bamberg and Adelheid). Götz is a free knight who owes allegiance only to the Emperor, not to the territorial princes; he defends a system of justice that depends on local traditions and is thus closer to nature and to the individual; but the most central of his values is freedom. Just before his arrest Götz joins Georg (who represents a hope for the future and has a practical, creative side to him that Götz lacks) to drink a toast to freedom:

> GÖTZ: Was soll unser letztes Wort seyn?
>
> GEORG: Es lebe die Freiheit!
>
> GÖTZ: Es lebe die Freiheit!
>
> ALLE: Es lebe die Freiheit!
>
> GÖTZ: Und wenn die uns überlebt können wir ruhig sterben.
>   Denn wir sehen im Geist unsere Enkel glücklich, und
>   die Kaiser unsrer Enkel glücklich. (*G-MA*, 1.1: 618)[31]

The idea of freedom is central to the kind of society from which Götz comes and for which he stands. What he means in practice becomes clearer when he goes on to conjure up one of the backward utopias in the play, moments when Götz retells stories from the past that give us a glimpse of a better world that is now lost. He recalls the festivities that used to be organized by the Landgrave of Hanau, in which there was harmony among powerful neighbors and harmony among the ranks of a hierarchically ordered society, a kind of extended family in which the individual is part of an organic network and is, therefore, in this sense free, despite inequalities. This political vision is often attributed to Justus Möser (1720–94), an administrator and writer in Osnabrück who was not a member of the Sturm und Drang circle but was admired by Goethe and emphasized the importance of local traditions. The title of one of his essays is symptomatic: "Der jetzige Hang zu allgemeinen Gesetzen und Verordnungen ist der gemeinen Freiheit gefährlich."[32]

Götz von Berlichingen shares with *Ugolino* the use of the idea of freedom as a central, controlling metaphor, but it explores a much broader range of meanings associated with that idea. Its root meaning derives

from the technical designation of Götz's status as a free knight who owes
his allegiance directly to the Emperor rather than to a territorial prince.
Götz's appeal to freedom as he dies is framed by two contrasting usages
of the term, which in effect color Götz's own usage. There is the response of those around him, to which we shall return, but earlier in his
final speech he predicts that his death will usher in an age of moral collapse: "Es kommen die Zeiten des Betrugs, es ist ihm Freiheit gegeben"
(*G-MA*, 1.1: 652–53).[33] Here the word *Freiheit* is used to denote the
license to act according to one's self-interest, irrespective of any higher
goals and irrespective of the needs of one's fellow human beings. This
kind of freedom is demonstrated, above all, by Götz's opponent, Adelheid, who is the sinister power behind the court of the Bishop of Bamberg and acknowledges no limits on her power to manipulate people:
everything is legitimate if it serves her self-interest. She encourages Franz
to think that they will both be free once he has murdered Weislingen for
her. She represents the perverted world of manipulation and deception
that is overtaking the world of Götz.

Götz and Adelheid never meet during the course of the play, and
Goethe organizes the conflict between them as a conflict between the
sets of values that they represent rather than a the dramatic encounter of
individuals. He uses the figure of Weislingen, torn between Götz and
Adelheid, to articulate the relationship between these two worlds. When
Weislingen is briefly reunited with Götz, he makes it clear how he had
deserted Götz in order to find freedom but now discovers that real freedom is only possible in the realm of Götz. The formulation in the first
version of the play is more explicit in its emphasis on the idea of freedom
and its antithesis, dependence:

O warum bin ich nicht so frei wie du! Gottfr[ied] Gottfr[ied]! vor dir
fühl ich meine Nichtigkeit ganz. Abzuhängen! Ein verdammtes Wort,
und doch scheint es als wenn ich dazu bestimmt wäre. Ich entfernte
mich von Gottfrieden um frei zu sein; und jetzt fühl ich erst wie sehr
ich von denen kleinen Menschen abhange die ich zu regieren schien.
Ich will Bamberg nicht mehr sehn. Ich will mit allen brechen, und frei
sein. Gottfr[ied] Gottfr[ied] du allein bist frei dessen große Seele sich
selbst genug ist und weder zu gehorchen noch zu herrschen braucht
um etwas zu sein. (*G-MA*, 1.1: 126).[34]

The subtlety of the portrait of Weislingen lies in the deep-rooted affection he feels for Götz and Götz's values and the way that the denial of
this affection leads to an aggressively desperate attempt to free himself
from Götz. Until he is visited by Marie and begins to understand the
truth of Adelheid, Weislingen thinks that the death of Götz will guaran-

tee his own freedom: "So verlischt er vor dem Andenken der Menschen, und du kannst freier atmen töriges Herz" (*G-MA*, 1.1: 642).[35] The consistency behind Weislingen's vacillation lies in his search for freedom.

There is also ambivalence in the figure of Götz. In his frustration with attempts to limit his freedom Götz allows himself to side with the rebellious peasants and thereby break the allegiance to the Emperor on which he had based his political position. He thus, however reluctantly, becomes party to their violence. Götz's iron hand is an image for the fact that he has become rigid and lost touch with the world since losing Weislingen to the Bishop and Adelheid. His failure — or refusal — to adapt is both his strength and his weakness, the reason why we admire him but also the reason why he must inevitably fail. The kind of freedom that Götz envisages is no longer compatible with the world as it is. His loss of freedom is, in a sense, the death of the true Götz; but his death also means that his search for freedom goes beyond the world in which he finds himself.

The search for freedom takes us beyond sixteenth-century Germany to Goethe's present, as is suggested by Lerse's reference in the last line of the play to the importance of Götz as a model for future generations who, it is implied, will need to struggle to recover their freedom. Or, perhaps, it will even take us beyond this our material existence. The play deals with the tragedy of historical change, and to this extent the idea of freedom is a social and political one. At the same time, Elisabeth responds to her husband's dying appeal to "Freiheit" with the words, "Nur droben droben bey dir. Die Welt ist ein Gefängnis" (*G-MA*, 1.1: 653).[36] On the face of it, this formulation is reminiscent of Gellert's interiorized understanding of freedom and, appropriately, makes use of the Christian idea that we only achieve freedom through harmony with the divine. Similarly, Elisabeth had earlier countered Götz's frustration at the imprisonment of his men with the words, "Laß sie gefangen sein, sie sind frei!" (*G-MA*, 1.1: 621).[37] But, as her discussion of Carl's education with Maria shows, the emphasis in Goethe's portrayal of Elisabeth is not on her piety, and the effect of these images is not to reduce the idea of freedom to that of orthodox Christianity but rather to universalize the tension the play has demonstrated between the ideal of freedom and the actuality of the world in which she and Götz have lived. Her words echo *Hamlet* as much as they echo the Bible. When Hamlet gives expression to his claustrophobic angst with the remark, "Denmark's a prison," Rosencrantz replies, "Then is the world one" (II, 2). Rosencrantz is here showing the absurd conclusion to which Hamlet's self-indulgent gloom leads, but, of course, the audience — and Hamlet — are aware that the words have a serious import: that things are absurd and that existence precludes freedom. And this meaning survives at the end of *Götz von Berlichingen*. The protest of the Sturm und Drang against restrictions of all kinds seems in Elisabeth's words to have become a metaphysical protest against the nature of existence.

Egmont is in its conception a Sturm und Drang play, and it is helpful in clarifying the idea of freedom that can be derived from *Götz von Berlichingen*, even if the explicitness with which the motif is treated may owe something to Goethe's later work on the play, which he did not complete until 1787. Again, the play revolves around the conflict between an individual dedicated to the defense of traditional rights, in this case the defense of local traditions in the Spanish Netherlands, and the cynical imposition of centralized power. It ends with Egmont going to his execution inspired by a vision in which he has seen himself crowned by his beloved Klärchen, who appears as the embodiment of freedom, announcing that his death will guarantee the liberation of the Netherlands. Like Götz, Egmont dies declaring the centrality of his faith in freedom: "ich sterbe für die Freiheit, für die ich lebte und focht und der ich mich jetzt leidend opfre."[38] But Egmont's tone at the end is more defiant than that of Götz, and the fact that the play ends with a Victory Symphony underscores the fact that the political meanings of the term are more to the forefront.

Nevertheless, critics have frequently pointed out that Egmont is shown to lack many of the qualities that are necessary for successful political leadership. His interview with his secretary and his ensuing discussion with Oranien show that he is warm-hearted and generous but also that he is impulsive and incapable of the longer-term planning that might produce real results. He is truly himself in the midst of battle or in the arms of Klärchen, but in the world of politics he is out of his depth. He misjudges people, he puts misplaced trust in King Philipp and the Order of the Golden Fleece, he even misjudges Klärchen to the point of entrusting her to Ferdinand just after the audience has seen how circumstances have driven her to suicide. If Egmont dies for freedom, it is because he embodies a system of values, a philosophy of life, that is the antithesis of those of the deathly, calculating Alba. He is a charismatic hero with a vision and a zest for life that goes beyond that of any other character on stage, except, perhaps, Klärchen; he is at ease among the common people but feels out of place at the court of Margarete. From the point of view of those who plan their lives, of course — Alba, Oranien, Graf Oliva, and Klärchen's mother — Egmont displays a devotion to the moment that can be criticized as short-sighted and impractical, but only as long as effectiveness remains the only criterion. *Egmont* is an experiment with a philosophy of life, one that is shown to be lacking in certain situations and unable to meet certain of the demands placed on it. There is an element of self-indulgence in Egmont's disregard for reality; but on the other hand, he demonstrates a warmth and intensity of living that we cannot help admiring, and it is the realization of these qualities that he is invoking when committing himself to the idea of freedom. In the words of H. G. Haile: "What the young Goethe calls *Freyheit,* a quality which suffuses the figure of Egmont, might best be called the tendency of a genius — or of a nation — to remain true to character."[39] At the same time, the play questions the value of this quality, and at its intellectual climax Alba, the sinister embodiment of rationalist control, challenges the notion of freedom on which Egmont has based his life: "Freiheit! Ein schönes Wort wers recht verstünde" (*G-MA,* 3.1: 305).[40] It is likely that this part of the play was written after Goethe's experience of practical politics in Weimar had given him the distance that allowed him to conceive of a figure questioning the content of the idea of freedom in such explicit terms. But even here, in *Egmont,* which appeared in the year before the French Revolution, the question is an expression of Alba's cynicism rather than the prelude to a definition of what freedom positively is. Alba knows that Egmont's instinctive spontaneity and closeness to the people is something that cannot be defined in words.

Lenz

Goethe's contemporaries were quick to see the essence of *Götz von Berlichingen* as the idea of freedom. Bürger's enthusiastic response was true to the spirit of Rousseau: "Frei! Frei! Keinem untertan als der Natur!"[41] Lenz's essay "Über *Götz von Berlichingen*" (On *Götz von Berlichingen,* written 1773–75, published 1901), also revolves around the idea of freedom in the play and makes it the basis of a set of philosophical and aesthetic principles. Lenz argues that the example of Götz reminds us of the freedom to which we all, as human beings, have access. The essay begins with an overwhelming account of humanity as unfree. Lenz describes socialization by parents and teachers and even falling in love as a mechanical process in which the subject is molded by impressions received from outside. He goes on to talk about the adult filling a role in society in the same way that a cogwheel fulfills a preordained function in a machine until it is worn out and replaced. This is an extraordinarily coherent expression of a modern, scientific account of mankind. Its central feature is the vision of the individual as passive, as purely dependent on social and biological forces, as unfree. According to Lenz, however, it is a vision of the life of people who fail to assert their freedom, and the ideologues of such people, the philosophers of the French materialist tradition, such as Helvétius. We all have within us, he argues, the potential for freedom; we just need to learn to assert our will through action, and by doing so we shall be asserting the fact that we are also essentially members of the kingdom of God. The significance of Götz to Lenz is that he is a character who asserts his freedom in precisely this way. By contrast with Weislingen, Götz retains his independence and is thus a model for each one of us.

Lenz's understanding of the idea of freedom is colored, on the one hand, by the Christian doctrines he had learned as a child and, on the other, by ideas that are reminiscent of those of Kant and may go back to lectures of Kant that he heard as a student in Königsberg, but he goes beyond both. The human being is for Lenz a hermaphrodite (*L-WB*, 2: 502) who belongs to a realm of contingency and dependence but at the same time belongs to a world of freedom. In his *Anmerkungen übers Theater* he outlines how it might be possible to form a "bridge" (*L-WB*, 2: 645 and 647) between the two. Thus, he argues that the artist imitates the freedom of God in creating the world inhabited by the work of art. Particularly relevant to his own writing is his argument that Aristotelian tragedy belongs essentially to a pre-Christian culture that because of its belief in fate did not know freedom and whose dramatic production is, therefore, incapable of responding to the individuality of human beings. The problem arises for Lenz when this model of dramatic form is transported into the modern, Christian world, as in the French neoclassical imitators of the Aristotelian tradition, where tragedy then effectively denies modern notions of spirituality.

Lenz's reflections on the philosophical implications of tragedy lead him to the distinction he makes between his own comedies, such as *Der Hofmeister* and *Die Soldaten,* and tragedies such as *Götz von Berlichingen.* Tragedy, as Lenz envisages it, celebrates the freedom of the individual. Comedy, on the other hand, portrays as ridiculous the person who fails to assert his freedom. Thus, the kind of fatalistic passivity characteristic of the classical and neoclassical tragedy is in the modern world only suitable for a comedy.[42] The consequence of Lenz's theory is that a comedy is led by the action, since the characters do not demonstrate the freedom to initiate action, whereas in tragedy the plot is led by character.

In *Die Soldaten,* for example, Lenz shows with extraordinary finesse the combination of social pressures that impel the characters to behave as they do. We are shown the mechanisms by which the soldiers themselves develop an aggressively masculine corporate identity that requires them to prove themselves by seducing middle-class girls, while Marie, the middle-class girl, is induced to aspire to higher social status, which she thinks she can achieve through her attractiveness. What is particularly telling is the way that Lenz traces the pattern of social pressures back through the minor characters to the family of Marie and to the soldiers surrounding her seducer, Desportes. Even the characters with good intentions and greater insight, the chaplain Eisenhardt and the Gräfin La Roche, allow their behavior to be determined by a social identity that, we infer, is no less based on self-interest than the crude egoism of Desportes and his fellow officers. Lenz exposes the social dynamic of human behavior as precisely as any naturalist; but he was aware that this was not an absolute necessity, that he was portraying a grotesque, fallen world that none of the characters had the ability of a Götz to rise above. The play ends with a scene in which it is suggested that the creation of state brothels would put the world to rights; but, despite Lenz's own interest in such reforms, it is unclear whether this plan should be understood as anything more than a picture of the absurd kind of response to be expected from those in authority, who are themselves locked into a world of unfreedom.

Lenz was aware that a play built on these kinds of assumptions was not a comedy in any conventional sense: he apologized for using what must appear an eccentric term (*L-WB*, 3: 395), but it reminds us (and the actors) that the point of the play is the absurdity of the way in which the characters acquiesce in the social pressures placed on them and thereby deny their own freedom. The play is, thus, centrally concerned with the idea of freedom, even though it remains implicit. The same principle applies to *Der Hofmeister,* but here we have the added complication of a scene (II, 1) in which one of the characters launches a defense of freedom:

> Ohne Freiheit geht das Leben bergab rückwärts, Freiheit ist das Element des Menschen wie das Wasser des Fisches, und ein Mensch der sich der Freiheit begibt, vergiftet die edelsten Geister seines Bluts, erstickt seine süßesten Freuden des Lebens in der Blüte und ermordet sich selbst. (*L-WB*, 1: 55)[43]

The irony of these words lies, as their rather hectoring tone suggests, in the fact that their speaker lacks, and fails to understand, the very freedom he is advocating. In this scene the Privy Councilor is trying to persuade Läuffer's father of the evils of private tutoring. In many ways he is right to do so, and his argument about the dehumanizing dependency to which a private tutor is subjected is convincing, but the Privy Councilor refuses to acknowledge the economic pressures that force Läuffer into this position. He understands the folly and the vanity of his brother, who hires Läuffer, but his insights into the necessity of freedom, like those of Eisenhardt and the Gräfin La Roche in *Die Soldaten,* are no guarantee of freedom.

Schiller

The idea of freedom plays an important part in Schiller's early writing and will help to define the way that writing belongs on the periphery of the Sturm und Drang. Freedom does not have the same theoretical position or the same explicitness as in his later writing, when he was responding to Kant and to the French Revolution and developed a notion of freedom as the essential link between the role of art and the ideal state of human existence. It remains, however, a fundamental gesture reflected in various ways in all his writing. *Die Räuber* concerns two brothers who, in different but equally misguided ways, attempt to assert their freedom and become in different ways alienated from their father, who, although enfeebled, represents the natural stability of the patriarchal order. Franz represents the abuses latent in determinists, whom Schiller, like Lenz, denounced as "entartete Sklaven, die unter dem Klang ihrer Ketten die Freiheit verschreien" (*S-NA,* 20: 121–22).[44] But if Franz represents the denial of freedom, then Karl represents the abuse of freedom, which is, in the end, closely related to it. As the choice of title indicates, it is Karl and his decision to join a band of robbers that bear the weight of the play's moral reflections. The play belongs to the tradition following *Götz von Berlichingen* that responded to public fascination with groups of people on the edge of society, ranging from vagabonds through secret societies to bands of robbers. These groups reflect, as does the robber band in *Die Räuber,* an urban middle-class longing to escape, an alternative to the repressive order of the state — even more so when they are seen to live in nature, away from the artificiality of an alienated existence in the town. As Crugantino, the vagabond hero of one of these texts, Goethe's *Claudine von Villa Bella,* tells Sebastian, civil society ("Eure bürgerliche Gesellschafft") makes both work and play acts of dependency, and for that reason he cannot, as a true individual, be part of it (*G-MA,* 1.2: 119).

One of the characteristics of the young Schiller is the particularly intense way in which he takes this motif and uses it in several discourses.[45]

The patriarchal family was often used in the eighteenth century as an analogy to the state, legitimating absolutist power with sentimental images of community and natural, benevolent authority. In *Die Räuber* Schiller links these ideas through the fact that Karl's decision to join the robbers is a response to his supposed rejection by his father and the fact that his father has political and judicial authority. It is characteristic of Schiller that, when Karl asserts the rights of the free individual against state, society, and family, he transcends each of these institutions by referring to the law, which suggests not only the particular laws of the state but also the idea of a stable society governed by law in general, and even moral law. In one of his first outbursts, before his estrangement from his father, Karl exalts this idea of freedom: "Das Gesez hat noch keinen grossen Mann gebildet, aber die Freyheit brütet Kolosse und Extremitäten aus" (*S-NA*, 3: 21).[46] He associates freedom with the flight of the eagle, with greatness and individuality, and contrasts it with images of constriction (palisades, once more) and servility, which are given a political twist when Karl uses coarse, uncourtly language to introduce anticourtly suggestions of nationalism and republicanism; but there is an element of posturing to all of this. A "second, improved" edition of *Die Räuber* has on its title page a vignette of a lion and the inscription "in Tirannos" (against tyrants).[47] This change shows that it was possible to understand *Die Räuber* as belonging to the tradition of antityrannical writing; but this title page was not authorized by Schiller, and the portrayal of Karl is more complex than such a slogan would suggest. Karl's outburst when we first see him is full of rhetoric. It is an expression of frustration rather than a statement of opposition, and we discover shortly afterward that, having written to ask his father for forgiveness, he is about to return home to Amalia.

When Karl receives the letter that, through Franz's deception, makes him believe that he has been rejected by his father, he adds the family home to his list of images of constriction (a cage), and allows his enthusiasm for freedom to brush aside all moral considerations:

> was für ein Thor ich war, daß ich ins Keficht zurükwollte! — Mein Geist dürstet nach Thaten, mein Athem nach Freyheit, — *Mörder, Räuber!* — mit diesem Wort war das Gesez unter meine Füsse gerollt — Menschen haben Menschheit vor mir verborgen, da ich an Menschheit appellirte, weg dann von mir Sympathie und menschliche Schonung! — Ich habe keinen Vater mehr, ich habe keine Liebe mehr, und Blut und Tod soll mich vergessen lehren, daß mir jemals etwas theuer war! (*S-NA*, 3: 32)[48]

Sympathy (pity, compassion) was for Rousseau, as it was for many writers of this time, the fundamental principle of natural human solidarity, and Schiller's formulation here shows how Karl's search for freedom has led him away from it and from the kind of freedom Rousseau envisaged.

As the play goes on to demonstrate, the robber band is marked by moral ambiguity. Both as a social structure and as a moral subject it is a highly problematic realization of Karl's ideal of a republic. On the one hand, Karl distances himself from the brutality in which some of the robbers indulge and responds to an ideal of sociability and solidarity when the band refuses to hand him over to the authorities: "Izt sind wir frey" (S-NA, 3: 73).[49] This positive representation of the life of the robber is extended by Kosinsky, who seeks in it the means of enforcing justice: "Männer such ich . . . die Freyheit höher schäzen als Ehre und Leben, deren blosser Name, willkommen dem Armen und Unterdrükten, die Beherztesten feig und Tyrannen bleich macht" (S-NA, 3: 81).[50] The reality, however, is different, and Karl is responsible, whether he likes it or not, for the suffering of the innocent caused by the less scrupulous in his band, such as his partial "reflection," Spiegelberg.[51] Karl is motivated by despair, that is to say, the disappointment of his belief in a moral universe.

Schiller has organized his play so that both sides of Karl, the moral and the immoral, the sociable and the antisocial, are inseparable from each other: Karl's pursuit of freedom, although in many respects an ideal, is, at the same time, deeply flawed. He can in individual cases create justice, but only at the expense of injustice. Karl is guilty of lacking faith in his father, and he can deny love, but, above all, his individualism turns out to be at the same time self-obsession. For example, he only accepts Kosinsky into the band when he sees in him a reflection of his own situation. He is tyrannical in his treatment of others in much the same way as Schiller's idealist Posa in Don Carlos, of whom he said that greatness of spirit often damages the freedom of others as much as does egoism or tyranny, since it does not consider other people as individuals (S-NA, 22: 170). Similarly, pride is implicit in Karl's decision to stand outside society and outside humanity and make the judgments on it that only God can properly make.

As he becomes conscious of this guilt, Karl realizes that he has failed to find freedom. When he returns to his home and recalls the social integration of society, the family, and love that he has foresworn, it is that lost potential for himself that now represents freedom, while he presents his existence as a robber as imprisonment:

Warum bin ich hiehergekommen? daß mirs gienge wie dem Gefange-
nen, den der klirrende Eisenring aus Träumen der Freyheit aufjagt —
nein, ich gehe in mein Elend zurük! — der Gefangene hatte das Licht
vergessen, aber der Traum der Freyheit fuhr über ihm wie ein Bliz in
die Nacht, der sie finstrer zurükläßt. (*S-NA*, 3: 87)[52]

Exactly this image is also found in Schiller's *Philosophische Briefe* (Philosophical Letters, 1786), where it denotes the dawning of reason that may
be the first step toward the self-realization of humanity, or "perfection."
Here it represents Karl's recognition of the potential that he has now
lost. The only way he can atone for the actions he took in claiming his
freedom, a selective and false freedom as a robber, is to free himself from
his dependence on the band by sacrificing Amalia and submit to the law
by handing himself over the authorities for punishment. Even at this
stage there may be an element of posturing, but his final sacrifice nevertheless expresses moral freedom by his decision to forego the kind of
freedom his outlaw existence promised. Whereas Franz, for all his belief
in control, was brought to suicidal despair by his emotions and his conscience, Karl, whose emotional outburst had propelled him into a wild
counterexistence, is now able coolly to decide on self-sacrifice. This
Schiller has attempted to show by exploring the psychological and philosophical entanglements of the idea of freedom in the play.

Many of Schiller's early works deal with the idea of freedom as a
central component of a complex of problems relating to the striving of
the individual for self-realization, but in *Don Carlos* it becomes part of
the overarching metaphor that compares the Spain of Philip II to a
prison. The parallels with *Hamlet* are inescapable. Like *Egmont, Don
Carlos* was written in stages that reflect the author's increasing distance
from the Sturm und Drang and, because of this distance, perhaps, he is
able to reflect with unusual clarity on themes that had emerged during
the Sturm und Drang. Carlos's friend Posa is committed to the idea of
freedom, but the play shows how, attacked from within and without, his
ideal is defeated by Philip, and even more by the cultural world of which
the king is merely a figurehead. The specific force behind the throne is
the Church, the antithesis of freedom, and at the end of the play the
Grand Inquisitor chooses annihilation in preference to freedom. In his
subsequent *Briefe über Don Carlos* (Letters on *Don Carlos*, 1788) Schiller
offers a critique of his play that focuses on the problematic nature of
Posa's ideal of freedom, and in the course of his discussion uses a striking
image of the role of the idea of freedom: "die schönsten Träume von
Freiheit werden ja im Kerker geträumt" (*S-NA*, 22: 141).[53] Like a dream,
freedom has no reality for the Sturm und Drang, but it does somehow

relate to reality. It is an idea that is evoked by a mind that experiences reality as restrictive and oppressive. At the same, there is a hint of irony in this comment: the word *"schön"* suggests not only the beauty (of nature or of art) that may communicate the idea of freedom to us but also a certain indulgence of the imagination that lies in these dreams of freedom. Dreams of freedom are utopian in that they look to a better world and may motivate us to strive for it, but they are also utopian in the negative sense that they are fantasies about an unattainable ideal that distract us from the reality around us and from any activity we might undertake to improve it.

Notes

[1] "I never doubted for a moment that I would renounce the traditional theater. The unity of place seemed to me an oppressive prison, the unities of action and time burdensome fetters on our imagination. I struggled free — and knew for the first time that I had hands and feet. And now when I saw what harm the keepers of the rules had done me in their dungeon, and how many free spirits there were still cowering there — my heart would have burst had I not declared war on them, had I not tried daily to destroy their prison towers" (*G-CW*, 3: 164).

[2] "The all too narrow palisades of Aristotle and Batteux."

[3] "We feel the need for a freer form and go over to the English side."

[4] "Each revolves around an invisible point . . . where the characteristic quality of our being, our presumed free will, collides with the inevitable course of the whole" (*G-CW*, 3: 165).

[5] This point is made in a review, either by Goethe or Schlosser, or both of them, in the *Frankfurter Gelehrten Anzeigen* of December 25, 1772, discussing "Alexander von Joch über Belohnung und Strafen nach türkischen Gesetzen." The openness of the idea of freedom to different meanings has contributed to its importance as an ideological tool in the development of European civilization: see Panajotis Kondylis, *Die Aufklärung im Rahmen des neuzeitlichen Rationalismus* (Munich: DTV, 1986), 24.

[6] "What blessedness within this prison!" (*G-CW*, 2: 69; many editions have "diesem" for "diesen").

[7] Goethe retained this focus on the idea of freedom when he completed *Faust II* some fifty-five years later: Faust's heroic final speech is the outline of a society predicated on the idea of freedom, but here, too, the vision is undercut by bitter ironies.

[8] "Where there is no freedom, all pleasure is killed."

[9] See Sigrid Weigel, *"Und selbst im Kerker frei . . .!" Schreiben im Gefängnis* (Marburg: Guttandin & Hoppe, 1982).

[10] See Diethelm Klippel, *Politische Freiheit und Freiheitsrechte im deutschen Naturrecht des 18. Jahrhunderts,* Rechts- und Staatswissenschaftliche Veröffentlichungen der Görres-Gesellschaft, n.s. 23 (Paderborn: Schöningh, 1976).

[11] "A friend of virtue prefers to be free but in chains than to serve slavishly at a prince's throne" (Christian Fürchtegott Gellert, *Gesammelte Schriften*, vol. 1: *Fabeln und Erzählungen*, eds. Ulrike Bardt and Bernd Witte [Berlin & New York: de Gruyter, 2000], 158).

[12] Letter of November 6, 1774; *Briefe an Goethe. Hamburger Ausgabe*, 2 vols., ed. Karl Robert Mandelkow, 2nd ed. (Munich: Beck, 1982), 1: 41.

[13] Immanuel Kant, *Werke in sechs Bänden*, ed. Wilhelm Weischedel, vol. 6 (Frankfurt am Main: Insel, 1964), 54, 54, and 60, respectively.

[14] Kant uses the terms "public" and "private" the other way around, because he imagines the emergence of a new public realm in which people will freely debate their views.

[15] For the performance of *Götz von Berlichingen* in 1804 and the performance of *Egmont* in 1806 Goethe cut important references to freedom. On the other hand, in 1810, a time when Napoleon was advancing across Europe, *Egmont* was performed with Beethoven's incidental music, which seemed to offer a rousing endorsement of heroic sacrifice for the sake of popular liberation.

[16] See Klopstock's cry, "Frei, o Deutschland, / Wirst du dereinst!" ("One day you will be free, O Germany"), in "Weissagung" (Prophecy), Friedrich Gottlieb Klopstock, *Ausgewählte Werke*, ed. Karl August Schleiden (Munich: Hanser, 1962), 122.

[17] "Freedom! The courtier does not know the idea, the slave! His chains rattle in silvery tones to him! On bended knee, with a bended soul he reaches out his cowardly neck for the yoke" (*Der Göttinger Hain*, ed. Alfred Kelletat, Universal-Bibliothek, 8789–93 [Stuttgart: Reclam, 1967], 173). See also his poem "Freiheitsgesang aus dem zwanzigsten Jahrhundert" (Song of Freedom from the Twentieth Century), 195–201, and his letter to Klopstock of March 15, 1774, 362–63.

[18] In the first version of the poem Stolberg lists the names of the heroes of liberation, Brutus, William Tell, Hermann, Cato, and Timoleon — in the published version he replaced Cato with Klopstock — but these are all interchangeable icons. See *Der Göttinger Hain*, 173–74. In *Dichtung und Wahrheit* Goethe records — whether accurately or not — his and his mother's mockery of this abstract idealization (*G-MA*, 16: 763–64).

[19] "The first germ of freedom is truly to feel that one is *not* free and to identify *which* bonds tie one. The strongest, freest people feel this most deeply and continue striving; crazed slaves, born for prison, mock them and, full of their elevated dreaming, remain lying in the mud."

[20] "We would not give up our hope . . . of growing more and more independent of external things, indeed of our own selves. The word *freedom* has such a lovely sound that we could not have dispensed with it even if denoted an error" (*G-CW*, 4: 364).

[21] Walter Hinderer, "Freiheit und Gesellschaft beim jungen Schiller," in *Sturm und Drang: Ein literaturwissenschaftliches Studienbuch*, ed. Walter Hinck (Kronberg: Athenäum, 1978), 230–56, here 233.

[22] "The human race is a uniform lot. Most people work the greater part of their time just for a living; and the little freedom which remains to them frightens them so that they use every means of getting rid of it" (*G-CW*, 11: 8).

[23] So, too, does Karl in Schiller's *Die Räuber* (*S-NA*, 3: 110).

[24] "Man is born free and everywhere he is in chains" (Jean-Jacques Rousseau, *Œuvres complètes*, 4 vols., eds. Bernard Gagnebin and Marcel Raymond [N.p.: Gallimard, 1959–69], 3: 351).

[25] "The more barbarous a people is — that is, the more alive, the more freely acting (for that is what the word means) — the more barbarous, that is, the more alive, the more free, the closer to the sense, the more lyrically dynamic its songs will be" (*GAL*, 155–56).

[26] "To see you together in this delightful intimacy gives me life."

[27] In the following discussion references are to the second version of the play, except where otherwise indicated.

[28] "Heavenly breezes. —— Freedom! Freedom!" (*G-CW*, 7: 82).

[29] "You were looking for Goetz? He's long since gone. Gradually they have crippled me more and more, my hand, my freedom, my possessions and good name. My head — what's that amount to? . . . And now it's not only Weislingen, not only the peasants, not only the death of the Emperor and not my wounds — it's all of them together. My hour is come" (*G-CW*, 7: 80–81).

[30] The effect in those last words of using the words of Christ is not only to compare Götz with Christ but also to suggest that he is dying for the numberless sins of the world (Mark 14: 41).

[31] GÖTZ: What should our last word be?

GEORG: Long live freedom!

GÖTZ: Long live freedom!

ALL: Long live freedom!

GÖTZ: And if that survives us, we can die in peace. For we'll see in spirit our grandchildren happy and the Emperors of our grandchildren happy (*G-CW*, 7: 54–55).

[32] "The present tendency toward universal laws and decrees is a danger to common freedom." Justus Möser, *Sämtliche Werke: Historisch-kritische Ausgabe*, ed. the Akademie der Wissenschaften zu Göttingen, 9 vols. to date (Berlin & Hamburg: Oldenbourg, 1943–), 5: 22.

[33] "There will come times of deception, deception has been given its freedom."

[34] "O why am I not as free as you! Gottfried! Gottfried! Before you I am entirely aware of my nothingness. To be dependent! A damnable word, and yet it seems as if I were destined for it. I left Gottfried in order to be free, and now I feel for the first time how dependent I am on those petty people that I seemed to govern. I shall never again see Bamberg. I shall break with all of them and be free. Gottfried! Gottfried! You alone are free because your noble soul is sufficient to itself and need neither obey nor command in order to be something."

[35] "So his light will be extinguished from human memory and you can breathe more freely, foolish heart" (*G-CW*, 7: 73).

[36] "Only on high, on high with you. The world is a prison" (*G-CW*, 7: 82).

[37] "Let them be captives, they are still free!" (*G-CW*, 7: 57).

[38] "I die for freedom, for which I lived and fought and for which I now passively offer up myself" (*G-CW*, 7: 150).

[39] H. G. Haile, "Goethe's Political Thinking and *Egmont*," *Germanic Review* 42 (1967): 96–107, here 100. See also Hans Reiss, "Goethe, Moser and the Aufklärung: The Holy Roman Empire in Götz von Berlichingen and Egmont," *Deutsche Vierteljahrsschrift für Literaturwissenschaft und Geistesgeschichte* 60 (1986): 609–44.

[40] "Freedom? A fine word, if only one could understand it!" (*G-CW*, 7: 132).

[41] "Free! Free! Subject to no one, only to nature!" Letter to Heinrich Christian Boie of July 8, 1773, in *Zeitgenössische Rezensionen und Urteile über Goethes "Götz" und "Werther,"* ed. Hermann Blumenthal (Berlin: Junker & Dünnhaupt, 1935), 37.

[42] This point is also made by the character "Lenz" in *Pandämonium Germanicum* (*L-WB*, 1: 269).

[43] "Without freedom life goes back downhill. Freedom is the element in which man thrives, like water is for the fish, and a man who relinquishes his freedom poisons the noblest spirits in his blood, stifles in the bud the sweetest joys of life, and murders himself."

[44] "Degenerate slaves, who, amid the sound of their chains, decry freedom."

[45] The intensity also lies in Schiller's language, which uses expressions and images taken from the Bible and from the tradition of exalted sentimentality, notably Klopstock, who himself drew on the Bible and on Milton's treatment of biblical themes.

[46] "The law never yet made a great man, but freedom breeds giants and extremes."

[47] See the illustration of the title page of *Die Rauber,* preceding this essay.

[48] "What a fool I was, to seek to return to the cage! My spirit thirsts for deeds, my lungs for freedom — murderers, robbers! at that word I trampled the law beneath my feet — men showed me no humanity, when to humanity I appealed; so let me forget sympathy and human feeling! — I have no father now, I have no love now, and blood and death shall teach me to forget that ever I held anything dear" (*SuD*, 203).

[49] "Now we are free" (*SuD*, 239).

[50] "Men, I am seeking, . . . who value freedom more than life and honour, whose very name, sweet sound to the poor and the oppressed, strikes terror in the valiant and turns the tyrant pale" (*SuD*, 247).

[51] The first part of his name, Spiegel, means "mirror."

[52] "Why did I come here? To hear like a prisoner the clanking chain wake me with a start from dreams of freedom — no, let me return to my exile and misery! — the prisoner had forgotten the light, but the dream of freedom flashed past him like the lightning in the night, leaving it darker than before" (*SuD*, 253).

[53] "The most beautiful dreams of freedom are dreamed in prison."

Goethe in 1776 (?), by Georg Melchior Kraus.
Courtesy of Freies Deutsches Hochstift, Frankfurt am Main.

Young Goethe's Political Fantasies

W. Daniel Wilson

To THIS DAY, THE IMAGE OF the young Goethe as a political firebrand persists. The usual story is that he was a driving force in the rebellious Sturm und Drang's rejection of the status quo, whether socially or politically defined. In reference works and literary histories we can read that he was part of the movement's supposedly "zunehmend offene Opposition gegen die feudalistisch-absolutistischen Fesseln der Zeit" (increasingly open opposition to the feudal-absolutist shackles of those days),[1] its struggle "um Befreiung von feudalen und absolutistischen Fesseln und um Herausbildung neuer, freierer Lebensverhältnisse," its "Impulse für eine grundsätzliche Opposition und . . . das Streben nach radikaler Erneuerung."[2] This view is based partly on Goethe's novel *Die Leiden des jungen Werthers,* in which the hero laments "die fatalen bürgerlichen Verhältnisse" (the awful civil conditions; *G-MA,* 1.2: 250), referring to class differences; or on the poem "Prometheus," which supposedly represents "Kritik an den bestehenden Herrschaftsverhältnissen" (criticism of existing conditions of sovereign authority)[3] or even "das Selbstbewußtsein der revolutionär gestimmten Kreise des Bürgertums" (the self-awareness of the middle-class circles that had a revolutionary consciousness).[4] To present this position, critics have to provide an ingenious interpretation (one that apparently did not occur to the contemporary readers of "Prometheus" after it was published against Goethe's will[5]) of what is essentially an apolitical poem that contains only *religious* heterodoxy. Or they have to ignore the fact that the young, unbalanced protagonist of Goethe's first novel rails against class distinctions but in the next breath admits that they are necessary and that they benefit him personally. Still, the legend of a politically "revolutionary" young Goethe persists. According to this account, only after his removal to Weimar in November 1775 did he accommodate to the dictates of feudalism and absolutism under the influence of the courtly and worldly Charlotte von Stein and his service to Duke Karl August of Weimar. The conservative, affirmative minister of state and best friend of the duke is almost always played off against the pre-Weimar upstart who refused to bow his head to any prince or nobleman.

There is no question that the Weimar Goethe was a proponent of the status quo. The problem lies in the depiction of the young, pre-Weimar Goethe as something of a political radical. There is, of course, a certain amount of ambiguous evidence for this view, as we shall see, but Goethe's attitude is never clearly oppositional, as many critics would have us believe. More important is the question of the *function* (or non-function) of his political beliefs in the public sphere of his day. Quite often Goethe voiced in letters, diaries, and other *unpublished* texts — including literary works — a political or social critique that he toned down in *published* works. He had an ambivalent attitude toward the political and social norms of his day, but he avoided expressing these views publicly and thus played no role in the emergence of a critical political discourse in Germany.

The lot of a German intellectual in the eighteenth century who had some kind of political and social awareness was a difficult one. These young people saw clearly the injustices and abuses around them: blatant class privilege within the system of feudalism, crushing poverty for the peasants who carried most of the productive weight of an essentially agrarian society, and the political system of (in most territories) absolute monarchy, which bolstered the feudal system and led to abuse of power, intrigues and corruption at courts designed to imitate Versailles, and immense waste of economic resources in the representation of the prince's power. Unlike France or England, which were unified realms, Germany was still a patchwork of hundreds of semisovereign territories, so that there was no cultural center to speak of in which intellectuals could meet and engage in political discourse, much less organize themselves to work against the status quo. Furthermore, the lack of copyright agreements among the various territories assured that writers could not develop a truly independent political stance, since they could not live entirely from their writings. They almost always had to make a living from a separate occupation, and in a land of hundreds of principalities, each seeking trained men to help their new bureaucracies modernize and rationalize public life, almost every intellectual found himself obliged to take a position that was dependent on the state in one form or another: bureaucrat, pastor, professor, teacher, officer, and so on. Thus, writers found themselves unlikely to express critique of a system that fed and clothed them and with whose interests they imperceptibly identified. Still, a few writers of this generation did publish sharp critiques of the status quo or, at least, of its abuses — at the fringes of the Sturm und

Drang, Christian Daniel Schubart and Gottfried August Bürger are the best examples.

In this most dissatisfying and contradictory situation, intellectuals might imagine overcoming the injustices and inequities of feudal and absolutist German principalities in three main ways:

1. True opposition was an entirely theoretical possibility, owing to the conditions of dependence mentioned above and to the lack of a solidly powerful middle class or peasantry that might challenge the domination of the nobility or the lack of political rights. Like the intellectuals, many middle-class burghers were dependent in an elemental way on absolutist courts for their livelihood. Only secret societies offered some hope of genuine opposition, but they were dominated by the privileged and adopted a variant of the model of change through "enlightened" absolutism (see below). Despite the impossibility of this alternative, literary scholars repeatedly make claims for the supposed oppositionality of movements such as the Sturm und Drang and, in particular, for the young Goethe.

   In Goethe, as in many other writers, we find the tendency — derived from a sometimes misguided understanding of Rousseau's early discourses — to seek fulfillment and authenticity by simplifying human relations through a "return to nature." Human beings and their social relations were envisioned as becoming closer to nature in two distinct ways, both of them deriving ultimately from an aversion to the perceived artificiality and corruption of courtly life.

2. The first of these movements toward nature has been called "secession." In this alternative, the dissatisfied turn their back on corrupt civil society or the wicked courtly world and retreat into "nature" — understood either in the narrow sense of a flight into the countryside and the landscape or in the wider sense of a retreat into the smallest social unit, the newly developing nuclear family, or into the popular cults of friendship. The secessionist alternative, the withdrawal from society, was championed by many writers in this period. Goethe, for example, expressed it, above all, in *Werther* and in thematically related reviews that he wrote for the periodical *Frankfurter Gelehrte Anzeigen* in 1772. In this alternative we find a political *gesture*, because many young "secessionists" were convinced that they were acting politically by withdrawing from a thoroughly corrupt society. But

secession should not be seen as a form of opposition or resistance; it left the social and political status quo untouched by simply fleeing from it. Besides, secession was ultimately an illusion; hierarchical and authoritarian structures were not actually left behind but were simply reproduced in the new idyll, as in the notorious case of the nuclear family. In the nineteenth century this illusion hardened into an ideology that persists even today. In Goethe the tendency to secession is often expressed as an aversion to "subordination," which is voiced not only by the fictive Werther but also by his author.[6] This stubborn independence bespeaks a lofty ideal of personal freedom that is hardly compatible with the notion of a life at court or as a "*Fürstendiener*" (servant of princes), as state officials were often contemptuously known.

3. Those young men — including both Werther and his author — who swallowed their pride and ultimately opted for the safe haven of service to a prince developed another model of serving nature, which I will call "naturalization." This option is a variant of the theory of "enlightened absolutism," the dominant political credo of eighteenth-century Germany and several other countries. In enlightened absolutism the sovereign adopts principles of the Enlightenment, inspired by enlightened advisers, and sets about applying these principles in reforms of society and the state. Ultimately, "enlightened absolutism" is a contradiction in terms, since the final consequence of Enlightenment would be democracy, and many of the adherents of enlightened absolutism (including Voltaire, who was disappointed by Frederick the Great of Prussia) ended by abandoning it. But many Germans convinced themselves that their princes could overcome the interests and dictates of power and devote themselves to the public good. In the "naturalist" variant of "enlightened absolutism," the prince is humanized, that is, *naturalized,* brought into contact with nature (however defined), and he then introduces "natural" human relations in society and state. We will follow the adventures of this notion through some of Goethe's works and activities both before and after the relocation to Weimar. At an individual level, these writers are certainly to be commended for refusing to withdraw from a true dilemma and for remaining engaged with society's ills. But the illusion associated with "naturalization," and with enlightened absolutism

generally, had a pernicious legacy in Germany and in most of the other states in which it dominated (Austria, Italy, Spain, and Russia). It cemented the deference to authority from above under the guise of social progress, of "enlightened" government, and thus strengthened the position of the authoritarian state and weakened the claim to human rights (which were considered unnecessary in such "enlightened" states) right into the twentieth century.

Despite the reputation of the Sturm und Drang generation as stalwart foes of "tyrants," many of them were just as inclined toward public service as Enlightenment writers. Some of them probably also favored the project of "naturalizing" enlightened sovereigns; Klinger's and Lenz's involvement in the antics of Goethe's first period in Weimar — discussed below — suggests that they, too, intended to introduce the Weimar duke to "nature" and thus to help turn his realm into a sanctuary of harmonious social and political relations. But there is little evidence on which to base a definite statement about their intentions, and Lenz — to take only the most investigated writer besides Goethe — favored a truly bizarre deformation of the idea of enlightened absolutism that reveals its inner contradictions. He wished to be ennobled in France and, thus, to marry a beloved woman from the high nobility, and his vehicle was to be an essay to be presented to the French minister of war in which Lenz proposed a system of marriage for soldiers that essentially would have resulted in state-sanctioned prostitution.[7] Thus, the deformities of thought to which their dilemma drove such men is evident quite apart from Goethe's no less grotesque plans.

As we have seen, the only real career option for a young, educated (and non-Jewish) German male of Goethe's day was state service. It seems that Goethe was determined for personal reasons to leave his hometown, Frankfurt, a nonabsolutist polity; and the large majority of other states where he could have found a position were absolutist principalities. Thus, he was careful not to offend Germany's princes, his potential future employers. Before we look at evidence of his interest in public service even during this pre-Weimar period and his model of "naturalization" in Weimar, we will examine those pre-Weimar works — both published and unpublished — that seem to show signs of political heterodoxy but that, on closer examination, fail to question the status quo in any fundamental way and, thus, kept Goethe's career options open.

A prime example of Goethe's wavering critical attitude is the glaring contrast between the two versions of his play *Götz von Berlichingen*. The first version, *Geschichte Gottfriedens von Berlichingen mit der eisernen Hand dramatisiert,* was written in six weeks in the fall of 1771. It contains scenes that portray with palpable empathy the sixteenth-century perpetrators of the Peasants' War and their resistance to feudal and absolutist oppression.[8] For example, one of the peasants describes a tyrannical feudal lord whom they have captured; he had victimized peasants who stole from his stock of hunting animals to relieve their hunger:

> Wie der giftige Drache, dein Mann, meinen armen Bruder, und noch drei Unglückliche in den tiefsten Turn warf. Weil sie mit Hungricher Seele seinen Wald eines Hirsches beraubt hatten ihre armen Kinder und Weiber zu speisen. — Wir jammerten und baten. . . . Er stund der Abscheu wie ein ehrener Teufel, stund er und grinste uns an. Verfaulen sollen sie lebendig und verhungern im Turn knirscht er. (*G-MA,* 1.1: 485–86)[9]

To be sure, this empathetic image of the peasant starved to death is mitigated somewhat, since his brother (the speaker) is about to wreak an almost sadistic revenge on the feudal lord despite his wife's piteous entreaties. So the rebellious peasant is using the same methods as the hated nobleman. But even if Goethe has not made the peasants' actions entirely justifiable from the point of view of a privileged reader, he has made them *understandable.* Not only that, but the nobleman Gottfried himself expresses approval of the peasants' struggle until it becomes counterproductive. In this play Goethe reveals remarkable solidarity with the perpetrators of one of the ruling class's lasting traumas, the Peasants' War. Since peasant revolts continued throughout the eighteenth century and were the most feared threat to absolutist power and aristocratic privilege, this was a bold piece of writing, indeed.

This version of the play was not published in Goethe's lifetime, however. He reworked it into *Götz von Berlichingen mit der eisernen Hand* in January and February 1773 and published it in June of the same year — his first important work, it immediately made him famous throughout Germany and, ultimately, abroad. It is still the version that is almost always read. In his later autobiography Goethe portrayed the impact of the play on young men: "Sie glaubten daran ein Panier zu sehn, unter dessen Vorschritt alles was in der Jugend Wildes und Ungeschlachtes lebt, sich wohl Raum machen dürfte" (*G-MA,* 16: 608: They saw in it a banner under which anyone who lives wildly and coarsely in his youth could assert himself). But these youthful rebels did not find in the work much political or social radicalism with which to identify, for in the published book the manuscript version's positive portrayal of the peasants is turned on its head. Gone are the speeches of men who articulately voice their legitimate complaints against an oppressive feudal regime. In their place we find bloodthirsty brutes who seem to have no real motive other than the sadistic pleasure in inflicting pain on noble lords — now fashioned as the victims, not the oppressors. The peasants murder, pillage, and plunder without the slightest legitimacy, since passages in which they justify themselves — like the one quoted above — have been omitted. It is no wonder that Goethe reported later: "Durch Götz von Berlichingen . . . war ich gegen die obern Stände sehr gut gestellt" (*G-MA*, 16: 752: Because of *Götz von Berlichingen* I was on a good footing with the upper classes). This is partly because Götz's resistance to princely absolutism hearkens back to an older ideal, the privileges of nobility and their ancient rights (*altes Recht*) vis-à-vis the new, rationalized state with its exclusive claim to sovereignty. The political message of the play is essentially a backward-looking one, though one that represented a common view in Goethe's day.

In a much less directly political sense, Goethe did have some reason to speak (in later years) of his "überfreie Gesinnung" (*G-MA*, 16: 670: excessively free views), not only in the mid-1770s[10] but also in his teen-age years as a student in Leipzig. There he fell in love with a woman much below his own station in life, Käthchen Schönkopf, and struck the pose of a man who experiences genuine love across class boundaries[11] — and despises princes who cannot enjoy such fulfillment. This fiery moral condemnation of princes comes in poems that — with one possible exception — remained in the poet's drawer. In the "Elegie auf den Tod des Bruders meines Freundes" (Elegy on the Death of My Friend's Brother) Goethe manipulates the facts to attack "die stolze Tyrannei" (the proud tyranny) of an (unnamed) prince who supposedly hindered a marriage (*G-MA*, 1.1: 111–13),[12] but he only circulated this poem among friends in the manuscript collection "Annette." A more complex poem, "Der wahre Genuß" (True Enjoyment), was actually published, albeit anonymously, in the *Neue Lieder* (New Songs) of 1769 (*G-MA*, 1.1: 140–42). Previous scholarship has always assumed that the poem was directed against Prince Leopold Friedrich Franz of Anhalt-Dessau, but this claim is based on little more than speculation and contradicts important passages in letters of Goethe and in the poem itself.[13] Rather, the poem is aimed at a generic "Fürst" (prince, in the sense of sovereign) who cannot experience true love because he abuses his power to achieve sexual gratification (a situation that had nothing to do with the Prince of Dessau). Unlike attacks on particular, named monarchs, abstract pathos against a generic prince was tolerated in German states. But

Goethe seems to have been unwilling even to have voiced this general criticism. His friend Behrisch, who worked as a tutor for the Prince of Dessau, objected to the apostrophe "O Fürst" in the poem; Goethe at first rejected Behrisch's "übertriebene Delicatesse" (exaggerated sensitivity) and kept the expression, but a few months later authorized Behrisch to change "Fürst" to "Freund" (friend).[14] In the published book, however, we find the original expression, "Fürst." Critics have assumed that Goethe changed his mind again and reverted to this politically critical apostrophe, but I find it much more likely that someone neglected to make the change that the poet authorized — especially since Goethe again used "Freund" when preparing a 1789 edition of his poetry, though he ultimately withdrew the poem from this collection.

Regardless of the circumstances, the poem is essentially a harmless invective against an unnamed and unidentifiable prince, the kind of vague critique that was not only permitted but was widespread in eighteenth-century Germany. The essential question is whether such works exhibit a fundamental critique of the status quo or of abuses of power (as do certain poems of Schubart and Bürger), and Goethe's clearly do not. Though the poem exhibits a similarly moralistic critique of unnamed princes as does Lessing's tragedy *Emilia Galotti* a few years later (1772), for example, Goethe's political acuity comes nowhere near that of Lessing, who, as Goethe later wrote, directed his "Piquen auf die Fürsten" (*G-MA,* 19: 216: barbs against the princes) in a radical form in this play — and *Emilia Galotti* is a prime example of the sort of sharp, fundamental criticism of absolutism that is found in much Enlightenment discourse but to which most Sturm und Drang writers never really aspired.

Those who portray Goethe as essentially predemocratic or presocialist in this period evoke what East German scholars called his "Verbundenheit mit dem Volk,"[15] his solidarity and empathy with the lower classes. Instances of this attitude in Goethe's correspondence, conversations, and works are legion. For example, in a letter of June 1, 1774, he calls the lower classes "die besten Menschen" (*G-HB,* 1: 161: the best people). Again and again we read that he enjoys the company of these simple people — in Sessenheim, for example, where he fell in love with the pastor's daughter Friederike Brion, a contemporary indicates that Goethe "kannte . . . viele Handwerker, wie er denn bei dem lahmen Philipp in Sesenheim Körbe flechten gelernt" (Grumach, 1: 188: knew many craftsmen and learned how to make baskets from the lame Philipp in Sessenheim). Of course, this admiration for the lower classes fed Goethe's aesthetic project, the rejuvenation of "high" literature through

fertilization from folk literature, as he reports in his autobiography regarding the acquaintance with Herder: folk poetry proved "daß die
Dichtkunst überhaupt eine Welt- und Völkergabe sei, nicht ein Privat-
erbteil einiger feinen, gebildeten Männer" (*G-MA*, 16: 440: that literature is a talent of the entire world and peoples, not the private inheritance of a few refined, educated men).

This attitude, however, remained on the level of an aesthetic project
and, at most, of congenial contacts with individuals from the lower
classes, but had no political consequences. Furthermore, even Goethe's
self-portrayal as a special friend of the unwashed simple people is contradicted in a few reports by others. For example, there is the "grotesque"
anecdote that Goethe ordered six peasant women in Sessenheim to
throw their straw hats into a bonfire; only one refused. Goethe then gave
each of the five compliant women two Taler — an immense amount of
money for a peasant — and their frowns turned to jubilation; the last
woman then threw her hat into the fire, but Goethe refused to give her
any money.[16] This story of the rich young man exhibiting his power over
the lower classes is matched by a report from Strasbourg, where the
student Goethe "discovered" Gothic art as an inspiration for modern
aesthetics:

> Er war bekanntlich ein großer Bewunderer unsres herrlichen Mün-
> stergebäudes . . . und stellte sich oftmals auf der Seite des großen Por-
> tals, wo es sich am vollkommensten ausnimmt, staunend hin. Einstmals
> soll er also mit übereinandergeschlagenen Armen, ganz in Bewunde-
> rung und Träumen, dagestanden haben. Da fährt ein Karrenzieher hart
> an ihm vorüber, sein Liedchen pfeifend.
>
> Goethe dreht sich zürnend herum und gibt dem verblüfften Man-
> ne eine derbe Ohrfeige mit den Worten: "Willst du staunen, Fle-
> gel?" — und weist ihn mit der Hand auf das Münster. (Grumach, 1:
> 186)[17]

In sum: there is no evidence that Goethe's attitude toward the lower
classes — ambivalent in itself, as such episodes show — had any political
implications that would have contradicted the heritage of his family's
privilege and power.

And nothing leads us to conclude that he was opposed to absolutism, either. To be sure, he sometimes indulged in radical *gestures* in this
realm, too. For example, Goethe later declared that in the above-
mentioned Frankfurt periodical to which he contributed in 1772 there
was an absolute attempt to break through all limitations,[18] and his autobiography claims that in the Sturm und Drang circle in Strasbourg critical remarks about sovereigns and their statesmen were freely expressed —

though generally against those in France (*G-MA*, 16: 405). This kind of political gesturing had no practical consequences for the target or for the source of the criticism. A Swiss republican, the literary critic Johann Jacob Bodmer, called Goethe, after a meeting with him in 1775, "ein Deutscher, der die Unterthänigkeit mit der äussersten Unempfindlichkeit erduldet" (Grumach, 1: 342: a German who tolerates political subordination with the most extreme indifference). Goethe's *publicly* expressed views correspond more with the deference to authority that Bodmer perceived. In his Strasbourg law disputation, for example, Goethe defends the principle that only the sovereign is entitled to make or even interpret laws — in contrast to many thinkers of his day, who championed the *Landstände* (estates) and the judiciary as counterweights to unadulterated absolutist power.[19]

So Goethe never really wavered in his loyalty to absolutist government, resisting democratic tendencies right up to his death a third of the way through the nineteenth century. It is, thus, no surprise that his political views were hardly limited to a negatively motivated reluctance to critique absolutism and feudalism. At least initially, he was fired by a positive desire to make a difference *within* absolutism, not *against* it. His views prepared the way for his career in the service of a young, apparently promising duke.

Goethe arrived in Weimar in November 1775, initially as a guest or protegé of Karl August, duke of the small Thuringian principality Saxe-Weimar-Eisenach. But even earlier in 1775 he had had — despite his obvious skepticism — increasingly positive experiences with princes and courts. One was his visit to the relaxed and liberal court of the Margrave of Baden, who seemed to treat the writer Friedrich Gottlieb Klopstock as an equal. Goethe's deep ambivalence toward courts, the idea of serving princes, and social conformity remained, but his aspirations underwent a profound shift in focus as a result of these experiences prior to going to Weimar. This change can be explained to a certain extent by the accommodations that courts made in the late eighteenth century to middle-class values (*Verbürgerlichung*). Goethe and other young "*Genies*" who visited the court at Karlsruhe were, as he later wrote, "gewissermaßen aufgefordert natürlich und doch bedeutend zu sein" (*G-MA*, 16: 767–68: more or less challenged to be natural and yet sophisticated) — that is, to be decidedly uncourtly but still somehow not to sacrifice civilization altogether. The seventeen-year-old soon-to-be-duke Karl August of Weimar, too, was part of this trend; Goethe tells us that he had proven himself "gemütlich" (*G-MA*, 16: 768: warm),[20] and thus, in the thinking of the *Genies*, as a kind of opponent (we would say today, a sham opponent) of courtly values. Goethe's thoughts were obviously guided by the idea of nature, his deity in these years. Was it the apparent secession from the corrupt world of traditional courts that fascinated him in these princes and statesmen, or was it the notion of "naturalizing" the polity by befriending or mentoring a humane prince? In his autobiography the older Goethe interpreted his first meeting with Karl August in December 1774 in the latter sense, and this version agrees with important biographical documents. But both alternatives were probably active in Goethe at this stage, as far as we can determine from his works, letters, and the previously neglected testimonies of others.

The upshot is that Goethe was thinking seriously about public service even before meeting Karl August or going to Weimar, as many documents (including the novel *Werther* and the play *Clavigo*) show. As early as the summer of 1773, soon after publishing *Götz von Berlichingen*, he was considering offers of a position as public servant in Frankfurt and then elsewhere (*G-MA*, 16: 703).[21] Particularly in letters to his friend Johann Georg Christian Kestner (1741–1800), who had an important public office, Goethe reacted ambivalently to concrete prospects of such a career, lamenting the requisite "subordination" but ultimately revealing keen interest and admiring Kestner's ability to cultivate the company of nobles and, thus, advance his career.[22] And Goethe defended life at court against his father's pronounced aversion, taking up the cause of the powerful ("die Partei der Großen," *G-MA*, 16: 688–89).

Right in the middle of the decisive events that led Goethe to Weimar — that is, after the meeting with Karl August in December 1774, with Klopstock on March 30, 1775, and into the period after the unexpectedly pleasant sojourn at the Karlsruhe court in May 1775 — Goethe took up again and completed a work that is essential for understanding his motivations. This is the singspiel (drama with music) titled *Claudine von Villa Bella* — a text that has been unjustly neglected by scholarship. In April 1775 Goethe dug up ("ausgegraben"[23]) the sketch for the work that he had begun the previous year, and he finished it in June.

Goethe's — by all accounts — wild demeanor in the period after he arrived in Weimar is prefigured in the character Crugantino. He is a renegade from the nobility who has fled society and lives as a "vagabond," so that here we clearly see the secessionist alternative of abandoning one's social class in an act of revolt against society. The following dialogue gives an impression of the pranks of the band of vagabonds:

CRUGANTINO: Was treibt ihr denn?

2. VAGABUND: Der Pfarrer hat heut ein Hirschkalb geschenkt
                 kriegt; das hängt hunten in der Küchenkammer.
                 Das wird ihm weggeputzt.

3. VAGABUND: Und die Hörner ihm auf den Perückenstock
                 genagelt. Sein Perückenstock mit der Fest-
                 perücke steht in der Ecke; verlaßt euch auf
                 mich! . . .

2. VAGABUND: Du steigst hinein, reichst mir den Bock heraus.
                 Wir lösen die Hörner ab, und geben sie dir.

3. VAGABUND: Für das übrige laßt mich sorgen! Auf der
                 Perücke muß das herrlich stehn, und ein
                 Zettelgen dran: — der neue Moses!
                           (*G-MA*, 1.2: 92)[24]

The similarity of this practical joke — and we hear in the play that there are other such "*Streiche*" — to the so-called *Genietreiben* (goings-on of the geniuses) in Weimar after Goethe's arrival there in November, the so-called Weimar Sturm und Drang, is striking. The duke himself was almost always one of the gang. I will give only one example of such antics, in which a pastor and wig also play a role:

> In Ilmenau badeten sie sich, umtanzten nackt zu 9 bis 10[,] der Her-zog an der Spitze[,] einen Pfarrer oder Madchen [*sic*] der vorbey ging, indem sie aus dem Wasser sprangen — Einen [*sic*] Glasmann gaben sie Senf und Fischbrühe zu essen — Göthe nahm ihm die Peruke [*sic*] ab — schor ihm mit einer Scheer sein Haar ab — Nachher liessen sie ihn unter die Plumpe [*sic*] lauffen, und hätten ihn beynah ersäuft.[25]

Other examples could be cited that underline this parallel. Incidentally, it seems to be precisely the wigs, which symbolized middle-class smug-ness, that irritated the *Genies* most; the infamous episode in which a merchant in Stützerbach was "skinned" could be mentioned.[26]

This striking similarity between fiction and reality appears to be more than a coincidence when we consider that there are *explicit* connections between *Claudine* and the Duke of Weimar and his antics with Goethe and others. In the first place, Goethe mentions his work on the play (before his removal to Weimar) in letters to Karl August's tutor, Carl Ludwig von Knebel.[27] More importantly, after he finished the work in June, he sent it to Knebel with the remark: "Hier schick ich lieber Kne-bel Claudinen; lesen Sie's unserm Herzog zur freyen Stunde" (*WA*, 4.2: 265).[28] Goethe thus declares Karl August to be an explicit addressee of

Claudine. And Goethe himself later associated the antics of the *Genies* in Weimar with this work. In a letter to Karl August of December 26, 1775, when the band of young upstarts was wreaking havoc in the duchy, the poet calls himself and them "Crugantino und Basko" — the "Spitzbuben und Vagabunden" (scoundrels and vagabonds) from the play (*G-HB*, 1: 203). Carl August Böttiger also reported on later conversations with Goethe that indicated that "Der Rugantino in Göthes Claudina von Villa Bella ist das Original, das Göthe damals spielte" (Grumach, 1: 477).[29] For earlier, positivistic scholars this parallel proved "wie sehr man während der ersten Monate nach Goethes Ankunft zu Weimar in der Claudinen-Sphäre lebte,"[30] but they did not find any further significance behind the *Genies* living out Goethe's fiction.

The meaning of the connection between the Weimar antics of the young firebrands and the plot of *Claudine* can be construed from other sources. The Weimar writer and pedagogue Johannes Daniel Falk, who wrote the description of the swimming party quoted above, reveals the reason behind this fun on the basis of later conversations with Goethe: "Alles das that Göthe kalt aus Plan, nicht aus Liebe zur Sache, sondern aus Idee den Herzog zu einem Naturmenschen zu machen. . . . Der Herzog sollte also ein Naturmensch werden und aus dem peinlichen Hof- und Philisterleben herausgerissen werden" (Grumach, 1: 478).[31] And then Falk gives an example of the practical realization of this idea: "Man grub sich die Kartoffeln aus der Erd, man kochte sie bey Reisig im Walde, schlief bey Mädchen im Walde, und machte Inschriften, an den Bäumen" (Grumach, 1: 478).[32] As outlandish as it sounds, this immersion in "nature" was supposed to make the duke into a "natural person." In another passage Falk reports: "Als der Göthe das erste Mal in Weimar war und der Herzog ihm den Vorschlag machte in Weimar zu bleiben: so sagte er, das ginge gar nicht an, dass er (ein Genie) in einer Stadt lebend [*sic*] könte. Dieß sey lauter erbermliches Philisterwesen: ein Genie der echte Naturmensch gehöre in die Natur, in Luft, Wald und Feld" (Grumach, 1: 412–13),[33] and Karl August thereupon bought Goethe his house outside the city.

Falk's report could be supplemented and confirmed by others, for example, that of the Weimar physician Christoph Wilhelm Hufeland (Grumach, 1: 473–74). In many reports by eyewitnesses life — that is, nature, in contrast to the court — is mentioned as one of Goethe's guiding concepts for the *Genie* excesses. This view corresponds to many well-known remarks by Goethe himself that portray contact with nature as a guiding principle. For example, Goethe says in his letter mentioned above that he and the other "vagabonds," who fashion themselves as

"Crugantino und Basko," are consorting with "natürlich guten Menschen" (natural, good people) in the country, "in der homerisch einfachen Welt" (in the simple, Homeric world). Goethe hints mysteriously at a programmatic aim of these events in a conversation with his Weimar neighbor Johann Joachim Christoph Bode, as reported by a third person:

> Er [Bode] habe Ihn [Goethe] gefragt, warum, da er Gutes stiften könte, er einen so gräßlichen Mißbrauch seines Postens machte, den Herzog im Fluchen, Zothenreißen pp ex professo unterrichtete u.d.g.? Goethe sey ihm hierauf um den Hals gefallen, hätte Ihm mit Rührung dießes unbegreifliche gesagt, "Freund, warte, warte auf den Erfolg, ich kann meine Absicht jezt nicht erklären, bald wird die Welt, Du und Weimar erkennen, daß ich einen Stuhl im Himmel verdienet habe." (Grumach, 1: 424)[34]

It must be stressed that the reasons that Falk and Hufeland give for the *Genie* capers under Goethe's leadership differ fundamentally from those voiced until now by scholars. At first biographers and researchers simply glossed over or ignored these episodes. But even today the facts are mentioned only selectively, and the harassment of the duke's subjects, especially, is almost completely left out of the accounts. Richard Friedenthal, whose Goethe biography of 1963 broke many taboos, is one of the few exceptions, not hesitating to point out the effect of the wildness on the populace: "Fratzenhaft ist das alles und nicht frei von dem unangenehmen Beigeschmack, daß es eben die Herren vom Hofe sind mitsamt Seiner Durchlaucht: Gegenwehr oder auch nur Murren gibt es nicht, der geneckte Untertan hat sich zu verbeugen und schweigend seine Kisten wieder den Berg hinaufzuschleppen."[35] Other scholars give this activity the most harmless epithets: earlier it was euphemistically called "die lustige Zeit in Weimar" (the fun time in Weimar),[36] and later the term "*Genietreiben*" (goings-on of the geniuses) became established, with the implication that the fun was somehow appropriate for an intellectual elite and, in any case, was beneficial to the necessary course of German literary history and the "*Geniezeit*" (genius period — another term for the Sturm und Drang). Others interpret Goethe and even Karl August as standing in opposition to the status quo, to courtly society and its values. These scholars seem to believe that Goethe and the duke freed themselves from their own power and privileged interests.

With obvious embarrassment at the great poet's behavior, generations of Germanists have taken the position that Goethe meant to win Karl August's confidence through these pranks, which were supposedly repulsive ("zuwider") to Goethe himself.[37] Goethe never said anything of the kind, but some scholars support this view with a remark by Goethe's older confidante Charlotte von Stein that, on closer examination, contradicts it. In a letter of March 6, 1776, she reports on a conversation with Goethe in which she admitted to him that she "wünschte selbst er mögte etwas von seinen [*sic*] wilden Wesen darum ihn die Leute hier so schieff beurtheilen, ablegen, daß im Grund zwar nichts ist als daß er jagd, scharff reit, mit der grosen Pleitsche klatscht, alles in Geselschaft des Herzogs. Gewiß sind dies seine Neigungen nicht, aber eine Weile muß ers so treiben um den Herzog zu gewinnen und dann gutes zu stifften, so denk ich davon; er gab mir den Grund nicht an, vertheitigte sich mit wunderbahren Gründen, mir bliebs als hätt er unrecht" (Grumach, 1: 409).[38] The report clearly indicates that these are not Goethe's reasons, because he defends himself with *other* reasons — which Charlotte von Stein either does not understand or rejects ("mit wunderbahren Gründen"), so that her interpretation is refuted as soon as she utters it.[39]

The difference between the two interpretations is fundamental. The view of Charlotte von Stein and most biographers assumes that Karl August was the instigator of the capers, that Goethe merely let the duke act out his "unbändige Natur"[40] (unbridled nature) and only joined in so as to guide him — that he was even a moderating influence[41] on the others. This thesis, too, contradicts the available documents, which clearly describe Goethe as the driving force behind the *Genietreiben* — which, after all, began only after he arrived in Weimar. Of course, some of these contemporary accounts of Goethe as the instigator stem from courtiers who were hostile to Goethe and blamed him for everything,[42] and von Stein could be counted among these.[43] But Falk and the other middle-class intellectuals also saw Goethe as the source of the "Ungezogenheiten" (immature pranks), as Goethe called them.[44] Wieland wrote: "Göthe lebt und regiert und wüthet" (Goethe lives and rules and ravages).[45] And finally, the *Genies* themselves saw Goethe as the ringleader; one of them, Lenz, put it succinctly: "Goethe ist unser Hauptmann" (*L-WB*, 3: 460: Goethe is our captain).

It thus seems clear that Goethe was the driving force behind the wild antics in his first months in Weimar, rather than simply taking part in order to indulge in the duke's immaturity and, thus, to bond with and influence him. Goethe imagined — and this is the second difference between the views of Falk and Hufeland, on the one hand, and the usual speculation (beginning with Charlotte von Stein), on the other hand — a philosophically grounded project, a "plan" (Falk), regardless of how unformed and fantastic it may seem today. This interpretation is bolstered not only by the evidence that Goethe was the instigator of the mischief but also by the fact that he had portrayed the kind of behavior displayed in Weimar months before arriving there, in *Claudine von Villa Bella*. This play — which, as we saw, Goethe commended to the duke as reading material and later associated with the *Genietreiben* — thus holds particular significance for understanding Goethe's project.

The few scholars who have taken a closer look at this play have appreciated the unique power that emanates from the main character. Hanna Fischer-Lamberg, a leading aficionado of the young Goethe, writes: "Crugantino . . . dem es allein um die persönliche Freiheit geht, ist der eigentliche Revolutionär im Goetheschen Jugendwerk."[46] There is no hint of a *political* revolutionary here. But Crugantino's credo of freedom is an impressive document of the young Goethe's impatience with social norms:

> Wißt ihr die Bedürfnisse eines jungen Herzens, wie meins ist? Ein junger toller Kopf? Wo habt ihr einen Schauplatz des Lebens für mich? Eure bürgerliche Gesellschaft ist mir unerträglich! Will ich arbeiten, muß ich Knecht sein; will ich mich lustig machen, muß ich Knecht sein. Muß nicht einer, der halbweg was wert ist, lieber in die weite Welt gehn? . . . wer sich einmal ins Vagieren einläßt, [hat] dann kein Ziel mehr . . . und keine Grenzen; denn unser Herz — ach! Das ist unendlich, so lang ihm Kräfte zureichen! (*G-MA,* 1.2: 118–19)[47]

Crugantino's perspective is socially defined: he is a nobleman. Therefore, his laments can be pinpointed more exactly in terms of the sociopolitical givens of Goethe's day. When he says, "Will ich arbeiten, muß ich Knecht sein," he means the two major career options suited to the nobility: service to the state either as a high official or as an officer. When he says, "will ich mich lustig machen, muß ich Knecht sein," he is referring to life at court, which through the lens of the (mainly middle-class) critique of the court current in Goethe's day was associated with morally despicable behavior such as intrigue and dissimulation but also with hierarchy. Both areas, public service and the court, represent for Crugantino an unacceptable limitation on personal freedom and a falsification of "heart," feeling, human nature. Crugantino seems, then, to be a typical "secessionist," in this case practicing secession from his own class. But at the end of the play comes the surprise: the rebel is reconciled with aristocratic society. The key to this ambivalence? Crugantino discovers that a noble family that lives in the countryside fulfills his ideals. The lord of Villa Bella, Don Gonzalo, invites Crugantino for an evening drink. In this intimate circle he surprises the young rebel with the following words: "zu meiner Zeit war's anders; da ging's dem Bauern wohl, und da hatt' er immer ein Liedgen, das von der Leber wegging, und einem 's Herz ergötzte; und der Herr schämte sich nicht, und sang's auch, wenn's ihm gefiel. Das natürlichste, das beste!" (101–102).[48] This "natural" idyll, in which the nobleman breaches class boundaries for the sake of natural desires and natural folk poetry, fires the outsider Crugantino's enthusiasm ("Vortrefflich!" [Great!]) and is then elaborated by Gonzalo: "Und wo ist die Natur als bei meinem Bauer? Der ißt, trinkt, arbeitet, schläft und liebt, so simpel weg; und kümmert sich den Henker drum in was für Firlfanzereien man all das in den Städten und am Hof vermaskeriert hat!" (102).[49] At this, Crugantino is beside himself: "Fahren Sie fort! Ich werde nicht satt, einen Mann von [I]hrem Stande so reden zu hören."[50] Nature must be experienced thoroughly and can be found, above all, among the peasants. These views are common to the Sturm und Drang writers, including the young Goethe, and they are expressed in many other places. For example, we have already seen that Goethe felt that "das gemeine Volck . . . doch die besten Menschen sind" (*G-HB*, 1: 161: the lower classes are the best people). At this point in his life the simple people dominated Goethe's thought — not as a political force but as a guiding principle, an inspiration for renewal of the upper classes, an idyllic fantasy. The misery and poverty of the lower classes do not figure in this equation; rather, the peasants — the victims of social inequality — are paradoxically idealized as models for secession from tainted reality and, thus, from social inequality.

Now, in 1775, these ideas are to be presented to the duke of Saxe-Weimar and lived out with him. What the duke was supposed to learn from this play, it seems, was, first of all, secession as a consequence of rejecting the court and conventional society in the name of nature and, second, the reintegration of nature into existing society as a weapon against class privilege.

It appears, then, that Goethe's thoughts were focused on elevating the duke above his class and power by activating in him behaviorial patterns that Goethe associated with the lower classes and social outsiders. In a superficial sense, Goethe seems to have succeeded: the duke learned coarse manners well. Charlotte von Stein mentions Goethe's "unanständges betragen mit Fluchen mit pöbelhafften niedern Ausdrükken" and then continues:

> gestern war er [i.e., Karl August] bey mir behaubtete daß alle Leute mit Anstand mit Manieren nicht den Namen eines ehrlichen Mannes tragen könten . . . daher er auch niemanden mehr leiden mag der nicht etwas ungeschliffnes an sich hat. Das hat er alles von Goethen. (Grumach, 1: 410)[51]

Taken by itself, the *Genietreiben* of the duke and his protégé could be understood as an imitation either of student behavior (that is, largely from the privileged classes) or that of soldiers (from the lower classes). But in fact, the conception evidently came from Goethe's reverence for the "Classe von Menschen . . . die man die niedre nennt" (class of people whom they call the lower one).[52] He is clearly thinking mainly of the peasants, as the remarks in *Claudine* and the association with peasants in these months indicate.

By a life close to the simple people and distanced from the court, the prince is supposed to be humanized — in Falk's word, to become a "*Naturmensch*" (natural person). Karl August was expected to erase the huge social and political barrier between himself and his subjects just as he attempted to nullify the social distance between himself and Goethe. In the end, that was impossible, but even modern biographers fall victim to this dream; they remark admiringly that in their association with the peasants in Ilmenau "streiften Carl August und Goethe die Fesseln von Stand und Geburt völlig ab" (Karl August and Goethe stripped off completely the chains of class and birth).[53] Other *Genies,* too, enthusiastically championed this idea of supposed classlessness — for example, a nobleman, Christian Graf zu Stolberg: "Der ganze Hof [i.e., at Weimar] ist sehr angenehm, man kann vergessen dass man mit Fürstlichkeiten umgeht" (Grumach, 1: 391: the entire court is very pleasant, you can easily forget that you're associating with princes).[54]

This "secessionist" step was, however, to be followed by a "naturalizing" one. Various documents indicate that the ultimate hope was that the new consciousness of these naturalized, genius princes would express itself in a more humane government. This hope was not expressed directly by Goethe in any of his own documents that have survived, but by his friends reporting on conversations with him in lofty phrases that point to the virtually utopian thrust of his expectations. The famous novelist Christoph Martin Wieland, who had expressed similar aspirations (though tempered with irony) in his then-celebrated novel *Der goldne Spiegel* (The Golden Mirror, 1772) and had immediately been hired by Karl August's mother as the young man's tutor in order to realize these dreams, saw Goethe almost daily during his first months in Weimar. Wieland wrote that Goethe had fallen prey to the "Magie" (magic) of Wieland's own earlier "verführerische[r] Gedanck[e]" (seductive idea), that of being able to achieve "Viel Gutes, im Grossen, auf Jahrhunderte" (much good, on a grand scale, for centuries) as a princely educator (Grumach, 1: 407). The utopian character of this project is clearly indicated by Wieland's metaphor: "wenn Goethens Idee statt findet, so wird doch Weimar noch der Berg Ararat, wo die guten Menschen Fuß fassen können, während daß allgemeine Sündflut die übrige Welt bedeckt" (Grumach, 1: 475: if Goethe's idea is realized, Weimar will become Mount Ararat, where good people can find a home while the Flood inundates the rest of the world).

This project is obviously an illusion — and even in 1775 this was evident to some. Wieland himself indicates in the same letter that this "Abentheuer" (adventure) was "beym Tagslicht besehn doch immer unmöglich" (if looked at in clear daylight, clearly impossible). The skepticism of the duke's former tutor was triggered not only by the human character of the "Fürstenkinder" (princely children) — of whom he writes in this letter that it is good that the addressee does not know them. Aside from the individual qualities of the prince, the whole project rested on a shaky foundation, on which some of Goethe's fictive characters had also found themselves dangerously poised: the assumption that power relations can simply be eradicated among "natural" people. For example, during his sojourn at court Werther had befriended a noblewoman, called simply "B.," who exhibited "sehr viele Natur mitten in dem steifen Leben" (*G-MA*, 1.2: 250: a great deal of naturalness in the midst of the stiff life) in courtly society — a metaphor of dangerous encirclement that, like Wieland's Mount Ararat metaphor, should tip us off to the impossibility of this idyllic denial of real power relations.[55] Sure enough, Werther's idyll comes crashing down around him. He is expelled from a dinner gathering of nobles, a "Verdruß" (annoyance) that is ultimately decisive in his decision to commit suicide. He is shown the door because he stays too long and does not notice that, as a commoner, he is not welcome. Before he leaves, he notices that Fräulein von B. ultimately conforms to her class's attitude toward commoners. In the first version of the novel (1774) Werther is puzzled by her behavior, and he stays too long "weil ich intriguiert war, das Ding näher zu beleuchten" (*G-MA*, 1.2: 254: because I was intrigued and wanted to find out more about this thing). The "Ding" (thing) is the persistence of power and class relations in human behavior, a reality that the dreamer Werther had obviously not expected. Goethe makes much clearer in the first version than in the second that the failure of the attempt to overcome class-based attitudes is responsible for the scandal of Werther's ejection and ultimately for his suicide (the latter version is, unfortunately, more often read, so that this pattern still goes unnoticed in scholarship on the novel). He realizes with great chagrin that Fräulein von B. cannot simply submerge with him in "ländlichen Scenen von ungemischter Glückseligkeit" (*G-MA*, 1.2: 252: rural scenes of unmitigated happiness) and leave behind the attitudes of her upbringing in the nobility. Ultimately, she remains loyal to her class. Götz von Berlichingen, too, shows that he cannot overcome the interests of his class by abandoning the peasants' struggle. Now, in his 1775–76 project of transforming the Duke of Saxe-Weimar into a sort of benevolent father, Goethe seems to have forgotten or repressed these insights in his most important works from the preceding years. He seems to be obsessed with the idea that he could form the duke into a person who would no longer heed the interests of his class and dynasty but would work for the good of all of society.

Utopian — even fantastic — though it was, the notion of immersing a prince in nature to achieve a more just society was part of a major eighteenth-century discourse. The theory of enlightened absolutism, after all, called for transforming the absolutist ruler, or at least his adviser, into a servant of all of society. Other writers before Goethe had explicated the idea of sending the ruler to consort with the simple people to enlighten him about true conditions among them and to remove him from the pernicious influences of the court and selfish advisers. One of the most important such works — though by no means the only one — was Wieland's *Der goldne Spiegel.* Goethe's inspiration to apply Rousseau's principles (from his book on education, *Emile,* 1762) to the "education" of a prince can be derived ultimately from the tradition of the "*Fürstenspiegel*" (mirror to princes), particularly François de Salignac de La Mothe Fénelon's *Les Aventures de Télémaque* (The Adventures of Telemach, 1699), right up to Wieland's novel. One passage from *Der goldne Spiegel,* which was published only three years before Goethe's arrival in Weimar and which Goethe knew well, will have to suffice: "Dschengis setzte sich also nichts Geringeres vor — und der bloße Vorsatz klingt schon widersinnig, so sehr hat er das allgemeine Vorurteil wider sich —, als den jungen Tifan . . . mitten unter lauter Hirten und Ackerleuten zu einem guten Fürsten zu bilden."[56] For the peasant, we learn, is "der echt[e] Sohn der Natur" (78: the true son of Nature). When Goethe wanders with the young duke through the forests, goes ice skating with him, rides horses with abandon and swims in cold water, leading him to parts of the duchy and to a class of people that the duke had only known from a distance, then, I think, we can perceive Rousseau's educational ideal, applied by Wieland to the prince — a typically German statist understanding of Rousseau's principles.

Goethe's conception is, so to speak, the Sturm und Drang variant of Wieland's state-oriented variant of Rousseau's anticourtly critique of culture. The prince is to come into contact with peasants — in a sense he plays the peasant, imitates their unspoiled, rough manners; he seeks out nature, forgets his class and his dynasty in the company of young *Genies* and is ultimately transformed into a "natural" person who then introduces natural social and political relations into his realm through enlightened reforms. Of course, in Goethe's Sturm und Drang version we find something new: the project is also directed against middle-class narrowness ("*Spießbürgertum*") and pedantry. We thus find an apparent twofold target of the project: courtly vices (conforming to the older tradition of critique of the court) and traditional middle classes (reflecting the Sturm und Drang's gesture toward social change). But this twofold attack is an illusion: ultimately, the project is directed against the powerless, against peasants and other unprivileged subjects, and only superficially against the privileged classes at court.

With these insights we can move closer to a political assessment of the *Genietreiben*. It quickly turned into a power play against Weimar subjects, in which the duke's authority and his and Goethe's power became the most important factors. Whether they harassed the duke's subjects, as in the case of the burghers of Ilmenau and the peasants they frightened by dressing up as ghosts, or whether they simply played with their power, as when they only revealed their identities after long conversations with unsuspecting subjects, the power of the duke and his privileged companions is the essential ingredient of all these antics. They thus became part of the age-old game of representation of the sovereign's power. Richard Friedenthal points out that, ultimately, this was a traditional pattern: "Ausschweifungen regierender Herren waren sonst nicht eben ungewöhnlich; sie waren die Regel. Das Ungewöhnliche in Weimar waren nur das Genietreiben, der 'neue Ton' und die Beteiligung eines jungen Dichters, der eben berühmt geworden war."[57]

The "new tone" was, thus, essentially a legitimizing strategy for the old excesses that merely appeared in a new guise. Sometimes they were simply the same excesses that had always provided diversion for ruling princes, as in the case of the paradigmatically aristocratic pastime of hunting, in which Goethe and the duke passionately indulged. Hunting was one of the most hotly contested of such princely entertainments, since the sovereign's proprietary game animals were allowed to roam freely over the crops of hapless peasants, who were not allowed to kill them. But other genial diversions that were originally conceived as opposition to Weimar's courtly manners soon conformed to the usual pattern of courtly pastimes, which, within the context of the Weimar economy, were expensive and extravagant. For example, at the beginning Goethe and his friends unceremoniously went ice-skating; but soon this activity, which had been unknown at court, was staged just like other amusements designed partly to represent the prince's power, and with correspondingly outrageous costs: "Der Teich, welcher nicht klein ist, wird rund um mit Fackeln, Lampen und Pechpfannen erleuchtet. Das Schauspiel wird auf der einen Seite mit Hoboisten- und Janitscharen-Musik, auf der andern mit Feuerrädern, Raketen, Kanonen und Mörsern vervielfältigt."[58] This sort of extravagance sounds much like the festivities of Duke Karl Eugen of Württemberg, who was criticized so roundly by Schiller — and by literary historians — for his profligacy, while Karl August has fared exceptionally well.

There is certainly no evidence that Goethe *intended* his and the duke's antics to fit into the ages-old pattern of princely abuse of his subjects — quite the contrary. But there is also no evidence that Goethe succeeded in divorcing the duke from his dynasty's interests. The *Genie* project was fatally flawed by its disregard for power relations — and Goethe himself had shown the consequences of this disregard in some of his fictional works, so he could have known better. At the end of his project stand a duke and his most trusted adviser, bonded to the interests of a petty absolutist state and its ruling family, without the progress and reforms that were Goethe's aim. But we should not be surprised to find such an outcome; as we saw, Goethe had never really managed to voice effective critique of the status quo, even in the pre-Weimar Sturm und Drang period in which he is reputed to have done so. His interests, like those of most of the young, brash *Genies,* were too bound up with the existing power structures. It is an object lesson in living in a difficult, oppressive time, with little outlet for reformative energies but literature and utopian fantasies.

Notes

1 Albert Vinzenz, "Sturm und Drang," in *Metzler Goethe Lexikon,* eds. Benedikt Jeßing et al. (Stuttgart & Weimar: Metzler, 1999), 473–74, here 473.

2 "For liberation from feudal and absolutist chains and for the development of new, freer conditions of life; impulses for a principled opposition and . . . striving for a radical renewal" (Hans-Dietrich Dahnke, "Sturm und Drang," in *Goethe Handbuch,* eds. Hans-Dietrich Dahnke and Regine Otto [Stuttgart: Metzler, 1998], 4: 1024–28, here 1025).

3 Hans Gerd Rötzer, *Geschichte der deutschen Literatur* (Bamberg: Buchner, 1992), 88.

4 Viktor Žmegač et al., *Scriptors Geschichte der deutschen Literatur von den Anfängen bis zur Gegenwart* (Königstein: Scriptor, 1981), 107.

⁵ On the controversy stemming from Jacobi's publication of the poem, see Jürgen Teller, "Das Losungswort Spinoza: Zur Pantheismusdebatte zwischen 1780 und 1787," in *Debatten und Kontroversen: Literarische Auseinandersetzungen in Deutschland des 18. Jahrhunderts*, 2 vols., eds. Hans-Dietrich Dahnke and Bernd Leistner (Berlin: Aufbau, 1989), 1: 135–92. The founding text in the GDR understanding of "Prometheus" as revolution is Edith Braemer, *Goethes Prometheus und die Grundpositionen des Sturm und Drang* (Berlin: Aufbau, 1968).

⁶ See Goethe's letter to Kestner, December 25, 1773 (*G-HB*, 1: 156). Note that letters will be cited where possible from *G-HB*, which makes corrections to the texts in *Werke: Weimarer Ausgabe*, 143 vols. (Weimar: Böhlau, 1887–1919), henceforth cited as *WA*.

⁷ See W. Daniel Wilson, "Zwischen Kritik und Affirmation: Militärphantasien und Geschlechterdisziplinierung bei J. M. R. Lenz," in *"Unaufhörlich Lenz gelesen . . .": Studien zum Leben und Werk von J. M. R. Lenz*, eds. Inge Stephan and Hans-Gerd Winter (Stuttgart: Metzler, 1994), 52–85.

⁸ For a more detailed analysis of the political implications of the two versions of this play, see W. Daniel Wilson, "Hunger/Artist: Goethe's Revolutionary Agitators in *Götz, Satyros, Egmont*, and *Der Bürgergeneral*," *Monatshefte* 86 (1994): 80–94.

⁹ "Just as the poisonous dragon, your husband, threw my brother and three other hapless men into the deepest tower, because, with hungry souls, they had stolen a deer from his forest in order to feed their poor children and wives. — We lamented and begged. . . . He stood there, the disgusting man, like a brazen devil, he stood there and grinned at us. Let them rot and starve in the tower, he spoke through grinding teeth."

¹⁰ The phrase refers to the period around July 1774: Goethe, *Begegnungen und Gespräche*, 6 vols. to date, eds. Ernst and Renate Grumach (Berlin: de Gruyter, 1965–), 1: 268; henceforth cited as Grumach.

¹¹ Käthchen Schönkopf was of the same class as Goethe, the "*Bürgertum*," but as the daughter of an innkeeper she was far beneath the station of the young patrician from Frankfurt's elite, which is why, in his letter to Wilhelm Carl Ludwig Moors of October 1, 1766, Goethe calls her "ein Mädgen, ohne Stand und ohne Vermögen" (*G-HB*, 1: 32: "a girl without class standing or fortune") and suggests that he could never marry her.

¹² On the unclear, but certainly falsified, historical circumstances surrounding Behrisch's brother, see the commentary in *G-MA*, 1.1: 805, and in Johann Wolfgang Goethe, *Sämtliche Werke: Briefe, Tagebücher und Gespräche*, 40 vols., eds. Hendrik Birus et al. (Frankfurt am Main: Deutscher Klassiker Verlag, 1985–99), I, 1: 786–87. The poem was written in April and May 1767.

¹³ On November 3, 1767, Goethe writes to Behrisch with moving empathy toward the tragic dilemma of the Prince of Dessau, who had a middle-class lover but was forced (by Frederick the Great) to marry a Prussian princess (*G-HB*, 1: 56). None of this has anything to do with the prince in "Der wahre Genuß," who buys love with money; none of the critics who assume the connection to Dessau has tried to explain this contradiction. They seem to have come to their conclusion based purely on Behrisch's objection to the apostrophe "O Fürst," but Goethe would not have called

Behrisch's objection "eine übertriebene Delicatesse" ("an exaggerated sensitivity"; see below) if the poem had had anything to do with the Prince of Dessau. When Goethe finally gave in to Behrisch's objection and change "Fürst" to "Freund," he was himself showing an "übertriebene Delicatesse" toward the political status quo; but this attitude is part of a pattern in these years, as I hope to demonstrate, and not a sensitivity to the Prince of Dessau, whom he would not have wanted to insult in the first place. On the more general point of the poem's critical tone, Gerhard Sauder argues that Goethe reverted to the more political addressee: "Für den Druck griff er [=Goethe] aber wieder auf die alte Anrede ['O Fürst'] zurück, ohne die das Gedicht seine kritische Absicht verliert" (*G-MA*, 1.1: 821: "For the publication Goethe used the older apostrophe ['O Prince'], without which the poem loses its critical intent"). This claim is speculative regarding the source of the use of "Fürst" in the printed version and is based on the assumption that Goethe cannot have wanted to soften the political impact of the poem — but that is exactly what he did in other works in this period. On Goethe's very positive relations with the Prince of Dessau, see the praise in his autobiography (*G-MA*, 16: 353 and 328).

[14] March 1768, *G-HB*, 1: 65. Goethe's earlier refusal to change the word is in the letter to Behrisch of December 15, 1767, *WA*, 4.1: 155.

[15] See Franz Hennicke, "Goethes Verbundenheit mit dem Volk: Anfänge einer zentralisierten Industrie im Herzogtum Sachsen-Weimar zur Zeit Goethes," *Goethe-Jahrbuch* 101 (1984), 360–62.

[16] Reported by J. V. Widmann, Grumach, 1: 167.

[17] "As is well known, he was a great admirer of our magnificent cathedral . . . and often stood, astonished, on the side of the great portal, where the building's effect is most perfect. Once he is said to have stood there with folded arms, lost in admiration and dreams. A carter passes close by him, whistling his ditty. Goethe turns around, enraged, and boxes the astonished man's ears roughly, with the words: 'Can't you gape at that, rascal?' — and points to the cathedral." The report is by A. Stöber.

[18] In the *Tag- und Jahreshefte* (Diaries, completed 1822) he states that the reviews in the *Frankfurter Gelehrte Anzeigen* display "Ein unbedingtes Bestreben, alle Begrenzungen zu durchbrechen" (*G-MA*, 14: 10: "An absolute tendency to break through all bounds").

[19] *Positiones Juris*, XLIII-XLIV: "Omnis legislatio ad Principem pertinet. Ut & legum interpretatio" (*G-MA*, 1.2: 555: "All legislative power rests in the prince. And the power to interpret the law"). See the commentary by Gerhard Sauder, 912.

[20] Peter Sprengel comments: "Die Einladung erging wahrscheinlich im September 1775" (*G-MA*, 16: 1062–63: "The invitation was probably issued in September, 1775"), but there is no reason to doubt that Karl August had made a preliminary invitation in Karlsruhe; Goethe reports on an even earlier invitation through the intermediary Kraus.

[21] Grumach dates these events to summer of 1773 (1: 237). Other passages of his autobiography in which Goethe mentions pre-Weimar possibilities of public service, particularly because *Genies* were in demand for such employment, include *G-MA*, 16: 748, 802, 829–30.

[22] See the letters from August and from December 25, 1773: *G-HB*, 1: 149–50 and 156.

[23] The term appears in a letter to Johanna Fahlmer of about April 10, 1775: *WA*, 4.2: 254.

[24]

CRUGANTINO:	What are you doing?
SECOND VAGABOND:	Today someone gave the preacher a fawn; it's hanging downstairs in the pantry. We're going to make off with it.
THIRD VAGABOND:	And we're going to nail the horns onto his wig-form. His wig-form with his fanciest wig is in the corner; you can count on me! . . .
SECOND VAGABOND:	You'll climb in the window and hand me the carcass. We'll remove the horns and give them to you.
THIRD VAGABOND:	Let me take care of the rest! That will look great on the wig, with a sign on it: "The New Moses"!

[25] Leaves from the notebook of Johannes Daniel Falk, first published in 1965 in Grumach, 1: 478 (the word "*liessen*" is unsure; part of the episode is confirmed by F. T. A. Müller, 479; on the girls, cf. 480): "In Ilmenau they went swimming; nine or ten of them, with the duke out in front, jumped out of the water and danced naked around a pastor or a girl who happened by; they gave a glazier fish broth with mustard to drink; Goethe took off the glazier's wig and cut off all his hair with scissors; then they made him run under a water pump and almost drowned him."

[26] Reported by F. W. H. von Trebra, Grumach, 1: 446.

[27] "Hab ein Schauspiel bald fertig" (*WA*, 4.2: 255: "I'm almost finished with a play"). Some commentators (including Karl Robert Mandelkow, *G-HB*, 1: 623) believe that the play to which Goethe refers here as almost completed is *Stella*. Others vote for *Claudine;* the older views are summarized in *Goethe über seine Dichtungen*, 2 parts, 6 vols., ed. Hans Gerhard Gräf (Frankfurt am Main: Rütten & Loening, 1901–14), 2.1: 99. As Gräf notes, both are possible, but Goethe's indication a few days earlier that he had "dug up" ("aufgegraben") *Claudine* makes it the best candidate. The Berlin Edition of Goethe's works, too, relates the passage to *Claudine: Werke*, 23 vols., ed. Siegfried Seidel (Berlin: Aufbau, 1961–78), 4: 667. Further, Goethe later indicated that *Claudine* was "früher fertig geworden" ("finished earlier") than *Stella* (*G-MA*, 1.2: 725). The term "*Schauspiel*" could easily refer to *Claudine*, which in the original version was called "ein Schauspiel mit Gesang" ("a play with song").

[28] "Dear Knebel, I'm enclosing *Claudine;* read it to our duke when you have an hour free." Of course, Karl August only became the duke on his eighteenth birthday, September 4.

[29] "Rugantino [the name given to the character Crugantino in later versions of the play] in Goethe's *Claudine von Villa Bella* is the original that Goethe played back then." The authenticity of this report, which was first published in 1965, is bolstered when Böttiger narrates the game of dice with Einsiedel that Goethe's letter of December 25–26, 1775, relates (*G-HB*, 1: 203).

[30] Gräf, *Goethe über seine Dichtungen*, 2.1: 100 (1903): "How much they lived in the *Claudine* sphere in the first months after Goethe's arrival in Weimar." More recently, Gertrud Rudloff-Hille, commenting in the Berlin Edition, finds even less to remark on in this passage: "Noch in den ersten Monaten nach der Ankunft in Weimar machte es Goethe Spaß, wie einer der Vagabunden zu leben" (4: 668: "Even in the first months after his arrival in Weimar Goethe delighted in living like one of the vagabonds").

[31] "Goethe did all of that from a coldly calculated plan, not because he loved doing it, but because of the idea of making the duke a natural person. . . . The duke, then, was to become a natural person and torn away from the miserable life at court among philistines." "*Peinlich*" ("miserable") is an unsure reading.

[32] "They dug potatoes out of the soil, baked them using kindling, slept with girls in the woods, and carved messages in the trees."

[33] "When Goethe came to Weimar for the first time and the duke suggested that he stay, Goethe said that he (a genius) could not live in a city. Nothing but philistines lived there; a genius, a genuine natural person, belongs in nature, in the open air, woods and fields."

[34] "[Bode] asked [Goethe] why he was making such awful use of his post, teaching the duke to curse, play pranks, etc., when he could do so much good? Goethe then fell into his arms and said the following incomprehensible words to him in an emotional tone: 'My friend, wait, wait for the outcome; I can't explain my intention now, soon the world, you and Weimar will realize that I have earned a place in Heaven.'" The author, writing to Countess Caroline of Hessen-Homburg in the fall of 1776, is unknown.

[35] Richard Friedenthal, *Goethe: Sein Leben und seine Zeit* (Munich: Piper, 1963), 219: "All of it is grotesque and not without an unpleasant taste, that it is the duke and the gentlemen from his court: there can be no resistance or complaining, the duke's vexed subject simply has to bow and silently drag his barrels back up the hill."

[36] See August Diezmann, *Goethe und die lustige Zeit in Weimar* (Leipzig: Keil, 1857).

[37] Karl Vietor, *Goethe: Dichtung — Wissenschaft — Weltbild* (Bern: Francke, 1949), 64.

[38] "[I] wished myself that he would abandon some of his wildness for which people here malign him; it really consists of no more than hunting, riding horses fast, cracking a big whip, all in the duke's company. I'm certain these aren't his own inclinations, but he has to do it for a while in order to win over the duke and then accomplish something good, that's what I think; he didn't tell me the reason for it, he defended himself with strange reasons, I still think that he's wrong." This report is cited by (among others) the two most important modern Goethe biographers: Nicholas Boyle, *Goethe: The Poet and the Age*, vol. 1: *The Poetry of Desire (1749–1790)* (Oxford: Oxford UP, 1992), 245; Karl Otto Conrady, *Goethe: Leben und Werk*, 2 vols. (Königstein: Athenäum, 1982; rpt., Frankfurt am Main: Fischer, 1988), 1: 318. Similarly, Heinrich Meyer, *Goethe: Das Leben im Werk* (Stuttgart: Günther, 1967), 216.

[39] Stein's interpretation is shared by Christian Felix Weisse in a letter to Johann Peter Uz, presumably in May 1776: "Man giebt Goethe hauptsächlich Schuld, daß er den

Herzog von Regierungsgeschäften abhalte und zu Polisonerien verführe. . . . Doch scheint es mir, wenn ich Goethe recht beurtheile, daß er dies nur zu einem Mittel wähle, sich dem jungen Herzog entbehrlich zu machen, und aus ihm ein Muster eines großen Fürsten zu bilden. Kopf hat er genug dazu" (Grumach, 1: 413–14: "They blame Goethe mainly for diverting the duke from his duties as ruler and leading him into pranks . . . But it seems to me, if I judge Goethe correctly, that he uses this only as a means of making himself indispensable to the duke and forming him into the epitome of a great prince. He is smart enough to do it"). With the phrase "Wenn ich Goethe recht beurtheile" ("if I judge Goethe correctly"), Weisse admits that he is speculating (he only stayed in Weimar for about ten days). Nevertheless, biographers like Boyle (245) adopt this interpretation. The mining expert Friedrich Wilhelm Heinrich von Trebra writes of the harassment of the merchant Glaser in Stützerbach mentioned earlier that Goethe's behavior during that week had "einen eignen, moralische hohe Zwecke aussprechenden Charakter" (!) ("a singular character that expressed a morally lofty goal"), Trebra relates how Goethe cut the face of the merchant out of a family portrait and put his own face through the hole to scare him when he came home, while the others rolled the man's barrels down the hill.) Trebra: "Bey solchen nicht zweydeutigen Merkzeichen, war es mir gar nicht mehr zweifelhaft, des freundschaftlich leitenden Genius [i.e. Goethe] Zweck war: durch einen, in überspannter Lustigkeit mit gemachten halben Schritt sich in die Möglichkeit zu bringen, von der andern Hälfte desto gewisser, den heran reifenden mächtigen Freund zurück zu halten, und so aus dem dicken Übel [probably a misreading for "Nebel"] der Zerstreuung im Unfug der Leidenschaft, zum lichten Sonnenstrahl der Besonnenheit, zum Genuß wahren und Nutzbringenden Vergnügens zu führen" (Grumach, 1: 445–46: "After such an unambiguous sign I no longer doubted that the goal of the guiding, friendly spirit [i.e., Goethe] was — through a half-step that he went along with in uninhibited fun — to make it possible for him to rein in his powerful, maturing friend that much more surely, and thus to lead him out of the thick fog of diversion in the craziness of passion to the clear sunlight of thoughtfulness, to the appreciation of true and useful pleasure"). Karl von Lyncker, too, uses the euphemistic phrase "sehr lustig[e] Vorfäll[e]" (Grumach, 1: 472: "very funny incidents") in Ilmenau. None of these contemporaries claims to have this opinion from a conversation with Goethe. The writer himself doesn't mince words when writing in his diary: on September 1, 1777, Glaser was "sündlich geschunden" (*WA*, 3.1: 45: "terribly skinned") by Goethe and friends.

[40] Curt Hohoff, *Johann Wolfgang von Goethe: Dichtung und Leben* (Munich: Langen-Müller, 1989), 228.

[41] Boyle, *Goethe: The Poet and the Age*, 1: 283. Boyle's source for this view — a remark by Böttiger from 1797 — does not say at all that Goethe moderated the behavior of others but only that he knew "wie weit ers [!] grade überal wagen dürfe" (Grumach, 1: 402–3: "how far he could go"). Conrady at first seems to distance himself from this interpretation: "Es gibt ein beliebtes Deutungsmuster für die stürmische Zeit des Herzogs mit seinem Dichterfreund: Goethe habe den Jüngeren in der Schlußphase des Reifeprozesses unvermerkt lenken wollen, und solche Führung sei wohldurchdacht gewesen" (1: 318: "There is a popular interpretation for the stormy period of the duke with his poet friend: Goethe supposedly wanted to guide the younger man imperceptibly in the final stage of his maturation, and this

guidance was supposedly well thought-out"). But then Conrady does speak of Goethe's positive influence, not in the form of educating a prince but of educating the "Privatperson" ("private person") Karl August — though he indicates that one should not assume a "wohldurchdachten Erziehungsplan Goethes" (1: 318: "well thought-out education plan of Goethe's") for the duke. Ultimately, Conrady portrays Goethe as the one who warns and moderates (1: 318–20). Nevertheless, Conrady seems to be on the right track when he remarks: "Den Beteiligten selbst kam es wohl so vor, als verwirklichten sie mit ihrem ungebärdigen Leben etwas vom zeitgemäß Unkonventionellen, als setzten sie die Schlagworte vom Genie und Naturhaften in private Praxis um" (1: 317–18: "The participants themselves probably thought that they were realizing something of the age's antipathy to convention, that they were transforming the ideals of genius and the natural into private reality"). But Conrady does not connect this notion to *Claudine* and, thus, to Goethe's concrete conception.

[42] See Goethe's letter to Johanna Fahlmer of February 19, 1776, *G-HB*, 1: 208.

[43] See her letter to Zimmermann, March 8, 1776, Grumach, 1: 410. Willy Andreas writes, regarding this letter: "Eine zuständigere Beurteilerin für diese Frühzeit von Goethe und Carl August kann man sich kaum wünschen" (*Carl August von Weimar: Ein Leben mit Goethe 1757–1783* [Stuttgart: Kilpper, 1953], 250: "One can hardly imagine a more competent judge of this early period of Goethe and Karl August"). See also, e.g., Karl von Lyncker, in Grumach, 1: 406.

[44] To C. von Stein, February 23, 1776: *G-HB*, 1: 209.

[45] To Merck, May 27, 1776, Grumach, 1: 425. Cf. Merck to an unknown addressee, September 1777: "Göthe gilt und dirigirt Alles" (Grumach, 2: 19: "Goethe counts for everything and directs everything").

[46] *Der junge Goethe: Neu bearbeitete Ausgabe in fünf Bänden*, ed. Hanna Fischer-Lamberg (Berlin: de Gruyter, 1963–73), 5: 435: "Crugantino . . . who is devoted only to personal freedom, is the true revolutionary in Goethe's early works." Conrady agrees with this view (1: 282). See also Gertrud Rudloff-Hille in the Berlin Edition: Crugantino "ist ein Empörer gegen die herrschende Feudalgesellschaft" (4: 668: "is a rebel against the dominant feudal society").

[47] "Do you know the needs of a young heart like mine? A young crazy guy? Where do you have a stage for my life? Your civil society is intolerable to me! If I want to work, I have to be a lackey; if I want to have fun, I have to be a lackey. Doesn't anyone who is worth anything have to go out into the wide world instead? . . . whoever devotes himself to being a vagabond has no goals and no boundaries; for our heart — o! it is infinite, as long as its powers last."

[48] "In my day it was different. The peasants were doing well, and they were always cheerfully singing a song that gladdened one's heart; and the noble lord wasn't ashamed, and sang along, if he wanted to. The most natural, the best!"

[49] "And where is nature if not with my peasant? He eats, drinks, works, sleeps and makes love, in a straightforward way, and doesn't give a damn how they dress it up in the cities and at court!"

[50] "Don't stop talking! I can't get enough of hearing a man of your class speak like that."

[51] "[Goethe's] indecent behavior, with curses and low-class, vulgar expressions. Yesterday he [i.e., Karl August] was at my house; he claimed that anyone with decency and manners doesn't deserve to be called an honest man . . . which is why he can't stand anyone who doesn't have something coarse about him. He has all of that from Goethe."

[52] To Charlotte von Stein, December 4, 1777: "Wie sehr ich wieder . . . Liebe zu der Classe von Menschen gekriegt habe! die man die niedre nennt! die aber gewiss für Gott die höchste ist" (*G-HB*, 1: 242: "How much I have again gotten . . . love to the class of people who are called the low! But who are for God doubtless the highest").

[53] "Hier [i.e., in Ilmenau, May 1776] mischten sie sich beim Vogelschießen unters Volk, schwenkten die Mägde beim Tanz in den Dorfschenken, trieben allerlei Schabernack. In Ilmenau und im nahgelegenen Stützerbach, wo man der Residenz am weitesten entrückt war, streiften Carl August und Goethe die Fesseln von Stand und Geburt völlig ab" (Andreas, 255: "In Ilmenau they mixed with the common people during bird shooting, danced around with girls in the village pubs, carried on all kinds of tomfoolery. In Ilmenau and in nearby Stützerbach, where they were farthest from the seat of power in Weimar, Karl August and Goethe tore off completely the chains of class and birth").

[54] During this time, Stolberg also wrote to Lenz: "Der Herzog ist ein herrlicher Junge, beide Herzoginnen, Mutter und Frau, sind zween Engel" (Grumach, 1: 391: "The duke is a splendid fellow, both duchesses, mother and wife, are two angels"), and to Miller: "Es ward uns sehr wohl in Weimar, so eine gute Fürstenfamilie habe ich nicht für möglich gehalten" (ibid.: "We got along wonderfully in Weimar; I would never have thought such a good ruling family possible").

[55] On the following, see W. Daniel Wilson, "Patriarchy, Politics, Passion: Labor and Werther's Search for Nature," *Internationales Archiv für Sozialgeschichte der deutschen Literatur*, 14.2 (1989): 15–44.

[56] Christoph Martin Wieland, *Der goldne Spiegel und andere politische Dichtungen*, ed. Herbert Jaumann (Munich: Winkler, 1979), 208: "So Gengis planned nothing less — and the very idea sounds absurd, since it contradicts a general prejudice — than forming the young Tifan into a good prince . . . in the midst of only shepherds and farmers."

[57] Friedenthal, 221: "Excesses of ruling princes had not been unusual; they were the rule. The unusual thing in Weimar was only the goings-on of the geniuses, the 'new tone,' and the participation of a young writer who had just become famous."

[58] Grumach, 2: 64: "The pond, which is not small, is lit up on all sides with torches, lamps and pitch lamps. The scene is augmented on the one side with oboe and janissary music, on the other side with fire wheels, rockets, cannons and mortars." This report is from J. F. Kranz to Elisabeth Goethe, dated February 16, 1778; for another description, see Grumach, 2: 64–65. Andreas plays down the financial costs of these entertainments when he castigates the "*Mißgünstige*" (dissatisfied people) who criticized the wastefulness (254).

"Wilde Wünsche": The Discourse of Love in the Sturm und Drang

Karin A. Wurst

LOVE IS A CENTRAL THEME in the literature of the Sturm und Drang. Modern criticism has recognized the importance of the role played by love in the formation of the modern middle-class identity that evolved during the period of transition between feudal society and the beginnings of modern society, and the high point of this transitional period was, it is now agreed, the eighteenth century.[1] This transition is characterized by the emergent cultural dominance of the middle class with its emphasis on individual achievements, on rational conduct, on the desire for self-determination, and on a specific ideal of the family.[2] It is especially the last point, the creation of what Lawrence Stone has termed the "companionate marriage," founded on a new notion of love "as an intensified affective bonding," that is important for the discourse of love in the Sturm und Drang.[3] This new ideal, described in the classic studies by Lawrence Stone and Edward Shorter, represents a paradigm shift to which literature made an essential contribution.[4] As we shall see, the literature of the Sturm und Drang embraces love as a central aspect of bourgeois identity driving the modernization process, while also pointing to the internal contradictions and the difficulties associated with this transition. In particular, the tension between socialization within one's family and its value system and the pursuit of individual wishes and desires, between the pull of community, on the one hand, and individualism, on the other, occupies the imagination of Sturm und Drang authors.

As the historical context for these discursive changes, social historians point to the new economic patterns that moved economic production for pay outside the household. This transformation, in turn, required different models of living together. In the separation of paid work from the household and the development of separate value systems for the worlds of work and family life, the family and its relationships took on a compensatory role.[5] If the sphere of work was characterized by efficiency, utility, and profitability, the family and the household were seen as the place where true happiness, harmony, and sympathetic sociability could be realized.[6] Sentimentalism (*Empfindsamkeit*), with its specific concept of love based on personal emotional attraction, represented a new framework for the orientation and understanding of the self, and this shift in mentality both contributed to and reacted against the transformation of feudal society into a functionally differentiated society.[7] The ideology of the family as a refuge, based on the value system of Sentimentalism, made the structural transformation of society possible because it compensated for the lack of social stability.[8] Here, in the private sphere, there was created a new interpersonal value system that governed the relationship between the individual and the individual's immediate circle of friends, the beloved, and the family.[9] Heightened sensibilities led to what has been described as the intensification of ego-reality,[10] a new kind of subjectivity in which the individual perceives his or her self-analysis as pleasurable. The complexity and individuality of the highly self-reflexive person became the indicators of a rich emotional life,[11] and this more complex subjectivity required the more complex love relationships explored in this essay. Tensions arise when the wishes of the individual clash with those of the larger society.

The intensified emotionality of the relationship between parents and children and the love between the couple made the family the predominant site for self-fulfillment and happiness. As the core of bourgeois intimacy, sentimentalized love between the couple and between parents and children came to dominate the private sphere. As the early studies by Reinhart Koselleck and Jürgen Habermas pointed out, the private sphere and its center, the family, constituted for the middle class an oppositional formation that challenged the cultural and political dominance of the nobility. The family was regarded as the realm of ideal human social interaction, where members were bound together by familial love and educated to become moral beings.[12] With the work of Michel Foucault and Niklas Luhmann, new attention was focused on the discursive construction of love within the context of social change.[13] Both studies develop broad, sweeping new conceptual models that allow the patterns or codes to emerge, but more recent studies have refined these models by pointing to the fact that the literature of eighteenth-century Germany not only established these new codes or patterns but, at the same time, also reacted to them in a (self-)critical fashion. Recent studies with their focus on individual textual analyses, therefore, explore not only how the patterns of these intimate relationships were established but also show that Luhmann's model needs to be differentiated for the German context; Jutta Greis and Walter Hinderer, for example, remind us of the centrality of *Empfindsamkeit* for the new concept of love.[14]

As the Sturm und Drang texts will show, love mediates uneasily between individualistic desires and the social framework, with its strong sense of familial love. The sentimental internalized ties of familial love denote, on the one hand, stability and personal grounding and, on the other, imprisonment. Although the focus of the present essay is on the concept of erotic love, it cannot be isolated from the context provided by familial love. Bengt Algot Sørensen, Karin A. Wurst, and Gail Hart have analyzed familial love as a form of intensive socialization, as the stabilizing core of bourgeois intimacy.[15] The tension between patriarchal and sentimental values is also at the core of two studies on the question of differences and tensions between the generations, Clara Stockmeyer's examination of social problems and Richard Quabius's study of the history of ideas.[16] Tracing the development of love from the alliance model to romantic love as a historically changing code of social communication, Niklas Luhmann bases his sociological study on a variety of textual materials from the seventeenth to the twentieth century in a European context and comes to the conclusion that the eighteenth century is a time of stagnation in the transformation of the paradigm of love.[17] Günter Sasse, who focuses exclusively on German literature of the eighteenth century, distinguishes three stages of love: rational (30–37), affectionate (38–47), and romantic (48–59). In the early Enlightenment the rational, reasoned selection of a partner was based on moral character as determined by a close and deliberate examination of the qualities of a potential partner. The choice not only emphasized the proper distribution of tasks and responsibilities between men and women but also served to discipline passion and sexuality. The second paradigm bases the relationship on emotional attraction and friendship.[18] As in the first paradigm, sexuality, which was limited to marriage, was domesticated.[19]

The conception of love created by Sturm und Drang authors cannot, however, be neatly categorized into these two historical paradigms. It is a hybrid and to a greater or lesser degree it displays traits of both paradigms; it also anticipates the paradigm of romantic love, which was not restricted to marriage and would later go on to celebrate the fusion of emotion, sensuality, and sexuality.[20]

The transformation from a stratified to a functionally organized social system was accompanied by the erosion of the family alliance model, in which families had arranged marriages on the basis of social and economic compatibility and interests. Marriage partners had tended to share similar expectations and rules of communication, and therefore similar goals in life. The decline of the family alliance model forced modern couples to negotiate these kinds of agreements themselves, making the couple responsible for initiating a successful partnership. As we shall see in many Sturm und Drang texts, these painful negotiations are at the center of the conflict, as couples transgress the family alliance model. Love can also embody the desire to escape or transcend the perceived limitations of a character's socialization within a particular class or offer an alternative to a life that is experienced as unsatisfactory, alienated, and meaningless. It can express the desire for a more authentic existence. Literature and, in particular, the literary discourse of love is the forum within which issues such as these could be negotiated and expressed.

Goethe's *Die Leiden des jungen Werthers* broke new ground in the discourse of love by fusing Sentimentalist traits with a new, qualitatively different sense of an all-encompassing power of love as the force of creation and life. In the celebration of love as an almost religious experience, we see a search for alternatives to bourgeois rationality, to materialism, and to the increasing bureaucratization of life. In this novel we see that the individual retreats not only from courtly life, with its focus on status and representation, but also from the emergent rationally organized and differentiated, alienated life of work and commerce. Modern romantic-erotic love becomes part of the search for a more authentic natural life, for an altered state of being, and for communication between highly individualized beings. As traditions based on the system of estates lose their power to provide their members with a stable unchanging identity, love increasingly becomes a medium for securing one's identity and orienting oneself in the modern world. It represents a form of compensation for the loss of social meaning by providing social grounding in a context of increasing individualization. The highly individualized self requires equally intense and exclusive relationships. This requirement decreases the likelihood of finding a suitable "soul mate" and increases the possibility that the subject desiring the most intimate communication remains without response. The stakes in personal relationships became enormous, as is suggested in *Werther*. The intellectual's disillusionment with his responsibilities at court, his sphere of work, prompt him to seek alternative outlets for his individuality. With his indulgence in literature, his abortive attempts as an artist, and his enjoyment of the simple life (letter of June 21, *G-MA*, 1.2: 217–18), he seeks to create a multifaceted, harmonious authenticity in his life. The experience of love is the culmination of his experience of nature and, thus, his search for more wholeness and immediacy in his life. As a unique form of friendship with a demand for exclusivity, love becomes one of the most important codes of communication, one whose rules allow the individual to express, construct, simulate, assume, and deny emotions.[21]

The motif of love at first sight is used as a symbol of a predetermined divine destiny, allowing the individual to isolate love from the moral discourse surrounding erotic attraction by idealizing it. Love is presented as a life force that creates both delight and a deep sense of "connectedness" to nature, while at the same time opening the abyss of despair when it is not reciprocated or is withdrawn. Werther's intense experience of nature in the famous letter of May 10 (*G-MA,* 1.2: 198–99) bespeaks a sense of cosmic unity in which the individual subject and his environment are in harmony. This, in turn, prepares him for the most powerful force binding man to nature, love.

Love as the culmination and intensification of the sentimental experience of an individual's soul, of the inner self in harmony with another or others — be it friends or lovers — and with nature is also at the center of Friedrich Heinrich Jacobi's *Woldemar* (1779). In this novel love is realized in a triangular relationship based on the deep friendship between Woldemar and Allwina and Henriette:

> Ich wandelte mit meinen Freundinnen sachte unserer Wohnung zu, sammelnd in mir alle Töne, die in meiner Seele angeschlagen hatten, daß sie nicht verhalleten, wenigstens nicht so geschwinde verklängen. Ein vieljähriges Gemisch dunkler Empfindungen ordnete sich in Melodie; und diese Melodie wieder in Accorde. In den schwingenden Sonnenglanz traten Sirius und Venus. Vor und nach erschienen die übrigen Sterne. Wir hörten die Musik der Sphären.[22]

Jacobi's imagery links the spiritual and the sensual aspects of love, represented respectively by the stars Sirius and Venus. Love purifies, clarifies, and intensifies what already exists diffusely in Woldemar's self and turns it into a melody, which finally becomes embedded in the harmony of nature through the symbol of the music of the spheres.[23] Love not only strikes a chord in the sensitive and receptive individual but also organizes and focuses the diffuse sensibilities into a pronounced and well-defined sense of harmony (harmonious music), which, the individual feels, connects him in turn to the surrounding cosmic harmony.

Carl in Klinger's *Sturm und Drang* also uses images from nature to convey how love affects the individual's sense of harmony (or disharmony). When the lovers Carl and Caroline are reunited after a long separation caused by a deadly feud between their families, Carl tells Caroline that heaven has formed a bond that no human hand can sever (*K-SD,* 27). During his separation from her he felt disjointed and alienated from a nature that he therefore perceived as hostile and frightening:

Die Nacht liegt so kühl, so gut um mich! Die Wolken ziehen so still
dahin! Ach sonst, wie das alles trüb und düster war! Wohl, mein Herz!
daß du dies Schauerhafte wieder einmal rein fühlen kannst! daß die
Nachtlüftchen dich umsäuseln und du die Liebe wehen fühlst in der
ganzen stillen Natur. Glänzet nur Sterne! ach Freunde sind wir wieder
worden! Ihr werdet getragen mit allmächtiger Liebe, wie mein Herz,
und flimmt in reiner Liebe, wie meine Seele. Ihr wart mir so kalt auf je-
nen Bergen! . . . So hieng ich oft an dir, Mond! und dunkel wards um
mich, da ich nach der reichte, die so ferne war. Ach, daß alles so zusammen gewebt, zusammen gebunden mit Liebe ist. (*K-SD,* 44–45)[24]

The text suggests that only the loving heart can grasp the harmonious
divine majesty of nature as a benevolent friend. Only when nature and
the soul are in harmony can Carl see how the universe is held together
by love. If that is not the case, then darkness, coldness, gloom, and the
hostility of nature become the correlates of the chaos and violent anger
that the alienated individual feels. The effects of love on a man's heart
enables him to feel "alles . . . was Schöpfung schuf, was der Mensch
fühlen kann" (*K-SD,* 46).[25] As part of himself, as the "Licht meiner
Augen" (*K-SD,* 45),[26] he needs (this) woman to instill the feeling of love
in him, which, in turn, allows him to grasp the essence and true meaning
of life, humanity's cosmic harmony. As Bruce Duncan has pointed out,
Carl is portrayed as incomplete: his love for Caroline allows him to
achieve wholeness, an authentic identity, while the loss of Caroline is a
loss of self for him.[27]

However, Duncan's conclusion, that the lovers as Klinger's "theatrical constructs, searching for wholeness" are "split fractured elements of
the same entity (Carl/Caroline)" (184), needs to be qualified to apply
only to Carl, to the male construct of identity formation. The text does,
indeed, portray the lovers as equal participants in love, whose hearts,
souls, and beings are one (*K-SD,* 27), for they belong to one class, grew
up together, and, after their families are reconciled, can truly reunite and
actually look forward to a life together. Nevertheless, it is Carl who uses
these images of unity and wholeness. The soliloquies of the lovers, who
employ the same imagery — the light/dark metaphors, moon, stars,
night, gloom — reveal a gender-specific portrayal of love. In keeping
with the traditional representation of the times, which saw women as
more in tune and closer to nature, Caroline is portrayed as part of nature:

Nacht! stille Nacht! laß dirs vertrauen! Laßts euch vertrauen, Wiesen
Täler! Hügel und Wald! Laß dirs vertrauen Mond und all ihr Sterne!
Nicht mehr nach ihm weinend, nicht mehr ihm seufzend, wandle ich
unter deinem Licht, sonsten trauriger Freund! Nicht mehr klagend

antwortest du mir, Echo, daß du keinen andern Widerhall, als seinen Namen kanntest. (*K-SD*, 45)[28]

By contrast with Carl, Caroline regards nature neither as an antagonist nor a path to grasping the essence of the universe but as her echo, a part of her that is as sad or as happy as she is. The construct celebrates "the feminine" as the less alienated, more natural state of being that can offer salvation to the modern male torn between the value systems of the public and the private spheres. The elaborate and particular construct of searching for wholeness through the power of love, which allows access to cosmic harmony and, with it, to the wholeness of an authentic self, is that of the male protagonist.

Not unlike Werther and Carl, Ferdinand in Schiller's *Kabale und Liebe* also regards love as the ultimate means to authentic experience. Steeped in the reformist Enlightenment philosophy of the middle-class university, he is deeply torn over his position in society. His trust in the values imparted during his earlier socialization at court has been shattered, plunging him into conflict with his father, whose intrigues, lack of morals, and ambitious designs of marriage repulse him. Ferdinand's celebration of erotic love, reflecting the young Schiller's own "philosophy of love," is the culmination of his sense of freedom from social conventions. His love is not the cause of his defiance but the effect, culmination, and intensification of his rejection of his initial courtly socialization. For Luise, erotic love at first sight awakens her nature, which brings out her potential for love, her "wilde Wünsche" (*S-NA,* 5N: 26: "wild desires"). She tries to reconcile her religious and moral upbringing with this intense experience of erotic love by regarding Ferdinand as sent by heaven to delight her, arguing that she can love God in his creation: "Ich wußte von keinem Gott mehr, und doch hatt' ich ihn nie so geliebt" (*S-NA*, 5N: 22).[29] While Luise's love brings out her nature, Ferdinand needs love, this particular kind of love, to create his own individuality, free from social conventions.

Ferdinand shares this fate with other Sturm und Drang figures, such as Julius in *Julius von Tarent,* who, as Helmut Koopmann has pointed out, insists on his own singularity.[30] However, Leisewitz also hints at another aspect of erotic love. Julius von Tarent's excessive passion is linked to a form of temporary insanity, an illness that hinders rational thought and action. It is seen as an affliction that the individual is unable to control. Indulging in these passions exposes the self to the dangers of the imagination; they "present the soul with fantasies that it cannot distinguish from reality,"[31] in effect, robbing the individual of all social orientation. Daydreaming and fantasizing represent a fertile ground for young love. As a boy Julius already took pleasure in daydreaming in solitude, and before he knew what love was, he already had a lovesick gaze. His heart was well prepared to receive love and the dreamer is overpowered by love, which gives his reveries a focus and begins to drive his whole being. In *Sturm und Drang* Carl uses a similar image to describe the necessity of love for the functioning of his "machine" (*K-SD*, 28). At the same time, he alludes to the precarious vicinity of insanity and salvation in this most powerful of all life forces when he argues that love holds this machine together, a machine that is in itself divided and, thus, precariously close at any given moment to its own destruction.

The metaphor of the machine suggests here an automatic response of the senses that the rational mind is unable to control; Julius knows that love cannot be set aside at will. Realizing his affliction, which cripples him in the larger social context of his familial responsibilities, he is aware that he is delirious with love and in need of guidance. As Hans-Jürgen Schings has shown, the eighteenth century regarded mood disorders as "reality-deficits" ("Realitätsdefizite").[32] Although the individual is aware of the affliction, he or she is powerless to end it and can but wait for the condition to subside.

The trope of passionate love as a form of temporary insanity also applies to Lady Milford in *Kabale und Liebe,* who offers a lengthy description of her state of mind as passion destabilizes her. Even though her passion is portrayed as an affliction, a bout of temporary insanity, she is still able carefully to orchestrate a cabal to get what she desires. Yet, in her plans she fails to take into consideration the fact that erotic love has to be based on reciprocity and cannot be willed, coerced, or forced.

As her love is rejected, she momentarily turns into an embodiment of fury. Like that of Bertha in Eleonore von Thon's *Adelheit von Rastenberg* (1788), Lady Milford's passion is transformed into murderous rage:

> Ich will über diese schimpfliche Leidenschaft siegen, mein Herz unterdrücken und das deinige zermalmen — Felsen und Abgründe will ich zwischen euch werfen; eine Furie will ich mitten durch euren Himmel gehn; mein Name soll eure Küsse wie ein Gespenst Verbrecher auseinander scheuchen; deine junge blühende Gestalt unter seiner Umarmung welk wie eine Mumie zusammenfallen — Ich kann nicht mit ihm glüklich werden — aber *Du* solst es auch nicht werden. (*S-NA*, 5N: 138–40)[33]

The fact that the momentary loss of reason through love can become destructive or self-destructive suggests "the frightening possibility that as paradigms change, individuals might actually remain completely un-integrated, grounded neither by the family alliance nor by sentimental love."[34] It is this existential danger that renders the stakes so high in the discourse of love. While Bertha gives in to this rage and kills her rival, who, not unlike Luise Millerin, has also already renounced her beloved for the sake of her marriage and her honor, Lady Milford rises above her fury. Her social position would be compromised if the marriage did not take place, and so, torn between pride and a rediscovered sense of virtue, she decides to renounce her love for Ferdinand, to withdraw her demand of marriage, and to leave the court and her dishonorable position.

What these plays share is that they pit love as the embodiment of internal, subjective values against the wishes of the more powerful, external "rationality" of familial and state interests. Individuality clashes with the collective values expressed by state authority, class, and socialization. Many Sturm und Drang texts oscillate between the celebration of erotic love as a utopian desire for an intensification of the self and as a means of escaping the limits of one's community and class. Yet, love turns out to be an ineffective means for transcending class boundaries that have been so deeply internalized. In *Kabale und Liebe* Ferdinand, Luise, and Lady Milford are unable to extricate themselves from their socialization and value systems. This leads to the misreading of motivations and contributes to the crisis.

After Lady Milford lost her home and family in England, she became the paramour of the prince. To accept a lifestyle financed with the blood, sweat, and tears of his subjects, she had had to suppress her sense of morality and justice. The conflict in her between the bourgeois sense of honor based on her original socialization in England and her external determination by her present position at court as the paramour of the prince is only dormant, not resolved. That is why she is bothered by the other women in the prince's life and by luxurious presents that are paid for by his abused subjects. She attempts to reconcile these two mentalities by giving away for humanitarian purposes the jewelry she receives from the prince as a gift. After all, she has only sold her honor to him, not her heart, and the precarious peace and stability in her soul are achieved only by suppressing her wilder desires. When she meets Ferdinand and falls passionately in love with him, her peace of mind is shattered. Yet, she uses the ultimate expression of instrumental reason, the court intrigue, to gain access to Ferdinand. She suggests to her lover that her marriage to Ferdinand would be the most opportune means of securing their relationship. This is, of course, not unusual, since a prince's paramours were often married off to lower-ranking members of the court. Yet, she does not follow the rules, since she does not see it as the traditional marriage of convenience. Once she is married to the beloved, in what she hopes will be an unconventional "middle-class" "*Liebesehe*" (love marriage), she plans to extricate herself from the court. She hopes that the reward (her marriage to a man she passionately loves) will make up for the time she has spent languishing in a dishonorable relationship. The moment she falls passionately in love with Ferdinand her sense of self becomes destabilized, and suppressed personality traits surface again, making her a deeply divided character.

The difficulty of liberating oneself from one's socialization is no less visible in the lovers Luise and Ferdinand. At first glance this play seems to go beyond the cliché of the nobleman as seducer of middle-class innocence. After all, both Luise and Ferdinand are deeply and honestly in love with each other, and their love seems to have the potential for escaping class boundaries, for, as Sasse points out, a relationship that disregards inheritance and possessions is in principle alien to a social order based on rank and birth (3). Yet both characters show that the force of their socialization into their original communities cannot be overcome by mere will power. Luise's comment "daß die Zärtlichkeit noch barbarischer zwingt, als Tyrannenwuth" (*S-NA*, 5N: 158)[35] suggests her inability to transcend her bourgeois identity despite her own heroic efforts to reconcile her love with her Christian belief and the bourgeois value system. In the end, it is her Christian belief and her duty as daughter that do not allow her to flee with Ferdinand or to commit suicide. As Rolf Peter Janz observes, these values that enslave Luise are socialized in the intimate bourgeois family, but Luise does not herself rebel against this double deformation of love in the family, the degradation of the wife and the subjugation of the daughter.[36] The text probes these issues, but Luise simply accepts them.

Ferdinand, too, is torn between two value systems. His education at the universities of the bourgeoisie has given him a critical awareness of the feudal abuses of power. Yet, the values which go hand in hand with this awareness prove ineffective, and even dangerous, in the context of the court, as the increasing intimacy of familial love makes him particularly vulnerable. His love for his father had kept him from publicizing the falsehoods with which his father gained his position as president, but this is a vulnerability that blunts his criticism and, in effect, makes him both an accomplice and a victim of the system he despises.

At the same time, there are layers of his personality that were formed at the court that lie beyond his education in bourgeois ideology and his enlightened sense of ethics. His image of women, formed at the court, makes him misread Luise's motivation for refusing to leave her father unprotected in his old age and at the mercy of the president. Failing to understand her sense of duty, he instead assumes that she refuses because of another man. His prophetic statement early in the play that he fears nothing but the limits of her love becomes self-fulfilling (*S-NA*, 5N: 24). He misreads the limits of her love as being based on the fickleness he attributes to her gender rather than to her absolute steadfastness in her core values of God and family. This misreading makes him an easy victim of the intrigue designed to make him believe that Luise is in love with the effeminate caricature of a courtier, von Kalb.

With less pathos and less differentiation than is found in Schiller's depiction of the mentalities that divide Ferdinand and Luise, Wagner's *Die Kindermörderin* also drastically portrays the incompatibility of value systems and the strong influence of socialization in one's class. In order to downplay any suggestions of attraction to a non-bourgeois lifestyle, Wagner turns the seduction motif of the traditional bourgeois tragedy into rape. Evchen Humbrecht's interest in Lieutenant Gröningseck is portrayed very sketchily. Although the play does not explicitly motivate her willingness to go to the masked ball with him, her embarrassment about her mother's behavior (her sloppiness and lack of worldliness) suggests an unspecified dissatisfaction with her middle-class lifestyle. Her mother seems to be more attracted to both the man and what he represents, and she is therefore the one who allows him to take them to the masked ball. This leads to the fateful visit to the brothel, where she is drugged and her daughter raped. After Evchen angrily reproaches her aggressor, he reluctantly agrees to marry her as soon as he is of age. Evchen withdraws emotionally and physically from her family and waits for him. In the meantime she learns that Gröningseck was not swept away by passion and, thus, did not lose control over his rational faculties but planned the whole "seduction" carefully, so that she is no longer able to consider marriage even if he were to return. She gives birth and, in despair, kills her newborn child. As it turns out, her father was prepared to forgive her, and Gröningseck was delayed by illness but ready to keep his promise. The way the plot thwarts this relationship is only the outer sign of the impossibility of such a union beyond class barriers. After all, by proposing marriage not only would Gröningseck have to give up his social identity, as Edward McInnes argues,[37] but so would Evchen. Even if we assume that she is attracted to him, a marriage based on passion would not be able to overcome Evchen's social identity as represented in her relationship to her parents and, especially, her father.[38] Her strong sense of shame at the loss of her virginity, even though it was by force, together with her remorse over her mother's death suggests how deeply she is socialized in the value system of her class and community.[39]

The improbability of the conversion of the rapist and crude drunkard into a sentimental lover and honorable would-be husband suggests that the most fundamental incompatibility of their social identities cannot be overcome by an optimistic Enlightenment ideology in the manner of Samuel Richardson (*Clarissa,* 1747–48). Evchen follows the model that Clarissa Harlowe provided and, at first, seems to succeed: she manages to shame her rapist into promising marriage. The unconvincing boldness of "offended virtue" has often been noted, most recently by Bruce Duncan. He argues that "these disjunctions are in fact consistent with the world that Wagner and other Sturm und Drang writers portray, one in which social expectations clash with human nature, and, at the same time, societal structures carry their own contradictions" (157). McInnes goes even further and suggests that Sturm und Drang writers try to "embody an awareness of society as an enclosing, shaping force at work in every aspect and at every level of the individual's existence, determining not just the circumstances of his environment but his seemingly most intimate experience" (270). The characters are not independent but are governed by the world around them.

The conversions of Evchen and Gröningseck, prompted as they are by the imitation of literary models, are shown to be inadequate paradigms for self-determination. By suggesting a reliance on the freely determined will in the face of an obvious determination by circumstances, this literary construct places the individual uncomfortably between idealism and materialism. According to the former, the individual determines his/her own destiny. In this case, the characters attempt to determine their destiny by, as it seems, freely choosing to adopt models created by literature. The latter view sees the individual as determined by discourses or social structures, as a victim of circumstances. The denouement of *Die Kindermörderin,* driven as it is by coincidence, certainly suggests the latter. Wagner's play acknowledges the idealist impetus to act as a self-determined, autonomous being: Gröningseck decides to change and Evchen transgresses her role as sexual and social victim and asserts her need for restitution. Yet both are also shown as determined by their long-term socialization in their class and cultural community. Pierre Bourdieu's concept of habit explains the interrelationship between the idealist and material tendencies by defining the tension as the dynamic interplay of structure and action, society and the individual. The symbolic features of social existence are entwined with the material conditions, yet without one being reducible to the other. Habit instills a "*sense pratique*" in the members of a group or class that causes people to react in certain situations in an almost unconsciously determined manner that has become second nature to them.[40] In this case the discourses they select for their self-determination, literature and the Enlightenment discourse of virtue, are inadequate for overcoming their socialization into their different peer groups. Evchen's value system, her strong sense of shame, does not easily transform into the libertine model of the fallen woman (at the beginning of the play), nor can we imagine the butcher's daughter as the wife of an officer or a nobleman. The same holds true for Gröningseck. His lifestyle as nobleman steeped in military culture, with its coarseness, drunkenness, and crude sexuality — he seems to be a frequent visitor to the brothel where he rapes Evchen — is not compatible with the domestic tranquility of a middle-class family. This fundamental incompatibility — which is not unique to this play but also informs Marianne Ehrmann's *Leichtsinn und gutes Herz: Oder die Folgen der Erziehung* (Folly and the Good Heart: Or the Consequences of Education, 1786) — becomes especially radical and apparent in Wagner's play because no attempt is made to elaborate a discourse of sentimental love between the couple. Andreas Huyssen has drawn from this fact the conclusion that the play is not about the intensification of the self through the power of love but about the victimization of woman, subject to the patriarchal order of state, society, family, and marriage.[41]

Evchen's socialization no longer firmly grounds her and fails to provide her with a stable position in society in which she knows the rules of the game (Bourdieu's "habit"). There is a piano in the household, and we know that she reads sentimental novels, so the transgressive activities of education that set out to replace the values of her socialization cannot truly erase the earlier habits, hard as she might try. The piano in the middle-class home attests to the gender-specific humanistic education as the female counterpart to the male neohumanist education in high culture (*Bildung*) at secondary schools and universities. The focus on *Bildung* was a means of leveling the playing field between the classes and communities, between those who acquired culture through their socialization and those who were in the process of newly acquiring it. Education and reading awaken desires without necessarily being able to fulfill them. They destabilize without offering new order and stability.

Several texts point to the role of literature and *Bildung* as a crucial element in bourgeois women's awareness of sentimental and erotic love (*Werther, Leichtsinn und gutes Herz, Die Kindermörderin*, and *Kabale und Liebe*). After all, their premarital experience in matters relating to love was mediated primarily though literature, which created modern sensibilities and desires. Social morality expected women to remain chaste until after marriage, while literature prepared the imagination for erotic love. When it comes to love, the middle-class fathers with some justification blame the expectations of their daughters on reading. For Lotte it was Klopstock, for Evchen it was Richardson, and for Gustchen and Fritz in *Der Hofmeister* it was *Romeo and Juliet* that initiated them into erotic love. The father in *Kabale und Liebe* also blames his daughter's transgression on her reading. The literary discourse in the tradition of Richardson's novels and Lessing's domestic tragedies imagined a new value system that transcends the barriers of primary socialization in the given community and produced a desire for the pursuit of the ideal of an autonomous self in which erotic love plays an important role.

In Ehrmann's *Leichtsinn und gutes Herz,* Count Treuberg falls in love at first sight when he sees the middle-class Lottchen reading by the banks of the river. After he seduces her, she, like Evchen, demands marriage and is even ready to use force. She threatens him with a pistol, which turns out not to be loaded — after all, as a woman she can only threaten and has no possibility of enforcement. The seduced, innocent Lottchen, displays the behavior patterns of another stock character of the bourgeois tragedy, the "*Machtweib,*" the woman with power and the desire to pursue her own goals. By fusing both types into one character the author suggests a more extensive habituation in the values of a community between city and country, between court and bourgeoisie. This, in turn, makes the non-tragic outcome more plausible. As Treuberg reluctantly agrees to marry her and sets out to secure his family's permission, she is almost raped by his wicked tutor but is rescued at the last minute by a young lieutenant. The model of bourgeois tragedy mutates into comedy. In the happy ending the father allows his daughter to marry the count, and we presume that all's well that ends well. Not surprisingly, the play is silent about the possibilities of their life together. Marriage itself is not a topic that tends to capture the interest of Sturm und Drang writers. In Lottchen, Ehrmann creates a character who is less firmly rooted in middle-class values than those of Schiller and Wagner. Her father's ambivalent class position — his former upper-class lifestyle in the city and his present indulgence in the simple life in the country — leads to her unique education in the city. Her character suggests an idealized femininity between nature and culture, an educated child of nature who embodies a fusion between the domestic virtues of the bourgeois value system and a certain level of upper-class lifestyle and *Bildung.* Her education has created a more significant basis for overcoming the limits — and the stability — of her class. As in the other plays, *Bildung* represents a crack in the habits, the socialization, of the middle-class family — or a moment for self-determination. Ehrmann's optimistic transcendence of class barriers is deeply steeped in the belief of the Enlightenment project in the possibility of education and historical progress.[42] She, therefore, offers a less pessimistic, and also less radical, vision than Wagner and Lenz. If Ehrmann takes the bourgeois tragedy in the tradition of Lessing to its final non-tragic, optimistic conclusion, Wagner and Lenz show its ineffectiveness and failure as a cultural model.

Evchen Humbrecht's transgression of the strictures of her class and community, which we suspect was inspired by the emancipatory discourse of literature, offers her no true freedom. Given her socialization in the patriarchal structures of family and community and their norms and values, her transgression leads to an even more radical enslavement by violent sexuality, which destabilizes her whole being. By avoiding a happy ending through intrigue and a chain of coincidences, Wagner suggests that Evchen's destabilization cannot be remedied by sentimental love across class boundaries. He radicalizes the pessimistic implications of the domestic tragedy as a genre. Ehrmann's departure from these genre conventions, on the other hand, affirms the Enlightenment belief in transformation through education. Her argument for education is directed at both the nobility and the bourgeoisie, and in her view it should lead to a leveling of class differences. As Helga Madland has pointed out, what the young nobleman Count Treuberg needs are better tutors with higher moral standards.[43]

In Lenz's *Die Soldaten* the influence of the literary discourse on the conception of love is alluded to but is deliberately set aside: the maternal character in the play, Gräfin La Roche, is apparently mistaken when she attributes Marie's transgressions to Richardson's *Pamela* (1740–41). Rather, they are motivated by economics and social advancement. After all, her community is in close contact with the noblemen of the officer class. Wesener sells luxury goods to officers, among others, and Marie's bourgeois fiancé, Stolzius, also makes his living providing the military with goods and services. Marie is attracted to Desportes's lifestyle, full of cultural entertainment and a degree of luxury. They frequent the theater, and he lavishes on her gifts for her adornment — even though he cannot afford these luxury items, and they probably stem from her father's store. Her love for the aristocratic suitor is her means of escaping the ascetic values of her class.[44] Even if social climbing is representative of her particular community and not the sign of an outsider, the fact that concealment and hypocrisy are necessary suggests that this is a time of instability when multiple layers of values are at play. It is no longer a case of individual rebellion; the play suggests that a stage of uneasy and unsettling coexistence has been reached between two value systems: on the one hand, the feudal order with its stable value system and, on the other, the modern functionally organized society with its less defined boundaries, which enables social mobility. Marie's attempts at writing in a style not her own, her uneasy shifting between linguistic registers, which frustrates her, suggests that her personality is destabilized by these conflicting value systems that she is unable to reconcile or integrate.[45] Unlike Ehrmann, neither Lenz nor Wagner seems confident that this destabilization can be remedied. Both authors can only offer a profound and complex critique of the modern condition: they do not provide us with a vision that could replace the stability of a patriarchal system.[46]

After all, neither Lenz's nor Wagner's plays suggest solutions of the question as to what models might be more appropriate for overcoming the perceived shortcomings of the middle-class lifestyle, which render it vulnerable to or complicit in seduction and victimization. Evchen's vague desire to escape her own socialization and the situation it has created is contained in her utopian wish to become a man and fight for freedom in America. This topos is not unique to Wagner: Klinger's *Sturm und Drang* is set in revolutionary America, and in Lenz's prose narrative *Der Waldbruder* the protagonist wishes to participate in the American Revolution. It has little to do with any specifically revolutionary fervor, however — it is even difficult to ascertain on which side the characters are or would be fighting — but is a rhetorical strategy that signals a strong, yet diffuse and unspecific wish for action. It is part of the desire for self-determination, with the ultimate goal of creating an autonomous self within a community of like-minded individuals. The vagueness of this dark desire, lacking as it does a specific goal and a direction, allows the topos to be used by both genders.

Jakob Michael Reinhold Lenz's *Der Hofmeister* offers the most critical view of the dangers of seductive literary fantasies. Gustchen's innocence is destroyed by a combination of Romeo and Juliet fantasies and an imitation of the Héloise and Abélard plot with her tutor. Although we are also dealing here with a relationship that transgresses class boundaries, the conflict is not simply a seduction of bourgeois virtue by the feudal transgressor but is, rather, a caricature of it. Läuffer, the middle-class tutor, is coerced into a clumsy affair with his employers' daughter, who is bored and frustrated in the absence of her beloved. While Läuffer laments his precarious social and economic situation in the household, Gustchen expresses her romantic frustrations. She slips into the role of

"Julie" and forces him into the role of Romeo, kissing his hand until he absent-mindedly reciprocates, while still engrossed in his own woes (*L-WB*, 1, 67–69). The relationship is induced by an indulgence in literary fantasies, which at the same time serve as surrogate communication. Läuffer and Gustchen never "speak their minds" but, instead, trade clichés. Lenz's assessment dismisses the literary discourse of love as a model for true emancipation and the pursuit of an authentic identity. Läuffer and Gustchen are unable to transcend the limitations of their circumstances. Lenz seems to be suggesting that the inner vacuum that his "lovers" are experiencing is an existential one, and cannot be remedied by the literary discourse of love. Läuffer's social and economic position as tutor is deplorable. He is a servant, he does not have the financial means and freedom to come and go as he pleases, and his students are difficult: there is no escape through which he could find a meaningful life outside of his duties.

For Gustchen, it is the limited range of action customary for women at the time that dictates that she should have a limited education and not much else in this conflict-ridden, unstable family, where the domineering mother insists on the privileges and lifestyle due to her class, while the father leans more toward a middle-class family and work ethic.[47] The discourse of love as the center of women's socialization is Gustchen's only sphere for action. The heroic descriptions of erotic love with its intensification of the whole being and its tropes and motifs of love at first sight, "*Seelenfreundschaft*" (spiritual love), divine destiny, and so forth are, however, empty promises in her confined situation; she meets only a limited number of men and has few options. She has to make do with mere imitations of dashing lovers, with coincidence and circumstance, rather than divine destiny. This portrayal strips the concept of love of much of its glamour by turning it into literary clichés. The characters are caught in a web of discourses ranging from Rousseauistic philosophy and literature (Werther, Romeo and Juliet, and Abélard and Héloïse) to social and economic ones. In addition, Läuffer senses his inability to reconcile his morality with the desire for sensual and sexual emancipation, and castrates himself. Yet, to avoid having the castration suggest any semblance of heroic renunciation, the author has Läuffer enter a farcical marriage of convenience. Thus, in *Der Hofmeister,* literature, although more obviously and crassly portrayed as a force of seduction than in other plays, turns out to be one of many ridiculous clichés that have no genuine role in the pursuit of authenticity, and even hinder it. Its false forms of communication take the place of potentially more authentic ones. This most radical of texts expresses a rejection of the literary construction of love as a valid means of achieving the status of autonomous subject.

Lenz dispenses with literature not only as imitation but also as a model to be imitated. This is a grave indictment of what he saw as the uncritical reception of literature. After all, literature was a central means of communication concerning middle-class values, and in this discourse love occupies a key position. Literary discourse helped to create new models for communication about love, for example, in Werther's and Lotte's emotional connectedness through the signifier Klopstock. *Der Hofmeister* seems to be more pessimistic about the usefulness of the discourse of love, which takes on a life of its own and begins to determine the actions of the characters. Literature is not regarded as giving expression to genuine emotion; instead, it is an inauthentic, copied discourse that shapes their action as a reaction to their varied and incoherent desires.[48] The characters cover up the banality of their relationship with the borrowed pathos of literature. The second-hand discourse of love masks a vacuum, an inner emptiness in the lives and lifestyles of both of them.

Overall, the literature of the Sturm und Drang embraces love as a central aspect of bourgeois identity driving the modernization process, while also pointing to the internal contradictions and the difficulties associated with the transition. We see how the concept of love negotiates uneasily between individualistic desires and the social context provided by the family with its strong forces of familial love. The conflicts that arise when the new concept of strong affective bonding within the family clashes with the individualistic desires of the couple remain unresolved. The difficulty of negotiating between different value systems, the courtly value system on the one hand and the bourgeois value system on the other, or between the demands of the emerging differentiated and functionalized modern society and individual desires becomes apparent in the depiction of love. The literary works show the self-reflexive formation of a new value system. As the individual retreats not only from courtly life, with its focus on status and representation, but also from the emergent rationally organized and differentiated, alienated life of work and commerce, love holds out the promise of a more authentic natural life. It claims to be a form of communication between highly individualized beings, offering a new form of social integration. However, while allowing glimpses of its utopian promise, the authors of the Sturm und Drang shied away from an unqualified celebration of love.

Notes

[1] For the role that love occupies in the development and stabilization of individuality, see Niklas Luhmann, *Liebe als Passion: Zur Codierung von Intimität*, 3rd ed. (Frankfurt am Main: Suhrkamp, 1983), 57. For the relationship between love and identity in the context of social and political change in the eighteenth century, see Günter Sasse, *Die Ordnung der Gefühle: Das Drama der Liebesheirat im 18. Jahrhundert* (Darmstadt: Wissenschaftliche Buchgesellschaft, 1996), 18. Siegfried J. Schmidt also points to the centrality of the eighteenth century in this development: *Die Selbstorganisation des Sozialsystems Literatur im 18. Jahrhundert* (Frankfurt am Main: Suhrkamp, 1989), 65. Ulrich Karthaus, in the most recent study of the Sturm and Drang, locates the literary period within a nexus of political, economic, and social changes, and links it to the beginnings of the modern industrial world with its increasing separation of work and home and the increasing predominance of the nuclear family over the extended family: *Sturm und Drang: Epoche — Werke — Wirkung* (Munich: Beck, 2000), 26. The discussion of love as a historical phenomenon has flourished in the last two decades, as Hans-Peter Schwänder has observed: *"Alles um Liebe?": Zur Position Goethes im modernen Liebesdiskurs* (Opladen: Westdeutscher Verlag, 1997), 8; there is, however, no comprehensive study of the role of love in the Sturm and Drang.

[2] Jürgen Kocka, one of the leading historians working on the emergent middle classes, emphasizes a specific middle-class culture ("bürgerliche Kultur und Lebensführung") as a unifying characteristic that drives the changes toward modern society: *Bürgertum im 19. Jahrhundert: Deutschland im europäischen Vergleich,* vol. 1 (Munich: dtv, 1988), 11–76, here 27–28. See also the modification of Kocka's model by, for example, Wolfgang Kaschuba, who argues for the inclusion of elements from "everyday culture" ("Alltagskultur"): "Deutsche Bürgerlichkeit nach 1800. Kultur als symbolische Praxis," in *Bürgertum im 19. Jahrhundert,* ed. Jürgen Kocka, vol. 3 (Munich: dtv. 1988), 9–44, here 18. Rebekka Habermas rightly criticizes Kocka's unacknowledged focus on male identity because the majority of his criteria do not apply to women, whose possibility for self-determination was limited: *Frauen und Männer des Bürgertums: Eine Familiengeschichte (1750–1850)* (Göttingen: Vandenhoeck & Ruprecht, 2000), 8. The present study will restrict itself to questions of family life and love and the tensions between these and self-realization and individualism.

[3] Lawrence Stone cites four characteristics of the new family ideal: "a) intensified affective bonding of the nuclear core at the expense of the kin; b) strong sense of individual autonomy and right to personal freedom and the pursuit of happiness; c) weakening of the association of sexual pleasure with sin; d) growing desire for physical privacy": *The Family, Sex and Marriage in England 1500–1800* (London: Weidenfeld & Nicolson, 1977), 22; see also his more detailed description, 325–404, and Dieter Borchmeyer, "Schwankungen des Herzens und Liebe im Triangel: Goethe und die Erotik der Empfindsamkeit," in *Codierungen von Liebe in der Kunstperiode,* ed. Walter Hinderer, Stiftung für Romantikforschung 3 (Würzburg: Königshausen & Neumann, 1997), 63–83. Of course, it is necessary to bear in mind the fact that the term *love* serves merely as a shortcut. Whether we regard love as a system of

communication or as a norm against which the emotions of individuals are measured, it is culturally produced, not a natural given. It changes historically, even though the terminology may remain constant.

[4] Edward Shorter, *The Making of the Modern Family* (New York: Basic Books, 1975). For the role of literature in these changes see also Bettina Recker: *"Ewige Dauer" oder "Ewiges Einerlei": Die Geschichte der Ehe im Roman um 1800* (Würzburg: Königshausen & Neumann, 2000), 9. Of course, as Heidi Rosenbaum points out, paradigms are artificial constructs that isolate typical patterns, they do not imply that "everyone" lived in conformity with the pattern: *Formen der Familie* (Frankfurt am Main: Suhrkamp, 1982), 308. The concept of love explored here is further limited to the literate middle-class elites. See, for example, Bengt Algot Sørensen, *Herrschaft und Zärtlichkeit: Der Patriarchalismus und das Drama im 18. Jahrhundert* (Munich: Beck, 1984), 45, and Karin A. Wurst, *Familiale Liebe ist die "wahre Gewalt": Zur Repräsentation der Familie in G. E. Lessings dramatischem Werk* (Amsterdam: Rodopi, 1988), 38–39. Only later in the nineteenth century does the new ideal of the family enter the mainstream. The discourse on love explores and anticipates models that over time could become social reality. Values and stated norms cannot simply be equated with actual social practices: rather, literature plays a creative part in an active process in the acquisition and negotiation of values. See also Rebekka Habermas, who cautions against a simple equation of norms and values with actual practices (11–12), while Sasse also points to the role of literature in this process of negotiation (10).

[5] See Rosenbaum, 272–75, and Karin Hausen, "Familie als Gegenstand historischer Sozialwissenschaft: Bemerkungen zu einer Forschungstrategie," *Geschichte und Gesellschaft. Zeitschrift für historische Sozialwissenschaft* 1 (1975), 171–209, esp. 201.

[6] Hausen characterizes the modern family as a refuge based on privacy, intimacy, humanity and freedom (198).

[7] See Nikolaus Wegmann, *Diskurse der Empfindsamkeit: Zur Geschichte eines Gefühls in der Literatur des 18. Jahrhunderts* (Stuttgart: Metzler, 1988), 23. Niklas Luhmann distinguishes between societies that are differentiated by stratification and those that are differentiated functionally, that is, by an increasing specialization of tasks and functions; it is in these latter that love in the modern sense of the term becomes responsible for the emotional dimension of life, for the happiness of the individual: *Gesellschaftsstruktur und Semantik: Studien zur Wissenssoziologie der modernen Gesellschaft*, vol. 1 (Frankfurt am Main: Suhrkamp, 1993), 9–11. Borchmeyer sees the crucial shift to the modern concept of love as taking place during the period of *Empfindsamkeit* (65). The present study explores the tensions between the formation of a code and a critique of it. Walter Hinderer also suggests that codes themselves are in flux and are self-reflexive: "Zur Liebesauffassung der Kunstperiode. Einleitung," in *Codierungen von Liebe in der Kunstperiode*, ed. Walter Hinderer (Würzburg: Königshausen & Neumann, 1997), 7–33, here 11; see also Wegmann, 50.

[8] Jutta Greis, *Drama Liebe: Zur Entstehungsgeschichte der modernen Liebe im Drama des 18. Jahrhunderts* (Stuttgart: Metzler, 1991), 7.

[9] The intersection of several powerful discourses created this form of sensibility with its emphasis on introspection, self-observation, and self-analysis. I define *discourse* as a functional unit that guarantees social communication by offering general patterns

of orientation that facilitate and simplify communication. The definition is derived from Michel Foucault, *Archäologie des Wissens* (Frankfurt am Main: Suhrkamp, 1973), and especially Niklas Luhmann, "Differentiation of Society," *Canadian Journal of Sociology* 2 (1977): 29–53.

[10] Wegmann, 87.

[11] With introspection emerged the discourse on sexuality. In what Michel Foucault has termed "confession," as a "ritual of discourse" in letters, autobiographical narratives, and literature, there came the "imparting of individual pleasures . . . reconstructing, in and around the [sexual] act, the thoughts that recapitulated it, the obsessions that accompanied it, the images, desires, modulations, and the quality of the pleasure that animated it": *History of Sexuality,* vol. 1 (New York: Random House, 1978) 61–63.

[12] Reinhart Koselleck, *Kritik und Krise: Eine Studie zur Pathogenese der bürgerlichen Welt* (originally 1955; Frankfurt am Main: Suhrkamp, 1973); Jürgen Habermas, *Strukturwandel der Öffentlichkeit: Untersuchungen zu einer Kategorie der bürgerlichen Gesellschaft* (Neuwied & Berlin: Luchterhand, 1962).

[13] In particular Foucault, *History,* and Luhmann, *Liebe als Passion.*

[14] See Greis, 9–13, and Hinderer, 11. In Germany, the paradigm of romantic love was intricately connected with the value system of Sentimentalism. As Hinderer (16–17) observes, Niklas Luhmann's innovative study, *Liebe als Passion,* which looks at the codification of love in a European context, does not sufficiently acknowledge the role of *Empfindsamkeit* in the German development of love.

[15] Bengt Algot Sørensen, *Herrschaft und Zärtlichkeit;* Karin A. Wurst, *Familiale Liebe;* Gail Hart, *Tragedy in Paradise: Family and Gender Politics in German Bourgeois Tragedy 1750–1850* (Columbia SC: Camden House, 1996).

[16] Clara Stockmeyer, *Soziale Probleme im Drama des Sturmes und Dranges: Eine literarhistorische Studie* (Frankfurt am Main: Diesterweg, 1922); Richard Quabius, *Generationsverhältnisse im Sturm und Drang* (Cologne: Böhlau, 1976).

[17] Luhmann, *Liebe als Passion,* 62.

[18] Greis argues that this is the dominant model in the eighteenth century and criticizes Luhmann for neglecting the drama (10).

[19] Sasse, 47.

[20] Paul Kluckhohn's comprehensive study (originally 1922) describes romantic love as the culmination and integration of many historically unresolved aspects of love: *Die Auffassung der Liebe in der Literatur des 18. Jahrhunderts und in der deutschen Romantik* (Tübingen: Niemeyer, 1966). The paradigm of romantic love should not be confused with the historical literary period known as "Romanticism." See in particular Borchmeyer, 65.

[21] See Luhmann, *Liebe als Passion,* 23.

[22] Friedrich Heinrich Jacobi, *Woldemar: Eine Seltenheit aus der Naturgeschichte,* vol. 1 (Flensburg: Leipzig, 1779), 86–87: "I walked with my women friends gently toward our house, collecting in myself all the tones which had resounded in my soul so that they did not die away, at least not so quickly. Years of mixed emotions became ordered into a melody, and this melody in turn into harmony. Sirius and Venus

entered the vibrating heat of the sun. The other stars appeared before and after them. We heard the music of the spheres."

[23] See Volkmar Hansen, "Sinnlichkeit in Friedrich Heinrich Jacobis *Woldemar* (1779) oder der Engelssturz," in *Sturm und Drang: Geistiger Aufbruch 1770–1790 im Spiegel der Literatur*, eds. Bodo Plachta and Winfried Woesler (Tübingen: Niemeyer, 1997), 149–56, here 153.

[24] "The night lies so cool, so nicely about me! The clouds drift by so quietly! Ah, otherwise how cheerless and gloomy everything would be! It is good, my heart, that you can again catch this pure feeling of awesomeness; good that the night air sighs around you and you feel love wafted through the vast stillness of nature. Shimmer, stars! Ah, we have become friends again! You are carried with almighty love, as is my heart, and you twinkle in pure love, as does my soul. You were so cold to me in the mountains! . . . So often have I clung to you, moon, but it went dark around me as I reached for her who was so far away. Ah, that everything is so woven together, so bound together by love" (*SuD*, 156).

[25] "All . . . that creation offers, all that a man can feel" (*SuD*, 158).

[26] "Light of my eyes" (*SuD*, 156).

[27] Bruce Duncan, *Lovers, Parricides, and Highwaymen: Aspects of Sturm und Drang Drama* (Rochester NY: Camden House, 1999), 182–84. See also Gerhard Kaiser, "Friedrich Maximilian Klingers Schauspiel Sturm und Drang," in *Untersuchungen zur Literatur als Geschichte: Festschrift für Benno von Wiese*, eds. Vincent Günther et al. (Berlin: Erich Schmidt, 1973), 15–35, here 26.

[28] "Night! Still night! Let me confide in you. let me confide in you, meadows! Valleys! Hills and forests! Let me confide in you, moon, and all you stars! No longer to cry over him, no longer to sigh over him. I wander under your light, my friend who was sad! No longer in wailing do you answer me, echo, you that knew no other sound but his name" (*SuD*, 157).

[29] "I knew nothing of God any longer, and yet I had never loved him more."

[30] Helmut Koopmann, *Drama der Aufklärung: Kommentar zu einer Epoche* (Munich: Winkler, 1979), 139.

[31] Duncan, 195.

[32] Hans-Jürgen Schings, *Melancholie und Aufklärung: Melancholiker und ihre Kritiker in der Erfahrungsseelenkunde und Literatur des 18. Jahrhunderts* (Stuttgart: Metzler, 1977), 30.

[33] "I will conquer this shameful passion, repress my heart and crush yours. I will cast rocks and chasms between you; I will rush like a fury through the middle of your paradise; when you kiss, my name shall make you part in terror as a ghost frightens criminals; when you embrace him, your young and blooming body will fall apart like a mummy. I cannot achieve happiness with him — but neither shall *you*."

[34] Karin A. Wurst, ed., *Eleonore Thons Adelheit von Rastenberg* (New York: MLA, 1996), xxvi.

[35] "That affection is more barbaric in its power of compulsion than the rage of a tyrant."

[36] Rolf Peter Janz, "Schillers 'Kabale und Liebe' als bürgerliches Trauerspiel," *Jahrbuch der deutschen Schillergesellschaft* 20 (1976), 208–228.

[37] Edward McInnes, "'Die Regie des Lebens:' Domestic Drama and the Sturm und Drang," *Orbis Litterarum* 32 (1977), 269–84, here 270.

[38] Scholars have remarked on the absence or unreliability of the mother in bourgeois tragedy. Sørensen has attributed it to the diminished social status assigned to wives and mothers in the hierarchical structure of the patriarchal family (17). In *Familiale Liebe* I have argued that the elimination of the mother allows for the forces of emotional socialization to be transferred to the father figure, who thus attains a social, economic, and, most importantly, an emotional hold over the daughter (132). Gail Hart makes the point that women "are good for facilitating significant male homosocial relations, and they do this by stimulating contacts and then disappearing" (xi).

[39] By using the concepts of class and community, I want to make clear that the concept of class — middle class or bourgeoisie — by itself is too broad as the middle class becomes increasingly differentiated. I refer to the resulting subgroupings as communities with their unique lifestyles and values.

[40] Pierre Bourdieu. *Distinction: A Social Critique of the Judgement of Taste* (1979), trans. Richard Nice (Cambridge MA: Harvard UP, 1984).

[41] Andreas Huyssen, *Drama des Sturm und Drang: Kommentar zu einer Epoche* (Munich: Winkler, 1980), 224.

[42] Helga Stipa Madland reads Ehrmann as an explicitly didactic writer: *Marianne Ehrmann: Reason and Emotion in Her Life and Works* (New York: Lang, 1998), 148.

[43] Madland, 144–45.

[44] Duncan (140) suggests that her behavior does not arise from subjective feeling but from social ambition, and foregrounds the hypocrisy of the middle class with its hopes for social advancement.

[45] See Paul Michael Lützeler, "Jakob Michael Reinhold Lenz: Die Soldaten," in *Interpretationen: Dramen des Sturm und Drang*, Universal-Bibliothek, 8410 (Stuttgart: Reclam, 1997), 129–60; Walter Höllerer, "Lenz: Die Soldaten," in *Das Deutsche Drama*, ed. Benno von Wiese (Düsseldorf: Bagel, 1958), 127–46; Bruce Duncan, "The Comic Structure of Lenz's *Soldaten*," *Modern Language Notes* 91 (1976), 515–23.

[46] Richard Quabius argues that Sturm und Drang writers essentially accepted that patriarchal authority in the form of conflict between sons and fathers could only be resolved if the sons gave in (61). Similarly, Sørensen argues that in Wesener Lenz attacks the weakness of patriarchal authority itself, since it does not protect its charges (152). However, it would be wrong to suggest that Sturm und Drang writers are nostalgic for patriarchal rule. Lenz does not advocate a return to the stability of patriarchy. Instead he is deeply concerned with the effects of destabilized systems and value systems in transition. Emptiness and vacuity as the consequence of destabilized value systems are therefore at the core of Lenz's works. They take the form of a lack of a center, disorientation, perspectival portrayals, and role playing. See Karin A. Wurst, "Lenz als Alternative: Einleitung," in *J. M. R. Lenz als Alternative? Positionsanalysen zum 200. Todestag*, ed. Karin Wurst (Cologne: Böhlau, 1992), 1–22.

[47] Sørensen gives a good description of the dysfunctional family, in which the authority of the patriarch is undermined by a superficial and arrogant wife (156–57).

[48] See Sasse, 26 and 188.

Discursive Dissociations: Women Playwrights as Observers of the Sturm und Drang

Susanne Kord

"A Heart with Testicles": The Gender of an Epoch

IN THE MOST RECENT EXTENSIVE STUDY of the Sturm und Drang, Bruce Duncan sums up the critical discussion of its women authors as follows: "According to the traditional critical consensus, no women can be numbered among the movement's members. Almost everyone agrees that the Sturm und Drang was both in fact and by its nature a wholly male enterprise. To talk about Sturm und Drang women has almost always meant to discuss only the female characters in the dramas."[1] While this is not entirely true — there are, in fact, several feminist works suggesting many female candidates for inclusion[2] — Duncan's remark intentionally describes not so much fact (the historical absence of women writers from the epoch) as fiction (the mythologization of the movement as inherently male in its reception). Critical literature has done its best to define the Sturm und Drang as "by its nature" wholly male in its three most central definitions of the movement: (1) the characterization of the Sturm und Drang as the sons' rebellion against paternal authority (fathers, the state, and God); (2) the depiction of its authors as a gathering of men joined together in exclusively male societies and friendships; and (3) the interpretation of the epoch as largely defined by a genius theory that has no relevance or application to women, refers exclusively to male idols (Prometheus, Christ, Shakespeare, Young, Ossian, Shaftesbury, and Rousseau), and finds its truest expression in drama — the genre in which women have long been held to be the least competent.[3] Unsurprisingly, these dramas are principally characterized by dominant and rebellious male heroes and conflicts among men (brothers, fathers, and sons).[4] As is true for any other literary movement, this "exquisitely masculine epoch," to cite Roebling's sarcastic wording (63), is, to a significant extent, being shaped through its own reception. But what is perhaps unusual about Sturm und Drang historiography — beyond the absolute and unequivocal exclusion of women writers from the movement in most criticism, which is not stated with comparable fervor for any other epoch in German literature — is the degree to which passionate identification permeates not only the works of its authors, but also those of its critics. Possibly inspired by the movement's own dictum that genius allows for no distinction between life and art,[5] critics of the movement, including modern scholars, routinely employ interpretive moves that would be considered methodologically questionable when applied to any other literary epoch. One prominent facet of this kind is the common identification of authors and characters,[6] a move in which the authors of the movement, that first generation of "angry young men,"[7] are themselves characterized as the *Kraftkerle* of their own fiction — extremists and individualists whose short-lived "outbursts of genius"[8] invariably ended in failure, loss of creativity, imprisonment, insanity, or early death.[9] Goethe alone, in many accounts the center of the movement, "overcomes" the juvenile tendencies of his wild youth and "outgrows" it to metamorphose into the Classical Goethe, a view that simultaneously relegates the entire Sturm und Drang to the status of puberty vis-à-vis the maturity of Classicism.[10] If such portrayals of the authors of the Sturm und Drang as youthful tragic heroes already bespeak the incompatibility of the movement with women or femininity in the minds of most critics, the movement's emphatic masculinity is frequently evoked in citations of its most central precursors. Lichtenberg's dictum of the "heart with testicles" as which humans would be seen if viewed exclusively through the lens of "our sentimental writings,"[11] Hamann's definition of the "passions" as "weapons of manhood" and his frequent castration metaphors,[12] usually cited as evidence of the movement's passionate language, indirectly illustrate once again the elementary fact that the Sturm und Drang was *the* movement in German literature that *by its very nature* excluded women from the ranks of its authors.

For feminist scholars the question may well be: what is to be gained from "including" women in the movement? The answer would depend on whether the movement is viewed as "historical" or as historically constructed. A view of the historical *epoch*, understood as a series of years, would in all likelihood confirm the complete absence of women as full participants in the movement. That epoch was marked by the literary activity of a small number of men working in loose association with each other, men who saw their work as aesthetic, not political,[13] and who defined their own significance largely in terms of their own exceptional-ity. Every single major Sturm und Drang manifesto, from Herder's Shakespeare essay to Goethe's Shakespeare speech to Lenz's *Anmerkungen übers Theater* — those writings, in other words, that are today considered most defining of the movement — was originally composed to address a small, select audience of initiates.[14] Bruce Duncan has pointed out that at the time, few of the major Sturm und Drang works were available in print (3), which would restrict the impact of these writings to the small circle of disciples among whom they were circulated. Just as our current definition of the "*bürgerliches Trauerspiel*," or domestic tragedy, clearly considered a significant genre of the age, rests on a textual canon of exactly four tragedies,[15] a fact that would certainly have to limit our ability to read this literary phenomenon as "representative" for the age, subsequent criticism overestimated the actual impact of the small circle of Sturm und Drang authors, mistook their aesthetic musings and dramatic depictions of boisterous rebels for political intent, and overread the Sturm und Drang as the "first democratic literary movement," a valiant critic of the corrupt aristocracy and a champion of Nature and the lower classes.[16]

If women are excluded from the Sturm und Drang *epoch*, there are of course ways of including them, as Helga Madland has suggested, into the Sturm und Drang *movement* — a move that implies understanding the Sturm und Drang not as a series of years but as a set of ideas.[17] But as Karin A. Wurst has pointed out, this decision invites its own set of problems, among them the inevitable devaluation of women's literature judged by criteria that were later established to describe a small body of literature by a select circle of men[18] — what's good for (a highly limited number of) ganders may not be good for the geese. Wurst is right to raise this objection — the trivialization of women's literature read in the context of traditional literary history can be amply demonstrated in reviews and "scholarly" treatments of women's literature.[19] More disturbing to me than the potential denigration of women's works is the limitation of interpretive possibilities that has often been the result of reading them from a "traditional" — that is, masculinist — scholarly perspective. The very fact that women's works were *not* at the "center" but at the "margins" of contemporary literary discourse, simultaneously participatory and excluded,[20] means that they wrote from a position of privileged marginality. They wrote sometimes as members, always as observers of the epoch and its aesthetic ideas; from a forced, but at times also a critical distance; and often with a complexity resulting from their observer status that critics who simply "compare" their works to standard works of the male literary canon are sure to miss. In the following inter-

pretation of "Sturm und Drang" dramas by women — Christiane Karoline Schlegel's *Düval und Charmille* (Düval and Charmille, 1778), Sophie Albrecht's *Theresgen* (1781), and Marianne Ehrmann's *Leichtsinn
und gutes Herz* (1786) — I will read them as plays by "observers" of the
movement, attempting to show their closeness to and, simultaneously,
their critical distance from major ideas of the Sturm und Drang. Ultimately, my interest in these plays is motivated less by a desire to "include" women in the Sturm und Drang than by the possibility of
discovering in their texts early critiques of the movement. Read simultaneously as literature and covert literary criticism, these plays may well
help us arrive at an understanding of what the Sturm und Drang means
to us as readers and why its canonization as that most emphatically male
of all literary epochs in German history is so central to this meaning.[21]
Since each of the plays in question has already been the subject of some
introductory studies, I would like to dispense with a further general
introduction and, instead, examine them with two aspects in mind that
can be read as self-conscious interactions with basic tenets of the Sturm
und Drang: the portrayal of the passionate/rebellious lover and the
dramatic treatment of spaces.

Rebels and Their Causes

Schlegel's bourgeois tragedy *Düval und Charmille*[22] portrays Düval, the
play's tragic lover figure, as a domestic tyrant endowed with matchless
egotism and blustering language in the best tradition of the Sturm und
Drang. Düval's decision to take his lover, Amalie von Charmille, into his
house, in which he continues to live with his wife Mariane, results in an
uncomfortable ménage-à-trois that the women endure out of love for
Düval and friendship for each other, and in severe damage to his reputation at the court. Düval, whom Wurst has identified as a combination of
the melancholy and the passionate rival brothers who are so often set
against each other in traditional Sturm und Drang drama (62), tends to
present the passionate side of his identity in interactions with others —
which are almost universally characterized by angry outbursts on his
part — and his melancholy side in monologues, during which he makes
the central decisions of the drama. The extent of his mistreatment of
both women, as well as of his son, Franz, can be measured by the trepidation with which they approach him (compare Franz's fears of making
his father angry by merely inquiring about his dinner plans: 98). Düval,
well aware of the situation, plays on these fears in order to keep his
household in line: "Keine Vorwürfe — wenn du mich nicht rasend ma-

chen willst" (98).[23] Since Düval's usual abusive behavior, as depicted by Mariane — "Wie er sonst dräute, tobte, schäumte, schreckte!" (99)[24] — has been modified under Amalie's calming influence, Mariane has learned to accept the situation and, clearly incited by fears that the raging Düval would rematerialize on Amalie's removal, even opposes attempts by the court to break up her husband's love affair: "Ihr hatte ich meine ruhigern, friedsamern Tage zu danken, die ich, seit sie ihn beherrschte, genossen. Durft' er nicht mich verlassen, hintergehen, mein Vermögen an andre verschwenden, mir hart begegnen? Niemand strafte ihn!" (107).[25]

Düval's character embodies several traits that were already emerging as, or would later become stock characterizations of, the movement's major heroes: like Goethe's Götz, he employs coarse language in defense of his rights against the aristocracy; like Goethe's Werther, he emphasizes the difference between his own emotional intensity and the "tödtende kalte Plauderei" (113: deathly cold chatter) of the "kalten Winterseelen" (112: cold wintry souls) sent to terminate his affair; like Schiller's Ferdinand in *Kabale und Liebe*, he employs all persuasion at his disposal to induce his lover to follow him to the ends of the earth and into death. And like both Werther's and Ferdinand's, his love is characterized by its intensity and an unconditionality that can conceive of no middle ground between absolute possession of the lover and death. As such, Düval is conceptualized as a conglomerate of characters that later came to symbolize the Sturm und Drang, characters that were, without exception, written to garner the audience's sympathy.[26] The crucial difference is that whereas the heroes of the Sturm und Drang are put on the defensive, Düval is, for the most part, portrayed as the man in power, since throughout the play he interacts much less with his superiors at the court than with the women under his control. Whereas the heroes of the movement are forced into desperate behavior by the extremity of the situation, Düval's abuses, while also related to the pressure under which he is placed by the court's intervention, are well within his range of normality, as we know from Mariane's allusions to the past. And whereas the Sturm und Drang emphasis is invariably on the heroes' despair, Schlegel places it squarely on her protagonist's abusive nature and shows the consequences of his behavior for the women under his influence in ways that no other drama of the period attempted. This is particularly true of the depiction of Düval's interaction with Amalie: in monologues he obsesses incessantly about the possibility of her being removed from his grasp; like a child, he would rather destroy her than permit her either to be temporarily placed in a convent, as the court plans, or to be married to someone else, as Düval's own feverish fantasies suggest. Ultimately, his goal is to force her into a lovers' suicide with him; in pursuit of this goal, he reveals himself a veritable expert at emotional blackmail. This scene is representative of the interaction between the lovers:

AMALIE: Meine Pflicht ruft.

DÜVAL: Deine Pflicht? — wenn Du in meinen Armen bist?
            (läßt sie ärgerlich los, und stößt sie ein wenig von
            sich) Gut, so geh nur, wenn dich deine Pflicht
            ruft. — Dieß ist das Erstemal, daß ich das höre! —
            Geh nur! geh ins Kloster! dahin wird sie dich auch
            schicken, deine Pflicht; und du wirst gehen, und
            denken, du hast viel, viel gethan, wann du in der
            Morgen- und Abendbetstunde, oder in der
            Festtagsmesse ein Gebet für den verlassenen,
            verspotteten, verzweifelnden, rasenden Düval mit
            trockenen Augen und kaltem Herzen gebetet hast.

AMALIE: *weinend.* Grausamer! — rede nicht so! lieber tödte
            mich!

DÜVAL: Ist das Ernst? Recht so, meine Mally! ich wartete auf
            diese Bitte. Hier! — (er thut ein klein zusammen-
            gewickelt Papier in ein Etuit, und giebts ihr) Ein
            kleines wohlschmeckendes — ein — jedes
            Herzensweh heilendes Pulver! Dieß nimm auf den
            Weg zum Kloster! Vergiß nicht! denke, daß dann
            dein Düval auch nicht mehr lebt!
            *Amalie ist betäubt und sprachlos vor Angst und
            Entsetzen.* (103–4)[27]

What is revealing about this scene is the different ways in which both lovers regard the lovers' language: what Amalie recognizes and employs as sentimental discourse — the exaggeratedly passionate vows of love and death customary in the Sturm und Drang — is taken literally by Düval. Thus forced to live up to her own declarations, Amalie is left with no room for maneuver; once caught in the web of that language, Düval forces her into a choice between suicide and — as he would see it — acknowledging the shallowness of her feelings. It is undoubtedly this dilemma that induces Amalie to go along with Düval's suicide scheme in the final scenes of the play, albeit with such obvious misgivings that Düval ultimately decides to kill her rather than trust in the strength of her convictions. His final ranting monologue is paradigmatic of those that characterize him throughout the play:

DÜVAL: *allein.* Ja, du bist schwach, weil du mich nicht liebst, wie ich dich. — Auch dieß war eitler Selbstbetrug! — Gut! Es war nicht in deinem Herzen so zu lieben. Was kannst du für dein Herz? Aber der Muth, deinen Düval nicht zu überleben, ist auch nicht in deinem Herzen! Es ist nicht deine Schuld — ein frommer Aberglaube an Chimären. Ich muß dir zu Hülfe kommen, es wäre zu viel für dich allein, das seh' ich. — (Pause. Mit Überlegung) Und sähe sie erst den Tod auf meiner blassen Stirn — in meinem brechenden Auge: wie würd' er sich mit zehnfachen Schrecknissen gegen sie rüsten! — Und das Gift — nähme sie es auch — ein unsicherer, langsamer, qualvoller Tod! Oder sie nähme Hülfe an, gewönne das Leben wieder lieb, — würde eines andern — des Grafen! — nein, nein besser, ein schneller leichter Tod! Das Stilet in meinem Stock — (137–38)[28]

The obvious question the play leaves open is whether or not the rebellion whose language Düval invokes so fervently in defense of his love against the court would be possible on the part of the women in defense against the abuses to which Düval subjects them. The play suggests this possibility by the reversal of a character constellation that the audience is initially led to expect: the potential rivals turn out to be close friends, the wife is closely identified with the new lover (by casting herself in the role of Düval's former, now abandoned, lover), and the traditional virtue-vice contrast that was so popular in contemporary drama by men[29] is undermined both by this identification and by the fact that Amalie is presented as *virgo intacta*. While both women are clearly under Düval's spell, Mariane brings to the relationship an experience with the man's character that could stand them both in good stead. She repeatedly attempts to warn Amalie, thus again emphasizing the similarity between her own situation and Amalie's rather than their difference in character: "Ach Amalie! Sie hören hier nicht die Eifersucht einer Frau, und wenn sie es noch zehnmal mehr Ursache hätte; nein, es ist bloß die Freundinn, die mit Ihnen spricht — Düval — hüten Sie sich vor Düval! Er ist ein ungestümer, heftiger Mann, seiner Leidenschaft nie Meister — — ein Wütrich, wenn er . . . St!" (120).[30] Mariane's panicked "St!," announcing Düval's arrival, demonstrates better than her words can convey the consequences for both women if they were surprised by him in such an exchange.

It is such scenes of attempted solidarity and exchange of information that serve to counteract Düval's ferocious vows of eternal love and inevitable death and that point to a possible alternative. Beyond the scenes in which Mariane attempts to warn Amalie, there are two allusions to this potential resolution of the play, which would propose Mariane's and Amalie's joint rebellion against Düval (rather than, for example, Amalie's marriage to the Count or her removal to the convent) as the alternative to the murder-suicide that ends the play. One is Mariane's and Amalie's joint excursion to a ball in which Düval does not participate. Düval responds to their absence from his direct control with such paranoia and later subjects the women to such intense questioning as to the lateness of their return that his behavior could only be justified, in the viewer's mind, by a suspected infidelity. This parallel seems appropriate in light of the fact that this ball is the only time throughout the play that the women have an opportunity to talk. Given the repeated interrupted scenes of warning earlier in the play, we might surmise that this opportunity was put to good use, that Mariane and Amalie have finally exchanged notes, possibly even arrived at a joint plan of action. This distinctly theoretical plot device is, however, immediately dropped on their return, in favor of the murder-suicide plot then initiated by Düval: as Mariane's earlier half-sentences of warning suggest, solidarity among women is possible only in the man's absence. The other allusion that the play makes to this potential women's rebellion is the fact that Amalie dies not in Düval's arms but in Mariane's. The difference between Mariane's and Amalie's potential rebellion against Düval and Düval's real rebellion against courtly intervention, between Düval's stormy rhetoric of love and death and the women's secret expressions of solidarity presumably exchanged offstage, is that the women's rebellion is limited to words, whereas Düval has the power and the callousness to put his words into action. But words matter in the sense that it is words and the actions they cause that have to be relativized and that are relativized in Amalie's dying act: Amalie's final journey to Mariane's door (139) and her death in Mariane's arms serve to illustrate the destructiveness of Düval's tempestuous discourse and negate unequivocally his fiction of the lovers' suicide.[31] The "moral" of the play — if, indeed, there is one — must then be seen in the universal condemnation not only of Düval's character and actions but also, and more significantly, of his words and *what they symbolize,* from each character on stage. In the final scene the servants, the officer rushing to the family's aid, Franz, and Mariane unanimously declare Düval's act a "murder" (140) — rather than, as he would have us read it, a sentimental suicide — thus putting the right word to the deed, thus denying the rebel his cause.

Albrecht's *Theresgen*, designated a "Schauspiel mit Gesang" (Play with Singing),[32] is the only drama by a contemporary woman that examines the applicability of the rebellious-lover concept to a female character. Theresgen enters the stage as a melancholy character;[33] her melancholia is not explained until the third act, when the audience is informed of her secret and doomed love for the Count. As Düval is placed between two women, so Theresgen is placed between two men: her hated suitor Franz and her hopelessly beloved Count Adolf. Both love stories play heavily on gender stereotypes, with the Theresgen-Franz association emphatically supporting traditional gender roles and the Theresgen-Adolf attachment silently subverting them. Theresgen encounters the Count sleeping on the banks of the lake; she falls in love with the image, barely saves the Count from drowning, and flees after he awakens and thanks her. This near-death scene sports some astonishing gender reversals,[34] with the Count cast in the role of both the beautiful image and helpless Ophelia ("Sein langes Haar schwamm schon im Teiche," 171)[35] and Theresgen as his valiant rescuer. Conversely, the association of Franz and Theresgen is defined by an intensification of traditional gender roles as they frequently appear in contemporary drama: all the men in Theresgen's life — Franz; her friend Andres; the Count; and her stepfather, Heinrich, whose primary character trait is his vicious hatred of Theresgen — join forces to coerce her into marrying Franz. The extreme lover of the Sturm und Drang is represented both by Theresgen, who loves the Count unswervingly, if hopelessly, and by Franz, who is equipped, much like Schlegel's Düval, with all the passionate rhetoric the viewer has come to expect from the great lovers of the movement. Oscillating constantly between the tragically melancholy lover in search of an early grave (146–47) and the passionate lover who has no qualms about forcing Theresgen into marriage against her will, Franz ultimately decides to accept her hand, despite his clear awareness of her distaste for him: "Theures Mädgen! Ein Leben voll Liebe und Dank, soll mir Vergebung schenken, daß ich sie an mein Herz reiße, deine sträubende Hand" (184).[36] Remarkably, audience identification with Franz's characterization as the unequivocal lover of the Sturm und Drang is frequently undermined, while that with Theresgen's parallel characterization is upheld. Franz's pathetic self-portrayal as the tragically unrequited lover for whom nothing is left but death is aptly undermined in a comment in which his sister reinterprets his stance as childish self-indulgence: "Ich glaube, Franz ist Schuld mit seinen Reden von Tod und Grab; gleich wollen die Leutgen sterben, wenns nicht nach dem Köpfgen geht" (147).[37] The same sentiment takes on a much different meaning when applied to Theresgen by her stepfather, who hates her virulently and frequently expresses his wish for her early death. "Man stirbt so leicht nicht" (180: One does not die so easily), he remarks immediately before Theresgen's suicide, in callous disregard of her real despair and her lack of alternatives. Rather than merely critiquing the rhetoric and predilections of the Sturm und Drang lover, the play is attempting to differentiate between the *literary* phenomenon (the ranting and raving of passionate lovers on stage, here played out in the character of Franz) and the social reality of those who are deprived of all choice in matters of love (the women whose consent is forced by an assembly of men, well-meaning and otherwise).

The play's astonishing conclusion is that the only possibility for Theresgen's survival lies in her inability to perceive that difference. Accordingly, a large portion of the play is spent in persuading Theresgen to mistake the literary discourse for reality. A key scene is that between Theresgen and her best friend, Lehngen, whose inability to see these connections enables her to function as Theresgen's happy and carefree alter ego:

THERESGEN: Vergieb mir, liebes Mädgen! ich kann mich nicht mit dir freuen — dort verstummte meine Freude.

LEHNGEN: Ach, immer Tod und Grab. Ich weis nicht, wie man im Sommer ans Sterben denken kann. Alles lebt und blüht.

THERESGEN: Ach stirbt und welkt. Immer steigt die zweyte Blume aus dem Sterbelager der ersten, und ihre Schöne welkt, wenn ihre Schwester erscheint. . . .

LEHNGEN: Das hab ich nie zuvorgedacht und war glücklich; reiß dich los von diesen trüben Gedanken, mach's wie ich, liebes Mädgen, schmücke dich mit der blühenden Rose, und denke nicht des welkenden Veilgens. (151–52)[38]

In other words, while the truth of Theresgen's words remains undisputed, what is required for her happiness is that selectiveness of perception that Lehngen has mastered so well: the unthinking ability to adorn oneself with the rose is predicated on one's refusal to consider the dying violet. In a similar manner, the Count suggests that Theresgen's salvation lies in inducing a misperception:

DER GRAF: Nein, Vater, das ist nicht die Art ein Mädgen zu zwingen, liebt sie Franzen nicht, wie es scheint, so wäre es grausam, sie zu binden, ohne ihr Zeit zu lassen, die Fesseln sich erträglich zu denken. Laßt uns die Ketten soviel als möglich unter Rosen verbergen, ist sie eigensinnig, laßt sie sanfte Bitten lenken, daß sie endlich selbst glaubt, sie giebt die Hand, wenn wir sie nehmen. (160)[39]

What would enable Theresgen to save her life is an astounding confusion of fiction with reality, a profound ignorance of her own feelings, and a fundamental misjudgment of what is being done to her. Essentially, what is required is Theresgen's misinterpretation of an act of coercion as a voluntary action on her part. As all the men in the play are well aware, such a profound perversion of feeling does not occur naturally but can only be the result of extensive indoctrination. Heinrich arrives at this conclusion when he presents Theresgen's problem as one of "education": because she was educated outside of the sphere of men — by a foster mother — she has never received the education that would predispose her to play the correct part in the love drama written by men. "Aus einer albernen Erziehung, die ihr die Edelfrau . . . gab welche dahin aus lief, nicht zu sagen, daß ein Mädgenherz bey einem hübschen Burschen mehr schlägt, als bey ihrer Großmutter, hat sie das dumme Zeug" (159).[40] Theresgen, in other words, has never been *told* that she is supposed to be indifferent in the company of her grandmother and all aflutter in the company of a man, and it is this lack of education — her lack of appropriation of the Sturm und Drang rhetoric and her inability to suppress what she knows to be true in favor of this fiction — that is her downfall. Because her perceived reality is invalidated in favor of this fiction, her rebellion remains, like that of Schlegel's women, limited to words: her most frequently recurring statement is the monotonous and unqualified "Ich kann nicht" (I cannot), simultaneously an expression of protest and refusal and a demonstration of her powerlessness. As is the case in Schlegel's play, her death subverts important conventions of the sentimental love death: her final exclamation — "Franz! Mein Vater!" (187: Franz! My father!) — is, of course, a direct allusion to the sentimental heroine's last words directed at the beloved man and/or father;[41] the rift between literary discourse and the reality of Theresgen's existence is stated once again in the fact that her final exclamation is directed at the men she hates the most and holds directly responsible for her death. In this she makes it clear that she kills herself not because of her unhappy love for the Count but to escape her forced marriage to Franz. What seems to emerge here is a program similar to the one conceptualized in Schlegel's play: the love rhetoric of the age is unmasked as a *literary* discourse, one that has no parallel, as scholarly readings by men's Sturm und Drang dramas would often seem to suggest, to a real or imagined social protest offstage, but one that, instead, emerges as a highly effective tool for the coercion of women.

If Schlegel's and Albrecht's dramas implicitly play on literary conventions of their day, Ehrmann's *Leichtsinn und gutes Herz oder die Folgen der Erziehung*[42] does so explicitly — most noticeably in its character constellation, which shows some marked parallels to that in Lessing's *Emilia Galotti*. At the center of the *Original-Schauspiel* (original drama), as Ehrmann dubs her play, are the aristocratic seducer Count von Treuberg and his evil adviser Mekler, juxtaposed to Lottchen Breiner and her father. Significant deviations from Lessing's formula include Ehrmann's emphasis on the difference in social rank between seducer and seduced — Lottchen and her father are members of the peasant class — and the unlikely happy ending, in which Lottchen and the Count marry with her father's consent. The story is one of seduction in more than one sense of the word: Lottchen's seduction by the Count mirrors the Count's seduction by the evil advice of his confidant Mekler. While the Count's intentions toward Lottchen are honorable from the beginning of the play — he repeatedly states his intention to marry her — Mekler dissuades him by recourse to the usual arguments with regard to rank and family. Mekler, who himself has sexual designs on Lottchen, induces the Count to abduct her, use her sexually, and ultimately abandon her; he also dissuades Lottchen's father, who has come to the Count's castle in search of her, from the pursuit by persuading Breiner of his intention to return Lottchen safely. Because both the Count and Lottchen's father are entirely deceived by Mekler's machinations, Lottchen can expect no aid from either of the men and decides to take action herself, and it is this aspect, coupled with her forthright language, that defines her as a heroine in the tradition of the Sturm und Drang.[43] Lottchen's character is conceptualized as an exact combination of the traditional bourgeois innocent and the aristocratic mistress that are so often juxtaposed in contemporary dramas by men:[44] at the outset of the play she is presented as the simple country girl who listens to Mekler's seductive talk with frank amazement and whose primary concern is to return to her household duties as quickly as possible (198). Once forcibly cast in the role of the aristocratic mistress by virtue of her abduction, seduction, and life in the Count's castle, however, she takes on that role with a vengeance. She demands that the Count make good his promise to marry her and does not hesitate to seize the nearest weapon when he continues to prevaricate:

LOTTCHEN: *(mit Ernst)* Des Priesters Segen muß noch heute über uns gesprochen werden, wenn ihre vierzehn Tage nicht eine Lüge von einer Ewigkeit sind.

GRAF: Wenn aber meine — —

LOTTCHEN: Keine Ausflüchte, oder Einwendungen! — Heute noch mit Ihnen zum Altar, oder Morgen mit mir in des Henkers Hände. Sind Sie das zufrieden? (sieht nach den Pistolen, die an der Wand hängen)

GRAF: *(verzagt stotternd)* Ihre Zudringlichkeit — —

LOTTCHEN: Ist sie etwa zu groß für meine Ehre? Siehst du Raubvogel, daß sie noch zu klein war. (nimmt eine von den ungeladenen Pistolen und hält sie ihm vor) Hier hab ich eine noch größere; heraus mit der Sprache verstockter Missethäter, oder ein Schuß macht uns beede unglücklich.

GRAF: Legen Sie ab, Sie sind rasend.

LOTTCHEN: Ja ich bin es. (drückt los) — Verfluchtes Werkzeug meiner Rache! (wirft die Pistole mit Heftigkeit zu Boden) auch du versagst mir den Dienst meine Ehre zu retten; auch du bist falsch! Nun dann, so sei alles wider mich verschworen, so bist du es nicht Gewissen (in der Raserei steigend) du sollst mich auffodern sein ewiger Verfolgungs-Geist zu seyn. Bei den Haaren will ich dich Weiberschänder vor das jüngste Gericht hinschleppen, alle bösen Geister sollen mir die Flüche einreden, die ich dir nachwerfen will; und mit teuflischer Freude will ich triumphiren, wenn ich dich vor meinen Augen verdammt sehen kann. (222)[45]

This scene is a significant reversal of similar scenes in other plays in that the weapon that is usually trained on the seduced daughter, precisely because the seducer is beyond reach, is here pointed squarely at the seducer — and not by the father but by the offended party herself. Lottchen's fruitless attempt to right her wrong can, of course, be interpreted as showing the inability of the woman to wield a man's weapon;[46] nonetheless, this remains the only play of which I am aware in which Orsina's suggestion that compromised virtue could strike back with more than words is played out to its logical conclusion. Whereas other heroines whose revenge is purely verbal, such as Orsina, or who direct their aggression at the female rival, like Marwood, pay for their actions by losing the audience's sympathies,[47] Lottchen, who vilifies her seducer verbally and attempts to kill him on stage, is ultimately reinstated in the audience's good graces. While the inefficacy of Lottchen's weapon throws her rebellion back to the level to which Schlegel's and Albrecht's heroines are limited from the start — that of words — the scene not only indicates how successfully Lottchen has appropriated the passionate language of the Sturm und Drang lover[48] but also endows her with his emotional volatility and potential for violence if pushed to the extreme.

In Ehrmann's play, unlike in Schlegel's and Albrecht's, this passionate language is taken seriously and defined as the principal expression of offended virtue. This is shown, on the one hand, in the fact that Lottchen's rebellion is presented as entirely justified, and, on the other hand, in the fact that this discourse is consistently mocked and vilified by Mekler, the play's evil schemer. In Mekler's mocking account, the Count's sincere love for Lottchen turns into a parody of Sturm und Drang passion: "Es ist ein wahres Vergnügen, wenn man den vollblütigen, schönen Grafen so nach Lotten seufzen sieht, wie da alles kocht! wie es wallt, daß ihm das siedende Blut aus den Wangen spritzen möchte!" (199).[49] In a similar perversion of Breiner's despair, expressed in the familiar dash- and exclamation-point-riddled Sturm und Drang style of half-sentences and exclamations, Mekler coolly advises, "Weniger Hitze, und mehr Gelassenheit" (215: less heat, more equanimity), thus representing himself as the voice of Reason and indirectly accusing Breiner of exaggeration.

Erziehung (education) is, as the title announces, a central concern of the play, and in the portrayal of this theme occurs perhaps the most significant of Ehrmann's interactions with contemporary discourse. For what this discourse would suggest — that Lottchen's misfortune is rooted in her faulty education, specifically in the undue influence exerted on her by romantic novels and in her education "above her station" in the city[50] — is subtly subverted in the play. These subversions are made all the more obvious by the fact that the audience is initially seduced into this faulty reasoning: Lottchen is shown repeatedly with a book (210); indeed, the Count first encountered her with book in hand (188); Breiner describes Lottchen's education as "über meinen Stand" (218: above my station); and the Count more than once alludes to Lottchen's education in the city, her reading, and her resulting "Schwärmerei" (189: sentimentality). But ultimately, it is not Lottchen's education that is faulted for her abduction and seduction but the Count's: in one of the key scenes of the play the Count shifts the blame from the victim, where traditional discourse would lay it, to where it belongs — the seducer, using and simultaneously perverting contemporary codes: "Meinem Hofmeister kann ich es nicht verzeihen, daß er mein weiches Herz zu keinem festen Karakter bildete. Tugend und Laster streiten um den Vorzug, und sehr natürlich, daß bei meiner verzärtelten Erziehung, bei'm Überfluß und besonders bei meiner Empfindung das letztere öfters mächtiger, als das erstere ist" (219).[51] Whereas Albrecht's solution juxtaposes natural feeling and "education," viewed as indoctrination and perversion of natural feeling, Ehrmann attempts a symbiosis in the happy ending, in which Breiner gives his consent to the marriage and invokes both Nature and Education in the ostentatious moral of the drama: "O Natur, Natur! — deine Wohlthaten sind unbegreiflich! — vor wenigsten Augenblicken war ich der gebeugteste, und nun — bin ich der glücklichste Vater! (lange Pause) Väter! Mütter! um dieser Thräne willen, gebt doch auf die Erziehung eurer Kinder acht!" (251).[52] In this conclusion Ehrmann again alludes to the two discourses she has employed throughout her play: as the Enlightenment, consistently evoked in the self-conscious interaction with Lessing's play, intercedes into what is otherwise a quintessential Sturm und Drang drama, so "Nature" can only be the benefactress of humans if linked with "education."

Where Ehrmann's play intersects with Schlegel's and Albrecht's is her depiction of her heroine in an extremely precarious position; the brutality with which the coercion of the woman in question is portrayed (see 195–97); the extremely negative portrayal of the male characters, in particular those guilty of this coercion; and the critical reflection of contemporary literary discourse. It is this last point that makes it possible to read these plays both from "within" the movement and simultaneously as positioned at a critical distance. Each play attempts to re-view the primary passions depicted in the movement (love and rebellion) from the viewpoint of the female character, with varying results. Perhaps the strongest critique expressed by these dramas is contained in the fact that Ehrmann's drama, clearly the least critical of these reflections, the sole — albeit not unequivocal — endorsement of Sturm und Drang predilections and mannerisms, and simultaneously the only play with a happy ending, was written from the vantage point of *hindsight,* at a time when the movement was already a thing of the past. It is also the most thoroughly literary treatment of the movement: the play, if read as literary critique, is less an example of the Sturm und Drang than a contemplation of both the Sturm und Drang and the Enlightenment. Despite the play's sympathetic portrayal of the forthright, blustering, and passionate characters, its ultimate moral calls on an Enlightenment element to guarantee the happy outcome: only "Education" can prevent the tragic ending that would inevitably ensue if "Nature" were left to take its course — and how close even Ehrmann's play comes to such an ending is suggested in the suddenness and apparent lack of motivation with which she imposes a happy ending onto a play that has, up to that point, exhibited purely tragic tendencies.[53]

Closed Rooms
and Wide Open Spaces

The dramatic treatment of space in all three dramas could productively be read as another indirect commentary on the dramaturgy of the Sturm und Drang. Whereas many Sturm und Drang authors saw their disregard for the Aristotelian unities of place, time, and action as paramount in their efforts at dramaturgic innovation, *Düval und Charmille* adheres to them precisely.[54] The setting throughout the play is the main room of Düval's and Mariane's home, with three doors leading off it: the one in the middle to Düval's private room, the one to the right to Mariane's room, the one to the left into the foyer (to the outside). Each room stands as a sign for a central aspect of the plot: Düval's private room for his illicit affair with Amalie, which is also the factor that makes this door off-limits to Mariane and Franz; Mariane's for the space into which she is banished in the absence of a family life with husband and son; the third door for the world outside of the family; and the common room — the only one into which the audience is granted insight — as the space in which family members interact with each other and with outsiders. Düval's door is centered in the same manner in which he is centered throughout the play.[55] The distribution of spaces throughout the play expresses in significant ways the meaning of the action performed in each space: just as Düval's lonely meals in his room signify his refusal to participate in family life,[56] so Mariane's and Amalie's single excursion to the outside could, as I have argued above, signify a potential attempt to break out of the rooms in which they are each closed in. In a dramaturgy in which rooms and doors are endowed with such meaning, it is significant that Amalie first enters the stage not through the door from the outside but from Düval's door,[57] a fact that already points to the firmness with which she is bonded both into the relationship with Düval and to the "place" she claims in the family. Düval's room is also the room that is ultimately fashioned into a "bridal chamber" (130) for the blood wedding Düval has in mind; Amalie's temptations to go along with Düval's plan and her simultaneous strong feelings of trepidation are physically expressed in the way she approaches and shies away from Düval's door in the scene before the murder (137–38). The fact that what takes place inside *is* a murder, rather than a joint suicide, is similarly documented in stage directions relating to the physical space the characters occupy: Düval "hat sich dem Kabinette genähert und steht einige Augenblicke schweigend still) — Sie regt sich — (er öffnet die Thüre, und indem er hineintritt, und das Fräulein nahe bey der Thüre gleichsam hindert herauszukommen) Bist du nun fertig, meine Liebe? — (er macht die Thür hinter sich zu, und man hört den Riegel vorschieben)" (138).[58] Düval's comment "Sie regt sich" (she moves) documents Amalie's last sign of life. Shortly thereafter, she enters the common family space mortally wounded. Amalie's final movements across the stage are equally expressive of action performed and of action that can no longer take place: "Die Kabinetthüre wird schnell aufgeriegelt. Amalie leichenblaß mit einem Schnupftuch ans Herz haltend kömmt heftig und wankend herein. Sie eilt nach Marianens Zimmer, kehrt aber schnell und taumelnd um nach der Thüre des Vorhauses" (139).[59] Already dying, Amalie flees Düval's room in an unequivocal dissociation from Düval's fiction of the lovers' suicide, but equally significant is her initial effort to seek help at Amalie's door, immediately abandoned for a final, and fruitless, attempt at flight *out of the house.* Clearly, what is being played out here in Amalie's final steps before she collapses and dies in the family's common room are the two suggested alternatives to the play's grim ending: the possibility of an association between the two women (which Amalie considers briefly but ultimately abandons) and the possibility of Amalie's complete removal from the family (the court's plan to enter her into a convent and the potential of marriage to someone else, alluded to in the Count's remarks and in Düval's ravings).

Rooms in Schlegel's dramaturgic world are, without exception, closed or locked: Düval regularly locks himself in to eat; he finally locks Amalie in to kill her; a great many of Mariane's tears, we are led to believe, are shed offstage in the privacy of her room. I do not view this as an expression of the secrecy of proceedings "behind closed doors," since both the affair and Mariane's reaction to it are made quite public: Düval and Amalie carry their affair quite openly into the family's common room, the same space Mariane occasionally occupies with her grief. Rather, I view the closed doors as a sign for the inability of each character to leave "his" or "her" room: Düval's inability to conquer his mad obsession with Amalie, Amalie's inability to disentangle herself from her association with both husband and wife, and Amalie's and Mariane's failure to arrive at a real understanding with one another. It is this aspect that I regard as, perhaps, the most radical conclusion of Schlegel's play: that the closed doors do not, as one might surmise in a drama about an illicit love affair, stand for secrecy (among lovers) but for imprisonment (of women), as well as the characters' severe limitations exposed within the given dramatic context (the love triangle).

In its use of space Albrecht's *Theresgen* seems to conform much more closely to central ideas of the Sturm und Drang. The play's dramaturgy of space subsists partly on the well-known opposition of the country versus the city: Theresgen, educated by a noblewoman in the city, remembers her tutor with great fondness and the city with equally intense aversion.[60] The entire play takes place outside, in "nature." Not only is Theresgen, the central character, never shown inside; she is also presented as removed from the village in her consistent localization in untamed nature: on the banks of the lake, in the forest, "outside" the village fences.[61] The only "civilized" space in which Theresgen is ever seen is, strikingly, the village cemetery. Theresgen's closeness to nature is underscored by the noticeable unity of outer and inner nature signified, for example, by the thunderstorm accompanying her final bout of despair (178). The most obvious example of the significance of nature in the play is the recurring water imagery: water stands simultaneously as the locus of fantasy and imagination (Theresgen's love for the Count, initiated on the banks of the lake, vis-à-vis the forced marriage prepared for her in the village) and as the locus of death both imagined and endured. Both love and death are central in Theresgen's vision of the Count. Lost in her observation of nature, of which the sleeping Count is an integral part, she nearly "forgets" that he is near drowning and saves him only at the last moment (171). Death by drowning becomes a recurring theme in the play: it is evoked in Theresgen's fantasy of the Count, reiterated in Heinrich's hate-filled remark that he would often have liked to have drowned his stepdaughter in a puddle (158), and ultimately achieved in Theresgen's death in the lake.

As is the case in Schlegel's play, spaces in *Theresgen* symbolically underscore the drama's central ideas: the principal aim of the play is to force her into the house. The ways in which Albrecht's play documents the relation of space and meaning is similar to Schlegel's and most strikingly revealed in the main character's inability physically to move from one space to another. Theresgen's weakness is both commented on by others — "Sie ist so matt Vater, daß sie kaum hier einige Schritte schwankt und hätte den Weg nicht aushalten können" (179)[62] — and evoked by

Theresgen herself in her recurring "Ich kann nicht" throughout the play. The "house" as a space is ominously thematized both as the ultimate site of civilization and, similar to the treatment in Schlegel's play, as the site of irrevocable captivity in an unhappy marriage. Theresgen's answer to Lehngen's entreaty to go "into your house" because the storm is approaching — "Nein, ich kann nicht ins Haus. O ich würde sterben!" (178)[63] — can thus be read as signifying a final refusal to enter that site that Schlegel's Amalie unsuccessfully tries to flee in her final scene, the site of bourgeois family life and patriarchal domination.[64] Ehrmann's *Leichtsinn und gutes Herz* is the only one of the three plays that makes extensive use of varied locales; similarly to Albrecht's play, it is characterized by a seemingly irreconcilable contrast between the country and the city. As it does in contemporary discourse, the country in her play signifies innocence and virtue, with the city standing for vice and corruption. One example of many is Breiner's idealizing depiction of country folk: "Wir wissen von keinen überflüßigen Wünschen, unsre Erziehung ist zu natürlich, als daß wir ihre Bequemlichkeiten nicht leicht entbehren könnten. Unbeneidete Freiheit, ist für uns ein Geschenk des Himmels. Das Geräusch der Stadt würde unsre unverdorbene Seele verstimmen" (193).[65] This juxtaposition is reiterated throughout the play: the Count falls in love when he encounters Lottchen at a brook (188); Lottchen's education in the city is mentioned several times as a potential endangerment of her virtue (189); and Breiner's idyllic country estate is visibly contrasted with Treuberg's castle, the sinister site of Lottchen's seduction. Once in the castle, Lottchen expresses her desire for a return to innocence in her yearning for "the wasteland" ("Einöde," 210), a space farther removed from civilization than even the "country." In a striking parallel to both Schlegel's and Albrecht's plays, the heroine's inability to move through space stands for her incapacity for self-defense; essential plot devices are played out physically, as in the following scene between Lottchen and her seducer:

LOTTCHEN:	*(zu Mekler).* Und nun leben Sie wohl. (Will gehen.)
GRAF:	*(hält sie zurück).* Bleiben Sie Lottchen! Bleiben Sie! Und sehen Sie mich zu Ihren Füssen, sehen Sie den, den Sie ohne Ihr Herz unglücklich machen.
LOTTCHEN:	Gott! Ich bin verlohren! — Ich muß — ja — ich muß fort.
GRAF:	Englisches Mädchen! Bleibe — oder du richtest mich zu Grunde.

> LOTTCHEN: Nein, lassen Sie mich, ich sauge Verderben aus Ihren Blicken. — Mein eigenes Herz veräth mich. — Weh mir! Ich kann nicht gehn, — kann nicht von der Stelle. (200)[66]

The essential difference from the earlier plays consists in the fact that Lottchen, whose ability to move is contested in this scene, ultimately regains her capacity to change places and thus change the outcome of the play — evidenced in her flight from the castle and her return to her father's home. And this ability takes on added significance by virtue of the fact that places in Ehrmann's dramaturgy not only symbolically represent dramatic action but also show a perceptible influence on dramatic character. Similarly to Albrecht's *Theresgen,* in which the heroine's inner turmoil is accompanied by a thunderstorm on the outside, Ehrmann dramatizes "Nature" as both a physical and a psychological space and proposes the parallelism of the two. Lottchen's otherwise implausible change from the innocent victim of seduction that she portrays in conversations with Mekler and the Count near her country home to the aristocratic mistress whose extreme language evidences both her recently gained "experience" and her bitterness over the loss of her innocence can only be explained by her respective positioning in each character's "natural" surroundings. Equally implausibly, Lottchen's return to "nature," to her country home, at the end of the play marks her return to innocence by virtue of her father's forgiveness and her marriage to her seducer. The identification of space and character, of inner and outer nature, is the sole factor that can explain the astounding fact that Lottchen succeeds where all of her dramatic precursors, from Sara Sampson to Emilia Galotti to Luise Millerin to Lenz's heroines, failed, thus becoming the only reformed "fallen virtue" in dramatic history.

Conclusion

Schlegel's, Albrecht's, and Ehrmann's dramas are undoubtedly not a perfect "match" if read from "within" the Sturm und Drang. Read as texts that were produced from a position as observer, however, it is precisely these discursive dissociations that must be seen as conscious interactions with basic predilections of the movement. Among the most central, in all three plays, are the use of language, the reinterpretation of the traditional feminine virtue-vice contrast, and the re-visioning of the rebellious male lover. In all of the plays the language used evokes clearly the passionate language of the Sturm und Drang lover, but each play

uses this motif in a different way: in Schlegel's play this language becomes a fatal trap for Amalie; in Albrecht's it stands for a fictional discourse that the heroine is expected to privilege over what she perceives
as reality; in Ehrmann's drama it is a sign for the characters' integrity.
Ultimately, however, even Ehrmann modifies her retrospective endorsement of Sturm und Drang passion in her allusion to education and edu-
cability, one of the most central ideas of the Enlightenment. If one reads
these plays, as I have tried to do, both as literature and as literary criticism, one might see in Ehrmann's conclusion a precursor of later criticism that views the Sturm und Drang not as diametrically opposed to,
but as a continuation and expansion of, Enlightenment ideas.[67]

Equally central is the reinterpretation of the traditional virtue-vice
contrast, expressed in men's plays by the common juxtaposition of the
bourgeois innocent with the aristocratic mistress. In the women's plays
the two roles are *identified,* rather than contrasted: in Schlegel's drama
Mariane and Amalie are viewed as points along the same trajectory; their
friendship stands in stark contrast to the bitter rivalry the audience is led
to expect and forcefully underscores the absence of this conventional
formula. Posited opposite Albrecht's Theresgen is not an aristocratic rival
but another woman of the same class; the difference between these characters is defined in terms of emotional predilections and character, not
in terms of moral qualities, sexual "innocence," or social rank. And
Ehrmann's heroine Lottchen embodies, in various scenes, both the
middle-to-lower-class victim of seduction and the sexually experienced,
embittered aristocratic mistress. The consequences are as obvious as they
are significant: by removing the rivalry between women that is so popular
in contemporary men's literature, the women playwrights redefine the
central dramatic conflict as one between women and men. It is in this
context, that of the reinterpretation of the female roles, that I see the
significance of the dramaturgy of space in each play. While all three
authors overtly allude to literary conventions, including those of the
Sturm und Drang, in their dramatization of space, the controversies
engaged in within contemporary literary discourse (the dramatic unity of
place, the country-city dichotomy, the exaltation of nature as both locale
and characterization) are hardly the primary concern of their dramas.
Instead, these conventions are used, consciously and skillfully, in the
dramatization of each play's central idea. All three plays conceptualize
spaces as fatal or near-fatal restrictions for the drama's female heroines
and endow them with symbolic meaning — even, in Ehrmann's case,
with the power to shape plot and character. In each play the heroine's
ability or inability to move through space becomes the primary indicator

of her ultimate potential for survival. In this way the plays shift the emphasis from the two most popular themes in contemporary discourse — the country-city (country-court, country-castle) dichotomy and its attendant dramatization in the juxtaposition of feminine virtue and vice — to the *consequences* of this taxonomy for women and to the implied question of what "space" exists for women beyond these dichotomies.

One of the most central re-visions of women's contemporary drama vis-à-vis the Sturm und Drang tradition is the reconceptualization of the male rebel-lover. In women's plays he is invariably portrayed as highly irrational and destructive for the woman or women under his control. In this he does not differ significantly from traditional depictions of the hero in plays of the movement. What is substantially different in women's dramatic conception of the rebellious hero is that he is not shown as rebelling *against* anything. None of their plays portray the corrupt aristocracy that traditionally furnishes the justification for the hero's rebellion: in Schlegel's play the court acts in loco parentis in trying to protect Amalie from Düval; in Albrecht's play the Count is portrayed as well-meaning, if tragically misled — he is, in fact, the *only* male character who insists that Theresgen not be forced to marry Franz against her will if she loves someone else. The Count in Ehrmann's drama contravenes his own resemblance to Lessing's prince in his initial intention to marry Lottchen and in the final scene, in which he dissociates himself effectively from his evil adviser and fulfills his promise. Whereas Lessing's play ends with the fundamental conflict between Odoardo and the prince, thus establishing the familiar context of oppression and rebellion emulated endlessly in traditional Sturm und Drang drama, the marriage of Lottchen and the Count, of peasantry and aristocracy, at the end of Ehrmann's drama serves as a clear refutation of Lessing's ending and, with it, of that context. This refutation, which I see as pivotal in all three plays, is more than merely an indirect reiteration that the central conflict in each play is gendered rather than class-based. It also effectively deprives the male hero-rebel in these plays of a cause for rebellion and thereby of the audience's sympathies. The male rebel, in stark contrast to traditional dramas of the movement, is no longer the point of identification for the audience; the identification is transferred to his victims. As is the case in traditional plays of the movement, the hero's despair is given extensive stage time in each play (in the form of Düval's ranting monologues, Franz's pathos-laden graveyard speeches, the Count's endless vacillations between virtue and vice), but — and this I see as the most radical deviation from the Sturm und Drang formula — what despair leads to, the death of the play's heroine, is no longer viewed with approbation. Because the traditional virtue-vice and bourgeoisie-aristocracy conflicts have been removed, the female corpse in these plays does not stand for anything; it has no symbolic value[68] and, therefore, also cannot serve the sublimatory function that the female corpse serves in traditional plays of the movement. While both Schlegel and Albrecht end their plays with this terse refusal of audience sublimation, Ehrmann withholds both it and its medium, the female corpse, in her seemingly unmotivated happy ending, an ending in which she also breaks every moral directive by rewarding, rather than punishing, her heroine's fallen virtue.

What emerges from Schlegel's, Albrecht's, and Ehrmann's adaptation of Sturm und Drang motifs is a highly critical view of the movement. Their changes provide an apt commentary both on the dramatic conventions of their day and on the symbolic signification of the movement as it was originally established in contemporary reception[69] and later perpetuated in scholarly discourse. Essentially, it is the male-centeredness of the movement, the centrality of the male hero, his close identification with the male author, and, above all, viewer sympathy with the hero's doomed rebellion that allows the audience to act as approving voyeurs of women's mistreatment and death and that invites the standard interpretation of women's subjugation as the sublimation of the hero's (author's, audience's) political powerlessness. By removing this context, women playwrights not only eliminate the essence of the movement while retaining its countenance but also forcefully dissociate themselves from an acknowledgment of the symbolic significance of Sturm und Drang literature, an acknowledgment that still furnishes the basis for our understanding of the movement.[70]

Notes

[1] Bruce Duncan, *Lovers, Parricides, and Highwaymen: Aspects of Sturm und Drang Drama* (Rochester NY: Camden House, 1999), 28. The nonexistence of women authors in the Sturm und Drang has most recently been stated by Inge Stephan, who cites the ideology of the masculine genius and its attendant homosocial modes of communication and interaction as a possible explanation: "Geniekult und Männerbund: Zur Ausgrenzung des 'Weiblichen' in der Sturm und Drang-Bewegung," in *Jakob Michael Reinhold Lenz*, ed. Martin Kagel (Munich: Text + Kritik, 2000), 46–54.

[2] Kirsten Krick problematizes the exclusive masculinity of the movement and lists Caroline Flachsland, Susanne Katharina von Klettenberg, Johanna Fahlmer, Agnes Klinger, Albertine von Grün, Friederike Brion, Sophie von LaRoche, Marianne Ehrmann, Maria Anna Sagar, Anna Luisa Karsch, and Christiane Karoline Schlegel

as female authors who could be counted as having contributed to the movement: Kirsten Krick, "Storm and Stress / Sturm und Drang," in *The Feminist Encyclopedia of German Literature*, ed. Friederike Eigler and Susanne Kord (Westport, CT & London: Greenwood, 1997), 495–96. Discussions of women's plays as Sturm und Drang dramas include Irmgard Roebling, "Sturm und Drang — weiblich: Eine Untersuchung zu Sophie Albrechts Schauspiel 'Theresgen,'" *Der Deutschunterricht* 48 (1996): 63–77, and Anne Fleig's chapter on Schlegel's *Düval und Charmille* in *Handlungs-Spiel-Räume: Dramen von Autorinnen im Theater des ausgehenden 18. Jahrhunderts* (Würzburg: Königshausen & Neumann, 1999), 205–27. Ruth Dawson has drawn a tentative connection between Sophie Eleonore Titzenhofer's play *Lausus und Lydie* and the Sturm und Drang's critique of tyrannical rulers in "Frauen und Theater: Vom Stegreifspiel zum bürgerlichen Rührstück," in *Deutsche Literatur von Frauen*, 2 vols., ed. Gisela Brinker-Gabler (Munich: Beck, 1988), 1: 421–34, here 427. Marianne Ehrmann has repeatedly been analyzed as a Sturm und Drang author, despite her chronological distance from the movement: Helga Stipa Madland, "An Introduction to the Works and Life of Marianne Ehrmann (1755–95): Writer, Editor, Journalist," *Lessing Yearbook* 21 (1989): 171–96, and "Gender and the German Literary Canon: Marianne Ehrmann's Infanticide Fiction," *Monatshefte* 84 (1992): 405–16; Edith Krull, "Das Wirken der Frau im frühen deutschen Zeitschriftenwesen," Diss. Berlin (1939), 237–75.

[3] So summarized by Roebling, 63. Critical literature on the movement that I have found useful, either for the completeness of its overview or for its concentration on different motives and themes in the movement, includes Rudolf Käser, *Die Schwierigkeit, ich zu sagen: Rhetorik der Selbstdarstellung in Texten des "Sturm und Drang" — Herder — Goethe — Lenz* (Bern, Frankfurt am Main & New York: Lang, 1987); Fritz Martini, *Geschichte im Drama — Drama in der Geschichte: Spätbarock, Sturm und Drang, Klassik, Frührealismus* (Stuttgart: Klett-Cotta, 1979); Martini, *Literarische Form und Geschichte: Aufsätze zur Gattungstheorie und Gattungsentwicklung vom Sturm und Drang bis zum Erzählen heute* (Stuttgart: Metzler, 1984); Martini, "Von der Aufklärung zum Sturm und Drang," in *Annalen der deutschen Literatur*, ed. Heinz Otto Burger, 2nd ed. (Stuttgart: Metzler, 1971), 405–63; Bruce Kieffer, *The Storm and Stress of Language: Linguistic Catastrophe in the Early Works of Goethe, Lenz, Klinger, and Schiller* (University Park & London: U of Pennsylvania P, 1986); Alan C. Leidner, *The Impatient Muse: Germany and the Sturm und Drang* (Chapel Hill & London: U of North Carolina P, 1994); Gert Mattenklott, *Melancholie in der Dramatik des Sturm und Drang*, 2nd ed. (Königstein: Athenäum, 1985); Henry J. Schmidt, *How Dramas End: Essays on the German Sturm und Drang, Büchner, Hauptmann, and Fleisser* (Ann Arbor: U of Michigan P, 1992); Walter Hinck, ed., *Sturm und Drang: Ein literaturwissenschaftliches Studienbuch* (Kronberg: Athenäum, 1978).

[4] Roebling, 63; Matthias Luserke, *Sturm und Drang: Autoren — Texte — Themen*, Universal-Bibliothek, 17602 (Stuttgart: Reclam, 1997), 13–14.

[5] Duncan, 22; cf. Matthias Luserke, *Die Bändigung der wilden Seele: Literatur und Leidenschaft in der Aufklärung* (Stuttgart & Weimar: Metzler, 1996), 220.

[6] For a paradigmatic example for the common conflation of dramatic authors and their characters, see Larry Vaughan, *The Historical Constellation of the Sturm und*

Drang, American University Studies, 1.38 (New York, Bern & Frankfurt am Main: Lang, 1985), who views the movement as driven by "young men aspiring toward Promethean stature" (178) and whose work aims to "analyze the revolt of the brothers — young Goethe, Lenz, Klinger, Wagner, young Schiller — against the father . . . [to] examine the (literary) movement to unseat entrenched aesthetic and social authority" (vi). What is actually a dramatic motif prevalent in the Sturm und Drang, the brothers' rebellion, is here misread as a psychological condition unproblematically transferable onto authors of the movement.

[7] Mark O. Kistler, *Drama of the Storm and Stress* (New York: Twayne, 1969), 11.

[8] H. B. Garland, *Storm and Stress* (London: Harrap, 1952), 23.

[9] For example Ferdinand Josef Schneider, *Die deutsche Dichtung der Geniezeit* (Stuttgart: Metzler, 1952), 35; Garland, 127–29 and 152–53; Kistler, 31–38; Gerhard Kaiser, *Aufklärung, Empfindsamkeit, Sturm und Drang,* 3rd ed. (Munich: Francke, 1979), 192–93; Luserke, *Sturm und Drang,* 9–10.

[10] Martini on Goethe in "Von der Aufklärung zum Sturm und Drang," 461–62: "Herzog Karl Augusts Einladung nach Weimar brachte dann den befreienden Ruf in ein größeres, weiteres Leben, in eine Fülle neuer Aufgaben und Pflichten, die für Goethe die Metamorphose zur tätig-geformten, sich selbst erziehenden Reife des Mannesalters, vom Sturm und Drang zur Klassik bedeuteten" ("Duke Karl August's invitation to Weimar brought him the liberating call to a greater, more unrestrained life, to a multitude of new tasks and duties, which meant, for Goethe, the metamorphosis into the actively forming, self-educating maturity of manhood, from the Sturm und Drang to Classicism"). Occasionally, Herder is cast in a comparable role: "Der ekstatische Jüngling Herder ist zum besonnenen Man gereift, der sich entschieden von dem Genieenthusiasmus seiner Jugend abwendet. . . . Das 'Dämonisch-Wilde' des Stürmers und Drängers Herder klärt sich ab zum 'Göttlich-Milden' des Humanitätsapostels." Herman Wolf, "Die Genielehre des jungen Herder," in *Sturm und Drang,* ed. Manfred Wacker, Wege der Forschung, 559 (Darmstadt: Wissenschaftliche Buchgesellschaft, 1985), 184–214, here 214: "The ecstatic youth Herder has matured into the level-headed man who decisively turns his back to the genius-enthusiasm of his youth. . . . The 'demonic wildness' of the Storm-and-Stress Herder settles into the 'divine mildness' of the apostle of humanity." On Goethe's centrality in the movement and consequences for the evaluation of the Sturm und Drang via Classicism, cf. Garland, 153; Kaiser, 192; Kistler, 23; Luserke, *Sturm und Drang,* 9; Edith Amelie Runge, *Primitivism and Related Ideas in Sturm und Drang Literature* (New York: Russell & Russell, 1972), ix and xi; Jörg-Ulrich Fechner, "Leidenschafts- und Charakterdarstellung im Drama," in *Sturm und Drang,* ed. W. Hinck, 175–91, here 189; Vaughan, 6; critically Andreas Huyssen, *Drama des Sturm und Drang: Kommentar zu einer Epoche* (Munich: Winkler, 1980), 22–25; Edward McInnes, *"Ein ungeheures Theater": The Drama of the Sturm und Drang* (Frankfurt am Main, Bern & New York: Lang, 1987), 11; Peter Müller, ed., *Sturm und Drang: Weltanschauliche und ästhetische Schriften,* 2 vols. (Berlin & Weimar: Aufbau, 1978), 1: xiv. Reading the Sturm und Drang from the Classical point of view almost invariably results in the same Goethe-centrism that has plagued scholarship on Classicism for so long. For a recent attempt at providing a more multi-faceted image of Classical

Weimar; see Burkhard Henke et al., eds., *Unwrapping Goethe's Weimar: Essays in Cultural Studies and Local Knowledge* (Rochester NY: Camden House, 1999).

[11] "Wenn eine andere Generation den Menschen aus unsern empfindsamen Schriften restituieren sollte, so werden sie glauben es sei ein Herz mit Testikeln gewesen. Ein Herz mit einem Hodensack" (Georg Christoph Lichtenberg, *Aphorismen, Schriften, Briefe*, ed. Wolfgang Promies in collaboration with Barbara Promies [Munich: Carl Hanser, 1974], 111: "If another and later species comes to reconstruct the human being from the evidence of our sentimental writings, they will conclude it to have been a heart with testicles," trans. Nicholas Boyle, *Goethe: The Poet and the Age*, vol. 1, *The Poetry of Desire (1749–1790)* [Oxford & New York: Oxford UP, 1992], 139).

[12] The quotation is taken from Johann Georg Hamann's *Aesthetica in nuce:* "Ihr wollt herrschen über die Natur, und bindet euch selbst Hände und Füße durch den Stoicismus, um desto rührender über des Schicksals diamantene Fesseln in euren vermischten Gedichten fistuliren zu können. / Wenn die Leidenschaften Glieder der Unehre sind, hören sie deswegen auf, Waffen der Mannheit zu seyn? Versteht ihr den Buchstaben der Vernunft klüger, als jener allegorische Kämmerer der alexandrinischen Kirche den Buchstaben der Schrift, der sich selbst zum Verschnittenen macht, um des Himmelreichs willen?" (Johann Georg Hamann, *Sämtliche Werke: Historisch-kritische Ausgabe*, 6 vols., ed. Josef Nadler [Vienna: Herder, 1949–53], 2: 208: "You wish to rule over nature, and bind your own hands and feet with stoicism in order to sing all the more movingly, in a castrato's falsetto, of Fate's diamond bonds in your poetic collections. If the passions are members of dishonor, do they therefore cease to be the weapons of manhood? Do you understand the letter of reason any better than that allegorical chamberlain of the Alexandrian Church [Origen] understood the letter of the Scripture, who made himself a eunuch for the sake of the Kingdom of God?") On Hamann's sexualized language, see W. M. Alexander, *Johann Georg Hamann: Philosophy and Faith* (The Hague: Nijhoff, 1966), 57–61, and James C. O'Flaherty, *Unity and Language: A Study in the Philosophy of Johann Georg Hamann* (Chapel Hill: U of North Carolina P, 1952).

[13] This is a contested area in Sturm und Drang research. There is a plethora of sources claiming the political relevance of the movement; paradigmatically, Klaus Gerth, "Die Poetik des Sturm und Drang," in Hinck, *Sturm und Drang*, 55–80, who asserts the movement's political significance as a vehicle for bourgeois emancipation and explains the uniqueness of the Sturm und Drang to Germany with the fact that the bourgeoisie in England and France enjoyed greater participation in political processes (57; cf. Duncan, 9, who claims the existence of parallel movements in both Britain and the Netherlands). While psychological connections of this nature are difficult to substantiate, it is important to note that all evidence for the political involvement or interest of Sturm und Drang authors is based on *literary* sources, primarily the occasional criticisms hurled at the aristocracy in dramas and the frequent treatment of the infanticide theme. Recent literature has painstakingly documented that the recurrence of this theme had nothing whatever to do with a political interest in either the status of women or that of the lower classes: Helga Stipa Madland, "Infanticide as Fiction: Goethe's *Urfaust* and Schiller's 'Kindsmörderin' as Models," *German Quarterly* 62 (1989): 27–38, and "Marianne Ehrmann's Infanticide Fiction"; Susanne Kord, "Women as Children, Women as Childkillers: Poetic Images of Infanti-

cide in Eighteenth-Century Germany," *Eighteenth-Century Studies* 26.3 (1993): 449–66; Germaine Goetzinger, "Männerphantasie und Frauenwirklichkeit: Kindermörderinnen in der Literatur des Sturm und Drang," in *Frauen — Literatur — Politik*, ed. Annegret Pelz et al. (Hamburg: Argument, 1988), 263–86; Barbara Mabee, "Die Kindesmörderin in den Fesseln der bürgerlichen Moral: Wagners Evchen und Goethes Gretchen," *Women in German Yearbook* 3 (1986): 29–45. There is also a sizable body of scholarship contesting the political dimension of the Sturm und Drang. Huyssen speaks of a "democratic genius-utopia" of the movement but views the fact that the rebellious heroes of Sturm und Drang drama are usually set far in the past, whereas contemporary dramas of the movement do not depict such characters but limit themselves to the portrayal of oppression and suffering (59, 78), as an implicit admission of the impossibility of "Selbsthelfertum" in "real life" (59, 79). Manfred Wacker reads the absence of political writings in the movement in much the same way (13); Duncan has pointed out that the members of the Sturm und Drang generation generally showed little interest in major political events of their day, including the first partition of Poland of 1772 or the Bavarian War of Succession of 1778–79 (30). Garland rather contemptuously posits the revolutionary rhetoric of the movement against its political inefficacy: "Genius, as they conceived it, was a pistol pointed at the head of authority. When it fired it went off with a formidable detonation, and proved only to be loaded with powder" (140).

[14] Martini, *Literarische Form*, 4.

[15] Gaby Pailer, "Gattungskanon, Gegenkanon und 'weiblicher' Subkanon: Zum bürgerlichen Trauerspiel des 18. Jahrhunderts," in *Kanon Macht Kultur: Theoretische, historische und soziale Aspekte ästhetischer Kanonbildungen*, ed. Renate von Heydebrand (Stuttgart: Metzler, 1998), 365–82, here 365–66 (hereafter cited as "Gattungskanon").

[16] For example, Kaiser, who sees the interest of Sturm und Drang authors in the "people" as rooted in the fact that many of them were themselves descendants of the lower classes (178). See also Werner Krauss, "Zur Periodisierung Aufklärung, Sturm und Drang, Weimarer Klassik," in *Sturm und Drang*, ed. Wacker, 67–95, here 73; in the same volume Wolfgang Stellmacher, "Grundfragen der Shakespeare-Rezeption in der Frühphase des Sturm und Drang," 112–43, here 129; Kistler, 11–14; Kaiser, 189–90; Runge, 14–32, 53–58, 122–23, 136–38, and 200–16; Schneider, 3; Müller, 1: xxiii, lii, lxvi, lxxiii and xcii; critically, Wacker's introduction, 8–13; Luserke, *Sturm und Drang*, 63 and 81–87; Leidner, 50–54; Hinck's introduction, ix.

[17] Madland, "An Introduction to the Works and Life of Marianne Ehrmann," 178.

[18] Karin A. Wurst, *Frauen und Drama im achtzehnten Jahrhundert* (Cologne & Vienna: Böhlau, 1991), 19.

[19] For some examples, see Susanne Kord, *Sich einen Namen machen: Anonymität und weibliche Autorschaft 1700–1900* (Stuttgart: Metzler, 1996), 135–70.

[20] Sigrid Weigel, "Der schielende Blick: Thesen zur Geschichte weiblicher Schreibpraxis," in Inge Stephan and Sigrid Weigel, *Die verborgene Frau: Sechs Beiträge zu einer feministischen Literaturwissenschaft* (Berlin: Argument, 1983), 83–137, here 85.

[21] Cf. Roebling, who views the inclusion of women's literature under the Sturm und Drang heading as potentially resulting in a differentiation of our understanding of the movement (64).

[22] Citations follow Wurst's edition of the play in *Frauen und Drama im achtzehnten Jahrhundert*, 96–140. First assessments of the play include Susanne Kord, *Ein Blick hinter die Kulissen: Deutschsprachige Dramatikerinnen im 18. und 19. Jahrhundert*, Ergebnisse der Frauenforschung, 27 (Stuttgart: Metzler, 1992), 100–2; Dagmar von Hoff, *Dramen des Weiblichen: Deutsche Dramatikerinnen um 1800* (Opladen: Westdeutscher Verlag, 1989), 49–52; Dawson, 430–31; Wurst, 58–69; Fleig, 205–39; Pailer, "'Gattungskanon' and 'Lasst uns die Ketten soviel als möglich unter Rosen verbergen . . .': Zum Problem der 'Zensur' in Dramen von Autorinnen des 18. Jahrhunderts," *Rundbrief: Frauen in der Literaturwissenschaft* 44 (1995): 39–44 (hereafter cited as "Ketten"). On Schlegel's correspondence with Gellert, see Regina Nörtemann, "Die 'Begeisterung eines Poeten' in den Briefen eines Frauenzimmers: Zur Korrespondenz der Caroline Christiane Lucius mit Christian Fürchtegott Gellert," in *Die Frau im Dialog: Studien zu Theorie und Geschichte des Briefes*, ed. Anita Runge and Lieselotte Steinbrügge (Stuttgart: Metzler, 1991), 13–32.

[23] "Do not reproach me — unless you want to drive me to madness."

[24] "How he formerly threatened, raged, foamed at the mouth, terrified others!"

[25] "To her I owe my calmer, more peaceful days, which I have enjoyed since she has possessed his heart. Could he not abandon me, deceive me, waste my property on others, mistreat me? Nobody would punish him!"

[26] Cf. Leidner, who has analyzed the dramatic situation of the Sturm und Drang heroes as one defined by "exonerative strategies" (53) and "extenuating circumstances" (62): "their authors attempt to reconcile impatient, Titanic self-assertion with principles an audience can share" (47).

[27] AMALIE: My duty calls.

DÜVAL: Your duty? — When you are in my arms? (angrily lets go of her, and pushes her away from himself). Very well, then go, if your duty calls you. — This is the first time I have heard this! — Go then! Go into the convent! It is there that it will take you, your duty; and you will go and think that you have done much, indeed much, when you have said a prayer for the abandoned, the ridiculed, the desperate, the fuming Düval with dry eyes and a cold heart during morning or evening prayers or during mass.

AMALIE, *weeping:* Cruel! Do not talk thus! Rather kill me!

DÜVAL: Do you mean it? Excellent, my Mally! I have been waiting for this request. Here! — (he puts a small wrapped-up piece of paper into a case and hands it to her) A little savory powder, one to cure all the heart's woes! Take this on your way to the convent! Don't forget! And think that when you do, your Düval is also no longer among the living! *Amalie stands stupefied and speechless with fear and horror.*

[28] DÜVAL, *alone:* Yes, you are weak, because you do not love me as I love you. — This, too, then, was vain self-deception! — Very well! It

was not in your heart to love like this. What fault is that of yours? But the courage not to survive your Düval is also not within your heart! It is not your fault — a pious faith in chimeras. I must come to your aid, it would be too much for you alone, that I can see. — (Pause. With deliberation) And if she saw Death on my pale face — in my dimming eye: how it would frighten her with tenfold horrors! — and the poison — even if she took it — an uncertain, slow, painful death! Or else she might accept help, learn to love life again, — marry another — the Count! — no, no, far better a quick and easy death! The stiletto in my walking cane —.

[29] Inge Stephan, "'So ist die Tugend ein Gespenst:' Frauenbild und Tugendbegriff bei Lessing und Schiller," in *Lessing und die Toleranz: Sonderband zum Lessing Yearbook,* ed. Peter Freimark et al. (Detroit & Munich: Wayne State UP, 1985), 357–74. For a more recent treatment of images of women in contemporary dramas by men, see Gerlinde Wosgien, *Literarische Frauenbilder von Lessing bis zum Sturm und Drang: Ihre Entwicklung unter dem Einfluß Rousseaus* (Frankfurt am Main & Bern: Lang, 1999).

[30] "Oh Amalie! My words are not those of a jealous wife, even if she had ten times more cause; no, it is only the friend that speaks to you — Düval — beware of Düval! He is a violent and impetuous man, never master of his passions —— a madman, if he . . . Sh!"

[31] Fleig arrives at a similar conclusion in her analysis of this scene (210).

[32] The play is cited after Wurst's edition in *Frauen und Drama im achtzehnten Jahrhundert,* 141–87. First interpretations include Roebling; Pailer; Wurst, 69–78; Fleig, 116–17; Dagmar von Hoff, *Dramen des Weiblichen,* 73–77, and her essays "Inszenierung des Leidens: Lektüre von J. M. R. Lenz' 'Der Engländer' und Sophie Albrechts 'Theresgen,'" in *"Unaufhörlich Lenz gelesen . . ." Studien zu Leben und Werk von J. M. R. Lenz,* ed. Inge Stephan and Hans-Gerd Winter (Stuttgart: Metzler, 1994), 210–24, and "Die Inszenierung des 'Frauenopfers' in Dramen von Autorinnen um 1800," in *Frauen — Literatur — Politik,* ed. Annegret Pelz et. al., 255–62.

[33] Dagmar von Hoff has analyzed Theresgen's melancholia in reference to Freud's theories and the eighteenth-century discourse of "Liebes-Melancholey" (*Dramen,* 73–77, and "Inszenierung des Leidens," 219–20).

[34] Pailer has interpreted this scene as a reversal of the process of imagination involving the poet and the muse; Theresgen's death, in her interpretation, is predicated by the gender-fixity of that process. Pailer considers the fact that only the woman who denies herself imagination can survive (Lehngen) — a "grotesque reversal" of the genius idea of the Sturm und Drang. Cf. "'Gattungskanon,'" 378–81; "Ketten," 43–44.

[35] "His long hair already floated in the lake."

[36] "Dearest girl! A life filled with love and gratitude shall earn me forgiveness for dragging your reluctant hand to my heart."

[37] "I believe this is Franz's fault, with all his talk of death and the grave; folks always want to die at once when things don't go according to their little heads."

[38] THERESGEN: Forgive me, dear girl! I cannot be happy with you — there, my joy fell silent.

LEHNGEN: Oh, always death and the grave! I don't know how one can think of death in the summer. Everything lives and blooms!

THERESGEN: Oh, everything withers and dies! The second flower always rises from the deathbed of the first, and her beauty withers as soon as her sister appears. . . .

LEHNGEN: I have never thought of this and I have always been happy; tear your thoughts from these sad ruminations; do as I do, dear girl, adorn yourself with the blossoming rose, and do not think of the withering violet.

[39] THE COUNT: No, father, this is no way of forcing a girl. If she does not love Franz, as indeed it appears, it would be cruel to bind her without giving her time to think of her bonds as bearable. Let us, as much as possible, hide the chains beneath roses. If she is recalcitrant, let her be swayed by tender pleas, until she finally believes herself that she has given a hand that we have taken.

[40] "She got all these silly ideas from a harebrained education given her by that noblewoman, which amounted to not telling her that a girl's heart beats higher in the company of a pretty boy than in that of her grandmother."

[41] See Sara Sampson's melodramatic final words, "Mellefont — mein Vater —." Gotthold Ephraim Lessing, *Werke*, 8 vols., eds. Herbert G. Göpfert et al. (Munich: Hanser, 1970–79), 2: 99.

[42] Citations follow Wurst's edition in *Frauen und Drama im achtzehnten Jahrhundert*, 188–251. Scholarly treatments of the text to date are limited to Wurst, 78–86; Helga Stipa Madland, "An Introduction to the Works and Life of Marianne Ehrmann" and *Marianne Ehrmann: Reason and Emotion in Her Life and Works* (New York: Lang, 1998), 135–48; and one brief and purely descriptive paragraph in Fleig, 109. For recent assessments of Ehrmann's other fiction and journalistic endeavors, see Madland, "Gender and the German Literary Canon" and *Marianne Ehrmann;* Krull, 237–75; Britt-Angela Kirstein, *Marianne Ehrmann: Publizistin und Herausgeberin im ausgehenden 18. Jahrhundert* (Wiesbaden: Deutscher Universitäts-Verlag, 1997); Maya Widmer, "Mit spitzer Feder gegen Vorurteile und gallsüchtige Moral — Marianne Ehrmann, geb. von Brentano," in *Und schrieb und schrieb wie ein Tiger aus dem Busch: Über Schriftstellerinnen in der deutschsprachigen Schweiz*, eds. Elisabeth Ryter et al. (Zürich: Limmat, 1994), 52–72; Doris Stump, "Eine Frau 'von Verstand, Witz, Gefühl, Fantasie und Feuer': Zu Leben und Werk Marianne Ehrmanns" and Maya Widmer, "'Amalie' — eine wahre Geschichte?," both in their joint edition of Marianne Ehrmann's novel *Amalie: Eine wahre Geschichte in Briefen* (Stuttgart & Vienna: Haupt, 1995), 481–98 and 499–515, respectively.

[43] Madland, "An Introduction to the Works and Life of Marianne Ehrmann," 176–78.

[44] As pointed out by Madland in *Marianne Ehrmann*, 145–47. On the traditional constellation of contrasting women characters in contemporary men's plays, see Stephan, "'So ist die Tugend ein Gespenst.'"

[45] LOTTCHEN *(earnestly):* If your fourteen days are not the lie of an eternity, the priest must bless us both even today.

THE COUNT: But if my ——

LOTTCHEN: No excuses, no objections! — Today with you to the altar, or tomorrow to the hangman with me! Are you content with that? (She glances at the pistols hanging on the wall.)

THE COUNT *(stuttering anxiously):* Your brazenness ——

LOTTCHEN: Is it too great for my honor? See, you vulture, that it was still not great enough. (she takes one of the unloaded pistols down and points it at him) Here is an even greater one, out with it, obdurate scoundrel, or one shot will make us both unhappy.

THE COUNT: Put it down, you are mad.

LOTTCHEN: Indeed I am (pulls the trigger) — Cursed means of my revenge! (throws the pistol down vehemently) you, too, refuse to aid me in restoring my honor; you, too, are false! Well then, may everything conspire against me, so it is not you, my conscience (increasingly frenzied) you shall summon me to be his eternal pursuer. By the hair will I drag you, defiler of women, before the seat of Final Judgment, all spirits of Hell shall urge on me the curses that I will hurl after you; and with devilish joy will I triumph when I see you damned before my eyes.

[46] Wurst explains this inevitable failure with the meaning of the weapon as a "symbol of male potency and societal power" (84).

[47] Huyssen, 83.

[48] See also the highly charged scene (232), in which she confronts Mekler with his treachery in very similar language as that employed in the scene cited above.

[49] "Truly, it is a pleasure to hear the full-blooded beautiful Count sigh for Lotte. How everything rages! How his blood boils, enough to make his hot blood burst forth from his cheeks!"

[50] Madland sees Ehrmann's critique of education in the play as targeting not clichés about the education of women but, rather, the common practice of employing private tutors (*Marianne Ehrmann,* 137–38).

[51] "I can't forgive my tutor for neglecting to mold my soft heart into a firm character. Virtue and vice still vie for dominance within me, and it is only natural that, given my pampered upbringing, my abundance of riches and especially my tender sentiments, the latter is often stronger than the former."

[52] "Oh Nature, Nature! Your benevolence is beyond human understanding! — only a few moments ago, I was the most despondent, and now — I am the happiest of fathers! (long pause) Fathers! Mothers! For the sake of this tear, attend well to the education of your children!"

[53] On Happy Endings and dramatic closure in eighteenth-century comedies by women, see Susanne Kord, "All's Well that Ends Well? Marriage, Madness and Other Happy Endings in Eighteenth-Century Women's Comedies," *Lessing Yearbook* 28 (1996): 181–97.

[54] My treatment of space in *Düval und Charmille* is indebted to the insights in Pailer's work ("Ketten" and "Gattungskanon"); Fleig has taken up this idea, as well (208–10).

[55] Pailer, "Ketten," 41.

[56] Pailer, "Gattungskanon," 371.

[57] Schlegel, 100; cf. Fleig, 209.

[58] Düval "has approached his room and stands in silence for a few moments) — She moves — (he opens the door, and in entering and apparently preventing Amalie, who is near the door, from coming out) Are you ready now, my dear? — (he closes the door behind him, and one can hear the bolt being shot.)"

[59] "The door to Düval's room is hastily unlocked. Amalie, deathly pale with a handkerchief held over her heart, enters vehemently, tottering. She rushes to Mariane's door, but hastily, reeling, retreats toward the door to the foyer."

[60] "Die Stadt war mir immer zuwider und ich wäre tausendmal glücklicher gewesen, wenn ich mit der lieben Verstorbenen hier auf ihrem Gute hätte leben dürfen" (150: "I have always abhorred the city and I would have been a thousand times happier if I had been permitted to live here on her estate with the dear departed").

[61] Cf. Roebling, 75–77. Roebling interprets the dramaturgy of space in the play as a "space beyond the fences" in the sense of Rousseau's critique of property (76–77). The central character in her analysis appears as Rousseau's "child of nature" who can only be "at home" in nature (75). My remarks on this theme are greatly indebted to her initial discussion.

[62] "She is so weak, father, that she can barely totter a few steps here and could not have endured the entire journey."

[63] "No, I can't go into the house — oh, I would die!"

[64] Thus Roebling, 76.

[65] "We don't know of any luxuries; our education was so natural that we can easily do without such comforts. To us, unenvied freedom is a gift from heaven. The clamor of the city would ill harmonize with our unspoiled souls."

[66] LOTTCHEN *(to Mekler):*   And now farewell. (*Turns to leave.*).

THE COUNT *(holding her back):*   Stay, Lottchen! Stay! And see me at your feet, see the man whom you will make miserable if you do not grant him your heart.

LOTTCHEN: God! I am lost! — I must — yes — I must go.

THE COUNT: Heavenly girl! Stay — or you will be my destruction.

LOTTCHEN: No, leave me, I see my ruin in your eyes. — My own heart betrays me. — Woe is me! I cannot go, — I cannot move from here.

[67] Recent literature on the link between the Sturm und Drang and the Enlightenment is briefly reviewed in Luserke, *Sturm und Drang,* 15–17. See also the essay by Gerhard Sauder in this volume.

[68] Pailer's comparison with Lessing's *Emilia Galotti* illustrates this aspect particularly well: "Whereas Emilia becomes a sign for the inevitable 'sacrifice' of women in the

stabilization of bourgeois culture, Mally remains, even as a dead body, a real woman. There is no symbolic signification of the female corpse" ("Ketten," 41).

[69] See Luserke, who cites several contemporary responses to and comments on the movement: *Sturm und Drang*, 23–34.

[70] I would like to thank Aida Premilovac for proofreading this essay and for making editorial suggestions.

Schiller and the End of
the Sturm und Drang

Alan Leidner

B Y THE END OF THE 1770s the Sturm und Drang had nearly run its course. Goethe had moved to Weimar in 1775 and had put his wild youth behind him, while in 1780 Lenz and Klinger left Germany for Russia, the former drifting in and out of madness and searching for employment, the latter to begin what would be an illustrious military career. But in January 1782 a drama appeared on the Mannheim stage that brought the spirit back to life. Its author was Friedrich Schiller, and his play, *Die Räuber* (published 1781), added a new dimension to the Sturm und Drang by not only depicting the turbulence of an eighteenth-century Germany out of order but also allowing audiences to luxuriate in the feeling that they could rise above the turbulence and even turn it to their own advantage. There followed three more plays in which he extended the tradition into the mid-1780s: the middle-class tragedy *Kabale und Liebe* (1784) and two historical dramas, *Die Verschwörung des Fiesco zu Genua* (1782) and finally *Don Carlos* (1787), during whose composition Schiller gradually moved away from the Sturm und Drang.

Friedrich Schiller was born on November 10, 1759, in Marbach in Württemberg. Although he had aspired to the clergy, at thirteen he was ordered to enroll in Duke Karl Eugen's new military academy in Stuttgart, where he studied medicine. He graduated in 1780 and was assigned to a regiment. But Schiller was more interested in a literary career, and when *Die Räuber*, his first play, was performed, he went absent without leave to attend the premiere. Produced by the Mannheim National Theater under its impresario Baron Wolfgang Heribert von Dalberg (1750–1806), it was a huge success, but the duke ordered Schiller to stop writing for the stage and focus on medicine. Defiant, Schiller deserted the regiment and never returned, hiding out in Bauerbach, near Meiningen, and later moving to Mannheim. In 1785, with the support of Gottfried Körner, a wealthy admirer, he went to Leipzig, where he wrote the poem "An die Freude" (Ode to Joy, 1785), the well-known celebration of universal brotherhood that was set to music by Ludwig van Beethoven (1770–1827) in the Ninth Symphony. Later that year he moved to Dresden and completed, among other works, *Geschichte des Abfalls der Vereinigten Niederlande von der spanischen Regierung* (History of the Revolt of the Netherlands against Spanish Rule, 1788). In 1789 he married Charlotte Lengefeld, and the following year he accepted an appointment to teach history at the university in Jena. The 1790s brought his great essays on aesthetics, a major work on the Thirty Years' War, and, finally, his return to drama with the *Wallenstein* trilogy (1798–99), *Maria Stuart* (1800), *Die Jungfrau von Orleans* (The Maid of Orleans, 1801), *Die Braut von Messina* (The Bride of Messina, 1803), and *Wilhelm Tell* (1804). He lived in Weimar from 1799 until he died, probably of tuberculosis, on May 9, 1805.

With *Die Räuber* Schiller serves notice that the problems that Lenz, Klinger, and Goethe raise about Germany have still not been resolved. What seemed viable in France and England was out of reach in this particularized feudal culture presided over by petty, pompous, and ruthless princes. The situation was not easy for a writer. Where were the admirable courtly models, the heroic figures with whom a national audience might identify, the joyful public from which the lightening grace of comedy might arise? Nothing was more important to German writers than to create a dramatic tradition that could vie with that of the French, for a great culture should be worthy of tragedy, the most venerable of literary genres. Yet, to have tragedy means to have heroes, and heroes and heroic feelings were a scarce commodity in Germany. The title character of Goethe's *Götz von Berlichingen,* faced with the politics of sixteenth-century courtly life, sees that his old sense of importance as an imperial knight, responsible only to the emperor, is slipping away. Klinger's Carl Bushy, alias Wild, of *Sturm und Drang,* the play that gave the movement its name, ends up searching for heroism on foreign soil, crossing the Atlantic to join the American Revolution so as to have the sensation of engaging in a struggle that seems significant. And for Lenz the feeling of a deficit of heroism was so acute that it led him away from traditional tragedy altogether and made him one of the founders of modern tragicomedy. With their hopes for self-actualization thwarted, feeling insignificant, and unable to dream of the heroic with the same conviction as the French, authors could, at least, give their frustration literary expression.

This frustration in the Sturm und Drang often takes the form of a futile reaching upward toward the infinite. Goethe's Werther drowns in a mystical love. In Klinger's *Sturm und Drang* Blasius tells us that Carl

Bushy walks around grabbing for heaven as if he wanted to pull it down to earth (*K-SD*, 34). The needs of these characters are deeper than even the grim German political situation can suggest, and classic works of the movement often contain an urge to extend oneself that seems more religious than political, as if the Sturm und Drang is expressing the needs of a place that has not yet had the same benefit of secularization as its eighteenth-century European neighbors. In its seemingly endless quest for transcendence, the urge to feel significant appears to have created an outbreak of forces resembling the frantic straining upward of the gothic. One sign of this is in the frequent repetition of words and phrases in a nervous, relentless logic of compulsion, a ceaseless activity with no beginning, no end, and no center. It is also found in Klinger's *Sturm und Drang*, where Carl Bushy, feeling the full weight of his disordered German world, says that he wants to be stretched over a drum or shot out of a pistol (*K-SD*, 8–9). Carl wants desperately to lift himself beyond himself, wants both to be an active individual in the world and to be connected to something eternal; but he finds it maddeningly impossible, and Klinger has no power at his disposal capable of solving this problem — no ritual and no political or moral power capable of helping him. And although Sturm und Drang writers could not help being drawn to the religiously colored poetry of the last generation, to Friedrich Klopstock, Albrecht von Haller, and Ewald Christian von Kleist (1715–59), most considered a plunge back into religion as out of the question. The only option Klinger had left to resolve the world out of order that he presented in *Sturm und Drang* was to have recourse to worn melodramatic devices. People return from the dead, a long-lost lover is found, and a feud is resolved by blaming it on a third party. The deus ex machina with which the play ends underlines the fact that Klinger has only artificial means at his disposal to deal with the debilitating German restlessness.

The longer view may provide some help in unraveling these problems. The sense of personal effectiveness and significance for which Germany longed in the Sturm und Drang, and for which its raging characters could supply only a poor substitute, was part of the new kingdom of freedom and sensation that human beings began to win for themselves at the dawn of the early modern era, when Europe emerged from the Middle Ages and began to breathe the air of Renaissance humanism and its new idealism about the worldly life. It was chivalric courtly culture, with its new personal ideals, that ushered in the second feudal age and the early modern period. But the rise of humanism, with its new kind of hope for mankind and its new versions of heroism, incorporated high-minded ideals derived from the Church itself. In this crucial transitional period, the purity of the ascetic ideal migrated from the monastery into the world, and it did so first with the troubadour and minnesinger, then in the great adventure of the Crusades. For our heroic action in the world must also be felt to be lofty. Humanism and heroism, then and now, can exist only when elevated above the selfish and mundane and only where human desires are blessed in one way or another with divine approval.

Of course, Germany has its classic age of courtly love lyric, as well, but France, in many ways the home of the Middle Ages, found itself better able to build on the culture of *courtoisie*. It was France whose feudal culture would eventually set the tone for the courts of Europe by turning the nobleman into a new secular bearer of piety, a figure who projected a glorious image of human possibility, a humanism conceived as higher than any that might have been imagined in the Hellenistic or Roman ages. The prince, who was the model for these new and liberating sensations of personal autonomy, represented an age moving away from the manor and into the world of trade and ambition and personal goals that was gaining acceptance in the early modern period but whose glory also required the continuing assumption of a bond with the eternal. The middle class also found itself needing this fictitious but enabling posture of mind, for with its power to reconcile activity in the world with piety it helped to ease the conscience of the merchant who, with his trade discouraged by the Church, had questioned his own piety as he worked in the commercial world.

But what happens when this life-enhancing force remains undeveloped? Through the Renaissance and the seventeenth century Germany's aristocracy remained backward not just economically but also in its ability to absorb and project this enabling spirit of early modern life. German principalities and bishoprics were too absorbed in petty squabbles and schemes ever to make the turn from religious to secular glory, a turn Germany's neighbor across the Rhine made handily, and this fumbled rite of passage became a prime cause of the frustration that accompanied the rise of Germany's national and literary ambitions in the second half of the eighteenth century. With this vital source of secular glory dammed up, ambitions failed to join with feelings that seemed eternal. Restless characters ventured into the world alone, possessed by the vague idea that there must be a unifying vision, some version of heroism, into which their peculiar energies might fit. And getting audiences to identify with frustrated, isolated characters who could not offer a vision that the spectators shared was almost doomed from the start. Dramatists had difficulty in getting their works staged, and it is no surprise that by the late 1770s the Sturm und Drang seemed to have played itself out.

But *Die Räuber* gave the movement new life. By the time he was seventeen Schiller was writing a turbulent and sometimes self-righteous poetry in which political oppression came under the gaze of an a acute sense of justice. He had been brought up in Swabian Pietism, a religion infused with the baroque extremes of damnation and salvation, worldly success versus mystical unity with God, and in these formative years his work seemed to derive its energy from a combination of enlightened idealism and baroque stringency. "Der Eroberer" (The Conqueror) creates an almost apocalyptic moral energy when a ruthless general's deeds are weighed at the gates of eternity and the young poet rejoices at being able to send him to hell. With his gift for rhetoric, Schiller pulls God mightily down to earth to balance the scales of justice. He is already in possession of two powers that will be essential to the alchemy of his drama: an unshakable ideal of human freedom and an all-or-nothing moral temperament.

Die Räuber begins at Karl Moor's family estate in Franconia. Karl, the first-born, is a handsome young man who has impressed many people with his high-spirited personality. Franz, his ugly brother, is so jealous of Karl that in Karl's absence he cooks up a plot to steal the family estate, as well as Karl's girlfriend, Amalia, for himself. Franz forges a letter, purportedly from an informer, that convinces his father that Karl has run up debts, robbed a young woman of her honor, killed her fiancé in a duel, and fled with the authorities on his heels. Franz receives permission to write Karl a mildly disapproving letter in their father's name but instead writes Karl that their father has disowned him. The letter reaches Karl at a bad time: he has just been reading Plutarch's *Lives,* and he is already railing against his own petty, hypocritical, unheroic age. Moreover, this day he happens to be with a particularly rough group of acquaintances who are considering forming a robber band. In these circumstances, Karl's terrible disappointment with a father he thought loved him — "Ist das Vatertreue? Ist das Liebe für Liebe? . . . Ich hab ihn so unaussprechlich geliebt!" (*S-NA,* 3: 31)[1] — drives him to assume the leadership of the band and take revenge on society for making such treachery possible. Karl sweeps through Bohemia, throwing a monstrous tantrum of arson, murder, and rape, a personal apocalypse to avenge his disappointed sense of righteousness. The band has a tremendous cohesiveness and sense of loyalty. When one town, which they have particularly ravaged, offers the entire band a pardon if they will turn Karl in to the authorities, they refuse. While the band plunders the villages of eastern Germany, back at Moor castle Franz tricks his father into thinking that Karl is dead, then locks him up in a tower so as to starve him and inherit the estate.

With this play Schiller was tapping into a capacity of his audience that he knew well, namely, its frustration with ideals that should be upheld but are not. And using this plot, which borrows elements from Shakespeare's *King Lear* and Fielding's *Tom Jones*, he discovers for himself the lengths to which Germany would have to go to bring its ideals, nourished over the centuries more by religion than politics, into harmony with reality. When Carl Bushy leapt into war five years earlier, Klinger was also showing us a world out of order, one that he tried to heal through love and peacemaking between two warring families. But Schiller wants to forge a consensus of a higher order than love, and to get it, there must be more than this world can offer right now. There must be an event of an apocalyptic order. *Die Räuber* is a very different kind of drama from what had come before because it actually offers an emotional solution to the problems faced by the Sturm und Drang, and one Germans were ready to accept, at least in the theater. The play is crafted so that, for more than four acts, an audience can take the side of a violent man who has a high conception of what the human community should be.

The play would never had worked if there had been any question about Karl's idealism. He is Karl, not Franz, and his high-mindedness must regularly come to the surface if audiences are to forgive his violence, and enjoy it. By act 3 Karl's idealism takes the form of lament for the murderous rampage on which he has led his men, and he realizes that his acts have ripped him from the fabric of humanity:

> Meine Unschuld! Meine Unschuld! — Seht! es ist alles hinausgegangen, sich im friedlichen Stral des Frühlings zu sonnen — warum ich allein die Hölle saugen aus den Freuden des Himmels? — daß alles so glüklich ist, durch den Geist des Friedens alles so verschwistert! — die ganze Welt *Eine* Familie und ein Vater dort oben — *Mein* Vater nicht — Ich allein der Verstosene, ich allein ausgemustert aus den Reihen der Reinen — mir nicht der süsse Name Kind — nimmer mehr der Geliebten schmachtender Blick — nimmer nimmer mehr des Busenfreundes Umarmung! *wild zurückfahrend.* Umlagert von Mördern — von Nattern umzischt — angeschmidet an das Laster mit eisernen Banden. (*S-NA*, 3: 79)[2]

When he returns home to Moor Castle in disguise, Karl uncovers his brother's treachery. The band attacks, Franz commits suicide, and when Karl reveals himself to his father, the shock of learning that the great robber is his own son kills him. In the last scene the robbers declare that they will not allow Karl to quit the band and marry Amalia, for he is in their debt, they say, and as evidence they bring up not only their recent rejection of the pardon they had been offered but also the continuing debt he has to those, such as Karl's best friend, Roller, who died under his command rather than disappoint him. They demand that Karl turn Amalia over to them as proof that he has abandoned this idea, but she begs the robbers to kill her instead. Just as they take aim, Karl declares that she will die by his hand alone, and he kills her himself, arguing that this sacrifice releases him from his obligations to his men. Finally, so as to help reconcile himself with the unspoken laws of humanity that he has offended, Karl determines to allow a miserably poor local man with eleven children to turn him in and collect the huge reward that has been offered for the great robber Moor.

Karl Moor had audiences swooning with delight, as if their own most cherished ideals had suddenly found a champion. What Schiller understood like no other writer of the Sturm und Drang was that from the start the movement had involved a restless, transcendental grabbing for meaning, and his accomplishment was to reveal that there was no quick solution to the problem that did not involve appealing to lofty absolutes. Love, negotiation, and deus ex machina are not enough. Through Karl, Schiller showed that glory, taken on purely secular terms, was impossible in Germany, and that the only kind of glory that could flourish there and that could respond to the rampant restlessness was one that was more religious and apocalyptic than political and secular. *Die Räuber* bridged the gap between national frustrations and uplifting theater, forging the kind of powerful relationship with an audience that, at this time, only a traditionally structured play could provide. Schiller's contribution is to go beyond merely creating a character who embodies spectators' own frustrations. He manages to make his hero's rampage forgivable, allowing spectators to identify with Karl's sense of righteousness while channeling the violence of his robber band into a powerful, morally resonant, cathartic experience. The play was a sensation when it premiered in January 1782. "Das Theater glich einem Irrenhause," wrote one reviewer the next day. "Rollende Augen, geballte Fäuste, stampfende Füße, heisere Aufschreie im Zuschauerraum! Fremde Menschen fielen einander schluchzend in die Arme, Frauen wankten, einer Ohnmacht nahe, zur Türe" (The theater was like a madhouse: rolling eyes, clenched fists, stamping feet, hoarse cries from the audience! Strangers fell, sobbing, into each others' arms, women staggered to the doors, close to fainting.)[3]

Although Karl possessed a thirst for violent revenge, what captured audiences was his almost holy quality. In act 2, scene 3, this man who claims that he lives between heaven and hell learns that some of his men had needlessly murdered women and children. In biblical tones he expels the worst perpetrator from the band and proclaims that the deed has poisoned his "finest works" (*S-NA*, 3: 65; *SuD*, 232). With Karl's pious side, Schiller harnesses a huge rhetorical resource in a deeply religious land. Yet, historically, this is in no way out of character for the Sturm und Drang. The principal writers of the movement had suspected from the start that the path out of German restlessness might lead through its religious tradition, and nowhere is their flirtation with religious points of view clearer than in their attraction to the Zurich clergyman Johann Caspar Lavater. When Schiller was barely ten years old, Herder and Goethe, and then Lenz, thought that they had found in Lavater part of the solution to the storm and stress they sensed at the center of their lives. He seemed to them to be a soul mate. In his writings and sermons he could masterfully illustrate the crippling deficit in our ability to enjoy our humanity, to enjoy people and be enjoyed by them, as he put it in volume three of his *Aussichten über die Ewigkeit* (Views on Eternity, 1768–73), our failure to turn the whole human race into one family.[4] Through an accepting demeanor and powerful rhetorical skills he was able to make Zurich's Church of St. Peter ring out with a spirit of divine reassurance even in this age that seemed so inadequate to German literary men. For Lavater, even though every individual was, as he thought, a species unto itself, every seemingly isolated individual was always still just a hieroglyph of God, which guaranteed that we had immediate access to the absolute. Still, to evoke a feeling through a well-orchestrated ritual within the walls of a church is one thing; to infuse such feelings into lived secular life, even in a deeply religious society, is another. *Die Räuber* creates an apocalypse that directs self-righteous violence toward human beings at large while lifting the praise of humanity in the abstract.

The moral world over which Schiller's noble hero presides is one as old as the Renaissance, when Europeans first gained the confidence to anoint the human mind as a privileged place where, even when sullied by our new ambitions, we could somehow still take on the role of a pure and noble humanity. The early modern European wanted autonomy, wanted to engage in trade despite the Church's warning, and wanted to indulge promiscuously in personal pleasures. But he did not want to relinquish the feeling that he was part of eternity. It was a situation that created two kinds of Renaissance humanism. One was a civic humanism. The sons of Florentine nobles and merchants were often sent to study moral philosophy, rhetoric, and history in preparation for a career of public service. But there was another kind of Renaissance humanism, a higher kind of humanism, and it existed in writers such as Marsilio Ficino (1433–99) and Giovanni Pico della Mirandola (1463–94).[5] Their Christianized Platonism looked away from the material and social realm in the conviction that this looking away allowed one to commune with the universe and enter into a pure and lofty love of mankind:

> Let us spurn earthly things; let us struggle toward the heavenly. Let us put in last place whatever is of the world; and let us fly beyond the chambers of the world to the chamber nearest the most lofty divinity. . . . Let us compete with the angels in dignity and glory. When we have willed it, we shall be not at all below them.[6]

It is not surprising that German humanists of the Renaissance, already living in a politically fractured land and forced to dream of an invisible *Reich*, were attracted to these intangible ways to bring unity to their world. When Johannes Reuchlin (1455–1522) traveled south to Florence in 1490 to meet Pico della Mirandola, the great German humanist and Hebraist quickly warmed up to his Cabbalistic mystical systems. Pico's system, Platonic, yet part of a religious tradition extending back to the early Christian church, could easily fit the needs of any time and place that wanted to erect a humanism beyond the misgivings of society. In the right circumstances this higher humanism, propelled by the right rhetoric, can be much more satisfying than real social relations. Here and in the Sturm und Drang it can be easier to remain incompletely secularized, easier to allow oneself the luxury of replicating the glory of the Middle Ages, than to choose the slower and duller path of civic progress to which Karl Moor resigns himself in the final scene of *Die Räuber*.

Schiller's next play, *Die Verschwörung des Fiesco zu Genua*, lacked the diabolical chemistry that made his first drama such a resounding success, and its January 1784 premiere in Mannheim was a failure. The play does continue the theme of heroism and its difficulty, however, and reveals how a would-be hero can be taken in by a sense of his own greatness. The title character is a champion of the republic of Genoa who evolves into an aspiring dictator. The play was quickly overshadowed by *Kabale und Liebe*, Schiller's third drama, which premiered with huge success in April of the same year in Mannheim and, with a different cast, in Frankfurt am Main. Schiller's only middle-class tragedy, *Kabale und Liebe* provides another example of the distorted heroism of a tainted idealism. It is set in Schiller's contemporary Germany and built on the clash between the aristocratic culture and its ruthless court intrigue, on the one hand, and a middle-class culture of love and feeling, on the other. Ferdinand, the son of the duchy's powerful President von Walter, is in love with Luise Miller, the daughter of a musician. But his father wants him to marry Lady Milford, a discarded and now inconvenient mistress of the duke. President von Walter has the eager assistance of his manipulative secretary, Wurm, who wants Luise for himself. Together they kidnap Luise's parents and extort her to write a love letter to another man, which they allow to fall into Ferdinand's hands. The plan works too well: convinced of Luise's treachery, Ferdinand despairs, flies into a murderous, idealistic rage, and poisons Luise and himself.

Once more, Schiller finds a way to build drama on a missing middle ground in Germany, that place where lofty ideals and lived life should be able to merge but do not. As early as act 2, when Ferdinand tells Luise that he would rather die than be separated from her, she is shocked by the look in his eye: "Mir wird bange! Blik weg! Deine Lippen beben. Dein Auge rollt fürchterlich" (*S-NS*, 5N: 72).[7] In the next scene Ferdinand's father has the Miller family arrested on trumped-up charges, leading Ferdinand to point his sword at Luise's breast and tell his father that he would rather see her die than be disgraced at the pillory. Both here and in *Die Räuber* Schiller manages to find his way out of the thicket of the earlier Sturm und Drang to a place where he can at least clarify the German situation. Like Karl, Ferdinand needs to be betrayed so that Schiller can present a time and place that are lacking in ways to merge lived action with high ideals. What he finds is that the only viable heroism in Germany is the one that takes advantage of our sometimes perverse human capacity, already demonstrated in Renaissance Neoplatonism, to enjoy soaring away from the very humanity we raise to the skies. In the case of *Kabale und Liebe* Ferdinand, on the one hand, wants to marry Luise because he thinks class differences are insignificant compared to the eternal laws of the universe, but, on the other hand, he is moved by this same supposedly honorable spirit to kill her when he suspects her of plotting against him.

Schiller continues to explore Germany's fractured heroism in *Don Carlos,* whose Marquis von Posa, like Karl Moor, is so concerned with humanity that he loses sight of human beings. In this rather long drama based on Abbé de Saint-Réal's *Dom Carlos: Nouvelle historique* (1672) Schiller moves into a politically detailed setting and ends up focusing on a figure who, instead of raging, channels his idealism into political shrewdness. The plot, which involves characters both historical and imagined, revolves around Posa's plot to topple the government of King Philip II of Spain, under whom the Spanish Inquisition reached its height. The plan is to install the crown prince, Don Carlos, in Philip's place and form an enlightened government. The key for Posa is to take advantage of the crown prince's emotions, particularly his lifelong fawning devotion to Posa himself. But first he has to deal with Don Carlos's love for his young stepmother, Elizabeth of Valois, a willing coconspirator and a woman Posa has to enlist to get the lad focused on the big picture. From his first meeting with the crown prince in act 1, the higher cause is all Posa can think of. He has no sympathy for the people with whom he deals; it is all about his dreams: his plan for Spain and how he will get the Netherlands out from under Philip's yoke. When he decides to use Elizabeth to kindle the flame of rebellion in Don Carlos, he does so without regard for the safety of either of them. As Schiller explains in the third of his *Briefe über Don Carlos,* Posa's relationship with the crown prince is heartfelt only because it lets him fall in love with his own ideas. Similar to Karl Moor in the Bohemian forest, Posa will not avail himself of the people around him, preferring instead to press an abstract idea into service. A colder, higher humanism is Posa's intellectual habitat. He soars above people.

The high point of *Don Carlos* is a brilliant scene in which Posa, meeting King Philip for the first time, predicts the fall of totalitarian governments such as his and the rise of human dignity. He reproaches the king for his brutal suppression of the Protestants in the Netherlands and, throwing himself at Philip's feet, challenges the king to launch a new era of human liberty: "Geben Sie Gedankenfreiheit" (*S-NA,* 6: 191).[8] You will not be truly human, he tells the king, until your subjects are as well. Philip is moved; he tells Posa that he has never seen a man like him, deciding on the spot that Posa is to be his close friend and adviser — a charge Posa accepts so as to further his aims. But a train of events threatens to derail the conspiracy, and as a last resort Posa writes a self-incriminating letter that he allows to fall in to the king's hands, intentionally martyring himself with the hope of inspiring the crown prince to follow through with the revolt. Don Carlos is, indeed, inspired, but his role in the plot is soon exposed as well, and the king must have him executed as an enemy of the state. To accomplish this end he turns Carlos over to the Inquisition. Philip, silently accepting the elderly Grand Inquisitor's derision for having been swayed by Posa's eloquent words about humanity, and capitulating to the same historical forces that robbed him of his wife and son, ends up himself a tragic figure.

During the four years it took Schiller to finish the play, and as he studied the history of the period, he grew less interested in writing about the emotional Don Carlos and his passion for Elizabeth and more absorbed in the intersection of ideals and politics that he was developing in the relationship of Posa and the king. As Schiller tells us in the first letter of the *Briefe über Don Carlos,* it was his own maturity that led him to find the emotional crown prince less interesting. Because of this change of focus in midcomposition and his use of blank verse in this play, *Don Carlos* is seen by critics as embodying Schiller's turn from the Sturm und Drang. Still, insofar as his turn away from Don Carlos to Posa and Philip preserves the frustrating incongruity of hyperbolic idealism and lived life, Schiller is continuing to respond to issues important to the tradition. In Posa's failure and Schiller's subsequent decade-long absence as a writer for the stage we may be seeing the author's realization that the all-or-nothing posture of mind of which he was a connoisseur and that seemed to sum up so much of the Sturm und Drang's frustrating essence was both an endless source of rhetorical inspiration and an attitude with no political future.

There may be no other time prior to the first half of the twentieth century when Germany looks so different from its neighbors. The Sturm und Drang shows us German humanism at the crossroads, and no one seems more aware than Schiller that there are two paths open to his countrymen: one is a glory for which they will pay dearly; the other is an enlightened but dull solution, which is, of course, the path Karl Moor must finally take. In his early drama Schiller leads Germany to the demons within its own conception of life. Perhaps that is why Goethe instinctively disliked *Die Räuber.* Karl Moor brings us face-to-face with our preference for conceiving humanity as something best cultivated through rhetoric rather than in a sober, workmanlike, and enlightened way. As in Franz Kafka's *Ein Hungerkünstler* (A Hunger Artist, 1922), there is a terrible secret hidden within the conception of humanity Karl represents: he never needed people anyway.

How does one get from Schiller's Sturm und Drang — the plundering of cloisters in *Die Räuber* and Ferdinand's brutal poisoning of Luise — to the grandiloquent "An die Freude," in which human brotherhood can be ours if we just dare to reach out to another person? The 1785 ode, made enormously popular by Beethoven, projects a class-dissolving, populist magic. When Schiller wrote it, his life had just taken a turn for the better — with Körner's help, he was on his way out of debt and feeling buoyant about his future. Thus, in "An die Freude" we see him forgetting the frustrations of the Sturm und Drang and granting himself a moment of pure joy. It is another high-wire act above real human beings, but in a new key. The evocation of a higher, truer, more beautiful realm presided over by an all-powerful being reminds us of *Die Räuber,* and in the tone of this poem we can almost hear the turgid language of Karl Moor. But "An die Freude" already lifts us beyond Germany's national problems and grants us a glimpse of the next decade, when Schiller will widen his gaze to explore themes more broadly European.[9]

Notes

[1] "Is this a father's devotion? Is this love for love? . . . I loved him so unspeakably!" (*SuD,* 202).

[2] "My innocence! My innocence! — Look! Everyone has gone out to bask in the peaceful sunbeams of spring. — Why must I, I alone, draw hell from the joys of heaven? All so happy, all kin through the spirit of peace! The whole world one family, a father there above — a father, but not mine — I alone cast out, I alone set apart from the ranks of the blessed — not for me the sweet name of child — not for me the lover's melting glance — never, never more the bosom friend's embrace. (*starting back wildly*) Set about with murderers, in the midst of hissing vipers — fettered to vice with bands of iron" (*SuD,* 245).

[3] Reinhard Buchwald, *Schiller: Leben und Werk,* vol. 2: *Der junge Schiller* (Leipzig: Insel, 1937), 352.

[4] Johann Caspar Lavater, *Aussichten in die Ewigkeit, in Briefen an Herrn Joh. Georg Zimmermann,* vol. 3, 2nd ed. (Zurich: Gessner, 1773), 92–93.

[5] See Charles G. Nauert Jr., *Humanism and the Culture of Renaissance Europe* (Cambridge: Cambridge UP, 1995), 52–94.

[6] Giovanni Pico della Mirandola, *Oration on the Dignity of Mankind,* trans. Charles Glenn Wallis (New York: Bobbs-Merrill, 1965), 7.

[7] "I am afraid! Look away! Your lips are trembling. Your eyes roll dreadfully" (Friedrich Schiller, *Plays:* Intrigue and Love *and* Don Carlos, The German Library, 15, ed. Walter Hinderer [New York: Continuum, 1983], 38).

[8] "Grant freedom of thought."

[9] A draft of this paper was read at the University of Kentucky in March 2001. I would like to thank the faculty and graduate students of the German department for their valuable suggestions.

The Sturm und Drang in Music

Margaret Stoljar

THE USE OF THE TERM *Sturm und Drang* in the historiography of music raises several questions. The most fundamental of these must be whether it is legitimate to adopt for music the established designation of a movement customarily regarded as purely literary. If such usage is prima facie acknowledged as acceptable, a theoretical basis for it remains to be worked out. Two axes might serve to focus the discussion in a preliminary way: the synchronic and the diachronic.

A synchronic approach examines musical phenomena during the period of the literary Sturm und Drang. Since the term is normally specific to German literature, the music to be considered will be that contained within the German cultural context, that is, written by German composers and, if vocal, using German-language texts. Stylistic aspects of this music will be analyzed to determine whether features comparable to those found in contemporary literature are present. Such features might include rapid changes in diction that produce violent contrasts, or marked emotional content. More generally, it will be asked to what extent the new forms are clearly a departure from the styles and conventions that have gone before.

This kind of typological analysis allows comparison between the literature and the music of a given period and contributes to a contextual profile of cultural change, where each of the arts is considered as a facet of a larger whole. But it stops short of explaining why certain stylistic features appear in music at that moment, and what aspects of contemporary music practice were necessary for their introduction. Musical change, perhaps more than innovation in literature or the visual arts, depends on the coincidence of aesthetic and material factors. The latter are found in the physical and social circumstances of performance. The technical modification or improvement of instruments and the spread of musical literacy in the later eighteenth century, for instance, both provide increased opportunity for innovatory composition, as well as the greater participation of a class of nonprofessional performers. These larger questions require one to explore the diachronic axis, the multiple historical developments that shape all music-making.

For the period of the 1770s and 1780s it can be shown that significant innovations in musical style and practice were being explored. Many of them are analogous or parallel to the central aspects of literary style that characterize the Sturm und Drang. On the one hand, simpler, more transparent forms and diction are used in what might be called the democratic mode; on the other, dramatic, turbulent expression appears as a revolt against established decorum. It can plausibly be argued that these are two sides of the same coin, that is, two responses to the desire of the late eighteenth century to break away from the artistic and social conventions of the preceding generation.

An explanation of these trends might seek to derive them from common cultural factors such as the gradual "embourgeoisement" of the arts since the middle of the century or the foregrounding of expressiveness, typically of sentiment. Beyond that, however, musical change can be said to demonstrate its own momentum as new forms grow out of the exhaustion of established practice or the desire to improve familiar techniques. Writing for solo instruments and orchestra introduced new dynamic effects, for instance, that allowed frequent changes in mood and intensity. It is in these stylistic experiments that the turbulent aspect of the Sturm und Drang in music is to be located. While formal and thematic characteristics of contemporary German literature may have played a role in shaping some dimensions of the new music, principally in the song with keyboard accompaniment, many factors intrinsic to performance practice were also at work.[1]

An example of the mutual influence of performance practice and composition can be found in the appearance of fully written-out accompaniments in music for solo instruments or voice. Baroque practice required the accompanist to improvise on the basis of numbers inserted in the manuscript to indicate the appropriate chords and intervals (known as the figured bass or continuo). This exacting discipline was largely beyond the abilities of the many amateur players who wished to enjoy the new music, while a written-out accompaniment simplified the technical demands on the performer. Together with the modification of keyboard and other instruments for greater flexibility and enhanced sound, these changes led to the widespread participation of amateur singers and players in music designed primarily for private performance.

At the same time, the introduction of public concerts in Leipzig, Vienna, and Berlin during the 1770s opened the way for new musical audiences and led many to try their hand at home. Music publishing, made incomparably more practicable by the invention of music printing by the Breitkopf family of Leipzig, began to assume mass proportions. Printed collections of keyboard pieces and songs were welcomed enthusiastically by the increasingly literate middle class, who were able to enjoy greater leisure for artistic pursuits — in particular, the cultivation of music in a domestic setting. This popularization of small musical forms is at one with the democratic aspirations of Sturm und Drang writers, who similarly spoke to a new middle-class audience.

Of the various kinds of music produced during the Sturm und Drang period, two were written for the voice, employing German texts. They are the German opera or singspiel and the solo song with instrumental accompaniment, usually for the keyboard. In the latter, where the texts used clearly demonstrate a Sturm und Drang style, such as the poetry of Klopstock or Bürger, the settings made by contemporary composers provide a ready starting point for a characterization of Sturm und Drang in music. Many of these settings display a wide emotional range and the frank expressiveness demanded by the new poetry. Some were able to incorporate dramatic or strikingly vigorous elements that matched similar qualities in the literary style. In the early singspiel, librettos were often translated from the French, so that direct links with the new German writing are absent. Nonetheless, ideological aspects of the Sturm und Drang are apparent, such as the trend toward less formality and greater accessibility in the arts. The first singspiels were performed by actors, not trained musicians, in a conscious move away from the conventions of the court opera.

In the case of instrumental music, analysis rests primarily on form and diction. If a Sturm und Drang style is sought, say, in the sonatas for solo keyboard of Carl Philipp Emanuel Bach (1714–88), it will be discovered in the repeated appearance of novel dramatic and highly contrasted devices. Similar stylistic innovations are apparent in his works for orchestra. Bach was writing for competent performers, but he, too, was aware that many enthusiasts for the new music needed greater guidance than accomplished professionals. Some of his keyboard sonatas are designated expressly "für Kenner und Liebhaber," that is, for the amateur as well as the professionally trained musician. While these works in no way compromise Bach's experimentation with radical diction, and some are technically demanding, they are printed with written-out ornamentation and dynamic marks (directions for louds and softs). Such additions were not customary in earlier practice, since new music was rarely printed, and accomplished performers were assumed to be able to improvise matters of style.

These innovations demonstrate the demand for music accessible to a new, musically literate public, and are witness to the readiness of a composer even of Bach's eminence to cater to it. In sum, two facets of the literary Sturm und Drang, its untrammeled desire for emotional expression and its movement away from formal diction toward greater openness and spontaneity, can be said to have their counterparts in contemporary music. To sustain this claim we need to look more closely at the musical life of the period: first, the new wave in music theater; then developments in instrumental music; and last, the creation of a new kind of keyboard song.

Music Theater

In his speech in praise of Shakespeare, *Zum Schäkespears Tag,* read to a private gathering in 1771, the twenty-two-year-old Goethe proclaimed his determination to rid the German theater of the constraints of classical conventions. The three unities cherished in the classical tradition, he declared, were nothing but chains that hindered the free movement of the imagination and turned all French tragedies into self-parodies. In the course of the next decade Goethe's own writing for the theater, especially *Götz von Berlichingen,* and that of his young contemporaries took German drama in radically new directions. A comparable movement had already begun in music written for the stage that was to introduce new styles in both content and form.

The drama with music, or singspiel, as it came to be known, would be established as a native form with texts in the German language and characters drawn from unpretentious village or town life. It takes shape as a kind of theater very different from the stylized presentation of mythological or historical subjects that was the norm in the Italianate court opera. The musical idiom of the new works is remote from the formality of the *opera seria,* with its virtuoso arias and accompanied recitatives. Just as the Sturm und Drang drama represents a conscious reaction against French classical models or the heroic history plays of the German baroque age, the new music theater, while initially modest in scope, shows a similar resolve to break new ground.

The last third of the eighteenth century did, indeed, see a first flowering of German opera. It would eventually take its place beside the Italian style that had long dominated the taste of the German courts and the more recently evolving French *opéra comique.* Although most texts were initially translated from Italian or French, the introduction of librettos written in German at the end of the 1760s indicates the start of a new momentum that found its culmination in Wolfgang Amadeus Mozart's (1756–91) *Die Zauberflöte* (The Magic Flute, 1791) and Beethoven's *Fidelio* (1805). The characteristics of these earliest librettos reveal the opening of music theater toward narratives and characters that are essentially different from earlier patterns. They include rustic themes, comic or farcical situations, and, significantly for the broader cultural history of the period, conflicts between upper- and lower-class figures that are generally resolved in favor of the more virtuous servant or countryman or -woman.

For these departures to be practicable, there had, first, to be innovations in theatrical enterprise that were directed toward a new public and made possible by changing economic circumstances. Additionally, an exhilarating sense of cultural novelty set up by major events in the theater, such as the striking success of Lessing's *Minna von Barnhelm* (1767) at its first production in Berlin, could not fail to reverberate among other entrepreneurs and audiences. Although the National Theater in Hamburg eschewed music theater as not worthy of serious attention, its wide prestige and the impact of Lessing's critical writing in the *Hamburgische Dramaturgie* were a stimulus to general receptivity to innovation in the theater.

The beginnings of the new German opera may be credited to the determination of a few theater troupes to establish themselves on a sounder and more enduring basis.[2] While traveling companies of actors had sometimes succeeded in obtaining stable engagements in the service of the courts, the upheaval of the Seven Years' War meant that many had been dissolved or forced to take temporary refuge away from their normal quarters. Such was the case with Koch's troupe in Leipzig, where a fresh start had to be made and audiences found for the theater he opened in 1766. Koch was able to persuade the Leipzig composer and musical pedagogue Johann Adam Hiller (1728–1804) to collaborate with the poet Christian Felix Weisse (1726–1804) in creating some new German-language operas in a popular style in imitation of the successful genre of French comic opera.

Koch's initiative established the form of the singspiel, often styled "drama with music." It is deliberately differentiated from the Italian opera by either of these designations, which indicate that musical numbers alternate with spoken dialogue. In its earliest incarnation, the spoken material provided the substance of the texts, since the actors who performed the roles were most comfortable with this emphasis. The dialogue was complemented with songs of a character appropriate for the amateur status of the singers, for the use of trained musical performers was rare in the early years of the new opera. Three of these works, *Lottchen am Hofe* (Lottie at Court, 1767), *Die Liebe auf dem Lande* (Love in the Country, 1768), and *Die Jagd* (The Hunt, 1770), were runaway successes and were published several times in keyboard reductions during the next decade. In particular, the many simple songs that punctuate the spoken dialogue became extremely popular. They represent a landmark in the evolution of the solo song at the keyboard that is an important social contributor to changes in the music practice of the period.

Weisse's librettos, although they are faithful adaptations of French models, introduce in the guise of light-hearted comedy some of the emerging themes of serious drama. An example is the contrast between the simplicity and innocence of rustic or middle-class life and the corrupting actions of aristocratic figures — a subject soon to be the focus of Lessing's tragedy *Emilia Galotti*. But all of these texts show the familiar stereotypes found in their French models. There are one or more pairs of innocent lovers, a scheming and lascivious older man with designs on the heroine, and, often, a benevolent prince who arrives when the lovers' situation seems hopeless and resolves the conflict in their favor. This enduringly popular pattern survives in many later works, for example, in *Die Entführung aus dem Serail* (The Abduction from the Seraglio, 1782), where a German libretto by Christoph Friedrich Bretzner (1748–1807) of Leipzig was revised by Gottlieb Stephanie (1741–1800) with Mozart himself. The opera, described as a singspiel on its first publication, contains passages of spoken dialogue, as did its modest forebears in Hiller's productions.

The most cursory comparison of the music of *Die Entführung aus dem Serail* with that of Hiller's settings that were so popular in Leipzig and later in published versions will point to significant differences. While Mozart was writing in Vienna for professional singers, especially in the female roles, who were as accomplished as any of his day, Hiller had in mind untrained actors or amateurs singing at home. These are the features of the earliest singspiel that allow it to be perceived as at one with the dawning movement of the Sturm und Drang. What will soon be apparent in the lyric of Matthias Claudius (1740–1815) and the young Goethe is a diction free of rococo artificiality. The songs that punctuated the singspiel spoke to a newly felt desire for artlessness and easy expressiveness in the vocal part, while the straightforward written-out accompaniments were within easy reach of the amateur player.

In the wake of the success of Hiller's and Weisse's comic operas, a great many new works were written and performed during the 1770s in Leipzig and, after the arrival there of the Koch troupe, in Berlin. Among the composers who produced new works for Koch and his successor Ludwig Döbbelin were two former students of Hiller's, Christian Gottlob Neefe (1748–98) and Johann Friedrich Reichardt (1752–1814). Neefe's comic opera *Die Apotheke* (The Apothecary's Shop, 1771) was performed in Berlin in the same year that Hiller's *Der Dorfbalbier* (The Village Barber) was presented in Leipzig with ten arias by Neefe. The central characters in both works are village tradesmen, figures who, together with a gallery of rustic workers or servants in aristocratic houses, were to become staples in German opera. It is already apparent that Neefe, still in his early twenties, was able to command a musical range and inventiveness that would outstrip those of his teacher Hiller. As will be shown in the discussion of the innovative song collections Neefe wrote later, his music provides material that can truly be described as characteristic of the Sturm und Drang.

Reichardt, a precocious talent who was appointed capellmeister to Frederick the Great in 1775 at the age of twenty-three, produced some German operas in the pastoral style, among them *Amors Guckkasten* (Cupid's Peep Show, 1772). Like many of its fellows, this work was published in a keyboard reduction but never performed on the stage. Reichardt enjoyed a long and often controversial career as a prolific musician and political journalist. In an early essay on the subject of German comic opera (1774) he argues for greater simplicity in writing for the voice.[3] In particular, he advocates through-composition, that is, a setting providing a different melody and accompaniment for each part of a song, rather than repeating identical forms for every stanza. Through-composition affords the music the flexibility to enhance the narrative or expressive content as it develops throughout the poetic text. The spontaneity allowed by this unconfined form, which Reichardt pursued in his own later song composition, shows the general movement of the period in music, as well as poetry, toward freer, more natural diction.

Goethe himself tried his hand at the singspiel during the 1770s. As a student in Leipzig he had enjoyed the popular operas of Hiller and Weisse, as he recalls in his autobiography *Dichtung und Wahrheit* (*G-MA*, 16: 352). The history of his own ventures in the form illustrates the interconnectedness of the musical and literary life of the period and the intricate paths through which one influenced the other. In late 1767 Christoph Willibald Gluck's (1714–87) Italian opera *Alceste* received its premiere in Vienna. The score was published two years later with a preface in which Gluck set out his conviction of the need for the music to serve the poetry faithfully, without unnecessary ornamentation. Coming as it did from the pen of the most celebrated opera composer of the age,

Gluck's aesthetic achieved considerable resonance in contemporary debates on the relation between poetic text and musical setting. Whether Mozart was familiar with Gluck's writing on this subject is not known, but with characteristic vehemence he expresses his own diametrically opposed belief in a letter to his father: "In an opera, the poetry must positively be the obedient daughter of the music."[4] It is as if Gluck's Olympian classicism is being confronted by the headstrong exuberance of youth.

In Weimar, where the celebrated Seyler troupe performed in the court theater, controversies over the most appropriate style for German opera were revived. On the prompting of Duchess Anna Amalia of Saxe-Weimar, herself a composer, the poet Wieland produced his own version of *Alceste* (1773), with a libretto in verse and music by a minor composer, Anton Schweitzer (1735–87). In an essay on the singspiel in his journal *Merkur*, Wieland put forward the view that although the singspiel as a native German form was to be distinguished from the Italian or French opera, it should aim for something other than the rustic style of the Hiller/Weisse works; he advocated mythological or idyllic subjects instead. Wieland's pretension (he compared himself to Euripides) and the stiffness of his *Alceste* were satirized by Goethe in his farce *Götter, Helden und Wieland*. Soon afterward Goethe began intermittent work on his own singspiels *Erwin und Elmire* and *Claudine von Villa Bella*.

Erwin und Elmire is an adaptation of a sentimental ballad from *The Vicar of Wakefield*. Goethe's libretto, first published in the journal *Iris* in March 1775, begins with a conversation between the lovelorn Elmire and her mother. The mother, urging moderation in all things, deplores affectation in the education of young women, specifically in musical taste. The subject is not pursued, but perhaps represents an echo of current discussions of musical style. Music for the songs inserted in the dialogue was provided by Goethe's friend Johann Anton André (1741–99), a versatile composer also remembered for his settings of Sturm und Drang poetry. *Erwin und Elmire* with his songs achieved considerable popularity, leading to his appointment as conductor at the Döbbelin theater in Berlin. Goethe directed the work himself in Weimar in 1776, with music by Duchess Anna Amalia.

While such performances were confined to those with access to the court theaters, publication of the songs allowed amateur musicians to reinforce their popular success. Goethe's second singspiel, *Claudine von Villa Bella*, like its predecessor subtitled "a drama with music," was completed in April 1775. The theme of the libretto differs markedly from the rustic style of the pioneering German comic operas and even from the middle-class, domestic tone of *Erwin und Elmire*. A "romantic" Spanish setting provides the background to a balladesque story of two brothers — one a melancholy dreamer, the other the leader of a band of outlaws — in love with the same woman. Of all the early singspiels it is the only one that can be said to show something of the character of Sturm und Drang drama.

The history of these works exemplifies the development of the singspiel from a play in the vernacular with spoken dialogue interspersed with songs to the more elaborate musical structure of the later German opera. The preparation of the first collected edition of his works prompted Goethe, more than ten years after writing the first versions, to rework the two singspiels in a more operatic form, with the spoken prose passages replaced by sung recitative. He records that it was Mozart who brought an end to the "innocent" period of German opera with *Die Entführung aus dem Serail*, which was performed in Weimar in 1785. Goethe could no longer be satisfied with the simple forms modeled on French operettas, despite their merit in having brought singable melodies to the German stage for the first time.[5] The revised version of *Claudine von Villa Bella* was later set by Reichardt but was not performed in Weimar until 1795 and never achieved much success.

Instrumental Music

While vocal music in opera or song shows readily identifiable ideological qualities that inform the verbal text and narrative content, these qualities are not transparent in instrumental music. What can be shown are changes in diction, such as new dynamic practice or the use of frequent modulations (key changes) within individual works. More than in vocal writing, the evolving chapter in German instrumental music is to be understood in the broader European context.

In an age of patronage that would persist until Beethoven's middle years around the turn of the century, musicians traveled constantly to further their careers or to study with renowned masters. The reputations of prominent virtuosi, even those, such as Carl Philipp Emanuel Bach, who did not travel extensively themselves, extended far beyond the cities or courts in which they worked through correspondence and the personal accounts of those who heard them. The English music historian Charles Burney's incomparable descriptions of musical life in the Low Countries and Germany provide an engaging and informative picture of the period.[6] His accounts emphasize the highly responsive character of the musical world, where knowledge of new styles of composition and performance spread rapidly.

For keyboard music Carl Philipp Emanuel Bach, second son of Johann Sebastian, is of particular interest in that his writing for his instrument illustrates a profound impetus for change in musical diction. As harpsichordist to Frederick the Great from 1740 to 1767 Bach consolidated the mastery of the keyboard that he had learned from his father. His treatise on keyboard playing is an exhaustive compendium of contemporary practice in technical matters such as accompaniment from a figured bass or ornamentation.[7] But it also includes a section on musical expression, where Bach insists on the need to play "aus der Seele" (from the soul) and to cultivate cantabile playing (playing in a singing style) by listening to fine singers. His insistence on the central importance of expressiveness was borne out by his own reputation as the foremost master of the clavichord in Europe.

The clavichord, most expressive of eighteenth-century keyboard instruments for its ability to prolong notes by a kind of finger vibrato, is acknowledged as the instrument most characteristic of the age of sentiment. In this sense it matched the desire of the Sturm und Drang generation to allow the articulation of personal feeling. It became the instrument of choice for the growing numbers of singers and players who practiced the new music for accompanied voice or keyboard. For solo playing the clavichord was prized for its sensitivity and sweetness, but its extremely quiet voice made it unsuitable for ensemble or orchestral music. This limitation meant that keyboard composers who wished to explore other dimensions of the new musical culture, such as dramatic or strongly contrasting effects, were obliged to turn to other media.

The harpsichord possessed the clarity and brilliance that the clavichord lacked; and its penetrating tone could be enhanced by the use of multiple registers, where more than one string is plucked by a single keystroke. This device allowed greater volume when playing with an orchestra and in solo recitals, but the change of registers was still cumbersome. Dynamic changes were made by operating pedals or hand stops and were generally only introduced between movements of a work. All these drawbacks disappeared with the arrival of the pianoforte, the growing acceptance of which after the middle of the century opened the way for far-reaching changes in keyboard writing.

Although a keyboard with hammers had been invented early in the eighteenth century, it was not until the 1760s and 1770s that instrument builders in Germany and England began to produce the pianoforte in large numbers.[8] Here was an instrument of greater power and flexibility than any that had gone before, apart from the organ. Considerable volume could be achieved through the action of the hammers on the strings, while dampers could control the length of the reverberation. The keyboard with hammers allowed rapid dynamic changes by simply increasing the force with which the keys were struck and by raising or lowering the sustaining pedal. By these means, today taken for granted, the composer could make use of two essential elements in the development of a new style of playing — greatly increased volume and the possibility of instantaneous dynamic variation.

The pianoforte provided composers and performers with an instrument with much greater volume than the clavichord and the flexibility and sustaining power that the harpsichord, as a plucked instrument, could not attain. By the late 1770s Emanuel Bach was introducing unprecedented dramatic effects in his six sets of keyboard sonatas, all but the first volume designated expressly for the "fortepiano."[9] Short forte and piano passages follow each other in quick succession, and dazzlingly fast tempi with repeated elaborate (written-out) ornamentation and virtuoso runs are present everywhere. While frequent modulations between relative major and minor keys within the movements point forward to similar effects in classical sonata form, Bach disconcertingly uses different and unrelated keys for each movement of these highly idiosyncratic pieces. In writing for orchestra, also, Bach introduced striking dramatic contrasts in works such as the sets of string symphonies published in the early 1770s.

An important impetus for change in orchestral writing at this time was the first-class orchestra maintained by the Duke Karl Theodor in Mannheim, celebrated for its bold use of crescendo and diminuendo. Many contemporary tributes to the impressive and novel effects achieved by the "Mannheim rockets" are recorded, and although this orchestra was disbanded in 1778, its bold experimentation left an enduring mark on musical experience. Burney recorded that here for the first time piano and forte "were found to be musical *colours* which had their *shades,* as much as red or blue in painting" (2: 96). The young Mozart also admired the Mannheim orchestra and was happy to find some of the same musicians in Paris during his visit in 1778. There he was present at the first performance of his "Paris" symphony (K. 297), writing delightedly to his father about the popular success of his daring use of piano and forte passages.[10]

In his keyboard writing, too, Mozart was experimenting with effects that could only be achieved on the fortepiano. During his stay in Paris, despite his complaints about a miserable instrument, he produced one of his most profound and troubled pieces for keyboard, the sonata in A minor (K. 310/300d).[11] The Fantasia in C minor (K. 475), written in

Vienna in 1785, shows even more revolutionary treatment of the keyboard, perhaps stimulated by the fine new fortepiano he had then acquired.[12] It will serve to illustrate how stylistic features thought of as typical of the literary Sturm und Drang have their counterparts in contemporary musical language. A dramatic opening unison passage for both hands introduces sudden dynamic alternation of *f* and *pp*, which is repeated throughout the first part. A middle *allegro* is based on strongly rhythmical octave chords in the left hand, accompanied by rapid sixteenth-notes in the treble. The section ends with fast-moving runs *forte*, with a final descending *rallentando* leading to an *andantino*. Far from resolving the tension, however, this short movement soon flows into a closing *più allegro* with dizzying thirty-second-note (demisemiquaver) phrases in both hands before a reprise of the opening dramatic section, marked toward the end *poco crescendo*, then *crescendo*, then *più crescendo*.

In larger-scale works such as the Adagio and Fugue in C minor (K. 546), written first for two pianos in 1783 and reworked for string orchestra in 1788, and the "Dissonance" quartet (K. 465) of 1785, the last of the set of six dedicated to Joseph Haydn, Mozart once more employs somber coloring and unorthodox harmonies that led to contemporary criticism of his "difficult" music. It is recorded that such departures from the customary kinds of musical themes and diction alienated many of Mozart's listeners.[13] These examples suggest that to extend the horizon of what is meant by Sturm und Drang in instrumental music it will not be enlightening to look for direct literary influences, as it may be in settings of contemporary poetry. For Mozart, as for Goethe, the arresting moments of tension and turbulence that precede or interrupt periods of serene mastery cannot adequately be understood as exploratory or transitional. Perhaps, rather, they are necessary peaks of intense emotional expression, yet always contained by the artistic discipline that the composer could impose on even the most impassioned material.

Keyboard Song

The dimension of the new music of the 1770s and 1780s that is closest to the literary Sturm und Drang is the solo song with keyboard accompaniment. Young composers of the same generation as the poets began to make settings for the new lyric poetry that was rapidly reaching a wide audience. Often, musical settings for individual poems were printed together with the text in the proliferating literary journals. Soon many collections of songs were being published, providing a wealth of material for performance in what was to be the most popular kind of music making for generations — the song at the keyboard.[14]

Just as the poetry of Claudius, Bürger, the young Goethe, and the Göttingen poets introduced a newly expressive, personal diction for the lyric, so, too, the songs of the young composers for the most part were cast in a similar style. Straightforward, singable melodies allowed performance by singers who were musically literate but not highly trained. The accompaniments, suitable for playing on any keyboard instrument to hand, were technically accessible and stylistically undemanding. In the absence of a keyboard they could be played on a harp, lute, or guitar. These were songs for domestic use, designed for a social context that endured throughout the century and beyond. In this respect they represent a clear departure from the kinds of writing for solo voice that preceded them, songs for religious use and operatic arias for virtuoso singers. In rarer instances some composers sought to extend the musical compass of their songs to emulate the more dramatic aspects of Sturm und Drang poetry. One such innovator was Neefe, who deserves special attention for the boldness and originality of his writing, beginning with his Klopstock songs.

One of the many parallels between the appearance of the Sturm und Drang lyric and its counterpart in the keyboard song is shown in the impact of the poetry of Klopstock. The publication of a collected edition of Klopstock's *Oden und Lieder* (Odes and Songs) in 1771 heralded a wave of enthusiasm unprecedented for a contemporary poet. Among the many tributes that followed were settings of his odes by several composers, led by two of the most prominent of the older generation, Gluck and Carl Philipp Emanuel Bach. Although born in Bavaria and based in Vienna, in a long career devoted to the composition of Italian and French opera the only time Gluck wrote for German texts was his setting of six Klopstock odes. Four of these songs were first published in the *Göttinger Musenalmanach,* "Wir und Sie" (We and They) and "Schlachtgesang" (Battle Song) in the issue for 1774 and "Der Jüngling" (The Youth) and "Die frühen Gräber" (Early Graves) in 1775. The first two songs mentioned, together with a setting of the patriotic "Vaterlandslied" (Song of the Fatherland), were described by the composer in a letter to Klopstock as German in character, and all of them as simple in style and easy to play. These attitudes mark Gluck's sympathy with the poet's intention to forge a new kind of German poetry.

Both issues of the journal also carried a Klopstock song by Bach. The first was "Vaterlandslied," one of the most popular of Klopstock's poems and one that enjoyed settings by many different composers. Bach's straightforward tune suits the somewhat naive character of the poem ("Ich bin ein deutsches Mädchen! / Mein Aug' ist blau, und sanft mein Blick"[15]). His second Klopstock song complements the sentimental mood of the poem "Edone" ("Dein süßes Bild, o Lyda, / Schwebt stets vor meinem Blick"[16]) with a more varied, dreamy melody in A minor, a favorite key for the often soulful songs of the period. These contrasting styles exemplify the dual character of Sturm und Drang song. At times it can be vigorous, democratic, imbued with the cultural nationalism espoused by Herder, the young Goethe, and many of their contemporaries. In other moods it illustrates the desire of the age of sentiment for free expression of feeling and ready indulgence in melancholy, as in the Petrarchan style of Ludwig Christoph Heinrich Hölty (1748–76).

Of younger composers working in the 1770s, three made major contributions to the evolution of the keyboard song: Neefe, Reichardt, and Johann Abraham Peter Schulz (1747–1800). All were interested in the new poetry and wished to write settings for it that could share in the spirit of the age. Neefe, who is remembered as the teacher of the schoolboy Beethoven, produced several collections of songs with keyboard accompaniment. Two of them, *Vademecum für Liebhaber des Gesangs und Klaviers* (Vade Mecum for Lovers of Song and Keyboard, 1780) and *Lieder für seine Freunde und Freundinnen* (Songs for His Friends, 1784), include settings of texts by Claudius and the young Göttingen poets. In his published diaries Neefe recorded his enthusiasm for the new writing that he found in the *Göttinger Musenalmanach* and other journals. As well, he paid tribute to Goethe in a series of songs headed "An Werther's Lotte," in which he set his own texts.

As the titles of these albums suggest, many of the songs are intimate in character, designed for the use of amateur performers at home. But Neefe's musical professionalism and his not inconsiderable ambition prompted him to explore more challenging kinds of writing. He found what he wanted in Klopstock's poetry, producing a collection of twelve songs in 1776. Neefe's volume, which preceded the publication of Gluck's smaller collection by nine years, enjoyed great success, leading to a second edition in 1785. In his preface Neefe declares that poetry of such revolutionary character demands a new style of music; indeed, he thought that no composer was capable of setting complex odes such as "Die Frühlingsfeier" or "Dem Allgegenwärtigen" (To the Omnipresent One). His own songs display a bold use of dynamic contrasts in the style of Carl Philipp Emanuel Bach and show his experimenting with more elaborate forms of accompaniment than were customary.

In "Gegenwart der Abwesenden" (Presence of the Absent One), which employs the sighing motif then familiar in established musical diction for the evocation of sentiment, a lament for the beloved is interrupted by a dramatic leaping interval of a sixth as the poem's tone changes to one of celebration. In "Die Sommernacht" (The Summer Night) Neefe introduces further innovation in his setting out of voice part and accompaniment on three staves rather than the usual two, where the right hand doubles the melody. The separate part for the right hand allows greater freedom and independence for both voice and keyboard in that a melodic line can be sustained above an accompanying rhythm. This development is especially useful when longer, more complex verse patterns are employed, such as are often found in Klopstock's lyric poetry.

Just as Bach, Gluck, and Neefe had responded to the appearance of Klopstock's *Oden und Lieder* with new, inventive songs, another landmark in the evolution of the Sturm und Drang song was the appearance of Gottfried Bürger's collected poems in 1778. Neefe's name is listed among the subscribers to this volume, and his *Vademecum für Liebhaber des Gesangs und Klaviers* includes seven Bürger settings. Perhaps because of the democratic convictions and the interest in freemasonry they shared, Neefe seems to have been particularly moved by the poet's savage expression of resentment at aristocratic exploitation of the peasantry. His appropriately strongly contoured setting of "Der Bauer an seinen durchlauchtigen Tyrannen" (The Peasant to His Excellency the Tyrant) is marked "Eifrig und mit starker Klavierbegleitung" (Vigorously and with strong piano accompaniment), inviting the performer to do justice to the extreme sentiments of the song. Bürger's short poems and ballads, including "Lenore," enjoyed more contemporary settings than those of any other poet of his generation. Other than in Neefe's songs, however, it cannot be said that the powerful rhythms and passionate feeling of his language found really adequate musical expression.

Of the North German composers who contributed to the flowering of the keyboard song, Schulz is the most memorable. In three song collections dating from 1779 to 1785 Schulz published new settings of poems by Claudius, Hölty, Bürger, and others of the Göttingen group. The collections were headed *Lieder im Volkston* (Songs in a Popular Tone) in an effort to make them accessible to as wide a public as possible. Like Neefe, Schulz was concerned to articulate his ideas on the relationship between poetry and song, on the one hand, and the musical style most appropriate to his own time, on the other. As a contributor to the widely read encyclopedia *Allgemeine Theorie der schönen Künste* (General Theory of the Fine Arts, 1771–74) the young composer had insisted on the need for simplicity and expressiveness in performance,[17] and he put these principles into practice in his song collections. They responded perfectly to the desire of a growing public, fired with enthusiasm for the new poetry and increasingly musically literate, for songs to perform at home.

Schulz's attractive melody writing employs a style he chose to describe as popular rather than as aspiring to high art. With their sympathetic, readily playable accompaniments, his songbooks had immediate success and were reprinted several times. In a preface to one of the later editions Schulz develops his idea of the *Volkston* (popular tone) in a discussion that brings out strikingly the distinction between authentic, anonymous folk song and the style he had created.[18] In striving for the maximum possible transparency and accessibility in his melodies, Schulz set out explicitly to create the appearance of familiarity. This is the quality that accounts for the enduring popularity of the folk song proper. Where it can be combined with the best of the new poetry, itself couched in readily accessible language and forms, the true *Volkston* may be achieved. Schulz, perhaps more than any of his contemporaries, was convinced of the moral and educational purpose of music and poetry as a force for good in society. He conceived his songs as a means for the widest possible audience to share in his progressive vision.

The most prolific of all the German song composers of the late eighteenth century was Reichardt, who is principally remembered for his settings of Goethe poems. With a few exceptions, however, these were written after the appearance of the first collected edition of Goethe's works (1787–90) and so fall outside the period being examined here. Reichardt's contribution to the Sturm und Drang keyboard song was made in the 1770s and 1780s with settings of many of the same poets chosen by Schulz. A typical volume is his *Oden und Lieder von Klopstock, Stolberg, Claudius und Hölty* (Odes and Songs by Klopstock, Stolberg, Claudius and Hölty, 1779). Something of a political hothead, Reichardt had written two volumes of musical memoirs in emulation of Burney.[19] Imbued with a spirit of cultural nationalism, his writing is often truculent and defensive of German musicians. Like the more temperate Schulz, Reichardt was convinced that the expression of sentiment is the true purpose of music, and that of all the arts song is the closest to nature. It is not surprising that Reichardt was a passionate admirer of Rousseau.

Almost half of the *Oden und Lieder* volume of 1779 was made up of settings of Hölty's intense, often melancholy, and always accomplished poems. Reichardt's sure musicality was able to match the poet's polished diction and depth of feeling. Several of the songs introduce Hölty's haunting motif of the dream bride, as in "An den Mond" (To the Moon). Reichardt chooses a strongly accented F minor tune, marked "Schwermuthsvoll" (in a melancholy tone). As in Neefe's Bürger settings, it is an example of the composer's imaginative use of dynamic indications, then not yet fully established in the Italian terminology that is now familiar. Another, more joyous poem of Hölty's, "Die Seligkeit der Liebenden" (Lovers' Bliss), is marked "Entzückt, hinströmend" (rapturous, flowing), setting the tone for a rapid, restless melody that seems to suggest a sense of abandon beneath the poem's still controlled four-line stanzas.

This example illustrates the versatility of Reichardt's song writing, in that, like Neefe, he seeks to give musical form to the more turbulent aspects of the Sturm und Drang. Yet in much of his published work at this time, he aims for the more readily singable style so ably represented by Schulz. In his published journal *Musikalisches Kunstmagazin* (1782), Reichardt praises Schulz's *Lieder im Volkston* for their popular qualities.[20] Notwithstanding his musical experimentation in many of the Hölty songs, Reichardt shared Schulz's conviction that music, like the other arts, should serve the wider goals of progressive education. His own more radical beliefs (he was to become one of the most passionate of German Jacobins) demonstrate that, like Bürger, Reichardt was not prepared to deny the arts an active role in the pursuit of political ends.

Is There a Sturm und Drang in Music?

This essay has explored three new kinds of musical writing in the decades of the 1770s and 1780s. It cannot be denied that these years saw an upheaval in the composition and performance of music in some ways comparable to the movement of the Sturm und Drang in literature, but whether it is appropriate to designate this phase as a musical Sturm und Drang is a matter of controversy.[21] On balance, its most plausible use seems to be in discussion of the general contours of cultural change in Germany during the 1770s and 1780s. In that context developments in music can be seen to be consistent with those in poetry and drama and all to be aspects of a movement running counter to formality and convention. Yet, the later profile of the arts shows divergences significant enough to undermine any attempt to find continuing parallel features. In particular, the wider European context of musical development as against the specifically German character of the literary Sturm und Drang demands a differentiated interpretation of these phenomena, although they are contemporaneous.

In literature the uninhibited, spontaneous quality of Sturm und Drang writing yielded to the more measured and artistically self-conscious forms of German Classicism. Given that the preeminent writers of the age, Goethe and Schiller, trace this development in their own work, it is not surprising that the Sturm und Drang has often been interpreted as the transient expression of impassioned youth, to be left behind with greater maturity. However valid this conclusion may be for literature, it cannot be sustained for music. Carl Philipp Emanuel Bach, whose later composition shows most unequivocally the kind of revolutionary diction that is typical of the Sturm und Drang, was at the end of his long career. His experimental writing was not superseded by new styles but contributed substantially to the development of the classical sonata, for instance. Both Neefe, as the teacher of the young Beethoven, and Leopold Mozart, in training his son, included the study of the younger Bach's keyboard works.

Unlike the democratic character of the Sturm und Drang, later developments in musical form and language reflect the increasing professionalism of performance as the age of patronage was succeeded by that of the public concert. The simplification or popularization of forms such as the singspiel and the keyboard song soon gave way to new, more elaborate writing in the development of German opera, song, and instrumental music. Virtuoso concert works such as the later piano sonatas of Mozart and Beethoven were not written for amateur performers, being far removed in technical complexity and emotional range even from the innovative keyboard writing considered earlier in this essay.

Goethe's perceptive observation on the transformation of German opera by Mozart underlines the brevity of its earliest phase, a phase that could not survive its transcendence in a work of the stature of *Die Zauberflöte*. Mozart's late operas may retain some traces of the singspiel in the use of spoken prose passages or unaccompanied recitative, but musically as well as thematically they are of a different order. A parallel process is apparent in the eclipse of the simple keyboard song with the appearance of Franz Schubert's brilliant settings of German poetry, with their demanding accompaniments, and in the rapid development of art song in the lied repertoire.

In the longer perspective of the second half of the eighteenth century the music written during the Sturm und Drang period appears as part of the gradual dissolution of the age of counterpoint. If the musical baroque can be considered a kind of cultural ancien régime, Sturm und Drang music looks forward to major transformations. The great wave of new music produced by classical and Romantic composers that succeeded it is still perceived as modern and retains its dominant place in concert repertoires and record sales. Nevertheless, the modest early phase of both German opera and art song, and the experimental instrumental writing that contributed to the flowering of the classical style, have their place in the larger history of music. They are pivotal moments that deserve attention both for their own sake and for the way they can illuminate the beginnings of the riches that followed.

Notes

[1] I have argued elsewhere for the central importance of performance practice in the evolution of musical forms: "*Speculum Ludi:* The Aesthetics of Performance in Song," in *Music and German Literature: Their Relationship since the Middle Ages,* ed. James M. McGlathery (Columbia SC: Camden House, 1992), 119–31.

[2] The following discussion of the Hiller/Weisse operas is indebted to the exhaustive survey provided by Thomas Bauman, *North German Opera in the Age of Goethe* (Cambridge: Cambridge UP, 1985). Bauman distinguishes these as "Saxon comic opera."

[3] Johann Friedrich Reichardt, *Über die Deutsche comische Oper* (1774; Munich: Katzbichler, 1974), 5.

[4] October 1781, written while working on *Die Entführung.* Cited in Peter Gay, *Mozart* (London: Weidenfeld & Nicolson, 1999), 106.

[5] See his account of the rewriting of the singspiels in Rome in November 1787 in *Italienische Reise* (Italian Journey; *G-MA*, 15: 520–22).

[6] Charles Burney, *The Present State of Music in Germany, The Netherlands and United Provinces,* 2 vols. (1772, 1775; New York: Broude, 1969).

[7] Carl Philipp Emanuel Bach, *Versuch über die wahre Art das Clavier zu spielen,* 2 vols. (1753, 1762; Leipzig: Breitkopf & Härtel, 1969).

[8] For an extended discussion of technical changes in keyboard instruments, see my *Poetry and Song in Late Eighteenth Century Germany: A Study in the Musical* Sturm und Drang (London: Croom Helm, 1985), 52–55.

[9] *Die sechs Sammlungen von Sonaten, freien Fantasien und Rondos für Kenner und Liebhaber* (1779–1787). In the first years of its wider use the instrument was known as the fortepiano from its ability to move rapidly between louds and softs.

[10] Gay, 34–36.

[11] One of Mozart's recent biographers describes the slow movement of this sonata as "a self-contained, windowless, protected space. . . . We note the striking contrasts, the darkening of mood, the piercing, almost Schubertian dissonances, the brooding intensity, the relentlessness of the rapid modulations through a shifting sequence of major and minor keys." Maynard Solomon, *Mozart: A Life* (London: Hutchinson, 1995), 187.

[12] Solomon, 298.

[13] Gay, 69–70. See Solomon, 200–203, for a commentary on the "Dissonance" quartet, "an unprecedented network of disorientations, dissonances, rhythmic obscurities, and atmospheric dislocations."

[14] For a comprehensive account of the Sturm und Drang song, see my *Poetry and Song in Late Eighteenth Century Germany.*

[15] "I am a German girl! / My eyes are blue, gentle is my gaze."

[16] "Your sweet image, O Lyda, / Floats ever before my gaze."

[17] Johann Georg Sulzer, ed., *Allgemeine Theorie der schönen Künste* (Hildesheim: Olms, 1967), 4: 375.

[18] Johann Abraham Peter Schulz, *Lieder im Volkston, bey dem Klavier zu singen,* 2nd ed. (Berlin: Decker, 1785). Cited in Max Friedlaender, *Das deutsche Lied im achtzehnten Jahrhundert: Quellen und Studien,* 2 vols. (1902; facsimile rpt., Hildesheim: Olms, 1970), 1.1: 256–57.

[19] Johann Friedrich Reichardt, *Briefe eines aufmerksamen Reisenden die Musik betreffend* (vol. 1, 1774; vol. 2, 1776; Letters concerning Music from an Observant Traveler).

[20] *Musikalisches Kunstmagazin* (vol. 1, 1782; facsimile rpt., Hildesheim: Olms, 1969), cited in Friedlaender, 1.1: 260: "Schulz' Sammlung kann wahrlich vieles dazu beitragen, daß unsere Nation von dem fremden, eitlen, üppigen Klingklang und Modesingsang zur Wahrheit und rührenden Einfalt zurückkehrt" ("Schulz's collection can, indeed, make a substantial contribution toward returning our nation from an alien, vain, and voluptuous tinkling and fashionable sing-song to truth and touching simplicity").

[21] See Ludwig Finscher's skeptical "Sturm und Drang," giving the historiography of the term, in *Musik in Geschichte und Gegenwart: Allgemeine Enzyklopädie der Musik,* 2nd ed., ed. Finscher, vol. 8 (Kassel & Weimar: Bärenreiter & Metzler, 1998), 2018–22. Finscher also quotes Walter Hinck's assertion, in his introduction to the critical anthology *Sturm und Drang: Ein literaturwissenschaftliches Studienbuch* (Kronberg: Athenäum, 1978), viii, that the term cannot be applied to music.

The Sturm und Drang and the
Periodization of the Eighteenth Century

Gerhard Sauder

The Concept of a Literary Period

THERE IS, NOWADAYS, agreement in the historical disciplines that epochs and periods are not phenomena that can claim existence in their own right: they are constructs and hypotheses developed by historians and, therefore, require continual critical reevaluation. The period within which the Sturm und Drang is situated is the Age of Enlightenment. Because of the short time within which it flourished, the Sturm und Drang can only be counted as a trend within the Enlightenment. Since the eighteenth century the concepts of period and epoch have been used synonymously to refer to a single span of time or a unique phenomenon,[1] but these terms would be imprecise as descriptions of the Sturm und Drang. The modern idea of an epoch became established through the tradition of German Idealism. It refers to a longer-term ensemble that develops out of one ensemble and points toward another one. Epochs and periods cannot be precisely dated, because their beginnings and endings are gradual. One of the particular features of the idea of an epoch is that it allows the temporal discontinuity of simultaneous histories, the experience of the acceleration, intensification, and temporalization of the world of experience, the openness to the future, and the multiplicity of perspectives that open up historical understanding.[2]

Phases of the Enlightenment: Sturm und Drang, Weimar Classicism, Romanticism

Modern scholars of the German Enlightenment interpret the Early Enlightenment, dating from 1680 to 1720–30, as a threshold between baroque and Enlightenment. The middle phase of the Enlightenment reached its high point between 1750 and 1770. At the same time there emerged trends such as the rococo and Sentimentalism (*"Empfindsam-*

keit"). The major debate about the nature of Enlightenment that took place in 1782–83 was not only an example of the necessary self-reflection and self-criticism but also a sign of a crisis. The Late Enlightenment had no clear profile, but, whereas the middle phase of the Enlightenment focused more on literature and philosophy, the Late Enlightenment devoted itself to socially useful activities and social reform, to praxis, and only came to an end in the first decades of the nineteenth century.

Early attempts to locate the Sturm und Drang within a history of literature understood it as a first stirring of so-called Pre-Classicism and looked everywhere for signs of a sharp opposition to the Enlightenment, but in the last decades virtually no scholars have wanted to see the Sturm und Drang as a preparatory stage in the development of Weimar Classicism. As also in the literary histories of other countries, scholars have become less convinced by attempts to interpret individual phases in terms of a single great moment in history. In France there are scarcely any supporters of the use of the term *Pre-Romanticism* to refer to Sentimental writing and the Late Enlightenment. In Germany, too, the use of Weimar Classicism as a reference point decades before it came into being has been criticized as a dubious kind of teleology. There is increasing support for the thesis that the Sturm und Drang is part of a broad and complex process of Enlightenment. The intertwining of the Sturm und Drang and the Enlightenment is certainly not straightforward, but the formulation I have suggested, "intensification and internal criticism of the Enlightenment,"[3] will serve as an approximate characterization of it. This formulation refers, on the one hand, to the acceleration of the way Enlightenment positions came to be voiced in radicalized forms in the 1770s. When dealing with the central concerns of this literature, the younger generation of writers frequently dispenses with the self-imposed rules of literary communication. On the other hand, one must not overlook the critical attitude that these young writers adopted toward many literary positions of the Enlightenment. This is what earlier attempts to construct a literary history turn into a sharp opposition, which seemed to make it easy to claim the superiority of the new literature over the already conventionalized writing of established authors. The Sturm und Drang should, therefore, be understood in a narrower sense and restricted to the 1770s, with a high point in 1776. The formulation I have proposed is also helpful in dealing with the many connections with positions adopted by the Enlightenment. It makes it more easily possible to come to terms with the tensions between individual authors and their works with respect to a tradition that was being overtaken, as well as with the discontinuities, especially those that emerged between the history of culture and of society in general, on the one hand, and the history of literature, on the other. It would be as mistaken to attempt a "definition" of the Sturm und Drang as it would be to attempt a "definition" of the important phases of the Enlightenment.

The Sturm und Drang is not merely a construction of literary historians; it was regarded at first by the participants themselves as a new "school" or "sect" led by Herder and Goethe. Several theoretical texts can be counted as programmatic statements of the Sturm und Drang, but on closer examination each of them is too selective and too individual to be able to stand for the whole range of activities evident in the movement. Strictly speaking, each of these young writers worked on his own account and increasingly only for himself.

Goethe's Use of Revolution as a Metaphor: The Periodization of the Sturm und Drang in the Nineteenth Century

The metaphor of the Sturm und Drang as a revolution goes back to Goethe's sketch of a literary history in book 11 of *Dichtung und Wahrheit:* "wir trieben uns auf mancherlei Abwegen und Umwegen herum, und so ward von vielen Seiten auch jene deutsche literarische Revolution vorbereitet, von der wir Zeugen waren, und wozu wir, bewußt und unbewußt, willig oder unwillig, unaufhaltsam mitwirkten" (*G-MA,* 16: 522–23).[4] If the nineteenth century, at least up to 1848, may be counted as an age of revolutions, it is not surprising that representatives of a critical, democratic historiography of literature such as Georg Gottfried Gervinus and Hermann Hettner took up this metaphor and, by contrast with Goethe, who only used it with reference to literature, gave it a political content.[5] Gervinus and Hettner understood the Sturm und Drang as the German counterpart of the French Revolution. At the same time, the ambivalence of this metaphor must not be forgotten. Only in certain respects can the story of the Sturm und Drang be read as the story of a revolution. When Gervinus interpreted the Age of Genius in terms of the Terror of the French Revolution, in which all authority was abolished, he was allowing the metaphor to lead him to false conclusions. It would not be easy to find a direct analogy between the Sturm und Drang and the Terror. Hettner was more cautious and withdrew the political implications. He preferred to speak in the same tone as Goethe of fermentation or of an adolescent phase in the evolution of Germany. This model, however, again looked forward to a classicism that would be reached when fermentation had been completed and adulthood had been reached.

In Wilhelm Scherer's classic positivistic history of literature of 1883 the ideas of literary revolution and Enlightenment are still connected, even if critical evaluations from the perspective of Classicism creep in: "Sturm und Drang! Genieperiode! Die Originalgenies! Unter diesen Namen pflegt man die deutsche Literaturrevolution und ihre Träger zu feiern oder zu verspotten."[6] Although the national trajectory of his historiography was self-evident to Scherer, and there was no doubt that the development proceeded toward its high point in the work of Goethe, we do not yet find any disparaging remarks about the literature of the Sturm und Drang as a whole. Negative judgments do not, it is true, wholly determine later presentations, but they are implied indirectly in the assessments of the period inasmuch as the literature of the 1770s is presented as having no relevance in its own right but only as *pre*-Classicism or *pre*-Romanticism.

Models of Periodization in the History of Ideas

Despite their brief companionship, the writers of the Sturm und Drang led separate existences in Strasbourg, Emmendingen, Frankfurt, Darmstadt, and Göttingen, and this fact was recognized at an early stage by histories of literature. In his celebrated study of 1914 Friedrich Gundolf adopted this separation as the structural principle of his portrait of the Sturm und Drang.[7] Herder and Goethe are presented as solitary models, followed by more or less detailed sections on the Sturm und Drang writers, who, by the standards applied to Goethe, are given predominantly negative assessments. At the same time, Gundolf is less interested in the individuals than in the "tendency" that they represent as a whole. Some of them, he claims, found the idea of nature in Shakespeare, while others found in Shakespeare the idea of freedom or passion. Gundolf understands the Sturm und Drang as "eine bestimmte Bewegung mit bestimmten Gedanken oder Gefühlsinhalten" or as:

> ein Tempo, als einen Wirbel des deutschen Geistes in welchen alles mitgerissen wurde was sich nicht bewusst entgegenstellte. Je nach ihrem persönlichen Temperament nahmen die verschiedenen Mitglieder des Kreises dasjenige aus Goethes Werken auf was ihnen am gemässesten war und verwandelten, d.h. erniedrigten, verzerrten oder übertrieben es. (226)[8]

The attitude of the circle around Stefan George (1868–1933), to which Gundolf belonged, is revealed in these verbs: they regarded the Sturm

und Drang as one more version of the rebarbarization of German literature. What the members of the Stefan George circle found particularly
repugnant was the closeness of the writers of the Sturm und Drang to
the lower social classes and their language, which was quite unheard of
in the early and middle phases of the Enlightenment. Heinrich Leopold
Wagner thus appears as a "gewandter Plebejer" (clever plebeian) and
"übler Litterat" (wretched scribbler), that is to say, as common: according to Gundolf, Wagner thought he saw nature everywhere, but, in
reality, he just saw what was vulgar. These Sturm und Drang writers,
Gundolf went on, had not shied away from allowing the lower and middle classes to speak their own language or from inserting vulgar expressions, coarse jokes, and swearing, irrespective of whether they were
appropriate or not. Wagner only knew "vulgar reality," and for that
reason his writings were entirely lacking in artistic or literary merit. His
version of *Macbeth* translated the enormity of myth into the plebeian
diction of a sensually alert but fundamentally vulgar scribbler. This,
Gundolf concluded, was private work and should not be counted among
the major documents of the history of ideas (227).

It is scarcely possible to imagine a greater gulf than that between the
modern assessment of Lenz and his condemnation by Gundolf. Lenz,
too, according to Gundolf, paid homage to the new ideal of naturalness
and found the best opportunity in contemporary sexual problems. The
Anmerkungen übers Theater is condemned as muddled and as consisting
in a confusion of ideas from Lessing and Herder about the French tradition and Shakespeare, obscured and distorted by the new style of the Age
of Genius, thrown together with no regard for logic (227). Lenz, with
his ascetic literary life, was distinguished from the rough coarseness of
Wagner by his power of imagination, which, however, Gundolf described
as a kind of disorder, a symptom of breakdown, an eccentricity rather
than the revelation of a world of dreams (229).

A further variant in the construction of a Sturm und Drang phase
was proposed by Paul Hankamer in 1930.[9] A chapter titled "Goethe und
die Zeit der deutschen Klassik" (Goethe and the Age of German Classicism) begins by treating the Sturm und Drang before going on to present Goethe, Schiller, and Jean Paul. Hankamer follows the tradition of
beginning his sketch of the Sturm und Drang with Hamann, who taught
Herder, as Hankamer puts it, to reject barren intellectualism and acknowledge a sense of the darker forces that nourish a spiritual culture
and the belief in the creativity that lies in feeling (220). All the basic
tendencies of the Sturm und Drang could be derived from the calm
critical judgments of Herder. For Hankamer there were only two circles

in which the Sturm und Drang came together as a literary group, the Göttinger Hainbund and the Strasbourg circle around Herder and Goethe. Both groups adopted revolutionary gestures and declared formlessness to be an artistic principle but wanted, above all, to have an effect in the moral and intellectual fields. One thing is unusual: Hankamer's reference to the Renaissance as a model for these young authors, from which he concludes that they interpreted their own breakthrough in terms of the historical period around 1500.

Periodization by the Denial of Tradition

The influence of book 11 of Goethe's *Dichtung und Wahrheit*, written in 1811, on histories of literature has already been mentioned. It was a source not only of evaluations and metaphors, such as the idea of a literary revolution, that were to be important for future histories but also of a methodological principle. Goethe allows his own epoch to emerge from the previous one through a process of abrupt confrontation, contradiction, and even radical negation. It is true that at the same time he speaks of a tradition that was to be surpassed by the younger generation, led by Herder and Goethe. Despite all individual differences in their aesthetics, the younger generation of writers were united in their rejection of doctrinal aesthetics (Gottsched) and systematic rationalism. They shared the awareness of a generation whose literary socialization reached back into the middle phase of the Enlightenment or the rococo and who were able to make a mark for themselves by radicalizing what they inherited from the Enlightenment. The denial of tradition must not be understood as a break with tradition: the denial of tradition presupposes a thorough knowledge of tradition.[10]

One of the preconceptions lying behind the characterization and periodization of the Sturm und Drang has been the assumption that there was a sharp opposition between Lessing, as *the* representative of the middle phase of the Enlightenment, and the younger generation of writers. On closer examination this assumption turns out not to be supported by the evidence. Lessing, evidently with good reason, held back from making a public judgment on this new literary trend. But he was too alert to developments within the arts not to follow — with some skepticism — the dramas, novels, poems, and literary theory emerging from Göttingen and the South German Sturm und Drang circles. As a critic with his roots in the Enlightenment, Lessing was unable simply to do away with the obligation of literature to contribute to a humane ethic and replace it with aesthetic innovation, the breaking down of taboos, or the claim of the individual to wide-reaching moral license. Nowhere in monographs on Lessing or in studies of the Sturm und Drang has there been any special note of the absence of explicit statements by Lessing on his young contemporaries between 1770 and 1781. Occasional judgments are to be found in letters and in conversations that have survived in notes by the person with whom he was speaking. Thus, we know that he was enraged by all the talk about genius, but his judgment on plays by Gerstenberg and Leisewitz, whom he knew personally, was positive. Klinger's early plays he considered dire, but he was somewhat more favorable toward Lenz, even if he considered that the latter had gone astray and had missed the opportunity to develop his talents. In the 1770s it was to Goethe's work that Lessing responded most intensively. He was an enthusiastic reader of *Werther,* only wishing that there could be a skeptical warning for the benefit of younger readers. He was much preoccupied by *Götz von Berlichingen* — and initially disapproved of the play. He read Goethe's shorter works, too. "Prometheus," which caused such public outrage, he declared an admirable poem. At the beginning of the 1780s Lessing's verdict on Goethe was approving and admiring, rather than negative. There were even occasional positive judgments on the other Sturm und Drang authors. Klinger, he said, must be matured to become a fine wine. Lessing's brother Karl regularly kept him informed about the new plays by the younger generation of writers. As far as they were concerned, Lessing continued to be a figure of literary authority who stood above criticism. The judgments of the younger generation on performances of *Emilia Galotti* were as positive as their reviews of the published text. The assembled members of the Göttinger Hainbund toasted Lessing, while those they considered a danger to public morals, such as Wieland or Voltaire, were roundly condemned. Lessing became friends with Friedrich "Maler" Müller, and throughout his life Müller retained his great respect for Lessing.

Even if Lessing was restrained as a critic of the younger generation and only communicated his judgments in private, however, there remain, despite many apparent points of agreement, several theoretical differences between them. The writers of the Sturm und Drang no longer accepted the poetics of Aristotle as a model, any more than they were willing to accept unquestioningly the supposed exemplary quality of the ancients. On the other hand, Lessing had drawn attention to Shakespeare in his *Briefe, die neueste Litteratur betreffend* (no. 17) and later in his *Hamburgische Dramaturgie,* and Shakespeare was *the* model of the Sturm und Drang writers, while Lessing's *Laokoon* (1766) became their secret literary manifesto. If Lessing was criticized at all, writers such as

Lenz and Matthias Claudius formulated their criticisms indirectly so that only the cognoscenti noticed the polemic. With respect to the aesthetics of reception in the Sturm und Drang, most of the writers of the younger generation went beyond Lessing's demand for moderation. The unleashing of passion will be discussed below as a characteristic of their work. The relationship between Lessing and the Sturm und Drang does not, as has often been supposed, demonstrate the discontinuity of German literature: on the contrary, it is a fine example of the formation of tradition across generations. In Lenz's *Pandämonium Germanicum* Klopstock and Lessing appear as father figures of the new writing and are allowed to express critical views.[11]

Surprisingly, the friction between the important representatives of the Enlightenment and the younger generation of authors was less intense than that between the latter and the advocates of a new conception of literature prepared by Karl Philipp Moritz and formulated by Goethe and Schiller in the 1790s. Only Lenz occasionally — for example, in his review of *Werther* — developed a train of thought that granted the fiction of the novel its own legitimacy and, thus, looked forward to the idea of the autonomy of art, according to which literature was to have absolutely no obligation to please or to be useful. The reception of the work of art that was intended by the writers of the Sturm und Drang — that it should encourage action, sentiment, or passion — contradicted the primarily contemplative reception of the autonomous work of art, which was supposed to be complete in itself. If a work of art was not to be determined by any external expectations, it was self-evident that the author was abandoning the claim to affect social reality by means of literary activity. The distance that, as a result of this theory, Goethe and Schiller developed to the products of their own youth led to their negative judgments on their early works — for example, in the case of Goethe in *Dichtung und Wahrheit*.[12]

A comparable construction of the period by means of negation is to be found in Tieck's introduction to his edition of Lenz.[13] It has the title "Goethe und seine Zeit" (Goethe and His Age), and Lenz is mentioned at the beginning in terms of his relationship to Goethe and then again only in a brief concluding section. Tieck devotes his detailed introduction almost exclusively to a reconstruction of the young Goethe's writing, for which he uses the metaphor of spring. Tieck leaps back over the works that appeared after Goethe's journey to Italy (1786–88) and finds in the Sturm und Drang the real sources of the Romantic tradition to which he himself belonged, a new literature that came into being after the French Revolution. The Classical works of Goethe that had exemplary value for Friedrich Schlegel and Novalis — *Wilhelm Meisters Lehr-jahre* (Wilhelm Meister's Apprenticeship Years, 1795–96), *Iphigenie,* and *Faust* — play no part in the genealogy that Tieck constructed with such radical partisanship and such violence to history. Tieck's introduction is, thus, a rare example of a period being constituted by negation at a distance of several decades. Bearing in mind Büchner's rediscovery of Lenz in the 1830s, the way Tieck harks back to the 1770s and the young Goethe and excludes the Classical period is one of the most unusual examples of reception contributing to the construction of a literary period.[14]

The Teleological Model
of the "German Movement"

The tendency to place rationalism and irrationalism in fundamental opposition to each other in the construction of literary history goes back to the positivists, but in the first decades of the twentieth century it became the basis for the only model that was used to distinguish the periods Enlightenment, Sturm und Drang, Classicism, and Romanticism. The term *rationalism* was used to characterize the Enlightenment as a period, while the Sentimental style of writing was traditionally understood as an opposition movement running counter to the rationalist Enlightenment. The essence of irrationalism, however, was to be found in the Sturm und Drang. At the beginning of the time when the methodology of the history of ideas dominated German studies, this scheme was given a political dimension and, at the same time, refined as a means for identifying literary periods. Herman Nohl was the first to use the concept of a "German Movement," and he did so in his lectures on the history of philosophy, beginning in 1908–9, which built on Wilhelm Dilthey's inaugural lecture in Basel discussing the three generations in the history of ideas in Germany between 1770 and 1830. Nohl was attempting to characterize the unity of a movement in the history of ideas that began in 1770 with the Sturm und Drang and that then revealed itself in early Classicism, continued without a break into Romanticism, and was finally reflected in the emerging systems of idealist philosophy. With this strong irrationalist movement, he claimed, the peculiarly German spirit had differentiated itself from the Enlightenment, which was oriented toward western Europe, and developed its own identity. After 1912 nationalist anthropology (*"Deutschkunde"*) included as one of its major goals the domination of German Studies by nationalist ideas, and in 1933 its representatives proudly referred to their particular contribution to the setting up of the "new State" under Adolf

Hitler, adopting the anti-Enlightenment gestures and the periodization of the German Movement. Heinz Kindermann was one of the most vociferous advocates of this thesis. He titled a study about the beginnings of the German Movement from Pietism to Romanticism with a phrase taken from the tradition of mysticism, "Durchbruch der Seele" (breakthrough of the soul).[15] This breakthrough, he argued, had been achieved in Pietism and the Sturm und Drang, which he described as the forecourt of the period of maturity in which the two peaks, Classicism and Romanticism, had found their fulfillment. This assessment and periodization of the Sturm und Drang from a teleological and nationalist point of view was retained into the postwar period. It is found in the four-volume study by Hermann August Korff, *Geist der Goethezeit* (Spirit of the Age of Goethe), a formulation rich in material and in quotations. Conceived as a pure history of ideas, the first volume, dealing with the Sturm und Drang,[16] appeared in 1923 and was revised in 1954. The literature of the Sturm und Drang is here located within a single major unit of the history of ideas. Korff argues that its first period, a cultural crisis, sees the breakthrough of the humanity of the age of Goethe. He sees the Sturm und Drang as apparently questioning the very principle of culture by confronting it radically with the ideal of nature (31). The shock that culture received after 1770 was not rooted, as the Enlightenment was, in the temporal but, like nature, in the eternal. At its deepest and most spiritual this was, for Korff, a religious shock (99–100).

It was a long time before histories of German literature abandoned this form of periodization, which was so closely associated with the history of Germany up to 1945. The tradition of a German Movement was no longer called by that name because of the denazification of German studies, but it nevertheless played a part in many presentations. The best-selling histories of literature that dominated the market in the postwar years were written by scholars such as Gerhard Fricke and Fritz Martini, who were suspended from their teaching duties because of their Nazi pasts.

Marxist Corrections:
The Continuity of the Enlightenment

Not until the middle of the 1960s was there a fundamental revision of the established periodization and assessment of the Sturm und Drang. Only then was the sharp contrast between an Enlightenment culture based on reason (rationalism) and a victorious culture of feeling (irrationalism) abandoned. The contributions to literary histories of the Marxists Georg Lukács and Werner Krauss produced a new overall interpretation of the Enlightenment and Sturm und Drang, although, admittedly, the categories Lukács uses to structure modern German literature need their own explanation and can only be understood within the context of a Marxist approach.[17] One of Lukács's main ideas is that the struggle against the miserable conditions in Germany was "progressive"; he calls "reactionary" the attempt to perpetuate these conditions in any form whatsoever. Lukács attacks the reinterpretation of the literary Enlightenment, which, he argues, was at best valid up to Lessing, after whom it was replaced by a revolt of feeling against reason. He believes that an attempt had been made to deny 1789, the peak of the Enlightenment, by seeking a conservative counterweight in the form of an irrationalist Romanticism that began with Hamann. Lukács understands the Sturm und Drang explicitly as a political force, inasmuch as the reason advocated by the Enlightenment proved its worth not least in the will to use criticism to negate inherited political forms. He wrote repeatedly about the lack of substance of the "Verstand-Gefühl-Konstruktion" (reason/feeling construct) that was revealed even in the work of Lessing, who set the totality of the bourgeois world of feeling and reason against the totality of the feudal absolutist world of feeling and reason (24–25). The unity of the Enlightenment movement consisted, according to Lukács, in German citizens gaining self-awareness and coming to the realization that it was necessary to struggle against petty absolutism and its ideology. The Enlightenment gave expression to the essence of the emerging bourgeois society, its revolutionary mission, which was encapsulated in the new ideology and literature emerging from the bourgeoisie. Lukács scarcely uses the term "Sturm und Drang." For him it is self-evident that the literature of the 1770s was an integral part of the development of the Enlightenment.

Even if this concept was lacking in subtle literary-historical distinctions, it had the virtue of offering a radical counterproposal that threw into doubt the periodization proposed by scholars in the first half of the century. Krauss, the distinguished theoretician and scholar of French culture, went further in the same direction. In his writings on the Enlightenment he analyzed both the German and the French traditions, for comparative literature was one of his specialties. In his account the Sturm und Drang follows after the critical direction of the Enlightenment, and he understands its essential features, reduced to a rather crude formula, as the cult of genius and Sentimentality. What are important are his general observations on the periodization of the Sturm und Drang in the context of the Enlightenment and his view that the Enlightenment did not come to an end with the Sturm und Drang but entered a new dynamic stage that, however, in no way changed, let alone reversed, its main goals. Krauss even goes so far as to see the Sturm und Drang as the fulfillment of the Enlightenment, rather than as an anti-Enlightenment movement. The Marxist perspective that Krauss adopted when redefining the relationship between Enlightenment and Sturm und Drang ascribes an important role to social processes. In the Sturm und Drang, he argues, the German Enlightenment formed a vanguard that challenged all the positions and values of the existing feudal society with a maximum of explosive force. The cult of the genius and the extreme insistence on individual personality embodied, for Krauss, the will to struggle, through which social groups, classes, and peoples constitute themselves.

The volume *Sturm und Drang: Erläuterungen zur deutschen Literatur* (Sturm und Drang: Elucidations of German Literature), produced by an East German collective, the first edition of which appeared in 1958 and the seventh in 1988, was intended, above all, for students.[18] Its high sales are, no doubt, also due to the popularity of the series among West German students in the 1970s and 1980s. The best-qualified literary historians of the GDR were asked for contributions, and where necessary the work of people described as "fortschrittliche bürgerliche Literaturwissenschaftler" (progressive bourgeois literary scholars) was also included. The chapters were structured according to genre, and there was nothing available in West Germany that was comparable with it in terms of range or detail. Irrespective of their Marxist basis, many passages must be read with skepticism simply because of our knowledge of the history of the idea of the Sturm und Drang. Once again, the starting point is the concept of a literary revolution, which since the time of the positivists had been used frequently and, for the most part, dubiously. The connotations of political revolution are intentional. As long as the concept is used often enough, so it seems, the adjective "literary" can be dropped. The authors, therefore, suggest, against their better judgment, that there is a necessary transition of the meaning to the realm of the political. The definition of the Sturm und Drang movement as a new phase of the Enlightenment comes straight from Marxist dogma:

> Es war die Aufgabe der Literatur als Bestandteil des werdenden Überbaus über der werdenden kapitalistischen Basis, dafür zu kämpfen, daß diese Basis zum Durchbruch gelangen konnte. Das Mißverhältnis bestand aber gerade darin, daß diese Basis nur keimhaft war und daß bis zu ihrem Durchbruch noch sehr lange Zeit vergehen sollte. (20)[19]

Although there are signs, even down to the formulations, that the authors are responding to "bourgeois" models of periodization (for example, the term "*Durchbruch*" taken from the title of Kindermann's book), they are thoroughly critical in their assessment of the Sturm und Drang. What they call the compromises the Sturm und Drang writers made with the aristocracy, and also the anarchic belief of the Sturm und Drang that they could take matters into their own hands, reveal for them the ideological weaknesses of the bourgeois intelligentsia of the time, while their orientation toward the lowest social classes and toward plebeian and peasant forces represented, on the other hand, a step forward in the direction of realism and the inclusion of a perspective based on real social and historical conditions (22). Counted among the slogans of the movement are such terms as human rights and rational thought, but also sensibility ("*Empfindung*"), which in the Sturm und Drang is intensified into feeling ("*Gefühl*") (23). Considering the way the authors use the catch phrase "literary revolution" at the beginning of their attempt to define and locate the Sturm und Drang, it is surprising that as they develop their arguments they use the idea of the "*Volk*" to specify typical positions of the Sturm und Drang, with no attempt to consider the way that these are mediated in literature. For example, they talk of the struggle for an alliance between bourgeois intellectuals and peasants and plebeians, or the struggle for positive action. These two positions mark off for them the territory within which the energy of the Sturm und Drang was to develop and, equally, to find its limits (30).

Arguments such as these ascribe to the writers of the Sturm und Drang a level of political consciousness and an intention to engage in social praxis that, in fact, existed only in a rudimentary fashion. The oft-cited alliance between intellectuals and plebeians is based on an early comment by Herder that occurs only at one point and is never repeated or varied in of his other writings (*H-SW*, 32: 51). By its dependence on political categories, the Marxist interpretation of the Sturm und Drang has constructed a trend that, at best, uses literary texts for occasional support. To the best of my knowledge, not a single study that has appeared since the unification of Germany has continued to espouse basic Marxist positions.

Attempts to Make Distinctions

A non-German Germanist such as Roy Pascal could be expected to produce a study of the Sturm und Drang that, without any Marxist objectives, would abandon traditional German schemes.[20] He rejects the teleology of positivism, the history of ideas, and nationalism, and attempts a presentation of the most important principles of the Sturm und

Drang and their development. His attempt is to describe not a complete system but, rather, an aspiration. He is convincing in his restriction of the movement to the years 1770 to 1778 and his allocation of Schiller to a special position.

In 1978 appeared a collection of essays edited by Walter Hinck that brought together the results of recent scholarship in all important areas.[21] The editor's preface and an essay by Christoph Siegrist on the question of periodization examine recent interpretations of the Sturm und Drang. Siegrist interprets the mutual relationship of Enlightenment, Sentimentalism, and Sturm und Drang in terms of their complementarity.[22] According to this perspective, the Sturm und Drang does not run counter to the Enlightenment but is a complementary variant of it. He rejects both the thesis that the Sturm und Drang was basically irrationalist and also the idealization of the Sturm und Drang as the culmination of the Enlightenment that was to be found in the literary scholarship of the GDR. This volume has formed the basis for many subsequent studies, which, following the increased interest in histories of literature, tend to begin with the eighteenth century, so that their treatment of the question of periodization has taken the new conclusions into account.

By the end of the 1970s something of a consensus had been reached on this matter. No one returned to older models. There even seemed to be a convergence of views with regard to the positions adopted by East German scholars in many individual studies. It was, therefore, all the more surprising when Peter Müller questioned this consensus in 1978 in his introduction to a two-volume collection of Sturm und Drang texts.[23] This substantial (124-page) essay, which attempts to avoid crass generalizations, returns to Goethe's designation of the period as a literary revolution. This metaphor, Müller argues, establishes the links with a complex transnational process of development and emphasizes the way in which the young Goethe and the writers of the Sturm und Drang were part of a set of prerevolutionary events. The importance of Rousseau and Diderot for the younger generation of authors is, for Müller, evidence of this hypothesis. In the continuity of Enlightenment literature, on which he continues to insist, he nevertheless sees a strong element of discontinuity. Since, however, when Goethe wrote about a literary revolution he did not exclude critical aspects, and since the Marxist-Leninist concept of revolution was, in any case, unthinkable without a revolution of the economic base, Müller decides to retain the term "Sturm und Drang" as the description of a period.

In 1980 Andreas Huyssen published a "commentary" in which he discusses in some detail questions relating to scholarly research into the

Sturm und Drang and the problems pertaining to its periodization; but when dealing with particular texts, he restricts himself to the drama.[24] He adopts Müller's hypothesis that the relationship between Enlightenment and Sturm und Drang was dominated by a discontinuity, which, he says, can be seen most easily in the drama and lyric poetry but is scarcely perceptible in sociohistorical developments. Huyssen argues for a position that excludes neither approach: it would be as wrong to speak of uninterrupted continuity as it would to speak of a sharp opposition. He thus understands the Sturm und Drang as offering the first radical critique of the middle-class Enlightenment, in the course of which it expressed both its links with the Enlightenment and also its criticism of the presumptuousness of the Enlightenment in claiming to be an authority above other authorities.

With his 1985 volume on the Sturm und Drang in the series "Wege der Forschung" (Paths of Investigation) Manfred Wacker had the opportunity to present the various strands of the latest debates, but for unexplained reasons the book only appeared after years of preparation and inevitably lagged far behind current discussions.[25] In his introduction Wacker is able to summarize the more recent positions up to Müller and report on the arguments about the periodization of the Sturm und Drang that had been published in the preceding years. He comments on Müller's avoidance of overgeneralizations but criticizes him for a certain arbitrariness in following different levels of argumentation (5). There is, however, no discussion of developments beyond Huyssen.

The example of several histories of literature shows that, by and large, the rejection of older teleological models of periodization is complete. Modern histories of literature are distinguished only by slight shifts of emphasis. As early as 1966 Gerhard Kaiser had drawn conclusions from recent scholarly debates.[26] He begins by characterizing the Enlightenment and the Sentimental style and identifying the middle classes as the social base of culture. The middle phase of the Enlightenment he presents as a literature "between" Enlightenment and Sentimentalism, and this discussion is followed by his sketch of Sturm und Drang literature. Kaiser takes as his starting point the relative unity of the Enlightenment as an epoch but allows for a complicated network of crosscurrents above the undercurrent that is the Enlightenment. In his 1976 revision of this study the principles he adopted are even more explicit.[27] Enlightenment and Sturm und Drang, he argues, cannot be understood simply as opposites. Their relationship is more that between evolution and a revolution that adds an explosive fulfillment and transformation of the old. Kaiser pays attention to sociological aspects when discussing the central ideas of the Sturm und Drang but is, in general, more indebted to the history of ideas in his approach. Viktor Žmegač's multivolume history of Germany literature includes a portrait of the Sturm und Drang by Hans-G. Winter under the unusual heading "Anti-Classicism."[28] He, too, integrates the Sturm und Drang into the Enlightenment, interpreting it as the literature of a small group of writers. He then returns to the metaphor of revolution and asserts that the Sturm und Drang did represent a revolution in the literary field.

In 1988 Ehrhard Bahr produced in collaboration with American scholars a three-volume history of German literature; here the Sturm und Drang is discussed under the heading "Late Enlightenment (or Sturm und Drang)."[29] The important quotations on which Krauss also relied are placed at the beginning of the chapter to justify the title: the Sturm und Drang is not to be understood as a linear development, and Bahr argues that the term "Late Enlightenment" is more suitable for bringing together a variety of contemporary tendencies of the age. Here, too, the accent is placed on the continuity of the Enlightenment.

The most substantial modern history of literature, the new version of Richard Newald's *Ende der Aufklärung und Vorbereitung der Klassik: 1750 bis 1832* (End of the Enlightenment and Preparation for Classicism: 1750 to 1832, 1957), includes a section by Sven Aage Jørgensen on the history of scholarly work on the Sturm und Drang in which he underlines the distance of modern scholars from older concepts such as "German Movement" and "Age of Goethe" and emphasizes the radicalism and critical force of the Sturm und Drang.[30] Here, too, he accepts Kaiser's formula that the relationship between Enlightenment and Sturm und Drang is that between evolution and revolution. He sees the Sturm und Drang as a youth movement. In this volume there also appears for the first time within a major presentation of the Sturm und Drang an attempt (by Per Øhrgaard) to distinguish different phases of the period between 1770 and 1776.

New Hypotheses

The Sturm und Drang has suffered from the decline of scholarly interest in the Enlightenment since the beginning of the 1990s. The positions outlined above have frequently been repeated. Only rarely has there been any exploration of new aspects that might have been introduced into the debates as a result of new methodological models. It is, for example, surprising that, despite the relatively widespread reception of Harold Bloom's theory of an "anxiety of influence" linked to an Oedipal conflict between fathers and sons, there has been no attempt to make use of it in the Anglo-Saxon world; his concept could long ago have been applied to the literature of the Sturm und Drang. Older studies of the generational problem or on the character of the Sturm und Drang as a youth movement could have played a part here, too.

Early in the 1990s Matthias Luserke and Reiner Marx presented new hypotheses in connection with research into the Sturm und Drang.[31] Linking hypotheses from Freud, Foucault, and Elias, they interpret the letters S and D (Sturm und Drang) as a coded reference to sexuality and discursivity (133). They understand the internal criticism of the Enlightenment along the lines of the formulation I have suggested, as a displacement of the critique of middle-class norms and forms of consciousness away from the Enlightenment critique of the court and the aristocracy and onto the advocates of the Enlightenment themselves. A middle-class identity was for these authors no longer a utopia but a reality that produced repression (140). Caught as it is in the dialectic of intensification and internal criticism, the Sturm und Drang must be understood as both emancipatory and compensatory (142). Finally, they interpret individuation and individuality as the response of the literary innovators of the 1770s to the process of embourgeoisement and the sexual repression associated with it in the eighteenth century. This makes it possible to offer an interpretation of the right of the individual to his or her passions and, at the same time, of the claim of the genius to uniqueness (145–50). Admittedly, these theses are rather simplified in the handy formula "S and D," but in their discussions of individual cases the authors succeed in incorporating many other elements of Sturm und Drang literature.

In his synthesis of current discussions of the Sturm und Drang, Roland Krebs has argued for the introduction of the concept of a literary avant-garde to replace a concept of revolution that has become rather questionable.[32] In the spirit of comparative literary history, he refers to an important study by Michel Delon, the expert in French studies who has pursued the history of the idea of energy in the period from 1770 to 1820.[33] This idea, Krebs argues, can be adapted and used as a central concept of the Sturm und Drang in the context of action, the "vita activa," and, in general, for an aesthetic based on action-oriented words.

In my study of Sentimentalism I have referred to the role of the passions in a definition of Sentimentalism and Sturm und Drang that pays due attention to the distinctions that need to be made.[34] A more detailed examination of the passions in the drama of the Sturm und Drang could also be of use, and Luserke has undertaken such an examination in a chapter of his second doctoral thesis.[35] He reaches the conclusion that the abandonment of control over the passions could only be expressed and explored in discursive form, that is to say, in the discourses of aesthetic theory and fiction. Ralph-Rainer Wuthenow is not merely concerned with the Sturm und Drang when he analyzes the various forms of passion in the philosophy and literature of the seventeenth and eighteenth centuries.[36] It is true that his study contains several chapters on the functions of the passions and the critique of rationalism in Hamann, Herder, Goethe, Lenz, and Heinse; but he declines to go beyond individual analyses and, for example, explain the difference between Sentimentalism and Sturm und Drang in terms of the release of passions in the discourses of the 1770s.

Recently, in a monograph on the Sturm und Drang, Luserke has extended the theses he developed with Reiner Marx on "S and D" and, at the same time, emphasized the function of passion in the texts of the Sturm und Drang, focusing on the distinction between Sentimentalism and the Sturm und Drang.[37] He restricts the latter to the decade from 1770 to 1780, without further distinctions, and insists that it is not a revolutionary movement. A detailed presentation of the history of the concept of the Sturm und Drang adds to the historical precision of this study, and in the assessment of precursors and influences it makes use of the latest scholarship.

The Philosophy of the Sturm und Drang; or, The Abandonment of Theory

The dissertation of Georg W. Bertram adds no substantial insights, despite the expectations its title raises, but the approach adopted by this most recent attempt to characterize the period is instructive.[38] The author is well aware of the eccentricity of his starting point when he interprets the Sturm und Drang in terms of modernity. He hopes to be able to bring this endeavor to a conclusion by ascribing to the period a perspective based on undifferentiated rationality, aware that, although he is unable to ascribe a unity to the period, he may be able to create the image of a discursive mechanism (8). Aware that the writers of the Sturm und Drang left no explicit programmatic statement of their intentions, the author nevertheless makes bold to discover what he calls a "philosophy of the Sturm und Drang" in texts dealing with the philosophy of language, the theory of history and the theater, and so forth. In this way, he argues, there emerges a context of nondifferentiation and discursive nonconstitution (9). But the Sturm und Drang also participates in the major themes of the philosophical discourse of modernity, namely, in questions relating to a connection between rationality and discursivity and to a connection between language and a framework of aesthetic values as guarantors of differentiation. Admittedly, he argues, a framework of aesthetic values is not stabilized in the discourse of the Sturm und Drang (9). The fluctuations in the reception of the Sturm und Drang determine its presence or absence in historical consciousness, and this phenomenon is itself one of the elements that must be included in what he calls a "panoramic interpretation" of the Sturm und Drang (11). The author too frequently relies on older secondary literature; he also thinks that he is able to achieve his goal by limiting himself strictly to the Strasbourg texts of Herder, Goethe, and Lenz. It is in these, he claims, that the specific identity of the period can be discerned. In the end Bertram is concerned with the "mechanism of the Sturm und Drang," which can evidently only be approached by a radical restriction of the body of texts under discussion. As a contribution to the philosophy of history it is remarkable that it fails to make use of three-quarters of the relevant material — for example, Kant. This, of course, also means that it fails to make use of most of the attempts that have so far been made to understand the period by discriminating among its individual discourses. The reference to Foucault's concept of "mechanism" ("*dispositif*") seems to fill a gap rather than to be a positive step forward.

With Bertram the discussion is set at so high a level that it fails to do justice to the facts of the historical epoch.[39] At the other extreme the synthesizing conception of the Sturm und Drang disintegrates into a number of disparate studies. In 1997 Bodo Plachta and Winfried Woesler presented a volume of essays with the title *Sturm und Drang: Geistiger Aufbruch 1770–1790 im Spiegel der Literatur* (Sturm und Drang: Spiritual Breakthrough 1770–1790 as Reflected in Literature).[40] Not only the generous time span but also the imprecise and apparently intentional archaism of the phrase "geistiger Aufbruch" (spiritual breakthrough) in the title shows that the arguments will be bounded by the traditional parameters. It is unclear as to where the spirit will emerge or where the transition of which the authors speak leads. Individual contributions, particularly those in comparative literature, are certainly useful, but, since this volume is the first for a long while to have tried to represent the latest scholarship on individual aspects of the Sturm und Drang, it is unfortunate that it missed the opportunity to establish new parameters.[41] The same is, unfortunately, also the case with a study guide for students by Ulrich Karthaus, that has just appeared.[42] It avoids a detailed discussion of problematic aspects and, instead of a subtle periodization, introduces Reinhart Koselleck's concept of the transitional period ("Sattelzeit"), which stands for the end of the early modern history but is not easily applied to the Sturm und Drang. The volume contains a wealth of references and information about individual texts, but there is scarcely any sign of an attempt to formulate the current state of scholarship. What is needed is a detailed critical review and assessment of the results of scholarly work on the Sturm und Drang. By contrast with other periods and trends within modern literary history, there is no such survey of the Sturm und Drang.

Translated by David Hill

Notes

[1] See Gerhard Krämling, "Periode, Periodisierung," in *Historisches Wörterbuch der Philosophie,* vol. 7, ed. Rudolf Eisler (Darmstadt: Wissenschaftliche Buchgesellschaft, 1989), cols. 259–61.

[2] See Reinhart Koselleck, "Das achtzehnte Jahrhundert als Beginn der Neuzeit," in *Epochenschwelle und Epochenbewußtsein,* eds. Reinhart Herzog and Reinhart Koselleck, Poetik und Hermeneutik, 12 (Munich: Fink, 1987), 269–82.

[3] See my introduction to *G-MA,* 1.1: 756, and, in greater detail, "Die deutsche Literatur des Sturm und Drang," in *Europäische Aufklärung, II. Teil,* ed. Heinz-Joachim Müllenbrock, Neues Handbuch der Literaturwissenschaft, 12 (Wiesbaden: AULA-Verlag, 1984), 327–78.

[4] "We drifted about on many a highway and byway, and thus, too, in several respects, the ground was prepared for that German literary revolution of which we were witnesses and to which, consciously or unconsciously, willingly or unwillingly, we relentlessly made our contribution."

[5] Georg Gottfried Gervinus, *Geschichte der poetischen National-Literatur der Deutschen,* part 4: *Von Gottsched's Zeiten bis zu Göthe's Jugend,* 2nd ed. (Leipzig: Engelmann, 1843), 413, 7, 10; Hermann Hettner, *Geschichte der deutschen Literatur im achtzehnten Jahrhundert,* vol. 2 (1869; Berlin: Aufbau, 1961), 14, 7, 15.

[6] "Sturm und Drang! Age of Genius! Original geniuses! These are the names that are commonly used to celebrate or to deride the German literary revolution and its supporters" (Wilhelm Scherer, *Geschichte der Deutschen Literatur* [1883; rpt., Berlin: Knaur, n.d.], 550). Compare the survey by Rainer Rosenberg, "'Aufklärung' in der deutschen Literaturgeschichtsschreibung des 19. Jahrhunderts," in *Aufklärungsforschung in Deutschland,* ed. Holger Dainat and Wilhelm Voßkamp, *Euphorion* (Beiheft) 32 (1999): 7–20.

[7] Friedrich Gundolf, *Shakespeare und der deutsche Geist* (1914; Godesberg: Helmut Küpper, 1947).

[8] "A particular movement with particular thoughts or feelings . . . an urgency, a whirlwind in the German spirit, dragging with it everything that did not offer deliberate opposition. According to their individual temperaments, the various members

of the circle took from Goethe's writing whatever suited them best and transformed it, that is, they debased it, distorted it, or exaggerated it."

[9] Paul Hankamer, *Deutsche Literaturgeschichte,* 3rd ed. (Bonn: Bonner Buchgemeinde, 1952).

[10] See Wilfried Barner, "Über das Negieren von Tradition. Zur Typologie literaturprogrammatischer Epochenwenden in Deutschland," in *Epochenschwelle und Epochenbewußtsein,* ed. Reinhart Herzog and Reinhart Koselleck, Poetik und Hermeneutik, 12 (Munich: Fink, 1987), 3–51.

[11] See my "Lessing im Sturm und Drang," in *Lessing und die Literaturrevolten nach 1770: 37. Kamenzer Lessing-Tage 1998,* Erbepflege in Kamenz, 18 (Kamenz: Lessing-Museum, 1999), 11–35.

[12] See my "Ästhetische Autonomie als Norm der Weimarer Klassik," in *Normen und Werte,* ed. Friedrich Hiller (Heidelberg: Winter, 1982), 130–50.

[13] *Gesammelte Schriften von J. M. R. Lenz,* 3 vols., ed. Ludwig Tieck (Berlin: Reimer, 1828).

[14] See my essay "Tiecks 'vernachlässigter Lenz,'" in *Jakob Michael Reinhold Lenz: Vom Sturm und Drang zur Moderne,* ed. Andreas Meier (Heidelberg: Winter, 2001), 37–46.

[15] Heinz Kindermann, *Durchbruch der Seele: Literarhistorische Studie über die Anfänge der "Deutschen Bewegung" vom Pietismus zur Romantik,* Danziger Beiträge, 1 (Danzig: Kafemann, 1928), 13. See also Mechthild Kirsch, "Heinz Kindermann — ein Wiener Germanist und Theaterwissenschaftler," in *Zeitenwechsel: Germanistische Literaturwissenschaft vor und nach 1945,* ed. Wilfried Barner and Christoph König (Frankfurt am Main: Fischer, 1996), 47–59.

[16] Hermann August Korff, *Geist der Goethezeit,* 5 vols. (Leipzig: Koehler & Ameland, 1954–57). Vol. 5 contains indices.

[17] Georg Lukács, *Skizze einer Geschichte der neueren deutschen Literatur* (Berlin: Aufbau, 1953; rpt., Neuwied & Berlin: Luchterhand, 1963), 21; the volume originally appeared in two parts with the titles *Deutsche Literatur im Zeitalter des Imperialismus* (1945) and *Fortschritt und Reaktion in der deutschen Literatur* (1947). Werner Krauss, "Zur Periodisierung Aufklärung, Sturm und Drang, Weimarer Klassik," in his *Perspektiven und Probleme: Zur französischen und deutschen Aufklärung und andere Aufsätze* (Neuwied & Berlin: Luchterhand, 1965), 234–65; rpt. in *Sturm und Drang,* ed. Manfred Wacker, Wege der Forschung, 559 (Darmstadt: Wissenschaftliche Buchgesellschaft, 1985), 67–95.

[18] Kollektiv für Literaturgeschichte im Volkseigenen Verlag Volk und Wissen, *Sturm und Drang: Erläuterungen zur deutschen Literatur,* 7th ed. (Berlin: Volk und Wissen, 1988).

[19] "It was the task of literature, as an element in the evolving superstructure above an evolving capitalist base, to struggle for the breakthrough of this base. The disparity, however, consisted in the fact that the base only existed in embryonic form and that it would be a long time before it fully came into being."

[20] Roy Pascal, *The German Sturm und Drang* (Manchester: Manchester UP, 1953).

[21] Walter Hinck, ed., *Sturm und Drang: Ein literaturwissenschaftliches Studienbuch* (Kronberg: Athenäum, 1978).

[22] Christoph Siegrist, "Aufklärung und Sturm und Drang: Gegeneinander oder Nebeneinander?" in *Sturm und Drang: Ein literaturwissenschaftliches Studienbuch*, 1–13.

[23] Peter Müller, ed., *Sturm und Drang: Weltanschauliche und ästhetische Schriften*, 2 vols. (Berlin: Aufbau, 1978).

[24] Andreas Huyssen, *Drama des Sturm und Drang: Kommentar zu einer Epoche* (Munich: Winkler, 1980).

[25] Manfred Wacker, ed., *Sturm und Drang*, Wege der Forschung, 559 (Darmstadt: Wissenschaftliche Buchgesellschaft, 1985).

[26] Gerhard Kaiser, *Von der Aufklärung bis zum Sturm und Drang 1730–1785* (Gütersloh: Mohn, 1966).

[27] Gerhard Kaiser, *Aufklärung, Empfindsamkeit, Sturm und Drang* (Munich: Francke, 1976).

[28] Hans-G. Winter, "Antiklassizismus: Sturm und Drang," in *Geschichte der deutschen Literatur vom 18. Jahrhundert bis zur Gegenwart*, ed. Viktor Žmegač, vol. 1.1 (Königstein: Athenäum, 1978), 194–256. On the matter of Winter's unacknowledged debt to Kaiser, see Kaiser, "Kein Kommentar zu einer Literaturgeschichte," *Euphorion* 73 (1979): 206–18.

[29] Ehrhard Bahr, "Aufklärung," in *Geschichte der deutschen Literatur. Kontinuität und Veränderung. Vom Mittelalter bis zur Gegenwart*, ed. Ehrhard Bahr, vol. 2: *Von der Aufklärung bis zum Vormärz* (Tübingen: Francke, 1988), 1–128.

[30] Sven Aage Jørgensen et al., *Aufklärung, Sturm und Drang, frühe Klassik 1740–1789* (Munich: Beck, 1990).

[31] Matthias Luserke and Reiner Marx, "Die Anti-Läuffer: Thesen zur SuD-Forschung oder Gedanken neben dem Totenkopf auf der Toilette des Denkers," *Lenz-Jahrbuch: Sturm-und-Drang-Studien* 2 (1992): 126–50.

[32] Roland Krebs, "Le *Sturm und Drang* comme avant-garde littéraire," in *Le Sturm und Drang: une rupture?* ed. Marita Gilli, Laboratoire Littérature et Histoire des pays de langues européennes, 42, *Annales littéraires de l'Université de Besançon* 597 (1996): 11–23. See also Krebs, "Herder, Goethe und die ästhetische Diskussion um 1770: Zu den Begriffen 'énergie' und 'Kraft' in der französischen und deutschen Poetik," *Goethe-Jahrbuch* 112 (1995): 83–96.

[33] Michel Delon, *L'idée d'énergie au tournant des Lumières: 1770–1820* (Paris: Presses universitaires de France, 1988).

[34] Sauder, *Empfindsamkeit*, vol. 1: *Voraussetzungen und Elemente* (Stuttgart: Metzler, 1974), 133–37.

[35] Luserke, *Die Bändigung der wilden Seele: Literatur und Leidenschaft in der Aufklärung* (Stuttgart & Weimar: Metzler, 1995), 223–36.

[36] Ralph-Rainer Wuthenow, *Die gebändigte Flamme: Zur Wiederentdeckung der Leidenschaften im Zeitalter der Vernunft*, Beiträge zur neueren Literaturgeschichte, 3.178 (Heidelberg: Winter, 2000).

[37] Luserke, *Sturm und Drang: Autoren — Texte — Themen,* Universal-Bibliothek, 17602 (Stuttgart: Reclam, 1997).

[38] Georg W. Bertram, *Philosophie des Sturm und Drang: Eine Konstitution der Moderne* (Munich: Fink, 2000).

[39] Siegfried J. Schmidt, *Die Selbstorganisation des Sozialsystems Literatur im 18. Jahrhundert* (Frankfurt am Main: Suhrkamp, 1989) is not a history of literature but a study of literature as a social system and avoids discussing periods, mental structures, discourses, and texts except through secondary sources. Nevertheless, there is no justification for the exclusion of the Sturm und Drang. Surely the Sturm und Drang is part of the process of modernization and functional differentiation in the eighteenth century. On one occasion, when discussing subjective individualism, Schmidt refers rather journalistically to the Sturm und Drang as a brilliantly expressive and irrational intermezzo (263).

[40] Bodo Plachta and Winfried Woesler, eds., *Sturm und Drang: Geistiger Aufbruch 1770–1790 im Spiegel der Literatur* (Tübingen: Niemeyer, 1997).

[41] This criticism does not apply to the catalogue *Sturm und Drang: Freies Deutsches Hochstift,* ed. Christoph Perels (Frankfurt am Main: Goethe-Museum, 1988). The well-informed contributions to this volume were intended primarily as commentaries on particular sections of the exhibition.

[42] Ulrich Karthaus, *Sturm und Drang: Epoche — Werke — Wirkung* (Munich: Beck, 2000).

Works Cited

Primary Literature

Bach, Carl Philipp Emanuel. *Versuch über die wahre Art das Clavier zu spielen.* 2 vols. Leipzig: Breitkopf & Härtel, 1969.

Baumgarten, Alexander Gottlieb. *Metaphysik.* 2nd ed. Halle: Hemmerd, 1783.

Blackwell, Thomas. *Enquiry into the Life and Writings of Homer.* London: Oswald, 1735.

Blumenthal, Hermann, ed. *Zeitgenössische Rezensionen und Urteile über Goethes "Götz" und "Werther."* Berlin: Junker & Dünnhaupt, 1935.

Brecht, Bertolt. *Gesammelte Werke.* 20 vols. Frankfurt am Main: Suhrkamp, 1967.

Burney, Charles. *The Present State of Music in Germany, The Netherlands and United Provinces.* 2 vols. New York: Broude, 1969.

Campe, Johann Heinrich. *Wörterbuch der Deutschen Sprache, Erster Theil, A- bis -E.* Braunschweig: Schulbuchhandlung, 1807.

Denis, Michael. *Die Lieder Sineds des Barden.* Vienna: Trattner, 1772.

Diderot, Denis. *Œuvres esthétiques.* Ed. P. Vernière. Paris: Garnier, 1959.

Eberhard, Johann August. *Allgemeine Theorie des Denkens und Empfindens.* Berlin: Voß, 1776; rpt., Frankfurt am Main: Athenäum, 1972.

Engel, Johann Jakob. "Die Bildsäule." *Schriften.* Vol. 1, *1801–1806.* Frankfurt am Main: Athenäum, 1971, 335–55.

Gellert, Christian Fürchtegott. *Gesammelte Schriften.* Vol. 1, *Fabeln und Erzählungen.* Ed. Ulrike Bardt and Bernd Witte. Berlin & New York: de Gruyter, 2000.

Gerstenberg, Heinrich Wilhelm von. *Ugolino.* Ed. Christoph Siegrist. Universal-Bibliothek, 141. Stuttgart: Reclam, 1977.

Goethe, Johann Wolfgang. *Begegnungen und Gespräche.* 6 vols. to date. Eds. Ernst and Renate Grumach. Berlin: de Gruyter, 1965–.

———. *Briefe an Goethe. Hamburger Ausgabe.* 2 vols. Ed. Karl Robert Mandelkow. 2nd ed. Munich: Beck, 1982.

————. *Briefe: Hamburger Ausgabe.* 4 vols. Eds. Karl Robert Mandelkow and Bodo Morawe. Hamburg: Wegner, 1962–67.

————. *Collected Works.* 12 vols. Eds. Victor Lange et al. New York: Suhrkamp, 1983–89.

————. *Der junge Goethe: Neu bearbeitete Ausgabe in fünf Bänden.* Ed. Hanna Fischer-Lamberg. Berlin: de Gruyter, 1963–73.

————. *Sämtliche Werke: Briefe, Tagebücher und Gespräche.* 40 vols. Eds. Hendrik Birus et al. Frankfurt am Main: Deutscher Klassiker Verlag, 1985–99.

————. *Sämtliche Werke nach Epochen seines Schaffens: Münchner Ausgabe.* 21 vols. Eds. Karl Richter et al. Munich: Hanser, 1985–99.

————. *Werke: Berliner Ausgabe.* 23 vols. Eds. Siegfried Seidel. Berlin: Aufbau, 1961–78.

————. *Werke: Weimarer Ausgabe.* 143 vols. Weimar: Böhlau, 1887–1919.

Gräf, Hans Gerhard, ed. *Goethe über seine Dichtungen.* 2 parts, 6 vols. Frankfurt am Main: Rütten & Loening, 1901–14.

Hamann, Johann Georg. *Sämtliche Werke: Historisch-kritische Ausgabe.* 6 vols. Ed. Josef Nadler. Vienna: Herder, 1949–53.

Herder, Johann Gottfried. *Briefe: Gesamtausgabe, 1763–1803.* 10 vols. Eds. Karl-Heinz Hahn et al. Weimar: Böhlau, 1977–96.

————. *Herders sämmtliche Werke.* 33 vols. Ed. Bernhard Suphan. Berlin: Weidmann, 1877–1913.

————. *"Stimmen der Völker in Liedern": Volkslieder.* Ed. Heinz Rölleke. Universal-Bibliothek, 1371. Stuttgart: Reclam, 1975.

————. *Werke.* 24 vols. Eds. Heinrich Düntzer and Anton Eduard Wollheim da Fonseca. Berlin: Hempel, n.d.

————. *Werke.* 10 vols. Eds. Günter Arnold et al. Frankfurt am Main: Deutscher Klassiker Verlag, 1985–2000.

————, et al. *Von deutscher Art und Kunst.* Ed. Hans Dietrich Irmscher. Universal-Bibliothek, 7497. Stuttgart: Reclam, 1968.

Hume, David. *A Treatise of Human Nature.* Ed. L. A. Selby-Bigge. 2nd ed. Oxford & New York: Oxford UP, 1978.

Jacobi, Friedrich Heinrich. *Woldemar: Eine Seltenheit aus der Naturgeschichte.* Vol. 1. Flensburg: Leipzig, 1779.

Johnson, Samuel. *The Yale Edition of the Works of Samuel Johnson.* 16 vols. to date. New Haven: Yale UP, 1958–90.

Kant, Immanuel. *Werke in sechs Bänden.* 6 vols. Ed. Wilhelm Weischedel. Frankfurt am Main: Insel, 1960–64.

Kelletat, Alfred, ed. *Der Göttinger Hain.* Universal-Bibliothek, 8789–93. Stuttgart: Reclam, 1967.

Klinger, Friedrich Maximilian. *Plimplamplasko der hohe Geist.* Ed. Peter Pfaff. Heidelberg: Schneider, 1966.

———. *Sturm und Drang.* Ed. Jörg-Ulrich Fechner. Universal-Bibliothek, 248. Stuttgart: Reclam, 1970.

———. *Werke: Historisch-kritische Gesamtausgabe.* 6 vols. to date. Eds. Sander L. Gilman et al. Tübingen: Niemeyer, 1978–.

Klopstock, Friedrich Gottlieb. *Ausgewählte Werke.* Ed. Karl August Schleiden. Munich: Hanser, 1962.

Lavater, Johann Caspar. *Aussichten in die Ewigkeit, in Briefen an Herrn Joh. Georg Zimmermann.* Vol. 3. 2nd ed. Zurich: Gessner, 1773.

———. *Physiognomische Fragmente zur Beförderung der Menschenkenntniß und Menschenliebe.* 4 vols. Leipzig & Winterthur: Weidmann & Steiner, 1775–78.

Leidner, Alan C., ed. *Sturm und Drang:* The Soldiers, The Childmurderess, Storm and Stress, *and* The Robbers. German Library, 14. New York: Continuum, 1992.

Leisewitz, Johann Anton. *Julius von Tarent: Ein Trauerspiel.* Ed. Werner Keller. Universal-Bibliothek, 111. Stuttgart: Reclam, 1965.

Lenz, Jakob Michael Reinhold. *Gesammelte Schriften.* 3 vols. Ed. Ludwig Tieck. Berlin: Reimer, 1828.

———. *Werke und Briefe.* 3 vols. Ed. Sigrid Damm. Leipzig: Insel, 1987.

Lessing, Gotthold Ephraim. *Sämtliche Schriften.* 23 vols. Eds. Karl Lachmann and Franz Muncker. Stuttgart: Göschen, 1886–1924.

———. *Werke.* 8 vols. Eds. Herbert G. Göpfert et al. Munich: Hanser, 1970–79.

Lichtenberg, Georg Christoph. *Aphorismen, Schriften, Briefe.* Ed. Wolfgang Promies in collaboration with Barbara Promies. Munich: Carl Hanser, 1974.

Loewenthal, Erich, and Lambert Schneider, eds. *Sturm und Drang. Dramatische Schriften.* 2nd ed. 2 vols. Heidelberg: Lambert Schneider, 1963.

Mendelssohn, Moses. *Gesammelte Schriften.* 24 vols. Eds. F. Bamberger et al. Stuttgart-Bad Canstatt: Fromann, 1971–97.

[Mercier, Louis-Sébastien.] *Neuer Versuch über die Schauspielkunst.* [Trans. Heinrich Leopold Wagner.] Leipzig: Schwickert, 1776. Rpt., ed. Peter Pfaff. Heidelberg: Schneider, 1967.

Moritz, Karl Philipp. *Werke.* 2 vols. Eds. Heide Hollmer and Albert Meier. Frankfurt am Main: Deutscher Klassiker Verlag, 1999.

Möser, Justus. *Sämtliche Werke: Historisch-kritische Ausgabe.* 9 vols. to date. Ed. Akademie der Wissenschaften zu Göttingen. Berlin & Hamburg: Oldenbourg, 1943–.

Müller, Friedrich. *Der dramatisierte Faust.* Ed. Ulrike Leuschner. Heidelberg: Winter, 1996.

———. *Fausts Leben.* Ed. Johannes Mahr. Universal-Bibliothek, 9949. Stuttgart: Reclam, 1979.

Musikalisches Kunstmagazin (vol. 1, 1782). Hildesheim: Olms, 1969.

Nicolai, Heinz, ed. *Sturm und Drang: Dichtungen und theoretische Texte.* Munich: Winkler, 1971.

Nisbet, H. B., ed. *German Aesthetic and Literary Criticism: Winckelmann, Lessing, Hamann, Herder, Schiller, Goethe.* Cambridge etc.: Cambridge UP, 1985.

Ossian. *The Poems of Ossian, &c. containing the poetical works of James Macpherson, esq., in prose and rhyme.* 2 vols. Ed. Malcolm Laing. Edinburgh: Constable, 1805.

———. *Works of Ossian.* London: Beckett & de Hondt, 1765.

———, et al. *The Poems of Ossian and Related Works.* Ed. Howard Gaskill. Edinburgh: Edinburgh UP, 1996.

Pico della Mirandola, Giovanni. *Oration on the Dignity of Mankind.* Trans. Charles Glenn Wallis. New York: Bobbs-Merrill, 1965.

Pope, Alexander. *The Poems.* Ed. John Butt. London: Methuen, 1963.

Reichardt, Johann Friedrich. *Über die Deutsche comische Oper.* Munich: Katzbichler, 1974.

Rousseau, Jean-Jacques. *Œuvres complètes.* Ed. Bernard Gagnebin and Marcel Raymond. 4 vols. N.p.: Gallimard, 1959–69.

Schiller, Friedrich. *Plays:* Intrigue and Love *and* Don Carlos. Ed. Walter Hinderer. The German Library, 15. New York: Continuum, 1983.

———. *Werke: Nationalausgabe.* 41 vols. Eds. Julius Petersen et al. Weimar: Böhlau, 1943–.

———. *Werke und Briefe.* 12 vols. Ed. Otto Dann. Frankfurt am Main: Deutscher Klassiker Verlag, 1988.

Schulz, Johann Abraham Peter. *Lieder im Volkston, bey dem Klavier zu singen.* 2nd ed. Berlin: Decker, 1785.

Smith, Adam. *Lectures on Rhetoric and Belles Lettres.* Ed. J. C. Bryce. The Glasgow Edition of the Works and Correspondence of Adam Smith, vol. 4. Oxford: Oxford UP, 1983.

Sulzer, Johann Georg, ed. *Allgemeine Theorie der schönen Künste.* Hildesheim: Olms, 1967.

Tetens, Johann Nicolas. *Philosophische Versuche über die menschliche Natur und ihre Entwicklung*. Leipzig: Weidmanns Erben & Reich, 1777.

vom Hagen, Johann Jost Anton, ed. "Über die Kochische Schauspieler-Gesellschaft." *Magazin zur Geschichte des Deutschen Theaters* 1 (1773): 72.

Wieland, Christoph Martin. *Der goldne Spiegel und andere politische Dichtungen*. Ed. Herbert Jaumann. Munich: Winkler, 1979.

Young, Edward. *Night Thoughts*. Ed. Stephen Cornford. Cambridge: Cambridge UP, 1989.

Secondary Literature

Adler, Hans. "Aisthesis, steinernes Herz und geschmeidige Sinne: Zur Bedeutung der Ästhetik-Diskussion in der zweiten Hälfte des 18. Jahrhunderts." In *Der ganze Mensch: Anthropologie und Literatur im 18. Jahrhundert*. Ed. Hans-Jürgen Schings. Stuttgart: Metzler, 1992, 96–111.

Alexander, W. M. *Johann Georg Hamann: Philosophy and Faith*. The Hague: Nijhoff, 1966.

Althaus, Thomas. "Ursprung in später Zeit: Goethes 'Heidenröslein' und der Volksliedentwurf." *Zeitschrift für deutsche Philologie* 118 (1999): 161–88.

Andreas, Willy. *Carl August von Weimar: Ein Leben mit Goethe 1757–1783*. Stuttgart: Kilpper, 1953.

Arntzen, Helmut. *Die ernste Komödie: Das deutsche Lustspiel von Lessing bis Kleist*. Munich: Nymphenburg, 1968.

Auerbach, Erich. *Mimesis: The Representation of Reality in Western Literature*. Princeton: Princeton UP, 1974.

Bahr, Ehrhard. "Aufklärung." In *Geschichte der deutschen Literatur: Kontinuität und Veränderung. Vom Mittelalter bis zur Gegenwart*. Vol. 2: *Von der Aufklärung bis zum Vormärz*, ed. Ehrhard Bahr. Tübingen: Francke, 1988, 1–128.

Baildam, John D. *Paradisal Love: Johann Gottfried Herder and the Song of Songs*. Journal for the Study of the Old Testament, Supplement Series, 298. Sheffield: Sheffield Academic Press, 1999.

Barner, Wilfried. "Über das Negieren von Tradition: Zur Typologie literaturprogrammatischer Epochenwenden in Deutschland." In *Epochenschwelle und Epochenbewußtsein*. Eds. Reinhart Herzog and Reinhart Koselleck. Poetik und Hermeneutik, 12. Munich: Fink, 1987, 3–51.

Barnouw, Jeffrey. "The Philosophical Achievement and Historical Significance of Johann Niclas Tetens." *Studies in Eighteenth-Century Culture* 9 (1979): 301–35.

————. "The Cognitive Value of Confusion and Obscurity in the German Enlightenment: Leibniz, Baumgarten, and Herder." *Studies in Eighteenth-Century Culture* 24 (1995): 29–50.

Bauman, Thomas. *North German Opera in the Age of Goethe.* Cambridge: Cambridge UP, 1985.

Beck, Lewis White. *Early German Philosophy: Kant and His Predecessors.* Cambridge MA: Harvard UP, 1969.

Bertram, Georg W. *Philosophie des Sturm und Drang: Eine Konstitution der Moderne.* Munich: Fink, 2000.

Betteridge, H. T. "Macpherson's Ossian in Germany, 1760–1775." Diss. London, 1938.

Bezold, Raimund. *Popularphilosophie und Erfahrungsseelenkunde im Werk von Karl Philipp Moritz.* Würzburg: Königshausen & Neumann, 1984.

Blackall, Eric A. "The Language of Sturm und Drang." In *Stil- und Formprobleme in der Literatur: Vorträge des VIII. Kongresses der Internationalen Vereinigung für moderne Sprachen und Literaturen in Heidelberg.* Ed. Paul Böckmann. Heidelberg: Winter, 1959, 272–82.

Blackwell, Richard. "Christian Wolff's Doctrine of the Soul." *Journal of the History of Ideas* 22 (1961): 339–54.

Blinn, Hansjürgen. *Shakespeare-Rezeption: Die Diskussion um Shakespeare in Deutschland.* Vol. 1: *Ausgewählte Texte von 1741 bis 1788.* Berlin: Erich Schmidt, 1982.

Borchmeyer, Dieter. "Schwankungen des Herzens und Liebe im Triangel: Goethe und die Erotik der Empfindsamkeit" In *Codierungen von Liebe in der Kunstperiode.* Ed. Walter Hinderer. Stiftung für Romantikforschung, 3. Würzburg: Königshausen & Neumann, 1997, 63–83.

Böttiger, C. A. *Entwickelung des Ifflandischen Spiels in vierzehn Darstellungen auf dem Weimarischen Hoftheater im Aprillmonath 1796.* Leipzig: Göschen, 1796.

Bourdieu, Pierre. *Distinction: A Social Critique of the Judgement of Taste.* Trans. Richard Nice. Cambridge MA: Harvard UP, 1984.

Boyle, Nicholas. *Goethe: The Poet and the Age.* Vol. 1: *The Poetry of Desire (1749–1790).* Oxford & New York: Oxford UP, 1992.

Braemer, Edith. *Goethes Prometheus und die Grundpositionen des Sturm und Drang.* Berlin: Aufbau, 1968.

Buchwald, Reinhard. *Schiller: Leben und Werk.* Vol. 2: *Der junge Schiller.* Leipzig: Insel, 1937.

Chapman, Malcolm. *The Gaelic Vision in Scottish Culture.* London: Croom Helm, 1978.

Clark, Robert T. *Herder: His Life and Thought*. Berkeley & Los Angeles: U of California P, 1955.

Conrady, Karl Otto. *Goethe: Leben und Werk*. 2 vols. Königstein: Athenäum, 1982; rpt., Frankfurt am Main: Fischer, 1988.

Corr, Charles A. "Christian Wolff and Leibniz." *Journal of the History of Ideas*, 36 (1975): 241–62.

Dahnke, Hans-Dietrich. "Sturm und Drang." In *Goethe Handbuch*. Eds. Hans Dietrich-Dahnke and Regine Otto. Stuttgart: Metzler, 1998, 4: 1024–28.

Darsow, Götz-Lothar. *Friedrich Schiller*. Stuttgart: Metzler, 2000.

Dawson, Ruth. "Frauen und Theater: Vom Stegreifspiel zum bürgerlichen Rührstück." In *Deutsche Literatur von Frauen*. Ed. Gisela Brinker-Gabler. Munich: Beck, 1988, 1: 421–34.

Delon, Michel. *L'idée d'énergie au tournant des Lumières: 1770–1820*. Paris: Presses universitaires de France, 1988.

Der große Brockhaus. Wiesbaden: Brockhaus, 1957.

Diezmann, August. *Goethe und die lustige Zeit in Weimar*. Leipzig: Keil, 1857.

Dülmen, Richard van. *Kultur und Alltag in der frühen Neuzeit*. Vol. 3: *Religion, Magie, Aufklärung*. Munich: Beck, 1994.

Duncan, Bruce. "The Comic Structure of Lenz's *Soldaten*." *Modern Language Notes* 91 (1976): 515–23.

———. *Lovers, Parricides, and Highwaymen: Aspects of Sturm und Drang Drama*. Rochester NY: Camden House, 1999.

Dürbeck, Gabriele. *Einbildungskraft und Aufklärung: Perspektiven der Philosophie, Anthropologie und Ästhetik um 1750*. Tübingen: Niemeyer, 1999.

Elias, Norbert. *Über den Prozeß der Zivilisation: Soziogenetische und psychogenetische Untersuchungen*. 2 vols. 6th ed. Frankfurt am Main: Suhrkamp, 1978.

Ellison, Julie K. *Cato's Tears and the Making of Anglo-American Emotion*. Chicago: U of Chicago P, 1999.

Fechner, Jörg-Ulrich. "Leidenschafts- und Charakterdarstellung im Drama." In *Sturm und Drang: Ein literaturwissenschaftliches Studienbuch*. Ed. Walter Hinck. Kronberg: Athenäum, 1978, 175–91.

Finscher, Ludwig. "Sturm und Drang." In *Musik in Geschichte und Gegenwart: Allgemeine Enzyklopädie der Musik*. ed. Finscher. 2nd ed. Kassel & Weimar: Bärenreiter & Metzler, 1998, 8: 2018–22.

Fleig, Anne. *Handlungs-Spiel-Räume: Dramen von Autorinnen im Theater des ausgehenden 18. Jahrhunderts*. Würzburg: Königshausen & Neumann, 1999.

Foucault, Michel. *Archäologie des Wissens*. Trans. Ulrich Köppen. Frankfurt am Main: Suhrkamp, 1973.

————. *History of Sexuality*. Vol. 1. Trans. Robert Hurley. New York: Random House, 1978.

Fox, Christopher, ed. *Psychology and Literature in the Eighteenth Century*. New York: AMS, 1987.

Fricke, Gerhard. "Das Humanitätsideal der klassischen deutschen Dichtung und die Gegenwart: Herder." *Zeitschrift für Deutschkunde* 48 (1934): 673–90.

Friedenthal, Richard. *Goethe: Sein Leben und seine Zeit*. Munich: Piper, 1963.

Friedlaender, Max. *Das deutsche Lied im achtzehnten Jahrhundert: Quellen und Studien*. 2 vols. Hildesheim: Olms, 1970.

Garland, H. B. *Storm and Stress*. London: Harrap, 1952.

Gaskill, Howard. "'Aus der dritten Hand:' Herder and His Annotators." *German Life and Letters*, 54 (2001): 210–18.

————. "'Blast, rief Cuchullin . . .!': J. M. R. Lenz and Ossian." In *From Gaelic to Romantic: Ossianic Translations*. Eds. Fiona Stafford and Howard Gaskill. Amsterdam: Rodopi, 1998, 107–18.

————. "Herder, Ossian and the Celtic." In *Celticism*. Ed. Terence Brown. Amsterdam: Rodopi, 1996, 257–71.

————. "'Ossian hat in meinem Herzen den Humor verdrängt'": Goethe and Ossian Reconsidered." In *Goethe and the English-Speaking World*. Eds. Nicholas Boyle and John Guthrie. Rochester NY: Camden House, 2001, 47–59.

Gay, Peter. *Mozart*. London: Weidenfeld & Nicolson, 1999.

Genton, Elisabeth. *J. M. R. Lenz et la scène allemande*. Paris: Didier, 1966.

Gerth, Klaus. "Die Poetik des Sturm und Drang." In *Sturm und Drang: Ein literaturwissenschaftliches Studienbuch*. Ed. Walter Hinck. Kronberg: Athenäum, 1978, 55–80.

Gervinus, Georg Gottfried. *Geschichte der poetischen National-Literatur der Deutschen*. Part 4: *Von Gottsched's Zeiten bis zu Göthe's Jugend*. 2nd ed. Leipzig: Engelmann, 1843.

Gillies, Alexander. *Herder und Ossian*. Berlin: Junker & Dünnhaupt, 1933.

Gode, Alexander. *On the Origin of Language*. New York: Ungar, 1966.

Goetzinger, Germaine. "Männerphantasie und Frauenwirklichkeit: Kindermörderinnen in der Literatur des Sturm und Drang." In *Frauen — Literatur — Politik*. Eds. Annegret Pelz et al. Hamburg: Argument, 1988, 263–86.

Greis, Jutta. *Drama Liebe: Zur Entstehungsgeschichte der modernen Liebe im Drama des 18. Jahrhunderts*. Stuttgart: Metzler, 1991.

Groom, Nick. *The Making of Percy's Reliques*. Oxford: Oxford UP, 2000.

Gundolf, Friedrich. *Shakespeare und der deutsche Geist.* Godesberg: Helmut Küpper, 1947.

Guthke, K. S. *Geschichte und Poetik der deutschen Tragikomödie.* Göttingen: Vandenhoeck, 1961.

———. "Repertoire: Deutsches Theaterleben im Jahre 1776." In his *Literarisches Leben im achtzehnten Jahrhundert in Deutschland und der Schweiz.* Bern & Munich: Francke, 1975, 290–96.

Guthrie, John. *Lenz and Büchner: Studies in Dramatic Form.* Frankfurt am Main: Lang, 1984.

Habermas, Jürgen. *Strukturwandel der Öffentlichkeit: Untersuchungen zu einer Kategorie der bürgerlichen Gesellschaft.* Neuwied & Berlin: Luchterhand, 1962.

Habermas, Rebekka. *Frauen und Männer des Bürgertums: Eine Familiengeschichte (1750–1850).* Göttingen: Vandenhoeck & Ruprecht, 2000.

Häfner, Ralph. "'L'âme est une neurologie en miniature': Herder und die Neurophysiologie Charles Bonnets." In *Der ganze Mensch: Anthropologie und Literatur im 18. Jahrhundert.* Ed. Hans-Jürgen Schings. Stuttgart: Metzler, 1992, 390–409.

Haile, H. G. "Goethe's Political Thinking and *Egmont.*" *Germanic Review* 42 (1967): 96–107.

Hankamer, Paul. *Deutsche Literaturgeschichte.* 3rd ed. Bonn: Bonner Buchgemeinde, 1952.

Hansen, Volkmar. "Sinnlichkeit in Friedrich Heinrich Jacobis *Woldemar* (1779) oder der Engelssturz." In *Sturm und Drang: Geistiger Aufbruch 1770–1790 im Spiegel der Literatur.* Eds. Bodo Plachta and Winfried Woesler. Tübingen: Niemeyer, 1997, 149–56.

Hart, Gail. *Tragedy in Paradise: Family and Gender Politics in German Bourgeois Tragedy 1750–1850.* Columbia SC: Camden House, 1996.

Hausen, Karin. "Familie als Gegenstand historischer Sozialwissenschaft: Bemerkungen zu einer Forschungstrategie." *Geschichte und Gesellschaft.. Zeitschrift für historische Sozialwissenschaft* 1 (1975): 171–209.

Haym, Rudolf. *Herder nach seinem Leben und seinen Werken dargestellt.* 2 vols. Berlin: Gaertner, 1877–85.

Henke, Burkhard, et al., eds. *Unwrapping Goethe's Weimar: Essays in Cultural Studies and Local Knowledge.* Rochester NY: Camden House, 1999.

Hennicke, Franz. "Goethes Verbundenheit mit dem Volk: Anfänge einer zentralisierten Industrie im Herzogtum Sachsen-Weimar zur Zeit Goethes." *Goethe-Jahrbuch* 101 (1984): 360–62.

Hettner, Hermann. *Geschichte der deutschen Literatur im achtzehnten Jahrhundert.* Vol. 2. Berlin: Aufbau, 1961.

Hill, David. "The Inner Form of *Aus Goethes Brieftasche*." In *Goethe at 250: The London Symposium. Goethe mit 250: Londoner Symposium*. Eds. T. J. Reed et al. Munich: Iudicium, 2000, 109–20.

Hinck, Walter, ed. *Sturm und Drang: Ein literaturwissenschaftliches Studienbuch*. Kronberg: Athenäum, 1978.

Hinderer, Walter. "Freiheit und Gesellschaft beim jungen Schiller." In *Sturm und Drang: Ein literaturwissenschaftliches Studienbuch*. Ed. Walter Hinck. Kronberg: Athenäum, 1978, 230–56.

———. "Zur Liebesaufassung der Kunstperiode: Einleitung." In *Codierungen von Liebe in der Kunstperiode*. Ed. Hinderer. Stiftung für Romantikforschung, 3. Würzburg: Königshausen & Neumann, 1997, 7–33.

Hoff, Dagmar von. *Dramen des Weiblichen: Deutsche Dramatikerinnen um 1800*. Opladen: Westdeutscher Verlag, 1989.

———. "Die Inszenierung des 'Frauenopfers' in Dramen von Autorinnen um 1800." In *Frauen — Literatur — Politik*. Eds. Annegret Pelz et al. Hamburg: Argument, 1988, 255–62.

———. "Inszenierung des Leidens: Lektüre von J. M. R. Lenz' 'Der Engländer' und Sophie Albrechts 'Theresgen.'" In *"Unaufhörlich Lenz gelesen . . .": Studien zu Leben und Werk von J. M. R. Lenz*. Eds. Inge Stephan and Hans-Gerd Winter. Stuttgart: Metzler, 1994, 210–24.

Hohoff, Curt. *Johann Wolfgang von Goethe: Dichtung und Leben*. Munich: Langen-Müller, 1989.

Höllerer, Walter. "Lenz: Die Soldaten." In *Das Deutsche Drama*. Ed. Benno von Wiese. Düsseldorf: Bagel, 1958, 127–46.

Huyssen, Andreas. *Drama des Sturm und Drang: Kommentar zu einer Epoche*. Munich: Winkler, 1980.

Irmscher, Hans Dietrich. "Goethe und Herder im Wechselspiel von Attraktion und Repulsion." *Goethe-Jahrbuch* 106 (1989): 22–52.

Janz, Rolf Peter. "Schillers 'Kabale und Liebe' als bürgerliches Trauerspiel." *Jahrbuch der deutschen Schillergesellschaft* 20 (1976): 208–28.

Jones, Robert W. "Ruled Passions: Re-Reading the Culture of Sensibility." *Eighteenth-Century Studies*, 32 (1999): 395–402.

Jørgensen, Sven Aage, et al. *Aufklärung, Sturm und Drang, frühe Klassik 1740–1789*. Munich: Beck, 1990.

Kaiser, Gerhard. *Aufklärung, Empfindsamkeit, Sturm und Drang*. 3rd ed. Munich: Francke, 1979.

———. "Friedrich Maximilian Klingers Schauspiel Sturm und Drang." In *Untersuchungen zur Literatur als Geschichte. Festschrift für Benno von Wiese*. Eds. Vincent Günther et al. Berlin: Erich Schmidt, 1973, 15–35.

———. "Kein Kommentar zu einer Literaturgeschichte." *Euphorion* 73 (1979): 206–18.

———. *Von der Aufklärung bis zum Sturm und Drang 1730–1785.* Gütersloh: Mohn, 1966.

Kantzenbach, Friedrich Wilhelm. *Johann Gottfried Herder in Selbstzeugnissen und Bilddokumenten.* Rowohlts Monographien, 164. Reinbek: Rowohlt, 1979.

Karthaus, Ulrich. *Sturm und Drang: Epoche — Werke — Wirkung.* Munich: Beck, 2000.

Käser, Rudolf. *Die Schwierigkeit, ich zu sagen: Rhetorik der Selbstdarstellung in Texten des "Sturm und Drang" — Herder — Goethe — Lenz.* Bern, Frankfurt am Main & New York: Lang, 1987.

Kaschuba, Wolfgang. "Deutsche Bürgerlichkeit nach 1800. Kultur als symbolische Praxis." In *Bürgertum im 19. Jahrhundert.* Ed. Jürgen Kocka. Vol. 3. Munich: dtv, 1988, 9–44.

Kieffer, Bruce. *The Storm and Stress of Language: Linguistic Catastrophe in the Early Works of Goethe, Lenz, Klinger, and Schiller.* University Park & London: Pennsylvania State UP, 1986.

Kindermann, Heinz. *Durchbruch der Seele: Literarhistorische Studie über die Anfänge der "Deutschen Bewegung" vom Pietismus zur Romantik.* Danziger Beiträge, 1. Danzig: Kafemann, 1928.

Kirsch, Mechthild. "Heinz Kindermann — ein Wiener Germanist und Theaterwissenschaftler." In *Zeitenwechsel: Germanistische Literaturwissenschaft vor und nach 1945.* Eds. Wilfried Barner and Christoph König. Frankfurt am Main: Fischer, 1996, 47–59.

Kirstein, Britt-Angela. *Marianne Ehrmann: Publizistin und Herausgeberin im ausgehenden 18. Jahrhundert.* Wiesbaden: Deutscher Universitäts-Verlag, 1997.

Kistler, Mark O. *Drama of the Storm and Stress.* New York: Twayne, 1969.

Klippel, Diethelm. *Politische Freiheit und Freiheitsrechte im deutschen Naturrecht des 18. Jahrhunderts.* Rechts- und Staatswissenschaftliche Veröffentlichungen der Görres-Gesellschaft, N.S. 23. Paderborn: Schöningh, 1976.

Klotz, Volker. *Geschlossene und offene Form im Drama.* Munich: Hanser, 1960.

Kluckhohn, Paul. *Die Auffassung der Liebe in der Literatur des 18. Jahrhunderts und in der deutschen Romantik.* Tübingen: Niemeyer, 1966.

Kocka, Jürgen. *Bürgertum im 19. Jahrhundert. Deutschland im europäischen Vergleich.* Vol. 1. Munich: dtv, 1988.

Kollektiv für Literaturgeschichte im Volkseigenen Verlag Volk und Wissen. *Sturm und Drang: Erläuterungen zur deutschen Literatur.* 7th ed. Berlin: Volk und Wissen, 1988.

Kommerell, Max. *Der Dichter als Führer in der deutschen Klassik*. Berlin: Bondi, 1928.

Kondylis, Panajotis. *Die Aufklärung im Rahmen des neuzeitlichen Rationalismus*. Munich: DTV, 1986.

Koopmann, Helmut. *Drama der Aufklärung: Kommentar zu einer Epoche*. Munich, Winkler, 1979.

Kord, Susanne. *Ein Blick hinter die Kulissen: Deutschsprachige Dramatikerinnen im 18. und 19. Jahrhundert*. Ergebnisse der Frauenforschung, 27. Stuttgart: Metzler, 1992.

———. "All's Well that Ends Well? Marriage, Madness and Other Happy Endings in Eighteenth-Century Women's Comedies." *Lessing Yearbook* 28 (1996): 181–97.

———. *Sich einen Namen machen: Anonymität und weibliche Autorschaft 1700–1900*. Stuttgart: Metzler, 1996.

———. "Women as Children, Women as Childkillers: Poetic Images of Infanticide in Eighteenth-Century Germany," *Eighteenth-Century Studies* 26.3 (1993): 449–66.

Korff, Hermann August. *Geist der Goethezeit*. 5 vols. Leipzig: Koehler & Ameland, 1954–57.

Koselleck, Reinhart. "Das achtzehnte Jahrhundert als Beginn der Neuzeit." In *Epochenschwelle und Epochenbewußtsein*. Eds. Koselleck and Reinhart Herzog. Poetik und Hermeneutik, 12. Munich: Fink, 1987, 269–82.

———. *Kritik und Krise: Eine Studie zur Pathogenese der bürgerlichen Welt*. Frankfurt am Main: Suhrkamp, 1973.

Krämling, Gerhard. "Periode, Periodisierung." In *Historisches Wörterbuch der Philosophie*. Vol. 7. Ed. Rudolf Eisler. Darmstadt: Wissenschaftliche Buchgesellschaft, 1989, cols. 259–61.

Krauss, Werner. "Zur Periodisierung Aufklärung, Sturm und Drang, Weimarer Klassik." In his *Perspektiven und Probleme. Zur französischen und deutschen Aufklärung und andere Aufsätze*. Neuwied & Berlin: Luchterhand, 1965, 234–65. Rpt. in *Sturm und Drang*. Ed. Manfred Wacker. Wege der Forschung, 559. Darmstadt: Wissenschaftliche Buchgesellschaft, 1985, 67–95.

Krebs, Roland. "Herder, Goethe und die ästhetische Diskussion um 1770: Zu den Begriffen 'énergie' und 'Kraft' in der französischen und deutschen Poetik." *Goethe-Jahrbuch* 112 (1995): 83–96.

———. "Le *Sturm und Drang* comme avant-garde littéraire." In *Le Sturm und Drang: Une rupture?* Ed. Marita Gilli. Laboratoire Littérature et Histoire des pays de langues européennes, 42. *Annales littéraires de l'Université de Besançon* 597 (1996): 11–23.

Kremer, Richard. "Innovation through Synthesis: Helmholtz and Color Research." In *Hermann von Helmholtz and the Foundations of Nineteenth-Century Science*. Ed. David Cahan. Berkeley: U of California P, 1993, 205–58.

Krick, Kirsten. "Storm and Stress / Sturm und Drang." In *The Feminist Encyclopedia of German Literature*. Eds. Friederike Eigler and Susanne Kord. Westport, CT & London: Greenwod, 1997, 495–96.

Krull, Edith. "Das Wirken der Frau im frühen deutschen Zeitschriftenwesen." Diss. Berlin, 1939.

Kühnemann, Eugen. *Herders Leben*. Munich: Beck, 1895. 2nd ed. Munich: Beck, 1912.

Lane, Richard D., and Lynn Nadel, eds. *Cognitive Neuroscience of Emotion*. New York: Oxford UP, 2000.

LeDoux, Joseph. *The Emotional Brain: The Mysterious Underpinnings of Emotional Life*. New York: Simon & Schuster, 1996.

Leidner, Alan C., and Helga S. Madland, eds. *Space to Act: The Theater of J. M. R. Lenz*. Columbia SC: Camden House, 1993.

Leidner, Alan C. *The Impatient Muse: Germany and the Sturm und Drang*. Chapel Hill & London: U of North Carolina P, 1994.

Linden, Mareta. *Untersuchungen zum Anthropologiebegriff des 18. Jahrhunderts*. Bern & Frankfurt am Main: Lang, 1976.

Luhmann, Niklas. "Differentiation of Society." *Canadian Journal of Sociology* 2 (1977): 29–53.

———. *Gesellschaftsstrucktur und Semantik: Studien zur Wissenssoziologie der modernen Gesellschaft*. Vol. 1. Frankfurt am Main: Suhrkamp, 1993.

———. *Liebe als Passion: Zur Codierung von Intimität*. 3rd ed. Frankfurt am Main: Suhrkamp, 1983.

Lukács, Georg. *Skizze einer Geschichte der neueren deutschen Literatur*. Berlin: Aufbau, 1953; rpt., Neuwied & Berlin: Luchterhand, 1963.

Luserke, Matthias. *Die Bändigung der wilden Seele: Literatur und Leidenschaft in der Aufklärung*. Stuttgart & Weimar: Metzler, 1995.

———. *Sturm und Drang: Autoren — Texte — Themen*. Universal-Bibliothek, 17602. Stuttgart: Reclam, 1997.

Luserke, Matthias, and Reiner Marx. "Die Anti-Läuffer: Thesen zur SuD-Forschung oder Gedanken neben dem Totenkopf auf der Toilette des Denkers." *Lenz-Jahrbuch. Sturm-und-Drang-Studien* 2 (1992): 126–50.

Lützeler, Paul Michael. "Jakob Michael Reinhold Lenz: Die Soldaten." In his *Interpretationen: Dramen des Sturm und Drang*. Universal-Bibliothek, 8410. Stuttgart: Reclam, 1997, 129–60.

Mabee, Barbara. "Die Kindesmörderin in den Fesseln der bürgerlichen Moral: Wagners Evchen und Goethes Gretchen." *Women in German Yearbook* 3 (1986): 29–45.

McFarland, Thomas. *Romanticism and the Forms of Ruin: Wordsworth, Coleridge, and Modalities of Fragmentation.* Princeton NJ: Princeton UP, 1981.

McInnes, Edward. "'Die Regie des Lebens': Domestic Drama and the Sturm und Drang." *Orbis Litterarum* 32 (1977): 269–84.

———. *"Ein ungeheures Theater": The Drama of the Sturm und Drang.* Frankfurt am Main, Bern & New York: Lang, 1987.

Mackenzie, Henry, ed. *Report of the Committee of the Highland Society of Scotland, appointed to inquire into the Nature and Authenticity of the Poems of Ossian.* Edinburgh: Constable, 1805.

McKenzie, Alan T. *Certain Lively Episodes: The Articulation of Passion in 18th-Century Prose.* Athens: U of Georgia P, 1990.

Madland, Helga. "Gender and the German Literary Canon: Marianne Ehrmann's Infanticide Fiction." *Monatshefte* 84 (1992): 405–16.

———. "Infanticide as Fiction: Goethe's *Urfaust* and Schiller's 'Kindsmörderin' as Models." *German Quarterly* 62 (1989): 27–38.

———. "An Introduction to the Works and Life of Marianne Ehrmann (1755–95): Writer, Editor, Journalist." *Lessing Yearbook* 21 (1989): 171–96.

———. *Marianne Ehrmann: Reason and Emotion in Her Life and Works.* New York: Lang, 1998.

Manning, Susan. "Henry Mackenzie and Ossian: Or, The Emotional Value of Asterisks." In *From Gaelic to Romantic: Ossianic Translations.* Eds. Fiona Stafford and Howard Gaskill. Amsterdam: Rodopi, 1998, 136–52.

Martersteig, Max. *Die Protokolle des Mannheimer Nationaltheaters unter Dalberg aus den Jahren 1781 bis 1789.* Mannheim: Dramaturgische Gesellschaft, 1890.

Martini, Fritz. *Geschichte im Drama — Drama in der Geschichte: Spätbarock, Sturm und Drang, Klassik, Frührealismus.* Stuttgart: Klett-Cotta, 1979.

———. *Literarische Form und Geschichte: Aufsätze zur Gattungstheorie und Gattungsentwicklung vom Sturm und Drang bis zum Erzählen heute.* Stuttgart: Metzler, 1984.

———. "Von der Aufklärung zum Sturm und Drang." In *Annalen der deutschen Literatur.* Ed. Heinz Otto Burger. 2nd ed. Stuttgart: Metzler, 1971, 405–63.

Mattenklott, Gert. *Melancholie in der Dramatik des Sturm und Drang.* 2nd ed. Königstein: Athenäum, 1985.

Maurer, Michael. *Aufklärung und Anglophilie in Deutschland.* Göttingen: Vandenhoeck & Ruprecht, 1987.

Maurer-Schmoock, Sibylle. *Deutsches Theater im 18. Jahrhundert*. Tübingen: Niemeyer, 1982.

Meek, Donald E. "The Gaelic Ballads of Scotland: Creativity and Adaptation." In *Ossian Revisited*. Ed. Howard Gaskill. Edinburgh: Edinburgh UP, 1991, 19–48.

Meinecke, Friedrich. *Die Entstehung des Historismus*. 2 vols. Munich & Berlin: Oldenbourg, 1936.

———. *Werke*. Vol. 5: *Weltbürgertum und Nationalstaat*. Munich: Oldenbourg, 1969.

Mensching, Günther. "Vernunft und Selbstbehauptung: Zum Begriff der Seele in der europäischen Aufklärung." In *Die Seele: Ihre Geschichte im Abendland*. Eds. Gerd Jüttemann et al. Weinheim: Psychologie Verlags Union, 1991, 217–35.

Meyer, Heinrich. *Goethe: Das Leben im Werk*. Stuttgart: Günther, 1967.

Mortier, R. *Diderot en allemagne*. Paris: Presses universitaires de France, 1954.

Müller, Peter, ed. *Sturm und Drang: Weltanschauliche und ästhetische Schriften*. 2 vols. Berlin & Weimar: Aufbau, 1978.

Nadler, Josef. "Herder oder Goethe?" In his *deutscher geist/deutscher osten: zehn reden*. Schriften der Corona, 16. Munich, Berlin & Zurich: Oldenbourg, 1937, 127–40.

Nauert, Charles G. Jr. *Humanism and the Culture of Renaissance Europe*. Cambridge: Cambridge UP, 1995.

Nörtemann, Regina. "Die 'Begeisterung eines Poeten' in den Briefen eines Frauenzimmers: Zur Korrespondenz der Caroline Christiane Lucius mit Christian Fürchtegott Gellert." In *Die Frau im Dialog: Studien zu Theorie und Geschichte des Briefes*. Eds. Anita Runge and Lieselotte Steinbrügge. Stuttgart: Metzler, 1991, 13–32.

Oberländer, Hans. *Die geistige Entwicklung der deutschen Schauspielkunst im 18. Jahrhundert*. Hamburg: Voss, 1898.

O'Flaherty, James C. *Unity and Language: A Study in the Philosophy of Johann Georg Hamann*. Chapel Hill: U of North Carolina P, 1952.

Pailer, Gaby. "'Lasst uns die Ketten soviel als möglich unter Rosen verbergen . . .': Zum Problem der 'Zensur' in Dramen von Autorinnen des 18. Jahrhunderts." *Rundbrief: Frauen in der Literaturwissenschaft* 44 (1995): 39–44.

———. "Gattungskanon, Gegenkanon und 'weiblicher' Subkanon: Zum bürgerlichen Trauerspiel des 18. Jahrhunderts." In *Kanon Macht Kultur: Theoretische, historische und soziale Aspekte ästhetischer Kanonbildungen*. Ed. Renate von Heydebrand. Stuttgart: Metzler, 1998, 365–82.

Pascal, Roy. *The German Sturm und Drang*. Manchester: Manchester UP, 1953.

————. *Shakespeare in Germany 1740–1815*. Cambridge: Cambridge UP, 1937.

Patterson, Michael. *The First German Theater: Schiller, Goethe, Kleist and Büchner in Performance*. London: Routledge, 1990.

Perels, Christoph, ed. *Sturm und Drang: Freies Deutsches Hochstift*. Frankfurt am Main: Goethe-Museum, 1988.

Pichler, Anton. *Chronik des großherzoglichen Hof- und National-Theaters*. Mannheim: Bensheimer, 1879.

Pinch, Adela. *Strange Fits of Passion: Epistemologies of Emotion, Hume to Austen*. Stanford CA: Stanford UP, 1996.

Plachta, Bodo, and Winfried Woesler, eds. *Sturm und Drang: Geistiger Aufbruch 1770–1790 im Spiegel der Literatur*. Tübingen: Niemeyer, 1997.

Plessner, Helmuth. *Die verspätete Nation*. 2nd ed. Stuttgart: Kohlhammer, 1959.

Porter, Roy. *The Creation of the Modern World: The Untold Story of the British Enlightenment*. New York & London: Norton, 2000.

Quabius, Richard. *Generationsverhältnisse im Sturm und Drang*. Cologne: Böhlau, 1976.

Rasch, Wolfdietrich. *Herder: Sein Leben und Werk im Umriß*. Halle: Niemeyer, 1938.

Recker, Bettina. *"Ewige Dauer" oder "Ewiges Einerlei": Die Geschichte der Ehe im Roman um 1800*. Würzburg: Kömigshausen & Neumann, 2000.

Reiss, Hans. "Goethe, Moser and the Aufklärung: The Holy Roman Empire in Götz von Berlichingen and Egmont." *Deutsche Vierteljahrsschrift für Literaturwissenschaft und Geistesgeschichte* 60 (1986): 609–44.

Reiter, Michael. "Pietismus." In *Die Seele. Ihre Geschichte im Abendland*. Eds. Gerd Jüttemann et al. Weinheim: Psychologie Verlags Union, 1991, 198–213.

Riedel, Wolfgang, ed. *Jacob Friedrich Abel: Eine Quellenedition zum Philosophieunterricht an der Stuttgarter Karlsschule (1773–1782)*. Würzburg: Königshausen & Neumann, 1995.

Roebling, Irmgard. "Sturm und Drang — weiblich: Eine Untersuchung zu Sophie Albrechts Schauspiel 'Theresgen.'" *Der Deutschunterricht* 48 (1996): 63–77.

Rosenbaum, Heidi. *Formen der Familie*. Frankfurt am Main: Suhrkamp, 1982.

Rosenberg, Rainer. "'Aufklärung' in der deutschen Literaturgeschichtsschreibung des 19. Jahrhunderts." In *Aufklärungsforschung in Deutschland*. Eds. Holger Dainat and Wilhelm Voßkamp. *Euphorion* (Beiheft) 32 (1999): 7–20.

Rötzer, Hans Gerd. *Geschichte der deutschen Literatur*. Bamberg: Buchner, 1992.

Rubel, Margaret Mary. *Savage and Barbarian: Historical Attitudes in the Criticism of Homer and Ossian in Britain, 1760–1800.* Amsterdam: North Holland, 1978.

Rudloff-Hille, Gertrud. *Schiller auf der deutschen Bühne seiner Zeit.* Berlin & Weimar: Aufbau, 1969.

Runge, Edith Amelie. *Primitivism and Related Ideas in Sturm und Drang Literature.* New York: Russell & Russell, 1972.

Saine, Thomas P. *Die ästhetische Theodizee: Karl Philipp Moritz und die Philosophie des 18. Jahrhunderts.* Munich: Fink, 1971.

Sasse, Günter. *Die Ordnung der Gefühle: Das Drama der Liebesheirat im 18. Jahrhundert.* Darmstadt: Wissenschaftliche Buchgesellschaft, 1996.

Sauder, Gerhard. "Ästhetische Autonomie als Norm der Weimarer Klassik." In *Normen und Werte.* Ed. Friedrich Hiller. Heidelberg: Winter, 1982, 130–50.

———. "Die deutsche Literatur des Sturm und Drang." In *Europäische Aufklärung, II. Teil.* Ed. Heinz-Joachim Müllenbrock. Neues Handbuch der Literaturwissenschaft, 12. Wiesbaden: AULA-Verlag, 1984, 327–78.

———. *Empfindsamkeit.* Vol. 1: *Voraussetzungen und Elemente.* Stuttgart: Metzler, 1974.

———. "Lessing im Sturm und Drang." In *Lessing und die Literaturrevolten nach 1770: 37. Kamenzer Lessing-Tage 1998.* Erbepflege in Kamenz, 18. Kamenz: Lessing-Museum, 1999, 11–35.

———. "Tieck's 'vernachlässigter Lenz.'" In *Jakob Michael Reinhold Lenz: Vom Sturm und Drang zur Moderne.* Ed. Andreas Meier. Heidelberg: Winter, 2001, 37–46.

Scherer, Wilhelm. *Geschichte der Deutschen Literatur.* Berlin: Knaur, n.d.

Schings, Hans-Jürgen. *Melancholie und Aufklärung: Melancholiker und ihre Kritiker in der Erfahrungsseelenkunde und Literatur des 18. Jahrhunderts.* Stuttgart: Metzler, 1977.

———, ed. *Der ganze Mensch: Anthropologie und Literatur im 18. Jahrhundert.* Stuttgart: Metzler, 1992.

Schmidt, Henry J. *How Dramas End: Essays on the German Sturm und Drang, Büchner, Hauptmann, and Fleisser.* Ann Arbor: U of Michigan P, 1992.

Schmidt, Siegfried J. *Die Selbstorganisation des Sozialsystems Literatur im 18. Jahrhundert.* Frankfurt am Main: Suhrkamp, 1989.

Schneider, Ferdinand Josef. *Die deutsche Dichtung der Geniezeit.* Stuttgart: Metzler, 1952.

Schwänder, Hans-Peter. *"Alles um Liebe?": Zur Position Goethes im modernen Liebesdiskurs.* Opladen: Westdeutscher Verlag, 1997.

Sen, Amartya. "East and West: The Reach of Reason." *New York Review of Books* 47 (2000): 33–38.

Sher, Richard B. "Percy, Shaw, and the Ferguson 'Cheat': National Prejudice in the Ossian Wars." In *Ossian Revisited.* Ed. Howard Gaskill. Edinburgh: Edinburgh UP, 1991, 204–45.

Shorter, Edward. *The Making of the Modern Family.* New York: Basic Books, 1975.

Siegrist, Christoph. "Aufklärung und Sturm und Drang: Gegeneinander oder Nebeneinander?" In *Sturm und Drang: Ein literaturwissenschaftliches Studienbuch.* Ed. Walter Hinck. Kronberg: Athenäum, 1978, 1–13.

Smoljan, Olga. *Friedrich Maximilian Klinger: Leben und Werk.* Weimar: Arion, 1962.

Solomon, Maynard. *Mozart: A Life.* London: Hutchinson, 1995.

Sommer, Robert. *Grundzüge einer Geschichte der deutschen Psychologie und Aesthetik von Wolff-Baumgarten bis Kant-Schiller.* Amsterdam: Bonset, 1966.

Sørensen, Bengt Algot. *Herrschaft und Zärtlichkeit: Der Patriarchalismus und das Drama im 18. Jahrhundert.* Munich: Beck, 1984.

Stellmacher, Wolfgang. "Grundfragen der Shakespeare-Rezeption in der Frühphase des Sturm und Drang." In *Sturm und Drang.* Ed. Manfred Wacker. Wege der Forschung, 559. Darmstadt: Wissenschaftliche Buchgesellschaft, 1985, 112–43.

Stephan, Inge. "'So ist die Tugend ein Gespenst': Frauenbild und Tugendbegriff bei Lessing und Schiller." In *Lessing und die Toleranz: Sonderband zum Lessing Yearbook.* Ed. Peter Freimark et al. Detroit & Munich: Wayne State UP, 1985, 357–74.

———. "Geniekult und Männerbund: Zur Ausgrenzung des 'Weiblichen' in der Sturm und Drang-Bewegung." In *Jakob Michael Reinhold Lenz.* Ed. Martin Kagel. Munich: Text + Kritik, 2000, 46–54.

Stockmeyer, Clara. *Soziale Probleme im Drama des Sturmes und Dranges: Eine literarhistorische Studie.* Frankfurt am Main: Diesterweg, 1922.

Stoljar, Margaret. *Poetry and Song in Late Eighteenth Century Germany: A Study in the Musical* Sturm und Drang. London: Croom Helm, 1985.

———. "*Speculum Ludi:* The Aesthetics of Performance in Song." In *Music and German Literature: Their Relationship since the Middle Ages.* Ed. James M. McGlathery. Columbia SC: Camden House, 1992, 119–31.

Stone, Lawrence. *The Family, Sex and Marriage in England 1500–1800.* London: Weidenfeld & Nicolson, 1977.

Stump, Doris. "Eine Frau 'von Verstand, Witz, Gefühl, Fantasie und Feuer': Zu Leben und Werk Marianne Ehrmanns." In Marianne Ehrmann, *Amalie: Eine wahre Geschichte in Briefen*. Ed. Stump and Maya Widmer. Stuttgart & Vienna: Haupt, 1995, 481–98.

Taylor, Charles. *Sources of the Self: The Making of Modern Identity*. Cambridge MA: Harvard UP, 1989.

Teller, Jürgen. "Das Losungswort Spinoza: Zur Pantheismusdebatte zwischen 1780 und 1787." In *Debatten und Kontroversen: Literarische Auseinandersetzungen in Deutschland des 18. Jahrhunderts*. Eds. Hans-Dietrich Dahnke and Bernd Leistner. Berlin: Aufbau, 1989, 1: 135–92.

Thomson, Derick. *The Gaelic Sources of Macpherson's "Ossian."* Edinburgh: Oliver & Boyd, 1952.

Tieghem, Paul van. *Ossian en France*. 2 vols. Paris: Rieder, 1917.

Troickij, S. *Konrad Ekhof, Ludwig Schröder, August Wilhelm Iffland, Johann Friedrich Fleck, Ludwig Devrient, Karl Seydelmann: Die Anfänge der realistischen Schauspielkunst*. Berlin: Henschel, 1949.

Vaughan, Larry. *The Historical Constellation of the Sturm und Drang*. American University Studies, 1.38. New York, Bern & Frankfurt am Main: Lang, 1985.

Vietor, Karl. *Goethe: Dichtung — Wissenschaft — Weltbild*. Bern: Francke, 1949.

Vinzenz, Albert. "Sturm und Drang." In *Metzler Goethe Lexikon*. Eds. Benedikt Jeßing et al. Stuttgart & Weimar: Metzler, 1999, 473–74.

Wacker, Manfred. *Schillers "Räuber" und der Sturm und Drang; Stilkritische und typologische Überprüfung eines Epochenbegriffs*. Göppingen: Kümmerle, 1973.

———, ed. *Sturm und Drang*. Wege der Forschung, 559. Darmstadt: Wissenschaftliche Buchgesellschaft, 1985.

Wegmann, Nikolaus. *Diskurse der Empfindsamkeit: Zur Geschichte eines Gefühls in der Literatur des 18. Jahrhunderts*. Stuttgart: Metzler, 1988.

Weigel, Sigrid. "Der schielende Blick: Thesen zur Geschichte weiblicher Schreibpraxis." In Weigel and Inge Stephan, *Die verborgene Frau: Sechs Beiträge zu einer feministischen Literaturwissenschaft*. Berlin: Argument, 1983, 83–137.

———. *"Und selbst im Kerker frei . . .!": Schreiben im Gefängnis*. Marburg: Guttandin & Hoppe, 1982

Wenzel, Stefanie. *Das Motiv der feindlichen Brüder im Drama des Sturm und Drang*. Frankfurt am Main: Lang, 1992.

Widmer, Maya. "'Amalie' — eine wahre Geschichte?" In Marianne Ehrmann, *Amalie: Eine wahre Geschichte in Briefen*. Eds. Widmer and Doris Stump. Stuttgart & Vienna: Haupt, 1995, 499–515.

————. "Mit spitzer Feder gegen Vorurteile und gallsüchtige Moral — Marianne Ehrmann, geb. von Brentano." In *Und schrieb und schrieb wie ein Tiger aus dem Busch: Über Schriftstellerinnen in der deutschsprachigen Schweiz.* Eds. Elisabeth Ryter et al. Zurich: Limmat, 1994, 52–72.

Wiese, Benno von. *Herder: Grundzüge seines Weltbildes.* Leipzig: Bibliographisches Institut, 1939.

————. "Der Philosoph auf dem Schiffe, Johann Gottfried Herder." In his *Zwischen Utopie und Wirklichkeit: Studien zur deutschen Literatur.* Düsseldorf: Bagel, 1963, 32–60.

Wilkinson, Elizabeth M., and Leonard A. Willoughby. "The Blind Man and the Poet: An Early Stage in Goethe's Quest for Form." In *German Studies Presented to Walter Horace Bruford.* London: Harrap, 1962, 29–57.

Williams, Simon. *Shakespeare on the German Stage.* Vol. 1: *1586–1914.* Cambridge: Cambridge UP, 1990.

Wilson, W. Daniel. "Hunger/Artist: Goethe's Revolutionary Agitators in *Götz, Satyros, Egmont,* and *Der Bürgergeneral.*" *Monatshefte* 86 (1994): 80–94.

————. "Patriarchy, Politics, Passion: Labor and Werther's Search for Nature." *Internationales Archiv für Sozialgeschichte der deutschen Literatur* 14.2 (1989): 15–44.

————. "Zwischen Kritik und Affirmation: Militärphantasien und Geschlechterdisziplinierung bei J. M. R. Lenz." In *"Unaufhörlich Lenz gelesen . . .": Studien zum Leben und Werk von J. M. R. Lenz.* Eds. Inge Stephan and Hans-Gerd Winter. Stuttgart: Metzler, 1994, 52–85.

Winter, Hans-G. "Antiklassizismus: Sturm und Drang." In *Geschichte der deutschen Literatur vom 18. Jahrhundert bis zur Gegenwart.* Vol. 1.1, ed. Viktor Žmegač. Königstein: Athenäum, 1978, 194–256.

Wolf, Herman. "Die Genielehre des jungen Herder." In *Sturm und Drang.* Ed. Manfred Wacker. Wege der Forschung, 559. Darmstadt: Wissenschaftliche Buchgesellschaft, 1985, 184–214.

Wosgien, Gerlinde. *Literarische Frauenbilder von Lessing bis zum Sturm und Drang: Ihre Entwicklung unter dem Einfluß Rousseaus.* Frankfurt am Main & Bern: Lang, 1999.

Wulf, Christoph. "Präsenz und Absenz. Prozeß und Struktur in der Geschichte der Seele." In *Die Seele: Ihre Geschichte im Abendland.* Eds. Gerd Jüttemann et al. Weinheim: Psychologie Verlags Union, 1991, 5–12.

Wurst, Karin A. *Familiale Liebe ist die "wahre Gewalt": Zur Repräsentation der Familie in G. E. Lessings dramatischem Werk.* Amsterdam: Rodopi, 1988.

————. *Frauen und Drama im achtzehnten Jahrhundert.* Cologne & Vienna: Böhlau, 1991.

————. "Lenz als Alternative: Einleitung." In *J. M. R. Lenz als Alternative? Positionsanalysen zum 200. Todestag.* Ed. Wurst. Cologne: Böhlau, 1992, 1–22.

————, ed. *Eleonore Thons Adelheit von Rastenberg.* New York: MLA, 1996.

Wuthenow, Ralph-Rainer. *Die gebändigte Flamme: Zur Wiederentdeckung der Leidenschaften im Zeitalter der Vernunft.* Beiträge zur neueren Literaturgeschichte, 3.178. Heidelberg: Winter, 2000.

Yolton, John W., et al., eds. *The Blackwell Companion to the Enlightenment.* Oxford: Blackwell, 1991.

Žmegač, Viktor, et al. *Scriptors Geschichte der deutschen Literatur von den Anfängen bis zur Gegenwart.* Königstein: Scriptor, 1981.

Contributors

BRUCE DUNCAN is Professor of German at Dartmouth College. He has published studies on Achim von Arnim, Gerstenberg, Goethe, Lenz, Lessing, Schiller, and topics of intellectual history, and has translated works by Arnim and Luise Gottsched. In 1999 Camden House published his *"Lovers, Parricides and Highwaymen": Aspects of Sturm und Drang Drama*. In addition to his literary studies, he has developed and written about programs for computer-assisted learning.

HOWARD GASKILL has recently retired as Reader in German at the University of Edinburgh. His publications include many essays on Hölderlin, and on Ossian and its German and European impact. He is the editor of *Ossian Revisited* (1991), *The Poems of Ossian and Related Works* (1996), and (with Fiona Stafford) *From Gaelic to Romantic: Ossianic Translations* (1998). He is currently editing a volume on the European reception of Ossian for the "Reception of British Authors in Europe Project" (School of Advanced Studies, London).

DAVID HILL is Senior Lecturer at the University of Birmingham, UK. He has written widely on German literature of the late eighteenth century, in particular on Lessing, Goethe, Lenz, and Klinger. He has edited *Jakob Michael Reinhold Lenz: Studien zum Gesamtwerk*, and is currently editing unpublished manuscripts by Lenz. He also works on the relations between music and literature, and is Reviews Editor of *Debatte. Journal of Contemporary German Affairs*.

WULF KOEPKE has recently retired as Distinguished Professor of German, Texas A&M University. He has published numerous studies on Herder and other authors from the period of Goethe, notably Jean Paul Richter. He has also worked on the earlier twentieth century, and has written on Lion Feuchtwanger and Max Frisch, on Exile Literature, and on the literature of the immediate postwar period.

SUSANNE KORD is George M. Roth Distinguished Professor of German at Georgetown University. She has written extensively on the subject of women's literature, history, and reception in eighteenth- and early nineteenth-century Germany. Together with Friederike Eigler, she has edited

The Feminist Encyclopedia of German Literature, and most recently she has completed a book about eighteenth-century peasant women poets.

FRANCIS LAMPORT has recently retired as a Lecturer in German at Oxford University and a Fellow of Worcester College. His publications include: *Lessing and the Drama*, *German Classical Drama: Theatre, Humanity and Nation*, and translations and articles on German literature and drama of the classical period (Lessing, Goethe, Schiller, Kleist etc.). His translation of Schiller's *Wallenstein* was performed by the Royal Shakespeare Company in 1993–94.

ALAN C. LEIDNER is Professor of German at the University of Louisville. He is the author of *The Impatient Muse: Germany and the Sturm und Drang*, co-author (with Karin A. Wurst) of *Unpopular Virtues: The Critical Reception of J. M. R. Lenz*, and the editor of volume 14 of The German Library, *Sturm und Drang*.

MICHAEL PATTERSON is Professor of Theatre at De Montfort University, Leicester. He has published several books and chapters on German theater, including *German Theatre Today*, *The Revolution in German Theatre 1900–1933*, *Peter Stein*, *The First German Theatre*, *German Theatre: A Bibliography*, *Georg Büchner: Collected Plays* (ed.). He is at present compiling *The Oxford Dictionary of Plays*.

GERHARD SAUDER is Professor of German Studies at the Universität des Saarlandes. Among the publications he has written are *Der reisende Epikureer* (1968) and *Empfindsamkeit*, vols. 1 and 3 (1974, 1980); among those he has edited are *Die Bücherverbrennung* (1983); *Der junge Goethe 1757–1775* (Vol. 1.1: 1985, Vol. 1.2: 1987); *Johann Gottfried Herder 1744–1803* (1987); and Georg Kulka, *Werke* (1987); he is also co-editor of the works of Maler Müller, of the Munich Goethe edition (*G-MA*), and of the *Lenz-Jahrbuch*.

MARGARET MAHONY STOLJAR has recently retired as Reader in German at the Australian National University and Honorary Visiting Professor at the University of New South Wales. Her books include *Athenaeum: A Critical Commentary*, *Poetry and Song in Late Eighteenth Century Germany: A Study in the Musical Sturm und Drang*, and *Novalis: Philosophical Writings*. She is a Fellow and former Vice-President of the Australian Academy of the Humanities.

W. DANIEL WILSON is Professor of German at the University of California, Berkeley. He has written on Wieland, Lessing, Lenz, and other writers of the late eighteenth century, but in recent years has worked particularly on the political role played by Goethe in Weimar society.

Publications include *Geheimräte gegen Geheimbünde: Ein unbekanntes Kapitel der klassisch-romantischen Geschichte Weimars, Unterirdische Gänge: Goethe, Freimaurerei und Politik,* and *Das Goethe-Tabu: Protest und Menschenrechte im klassischen Weimar.*

KARIN WURST is Professor of German at Michigan State University. Her main research interests lie in the late eighteenth century, particularly in questions concerning aesthetics and gender, and the relationship between the two. She has published widely on Lessing, on Lenz (including, with Alan Leidner, *Unpopular Virtues: The Critical Reception of J. M. R. Lenz*), and on women's writing in this period.

Index